THE FOURTH STAR

★★★★

Dispatches from Inside
Daniel Boulud's
Celebrated New York Restaurant

LESLIE BRENNER

THREE RIVERS PRESS

NEW YORK

Published by Three Rivers Press, New York, New York.
Member of the Crown Publishing Group, a division of Random House, Inc.
www.randomhouse.com

THREE RIVERS PRESS and the Tugboat design are registered trademarks
of Random House, Inc.

Originally published in hardcover by Clarkson Potter/Publishers,
a division of Random House, Inc., New York, in 2002.

Printed in the United States of America

Design by Maggie Hinders

Library of Congress Cataloging-in-Publication Data
Brenner, Leslie.
The fourth star ; dispatches from inside Daniel Boulud's
celebrated New York restaurant / by Leslie Brenner.
1. Daniel (Restaurant). 2. Boulud, Daniel. I. Title.
TX945.5.D36B74 2002
647.957471—dc21
2002022455

ISBN 1-4000-4803-6
10 9 8 7 6 5 4 3 2
First Paperback Edition

CONTENTS

On ne fait pas d'omelette sans casser d'œufs.

(You can't make an omelette without breaking some eggs.)

PROLOGUE

THIS BOOK CHRONICLES a year behind the scenes at the New York City restaurant Daniel. Although the choice of the dates I would cover—January through December 2000—was somewhat random, it also seemed to me nice and round, the first or last year of a millennium, depending on one's point of view.

When I approached Daniel Boulud in June 1999 to find out whether he'd consider agreeing to let me spend a year at Daniel in order to write a book, he acceded immediately. "Maybe you should think about it," I told him. "I can call you in a week or so." But he didn't need time to decide; he readily agreed to give me full access to every area of his restaurant. "It probably won't all be pretty," I warned him, but he was undeterred. Mr. Boulud never asked to exercise any kind of approval on a draft, nor even see a manuscript. As the manuscript went to page proofs, neither he nor anyone in the Dinex Group, the company that owns Daniel, had seen any of the material.

It wasn't easy deciding how best to render such a place as Daniel in a narrative. The reader, I felt, would be much more interested in seeing and hearing what was going on in the kitchen, the dining room, or the reservations office than he or she would be in hearing about my role in the story. I didn't want to interfere in what would happen during the course of the year by interrupting with constant questions any more than I could imagine breaking into a narrative to weigh in on how Leslie Brenner fit into all of this. Seeking the most natural possible flow for the dialogue and action, I decided to simply let the story unfold, dutifully recording what I saw and heard. The traditional third-person-narrative, fly-on-the-wall point of view seemed to me much more appropriate than a first-person account would have been.

But how to do so faithfully? Using a tape recorder to capture the proceedings was impractical, for I'd have thousands and thousands of hours of tapes to transcribe. And even if I could do so, it would be impossible to distinguish who was saying what when there were frequently twenty people talking (or shouting!) at once.

I settled on the method I've always used as a journalist interviewing subjects: I took notes in shorthand. This way I could get down every word verbatim while adding notes about what was going on visually. The only little snag was that I don't take shorthand in French, so anything in that language had to go down longhand.

Therefore, everything I've attributed to an individual was actually said by him or her. I've used the real names of all the Daniel and Dinex Group employees, as well as various vendors, who were aware at the time that I was writing this book, and certain public figures. The only names I changed were those of Daniel guests, in order to protect their privacy.

While in the kitchen I wore whites, which helped me blend in. In the dining room I dressed as an assistant captain. At the front desk I dressed as a hostess. Although I was always furiously writing away in my notebook, I think my uniforms helped the staff forget my presence and focus on their work.

As at the restaurant, many characters come and go from this narrative over the course of a year. Just when you feel you're getting to know and love the lunchtime *saucier*, poof! he quits. That charming busboy who doesn't appear until page 270? He wasn't hired until September. Rather than melding several employees into one in order to serve the dramatic purposes of a narrative, I have opted to keep it real.

Nor was it always evident to me why people were saying or doing what they were saying and doing. When a chef blew up at the soup cook, for instance, I didn't always know what had caused the outburst. Since the soup cook probably didn't know why the chef blew up, either—and I could hardly stop service and ask him to explain, in any event—I let the incident speak for itself.

Confining the narrative to the year 2000 posed its own challenge. The concept of the book was that I would spend one calendar year in the restaurant and then chronicle that year. In keeping with that plan, I stopped visiting Daniel after December 31, at which point I began writing. Unfortunately, that meant that I missed William Grimes's series of visits in early 2001 that led to his momentous *New York Times* review in March. Rather than try to reconstruct what happened during those visits, relying on unreliable secondhand accounts from Daniel's staff, I decided to stay true to the concept; I left them out.

However, I did return on Wednesday, March 14, 2001, the day the *New York Times* bestowed on Daniel its fourth star.

When chef-owner Daniel Boulud opened the restaurant Daniel in January 1999, he was one of the most critically acclaimed chefs in New York City, and one of the longest-running four-star chefs in New York City. In New York, being a four-star chef is generally understood to denote those who have earned a four-star review from the *New York Times*. At any given moment in contemporary Gotham history, such honors are accorded no more than five or six restaurants. These are the restaurants that soar above all others, headed by chefs who consistently turn out extraordinary food—food that is, in other words, more often sublime than merely delicious.

In general, there's not much disagreement among New York's food cognoscenti about which venerable kitchens will attain—and maintain—the cherished quadruple-star rating: The restaurants that garner it set themselves apart so clearly that the distinction is fairly obvious. In 1999, Le Bernardin, Le Cirque 2000, Chanterelle, Jean Georges, and Lespinasse were the reigning four-star establishments. It was expected by all that with the opening of his much-heralded new restaurant, Daniel Boulud would regain his place among New York's four-star chefs, for he was clearly one of them.

To be sure, French-born Daniel Boulud was accustomed, by this time in his career, to critical superlatives. When he came to Sirio Maccioni's famed eatery Le Cirque in 1986, that restaurant, as much a favorite with the Park Avenue crowd as it was with former presidents, held only the distinction of three stars from the *New York Times*. When the thirty-one-year-old Boulud took over the range, fresh from a two-year stint as executive chef at Le Régence in Manhattan's Plaza Athénée Hotel, people started coming to Le Cirque for something other than the scene: For the first time, they came for the *food*. And the fourth star followed in early 1987.

Boulud had trained in France, land of a slightly different rating system. There, the red *Guide Michelin* grants one star (or *étoile*, or *macaron*) to restaurants its reviewers have deemed *"une très bonne table dans sa catégorie,"* that is to say, very good. Two stars go to excellent restaurants that merit a detour on a road trip. The *ne plus ultra* is three stars from *Michelin*, indicating that the establishment is one of the very best restaurants in France, worthy of a voyage in and of itself.

Boulud, who was born in a small village outside of Lyons, had learned to cook, and then grew as a cook, in a number of *Michelin*-starred restaurants, including Georges Blanc's La Mère Blanc in Vonnas, Roger Vergé's Moulin de Mougins in Mougins, and Michel Guérard's Les Prés d'Eugénie in Eugénie-les-Bains, all possessors of the cherished three-star designation in the *Guide Michelin*. Boulud's very first job, at the age of fifteen, was as an apprentice at Gérard Nandron's eponymous restaurant in Lyons, which had two stars.

In the early nineties, the restaurant widely considered to be New York's best in terms of cooking was the small, elegant downtown restaurant Bouley, owned by American chef David Bouley. When Bouley closed in the fall of 1995, New York's gastronomic world flew into a state of confusion, not knowing exactly how to function if there was no single "best" restaurant. The following year, one New York monthly, *Avenue* magazine, asked me to dope out the competition for best restaurant in New York City for their October issue. Some contenders were obvious. Both Le Bernardin, the Midtown seafood palace presided over by chef Eric Ripert and owned by Maguy Le Coze, the sister of the late founding chef, Gilbert Le Coze, and Lespinasse, the very formal gold-flecked Louis XVI dining room in the sumptuous St. Regis Hotel, with Gray Kunz at the stove, doing his daring Southeast Asian takes on classic French, had four stars from the *New York Times*. But I saw Le Bernardin's all-seafood menu as somewhat limiting, and the early dynamic energy Kunz brought to Lespinasse had since dissipated.

Jean-Georges Vongerichten, another New York chef cooking at a level up with Boulud, Kunz, Ripert, and Delouvrier, had not yet opened Jean Georges, but construction at the new Trump Hotel on Columbus Circle was proceeding apace. Vongerichten was breaking out of the bistro format he'd established at JoJo, his charming and personal Upper East Side French restaurant; from the impressive activity on the enormous construction site, it looked as if this would be big. And accordingly, some in the food world already knew that it would be very important indeed. ("Though it might seem wacky to include a restaurant that hasn't even opened yet on my list of top contenders," I wrote, "Vongerichten's track record is so strong and he's cooking so extraordinarily well that it's safe to predict he is on the verge of greatness.") Still, the restaurant was, at that moment, unproven.

My dark horse was Les Célébrités, the small, elegant restaurant in the

Essex House, where Christian Delouvrier was chef. (Delouvrier did go on to earn four stars, but not until he left Les Célébrités and took over the kitchen at Lespinasse, in the wake of Gray Kunz's departure.)

So that left Daniel, the ninety-seat restaurant Boulud had opened in the Surrey Hotel in 1993. "The food at Daniel is superb," I wrote, "the dishes polished and distinctive. Chef-owner Daniel Boulud makes each ingredient sing in the harmonic synergy of the finished dish." There were some flaws, however. The kitchen and dining room were both cramped, the bar area tiny and unwelcoming. At a number of tables, wait staff would routinely bump into the backs of chairs. "Still," I added, "the service is impeccable, and the coziness makes one feel privileged to be there."

Finances, at least according to a number of his fellow chefs, were difficult, too, at the time for Boulud. The way another New York chef, Aureole's Charles Palmer, put it at the time, "Daniel's got a hugely successful restaurant, but he's never going to make much money because it's too small and his overhead is too high." When I read back Palmer's quote to Boulud in preparation of the article, he told me, "It's great to be the best, but if you don't make money, you might not be able to *stay* the best."

Was it time for Boulud to think about opening a new restaurant, when this one was only three years old? "My goal is not to be number one," Boulud told me at the time. "It is to be one of the best French restaurants in New York and maybe *the* best French restaurant in New York. I want to grow. Who knows— maybe in a couple of years I may want to change the whole thing and turn it upside down."

Two and a half years later, that's exactly what he did.

By 1998 Boulud had closed Daniel, had reopened the restaurant as Café Boulud, and was preparing to open an incredibly ambitious new restaurant in a nearby location.

The opening of the luxurious new Daniel in January 1999 was auspicious for a number of reasons. For one thing, its $10 million price tag attracted quite a bit of attention. So did the fact that the site Boulud chose—the Mayfair Hotel—was the same site that Le Cirque had occupied until Sirio Maccioni moved it fifteen blocks downtown to the Palace Hotel a year and a half earlier.

But mostly, and this escaped most of the New York and national food press at the time, Boulud intended to do something that had never been done any- where in the world before: At the new Daniel, Boulud would attempt to produce four-star cuisine, food that must be gorgeous, original, amazing—even, one hoped, transcendent—on a completely unprecedented scale, serving up to 380 diners a night, plus another eighty in the banquet room. No one even knew whether such a feat was physically possible.

The press skewed the story as a financial crapshoot: Could a restaurant that was so expensive to create ever hope to be profitable? "A high-stakes gamble," was how Peter Kaminsky characterized it in a *New York* magazine cover story that ran two weeks before the restaurant opened. DANIEL BOULUD BETS THE FARM, shouted out the cover, and more quietly, "The city's premier chef is staking $10 million on the ultimate French country restaurant."

In fact, Boulud and his partner Joel Smilow were never really worried about the money; they didn't see it as risky for their company, the Dinex Group. According to Lili Lynton, Dinex's business consultant and a partner with a 5 percent stake (Boulud and Smilow are equal partners, dividing the remaining 95 percent), the only danger would have been if the economy collapsed soon after the restaurant opened. Under the operating structure they had created, they had plenty of cushion.

Nor would it be a French country restaurant exactly. Rather, it would feature Boulud's ultra-contemporary take on French food, some of which draws its inspiration from the French country dishes of Boulud's childhood. But there would be other influences as well, particularly Italian, Japanese, and American.

The ambitious nature of Boulud's dream restaurant, as well as the food itself, held considerable cultural significance.

At the end of the twentieth century, culture in America was in a curious state. Traditional fine arts—painting, photography, sculpture, music, theater, dance, and literature—had become lackluster and static, as were cinema and fashion.

Had all the new ideas been channeled off into cyberspace?

Yet oddly, the living arts flourished. Architecture was vibrant, as was interior design. This wasn't just a reflection of the nesting trend of the early 1990s; this was living with flair, with style. And nowhere was this desire to live life artfully more obvious than in the realms of cooking and dining. The American food revolution that had been fomented some forty years earlier had finally brought gastronomy to a point where anyone who had the means and knew where to look *could* eat very well.

Furthermore, Americans were becoming interested in the art of dining, of sitting at table. We thought about food more, and even if we weren't cooking more, we were buying an awful lot of cookbooks, dreaming perchance of food.

Chef Daniel Boulud came to the United States in 1981 and would develop his art, his style, over the next twenty years. By the year 2000, he was a mature artist working at the top of his game. And he *was* an artist. The chef as a creative talent was a relatively new idea, at least in America, where for the longest time, cooks were cooks and portions were never big enough. Nor was Boulud the only chef who inhabited such an exalted position: His peers over these years, chefs such as Thomas Keller, David Bouley, Gilbert Le Coze, Eric Ripert, Charlie Trotter, and Gray Kunz, were artists as well. Many of their *sous-chefs* were highly creative talents in their own right, destined to become the major culinary artists of tomorrow.

The restaurants of these gifted chefs function much like the workshops of master painters such as Rembrandt. The artist has a master plan, which is executed by talented apprentices. Daniel was, and is, no different.

Even so, when it opened, there was a real question as to whether Boulud—or indeed anyone—could pull off the kind of inspired cuisine for which he had become known on such an extraordinarily grand scale. Boulud was a visionary, yes, and a four-star chef at the original Daniel, but that restaurant produced four-star food for only ninety seats. The other restaurants considered the country's best are also relatively small. French Laundry in the Napa Valley has only sixty-two seats; Bouley's erstwhile eponymous restaurant accommodated eighty-five; Jean Georges seats seventy. It may not seem immediately obvious, but it's much easier to cook brilliantly when you're cooking for just a few.

The grand new Daniel opened in the middle of January 1999 to much fanfare; expectations ran appropriately high. And on Friday, January 29, when *Times* critic Ruth Reichl weighed in with an advance word (not a review) in her "Diner's Journal" column, those of us who hadn't yet been lucky enough to snag a table flipped open the paper with eager anticipation. "How's the food?" she wrote, asking the question that occupied us all. "Do you really need to ask?" she continued. "If you were a fan of Daniel, you know what to expect: first-rate French food from a talented chef at the peak of his powers." Surely a full-scale review and the requisite four-star rating were just a matter of time.

Two months later, however, Reichl announced that she was leaving her post to become editor-in-chief of *Gourmet* magazine, and all bets were off.

The food world waited tensely to see who would replace her. The *New*

York Observer's "Off the Record," a widely read publishing industry gossip column, reported that the *Times* was likely to hire someone from outside the paper, though possible candidates at the *Times* included Eric Asimov, who penned the paper's "Under $25" restaurant column, and William Grimes, the dining section's highly literate and physically nondescript star feature writer. Grimes intimated that he wasn't interested in the job, stating, "I'm not really a reviewer. I'm a feature writer and reporter. To be a restaurant reviewer you have to be out there eating like an unleashed swine every night."

A few weeks later the announcement was made: Grimes would be the new *New York Times* food critic. His first review appeared on May 19: Coach House, a historic restaurant reinvented by chef-owner Larry Forgione. The review was measured and just-sounding; the assessment, two stars. The following week, Grimes reviewed Roy's New York, the Manhattan outpost of the well-known Hawaiian chef Roy Yamaguchi. "Time has not been kind to Mr. Yamaguchi," he led off his third paragraph. "His freewheeling style has become reckless." And it got worse from there. No stars, just a perfunctory "satisfactory" rating. A collective shudder went up from restaurant kitchens around the city as chefs gave an empathetic wince on behalf of the well-liked, widely respected chef. During her tenure Reichl had awarded very few "satisfactory" ratings; would Grimes's bar be set unrealistically higher?

On Wednesday morning, June 2, gastronomes throughout the five boroughs of New York City eagerly grabbed the dining section to read Grimes's third review. AT THE NEW DANIEL, ran the headline, INVENTION MEETS RESTRAINT. Its placement on the first page of the dining section signaled that this could well be, for Boulud's new restaurant, the all-important four-star review.

The opening paragraphs were enthusiastic. After an attentive, fawning overall description of the restaurant, Grimes described an oxtail terrine as "a dish that could inspire a crime of passion." A couple of paragraphs later, he noted, "He has one foot firmly planted in his family's farm near Lyons, and there's a headlong inventiveness to his cuisine, but at heart he remains a classicist who prizes harmony, refinement and restraint." Such praise from one not given to superlatives augured well for the ultimate assessment. Yet when the review's avid readers flipped inside to the continuation of the review, a shocking verdict greeted them: three stars.

It is on this uncomfortable note that our story begins, seven months later.

One

DANIEL BOULUD, THIS IS YOUR DAY

Thursday, January 4, 2000

THE FOURTH DAY of the new millennium. But to the chefs and captains at Daniel, the line cooks and dishwashers, the sommeliers and maître d's and bakers and office assistants and reservationists and publicists and runners and busboys, it's business as usual. Behind them: the $650-a-head four-course New Year's Eve millennial gala dinner they turned out five nights earlier; before them: 354 covers, a busy Thursday night.

It's 5:20 P.M., and in the main kitchen on the ground floor, the cooks are going through their last-minute preparations: tucking square stainless-steel canisters of garnishes, cut earlier that morning, into refrigerated units at their knees, completing their *mise en place*. In a restaurant kitchen, cooks prepare everything they can hours before they have to actually begin a meal service. The *mise en place* is the organizational foundation of the professional kitchen; without it, the cook, and therefore the restaurant, would be lost. To accomplish it, cooks have been downstairs in the prep kitchen since five o'clock this morning, simmering stocks, making sauces, cutting garnishes, peeling, slicing, dicing vegetables, portioning out meats, poultry, and fish. Now they arrange all their prepared ingredients within arm's reach so no time will be wasted as they cook during the press of dinner service. The first seating will begin at 5:45, unfashionably early in New York, where everyone wants to dine at eight, but at a restaurant as hot as Daniel, one takes what one can get. For despite the fact that Daniel received only three stars from the *New York Times* seven months earlier, Boulud's tremendous talent is lost on no one.

Many culinary-world insiders feel that Grimes's three-star pronouncement was ill-deserved. Some think he reviewed Daniel too soon after opening, before the ambitious restaurant had a chance to find its rhythm, solve early staffing problems, and work out kinks. Others postulate that in his closely watched first reviews, Grimes didn't want to do the expected. There had been talk of star-inflation under Reichl's tenure; perhaps Grimes was eager not to fall victim to the same criticism. So where exactly did Grimes find fault with Daniel in the fateful review? "Mr. Boulud has painted himself into a corner, of course," he had written. He went on to explain that Boulud had already "earned an unassailable reputation as one of the city's most brilliant talents. By now," he continued, "diners expect nonstop fireworks when he gets within fifty feet of a stove, and he has encouraged those expectations, promising to outdo himself at the new Daniel." Grimes apparently did not get those nonstop fireworks. But are *nonstop* fireworks a prerequisite to a four-star review? In a system in which four stars is the maximum, should the attainment of four stars require not only perfection but ceaseless stupefaction and dazzlement, or should it be enough to be one of the three or four best restaurants in the city?

The *Times* review notwithstanding, in January 2000, Boulud is still widely considered to be one of New York City's best chefs—and in fact one of the best in the country. Not only has Daniel received four stars from the *New York Observer* and the *Daily News*, but it was also named best restaurant in New York City in a *Gourmet* magazine readers' poll and voted top restaurant in the country by *Food & Wine*'s readers. In the *Robb Report*, influential critic John Mariani named Daniel Boulud best chef—not just in the country, but in the *world;* the *International Herald Tribune* has dubbed Daniel one of the ten best restaurants in the world as well. Tables, therefore, are not easy to come by.

In the *garde-manger,* a corner of the kitchen just large enough to allow three to stand comfortably, a cook pipes a little puree of white mushroom in a star shape onto tiny homemade potato chips, his head bent myopically close to his work. Another pulls only the tenderest pale yellow-green leaves off of celery hearts. It is in here that all the salads, cold appetizers ("cold apps"), and canapés are assembled. (In restaurant-speak, *canapés* refer to small *amuse-gueules,* the tantalizing little hors d'oeuvres that are placed in front of diners in advance of their first courses.)

Throughout the kitchen, cooks work quickly, meticulously. All wear white jackets topped with white aprons, checkered pants, bare heads. Unlike the line cooks, whose aprons cover their chests, the *sous-chefs* fold down the bib part to reveal their name stitched on their jacket; otherwise, only their shoes belie individuality. Some, mostly the French cooks, wear worn-looking clogs; the rest wear running shoes. A vague nervous energy underlies the quiet activity. A young cook at the soup station pours soups into cylindrical stainless-steel *bain-marie* inserts, then places them in hot water: Jerusalem artichoke velouté, curried cream of cauliflower and apple. He organizes his garnishes—cubes of foie gras and sage-garlic croutons for the velouté, shrimp and coriander for the cauliflower—and places them conveniently within reach in shoulder-height crannies.

Although the kitchen is large by New York City standards—a full 1,750 square feet, with soaring thirteen-foot ceilings in the pickup area—so is the dining room, which can deliver up to 140 "covers" or meals per seating, up to 380 per service. The kitchen staff is also large, with fifteen or so cooking in the main kitchen at any one time, and a total of forty cooks on the payroll. It is said that in traditional French cooking nothing is ever wasted, a practice that even restaurants at this level abide by; here in Daniel Boulud's kitchen, space, too, is at a premium, and not a cubic inch goes unused.

To the cashmere-coated and fur-wrapped diners who slide from cab to curb as they arrive at the restaurant, Daniel sweeps into view from another angle. It's cold outside, and melancholy traces of the day's crystalline blue sky still streak the chilly evening air of January. At least the days have begun to lengthen. As one couple pushes through the heavy revolving doors of the former Mayfair Hotel, there's a little puff, a slight change of pressure; they leave winter behind and gently enter another world. On the left, a smiling face peeks out from the Dutch door of a discreetly tucked-away coat check; its occupant emerges, arm crooked to receive wraps. At Daniel, one is cared for, attended to. Or as the French say, *soigné*.

The lucky diners glide past the whimsical tables of the entryway lounge, passing the bar on the left, with tender strains of Ella Fitzgerald issuing forth. A tall, dark (of course), and imposing Frenchman nods gravely, smiling a little underneath it all, and ushers them to the front desk.

"Good evening," bids an elegant young Asian woman, her hair caught up in a chignon. She's dressed in black, a tailored jacket, bare at the neck save for a delicate gold necklace. She raises her chin expectantly. They give their name, she receives them politely, with reserve, yet somehow she seems honestly happy to see them this evening. She leads them to the entrance to the dining room, where they're met by a polished maître d'.

Now they're poised to enter an idealized Venetian villa of a dining room, swathed in deep tomato-soup reds and saturated blues, pale roses, burnished golds, velvet and brocade, alabaster and terra-cotta, with soaring ceilings and graceful pillars—Shakespearean Italy as imagined, perhaps, by Franco Zefferelli. A look upward at the arch above the mahogany doors marking the entry reveals a gold-leafed inscription: DANIEL — MCMXCVIII.

This chef, one understands, wants to be remembered.

The maître d' shows them to their table, pulling out their chairs. An assistant captain comes to welcome them, offers an apéritif. Nothing is rushed: The idea, after all, is to relax and enjoy. Before long, the captain—a handsome Frenchman, more likely than not—arrives bearing long, carnelian-red menus in both arms, menus that contain the blueprint for the most magnificent meal imaginable.

They will enjoy. And they will pay: Appetizers at dinner here run from sixteen dollars to twenty-eight, or even $140 if you opt for an ounce and a half of Beluga caviar; main courses range from thirty-three to thirty-eight dollars. The average dinner cover, meaning the cost of a meal for one person, including beverages, but not including taxes and gratuities, is $184. Dinner for two, including tax and an 18 percent tip (standard in a restaurant of this caliber), averages $465. But this happy couple needn't worry about that; they just take it all in.

"Two pree-fee soup, followed by two pree-fee veal!" shouts executive chef Alex Lee in the kitchen, sticking a ticket (also known as a dupe) up on the board in front of him. "Pree-fee" is restaurant shorthand for an item from the *prix fixe* (actually pronounced *pree-feex*) menu. "A terrine and a ravioli followed by a paupiette and a beef!" and another ticket goes up. Lee stands at what is known as the pass—the broad counter, topped with a two-sided slanted board for holding tickets, with room to slide finished plates onto large trays in the pickup area, the opposite side of the counter. There runners pick up the trays, backing through the swinging "out" door that leads to the service area of the dining room (out of diners' views), and then to the tables.

This is where the ranking chef in the kitchen—whether it's Boulud himself, Alex Lee, or a *sous-chef*—stands, facing the runners, calling out orders to the line cooks behind him, "expediting," acting as sort of a traffic cop throughout the service. Controlling traffic from the runners' side is a head runner, also known as the expediter, who communicates with the chef on one side and the team of runners on the other. He keeps track of which tables are eating which courses, which plates have gone out, and which should go out next. Although the expediting chef often changes several times during service, the expediter on the runners' side does not.

Another ticket comes in. "Ordering one tuna tartare and one terrine, followed by one rabbit and one *pintade!*" shouts Lee, reading it. The line cooks behind him scramble. The *saucier*, the cook responsible for the meats and their attendant sauces, browns two boned baby legs of lamb, each rolled tightly into a tidy log and tied with cotton string; herbs are tucked in place. He tips the straight-sided copper *sauteuse* toward himself and rhythmically spoons the fats and juices that fall back over the meat with a *click, click, click, click* as the spoon hits the side of the pan.

At Daniel a tremendous amount of attention is paid to every dish. That may be the most remarkable thing about this particular kitchen: Boulud has the resources, both in terms of manpower as well as money and space, to focus on each plate in a way that's impossible in most restaurants, where normally everyone does a few plates at once. Boulud's dishes often involve long lists of elements, each of which requires special preparation, even if it is just a garnish, such as tomato confit or a powder of dried Meyer lemon zest that dusts a plate, adding a new dimension of flavor should a forkful happen to sweep through it. In this way, Boulud's kitchen more closely resembles that of a French two- or three-star establishment, with their large brigades, than most American restaurants.

The *entremétier* working next to the *saucier* is responsible for his vegetable garnishes. He dollops some sauce on a plate, then tosses some herbs in the vegetables and shakes. On the fish line, a young American cook—the *poissonnier*—sautés scallops.

"Did you put the garlic in there?" asks Lee.

"Yes, I did, Chef," says the *poissonnier*.

"You should get a little more color on them," says Lee, looking into the pan.

The *entremétier* makes the contents of his pan leap—the word *sauté* derives from the French *faire sauter*, "to make jump." On the counter by his elbow, a squat metal ring sits in the center of a soup plate, filled with onion confit that's been deglazed with a little red wine. The ring is used to keep the onions in place as the dish is assembled.

"Nicki, turn that down please," shouts Lee to the cook working the soup station as he fiddles with the scallops in the fish cook's pan. "This way you get the better seal," he explains to the fish cook. Lee arranges five scallops atop the onions, removes the metal ring, then puts more onion confit on a dish, topping it with two scallops. "This is all the flavor here," he says, referring to the scallop juices he now pours back into the pan with some potatoes that will also garnish the dish. "Nicki," he calls, "you're going to get a little *passoire* for that." *Passoire* is French for colander; in restaurant kitchens it's the preferred word.

Teaching is part of the role of a chef, and Alex Lee is known among his present and former charges—Daniel alumni around the country—as a formidable teacher, as generous with suggestions for improving technique as he is ready to share his encyclopedic knowledge of ingredients. Lee, who has been working with Boulud since 1989, when he joined him at Le Cirque, is a solidly built, physically fit Chinese-American man. Of medium height and dark honey-skinned, Lee has short, thick black hair that sticks straight up on top; his full lips lend an air of sympathy. The thirty-five-year-old chef is tough with his cooks, but fair, and they love him.

Another cook brings in a huge sheet pan holding prepped pieces of meat, covered with another sheet pan. "Did you dry it?" asks Lee, glancing over. "Is it dry?"

"Yes, Chef. . . ."

The cook reaches into a five-by-seven stainless-steel box of sea salt, strews it over the meat with generous fingers. Now the reason for the second sheet pan becomes evident: He clamps top and bottom pans together with both hands, and inverts the whole thing, eliminating the need to flip fifty or sixty pieces of meat individually. He salts again.

"Ordering on 31," thunders Lee, moving back to the pass as another ticket comes in. "Pree-fee risotto, pree-fee salad, followed by pree-fee veal, pree-fee cod."

Ironically, though some of the kitchen's most exacting work goes on in the *garde-manger,* it is here that many cooks begin when they come to work at Daniel. The canapé cook puts the finishing touches on artichoke leaves filled with artichoke puree, topped with duck prosciutto. Daniel's customers love vegetable canapés. A classic French restaurant would serve only the artichoke heart and crown; here, using the leaves for a canapé means nothing is wasted.

Across the small cranny from the canapé cook, Armand, the *chef garde-manger,* sauces a plate, arranges strips of marinated raw tuna in a perfect rectangle onto the sauce, places several pieces of sautéed veal sweetbreads on top of the tuna. This tongue-in-cheek take on *vitello tonnato* looks like a painting. He garnishes it with baby mâche (lamb's lettuce) and celery leaves. He turns to a dark sauce in a metal container in a *bain-marie* of ice, sticks in his finger, and tastes. This will be used for a different dish; he's just checking the seasoning.

"An illegible ticket!" shouts Lee, stretching as he tries to read an order on the board. It's the first time he's raised his voice this evening, but it won't be the last. Squinting, he finally deciphers the order, barking it out. Everyone does a momentary heads-up to hear it. They never know whether a given order will concern their station, so everyone must listen well whenever one is called. "Be careful," Lee warns the brigade behind him, "you're going to get a little hit now." He pops three, four, five tickets onto the board. "Three risotto on table 12, no shellfish. Followed by *vitello,* lamb, beef, and duck tasting."

"Pick up 31, Chef!" shouts the *saucier.*

"Thirty-one, out!" yells Lee.

"Thirty-one already left?" says a line cook.

"Two chestnut, two consommé coming?" yells Lee.

"Yes, Chef!"

"Two mushroom?"

"Yes, Chef!"

"Ordering one tuna, two terrine, and a ravioli! Ordering one duck, two lamb, one rare, one medium-rare, one bass. Two pree-fee crab working?"

"Yes!" shout the two *garde-manger* cooks in unison.

"Vamano, vamano!" shouts Lee. (This is kitchen Spanish, not textbook Spanish.)

"Ordering one tuna, one crab, and two ravioli, followed by two sea bass, one veal, and one lamb, rare!"

Daniel Boulud, the white-jacketed sovereign who presides over this productive realm, is up in the "skybox," his glassed-in office overlooking the kitchen. He's chatting with a visiting chef from Denver.

"One chicken, no onion, no garlic, no chives," shouts Lee from down below. "And a vegetable side! Three lobster, Dungeness crab is up on 65!" He puts up another ticket: "Ordering three on 34: three pree-fee artichoke, followed by three pree-fee crab, two pree-fee bass, and one pree-fee swordfish, followed by one pree-fee swordfish and two pree-fee lamb! *Vitello,* crab, and sardine tasting, working?"

"Yeah, Chef!" yells a cook. Lee swigs from a two-liter bottle of Evian and starts shouting commands in French. Things become tense.

"*Attention—chaud!*" cries a line cook, delivering two plates to the heavy silver trays on the pass.

"Two pree-fee bass coming?"

"Yes, Chef!"

A barely perceptible beat as Boulud descends the stairs leading down from the skybox with the visiting chef.

At the bottom of the steep stairs, Boulud kisses the visiting chef on both cheeks, and as his friend leaves through the double swinging door leading to the service exit, Boulud takes his place at the pass, picking up a ticket from a spindle next to the board. Lee migrates to the *garde-manger*. Spoon in left hand, damp cloth in right, Boulud wipes the edges of a couple of plates ready to go out.

"Ordering, please!" booms Boulud. Though he's not tall, he's imposing, and the kitchen undergoes a perceptible change when he steps in. His weighty voice is almost operatic, coming up from deep inside him. He doesn't need to shout, it's so profound. The baritone carries well, and though Boulud has a French accent, it's not extreme. He is handsome, dressed in crisp whites, very white, his jacket accented with royal blue piping; gray slacks, sleek Italian leather shoes complete the picture. "Two smoked salmon, one tuna-caviar, one *ballottine,* followed by two sole, one lamb medium, and one pheasant."

"Right behind you!" says Armand, stepping around Boulud with two plates from the *garde-manger.* Now Boulud moves to the soup station, tastes the soups, conferring with the soup cook as Lee steps back to the pass.

The fish cook wrings his hand, grimacing. A burn. Bare-handed, he has just grabbed a bowl sitting on a hot surface.

"Okay?" asks David, his *entremétier.*

"Yeah. I had the bowl sitting up there," says the *poissonnier,* indicating the hot top of the range. "Complete idiocy."

"Armand! Armand!" shouts Lee. "*Les crabes—ils manquent un peu de sel, hein?*" The crab salads are undersalted.

Boulud appears in the *garde-manger,* tastes the crab salad, picks up three plated orders of it, wipes the edges. He's now moving very fast. The bank of video monitors between the pass and the *garde-manger* show a full dining room. Boulud calls to Armand to bring him vinegar—it appears in a flash in a plastic squeeze bottle. Boulud squirts it onto three crab salads. They weren't only undersalted, they also lacked the vinegar's acid note.

Boulud quickly sauces three squab plates. Lee steps in and takes over. A huge flame jumps up on a meat burner as the *saucier* sautés. He blows on it. The tension is electric. "Everybody out of my station, okay?" says the *saucier*, edgily. If he can't concentrate and keep his rhythm, all is lost.

Boulud starts yelling next, to a *sous-chef:* "*Il n'y a pas d'organisation. Le pigeon, par exemple.* The squab. Do you agree or not?" It is that *sous-chef's* responsibility to plate the dishes coming out of the meat station, and if the station gets behind this early in the service, the whole kitchen will be thrown off.

The *sous-chef* mutters something.

"And now they're all complaining!" Boulud continues angrily. The *garde-manger* cooks glance over to see what the commotion is. "Okay?! A chicken, please!"

Boulud turns to the tickets on the board.

"There's no more fish special," shouts Lee. "That's eighty-six, okay?"

"Ninety-five is Mr. Bill Blass," says Boulud. "Who took the order?" The famous clothing designer, a regular, is sitting at a table in the lounge.

"The cocktail waiter," says another waiter.

Boulud looks at the video monitor trained on the lounge and picks up the phone. "*Allo? Bill Blass est là. . . . Trois canapés VIP pour Bill Blass. . . .*" He looks around. "*Omar! Quatre-vingt quinze ou quatre-vingt seize?* Who took the order?" Pushing buttons, he zooms in on camera 8. "Sixty-two is you, George? There will be an extra course for 62." With sixteen video cameras hidden throughout the dining room and lounge areas, Boulud can literally zoom in on a table to see how the glazed spiced squab is going down or whether a table of VIPs has finished its complementary extra course. Although such systems will become more common in restaurant kitchens over the coming year, they are as yet quite rare. Boulud did have one, however, at the old Daniel.

George, the server assigned to table 62, comes in. "For Bill Blass," he asks Boulud, "can you do some crispy sweetbreads?"

"Of course," says Boulud. "Ask him if he wants *persillade*. We did that for him at lunch once. Ask him if he likes a little garlic." He hands a soup plate back to Nicki, who had just sent it out. It's chipped.

"What are you doing?" screams Lee suddenly to a runner. "*Tu prends pas une assiette toute seule!*" You don't take a plate out by itself! Orders must be kept together so the entire party is served simultaneously.

"*Ça commence à m'emmerder complètement. . . .*" mutters Boulud. This shit is really beginning to bug me.

On the other side of the swinging doors, of course, the diners haven't the least suspicion of the cacaphonous yet concentrated frenzy of the kitchen. The carpeted and upholstered dining room, swathed in silk and brocade, softens voices, muffles noise. It is a world apart: a world for civilized conversation, for enjoyment of the pleasures of the table.

In describing Boulud's food, one finds oneself grasping at contradictions. It is at once extremely elaborate and startlingly simple. A dish may encompass a long list of ingredients, but the primary flavors work so harmoniously together that it seems artless. Balance is of the utmost importance. Each dish is a thing of beauty: not particularly architectural or showy, but artfully designed and eminently appetizing. The phrase "embarrassment of riches" might have been invented to describe the gustatory pleasures here, for they are so many and so varied.

Boulud is known as a master of classic terrines and *ballottines*, and his range in the *garde-manger* is tremendous, from a painterly presentation of tuna carpaccio with crispy sweetbreads, set off by a garnish as miraculously simple as celery leaves, to a lusty *ballottine* of duck foie gras with rhubarb confit, spiced hazelnuts, and a tangle of upland cress. Soups are silken essences of peas or intense wild mushroom veloutés, made luxurious with hidden treasures, depending on the soup and the season—foie gras or lobster or maybe smoked salmon. The risottos, a specialty here, are light and frothy, imbued with the deep flavor of the best stocks.

Boulud loves sardines and anchovies and frogs' legs and squab, featuring them in gorgeously structured dishes, resplendent with the vegetables that best express the season: favas and morels in the spring perhaps, or porcini and salsify in the fall. And oh, when those truffles start raining down upon the dishes in late autumn, turning from white to black as winter sets in, it is luxury itself.

Great chefs love fish—it has often been said that's where they best show off their creativity and technique, and at Daniel that's no exception. Fish is an event here, and Daniel's preparations often feature meat *jus* or wine sauces, giving them depth of flavor; with their gorgeous garnishes (the spectacular melanges of vegetables are enough to feast on by themselves), these are fish to contend with. And although meats can sometimes be anticlimactic at such gastronomic temples, at Daniel one has the sense that Boulud's soul resides in the rich pork belly, the glorious short ribs, the racy squab. Their sauces pull these meat dishes up into the realm of the sublime.

The menu is copious—even overwhelming—and it changes frequently. At lunch and dinner, *prix fixe* menus are offered along with à la carte items and chef's tasting menus of varying complexity. Sometimes there are special seasonal menus as well, such as a "celebration of truffles." A long list of market specials, "Les Plats du Marché," changes daily, depending on the products that have come in and the whims of Alex Lee and his *sous-chefs*. Beneath the list of specials there is always "Le Plat Classique"—something along the lines of Confit de Canard à la Sarladaise (duck confit with sautéed potatoes in the classic preparation from Sarlat) or Poitrine de Porc aux Lentilles et Racines de Saison (braised pork belly with lentils and seasonal root vegetables). Twice each season, Boulud changes the menu completely, though there are signature dishes that always remain and others that appear and reappear according to the season.

What's amazing about this restaurant is the range one experiences at table. Eating at Daniel is like going on a journey through every flavor and texture and temperature sensation, through every kind of food, from west to east and back again. The bread alone is a miracle—if it weren't for all the other gustatory delights, one would happily eat it all day. The cheese trolley is worthy of a visit all by itself. And the wine list is a document that any oenophile would be happy to read in bed.

Desserts are every bit as appealing as what comes before; here, too, harmony and balance are key. And after the *tartes Tatin* or chocolate-passionfruit bombes or *Dacquoises* and the *pyramides glacées* comes a gleaming silver tray of petits fours—the fragile *pâte de fruit*, the tender homemade marshmallow, the coconut *rocher*, and then, ah, the chocolates, *fait maison*—the best dark chocolate filled with bergamot and orange or cinnamon *ganache*. Or try, won't you, an Armagnac truffle? One couldn't possibly after all that one's already eaten, but then really, who could resist? And finally, when all is said and done, those magical, ethereal, warm madeleines appear, nestled in a lotus blossom made of linen.

Wednesday, January 12

THE DAY STARTS early for Fay, the lunchtime *saucier*. She leaves her apartment in the Kensington neighborhood of Brooklyn at five-thirty in the morning, catching the Q train into Manhattan. At that ungodly hour, she always makes sure to sit in the middle car—the one with the conductor—where there are actually quite a few people, faces she sees every day.

When Fay arrives at the restaurant thirty or forty minutes later, the meat and bones she needs are in the walk-in, and she heads downstairs to the prep kitchen to start her *jus* and her short ribs. Lupe, the butcher, comes in at eight A.M. and hands her the rest of the meats she'll need for lunch service; these she ordered at the end of her shift the day before from Jed, the steward responsible for purchasing. The *saucier* is responsible not only for preparing all of the sauces, but also for cooking all of the meats and poultry during service. At ten A.M. she loads the meats and other ingredients onto a metal cart, wheels it out of the prep kitchen, along a corridor, into an elevator, and brings it to the upstairs kitchen, where she'll set up and make the sauces for lunch.

Fay grew up in Massachusetts, wanting to be a doctor—a pathologist, to be exact. She loved physiology, especially dissecting things. Plans changed in high school when she started dating a guy who went to Johnson & Wales, the well-known cooking school, and she decided to do the same. "You can't do this to your life," a guidance counselor told her at the time, but she enrolled anyway. When she came to work at Daniel, just a couple months after it opened, Boulud proposed that she work in the pastry kitchen. Although Fay loves to bake, she never wanted to be a pastry chef; she prefers the energy and chaos of being on the line to the more predictable discipline of the pastry kitchen. So she convinced Boulud to let her start as *saucier*. Now she finds cutting up meat as satisfying as cutting up bodies, and although this is a man's world, she holds her own.

Upstairs in the skybox, Boulud's offices, the reservation list lies on Boulud's desk. A copy will be placed in ten different stations throughout the restaurant, including the kitchen. The list for today's lunch shows that Helen Frankenthaler is seated in the lounge, where lunch and dinner are also served. Amazingly, there's no indication that anyone knows that she's a world-renowned painter.

The skybox is divided into two rooms. At the top of the steep flight of industrial metal stairs is a small office with three desks; beyond that, through a door, is the chef's denlike office. In the front office, the desk that is usually unoccupied is Boulud's. On it: telephone, books, file folders, several snapshots of Alix, Boulud's ten-year-old daughter. There's also a black leather binder with lettering on the front that announces: DANIEL BOULUD "THIS IS YOUR DAY."

To the left of the entry is the desk of Hilary Tolman, Boulud's assistant, and along the facing wall, another desk. Tall cherrywood closets line the far wall; opening them reveals seven or eight beautifully pressed chef's jackets, all Boulud's. Tolman's coat hangs alongside them.

Hilary Tolman doesn't fit the picture of a typical chef's assistant. Bright and serious, tall, blond, and slim, the thirty-five-year-old looks and sounds as American as apple pie, yet when she speaks French, what comes out sounds like native *Parisienne*. Surprisingly, Tolman grew up neither in France nor the United States, but in Japan, spending her first seventeen years in Tokyo. Her father, originally from the Boston area, worked as a diplomat; her mother hailed from the Washington, D.C., region, so the family spoke English at home. However, Tolman attended French schools in Tokyo from kindergarten to high school, and by the time she left for the United States to enroll as a freshman at Smith College, of the three languages she spoke fluently, English was the one with which she felt least comfortable. After graduating college and attending business school, she worked as an investment banker for a number of years and then moved to Paris, where she met her husband (she sometimes goes by the name Tolman-Michon), and the two founded an executive recruiting company. When her husband died, tragically young, of pancreatic cancer, Tolman came to New York, at loose ends. One evening at a party she bumped into a friend, Georgette Farkas, who happens to be Daniel Boulud's director of public relations and marketing. Georgette sensed it might do her friend good to get out of the house. "Are you looking for something to do?" she asked Tolman, then told her that Boulud was looking to hire an assistant. "You love food so much. This could be a fun experience for you."

"I don't really want to be somebody's assistant," replied Tolman, who was accustomed to having her *own* assistants. Yet she agreed to meet Boulud for an interview. She was surprised to find that Boulud gave her an hour and a half of his undivided attention. Impressed by his energy and intelligence, Tolman decided to give it a go. Boulud, sensitive to her situation, agreed to hire her, though she would commit to just one year. Two years later, she's still working for him. The perks don't hurt: One of them is being allowed to order two meals a day from the menu.

Boulud's inner office is another small square room, this one perched over the kitchen. A glossy mahogany table extends out from the left-hand wall, with banquette benches on either side, like the dining table of an exquisite yacht. From here, Boulud can look directly down onto the kitchen while conferring with colleagues, being interviewed by journalists, or otherwise taking care of business. This catbird seat is a real luxury; in most restaurants, the chef's office is a tiny, windowless nook with no direct connection to the kitchen.

Today the chef sits taking a phone call and rewriting a menu at the same time.

The call is from Shelby Bryan, who will be hosting a fund-raising dinner for the Democratic National Party next month; he'd like to have it in the private dining room at Daniel. Bryan is one of the Democratic Party's largest fund-raisers, as well as one of its most generous donors—he has given an estimated $500,000 to the party. Boulud jots down *5:45–8:00, 2/24* and assures Bryan it will be no problem. President William Jefferson Clinton is to be the guest of honor.

In fact, Boulud already has an event scheduled in the Bellecour Room, the restaurant's banquet room, for that evening—a party for CBS, beginning with cocktails from seven to eight. Boulud puts in a call to CBS, suggests delaying the cocktails a little—making it seven-thirty to eight-thirty. He proposes moving the cocktail portion of their event to the lounge, where he promises to seat thirty people comfortably. "Okay," he says. "Do you think I could have your answer in a couple of hours?" Boulud is completely unflustered by the conflict.

Nor is he unaccustomed to cooking for world leaders: At the tender age of fifteen, he cooked for Georges Pompidou and Valéry Giscard d'Estaing. At the time, he was an apprentice at the *Michelin* two-star Nandron, in Lyons, and he had a special pass to enter the Préfecture du Rhône and the Lyons city hall in order to cook for dignitaries. He cooked for Ronald Reagan when he was working in Washington, D.C., in the early 1980s. In 1998 he was chosen to cook for *Time* magazine's seventy-fifth-anniversary celebration at Radio City Music Hall. *Time* invited eighty-four people who had appeared on its cover, giving Boulud the opportunity to cook for Mikhail Gorbachev, the Queen of England, and President Clinton, among others. (Although he got an even bigger kick when Sharon Stone recognized *him* across the room and waved prettily to him.)

Al Gore dined here at Daniel last fall, and Yassir Arafat a few months before that. When Arafat came, snipers patrolled the rooftop of the brownstone across the street. Arafat's security team wanted to have dogs sniff through the kitchen, but here Boulud drew the line. Although the *New York Times* reported it was health-related concerns that kept the dogs out of the food preparation areas, in fact Boulud simply wouldn't allow it.

Boulud had also cooked for Clinton at a fund-raiser at Bruce Wasserstein's estate out in the Hamptons the previous fall. The president honored the chef by coming to meet him in the kitchen, where he spent ten minutes chatting before going back to schmooze the sixty party faithfuls who had spent twenty-five thousand dollars a plate to dine on Boulud's victuals.

After finishing with Bryan, Boulud starts to flip through a stack of papers, then phones downstairs to inquire about someone who has applied for a chef position; Alex Lee has asked the prospective cook to come in and "trail" for a few days. Trailing is in effect a short tryout in which the cook follows one of the line cooks, stepping in to help when asked to. In this way, Lee and Boulud can take a measure of his skills before making a commitment. "What about this Blake somebody?" Boulud says into the phone. "What is he flying his résumé around for?" He continues flipping through the papers as he talks. "What is he looking for?" asks Boulud. "A stable position, or something else? What is he looking for salary-wise?" Boulud listens. "Okay, when? You don't know? Because we need one or two strong guys here."

Now, holding the résumé, he punches Blake's phone number, gets his machine. "Hello," he says, "this is Daniel Boulud. If you could call me, I'd like to have a word with you and know a little bit what you're planning to do. I just want to know what date was decided and when you want to come, and maybe before we could have a little talk."

Boulud punches more buttons, calling Lee again. "Joseph Gabriel, New England Culinary Institute," he says. "He's coming in on the nineteenth to trail, but he has trailed here before, no? Did we promise him a job? Is he coming?"

Michael Lawrence, the dining room director, comes in with a beige tablecloth and waits for Boulud to finish his call. Lawrence, a good-natured Louisiana native, has infinite patience, yet he always wears a pained, world-weary expression. "We're short on seventy-twos, Chef," he says. "Seventy-two" refers to a seventy-two-inch tablecloth. "Do you want to use this one instead?"

Boulud looks at the alternative tablecloth and picks up the phone, calls his director of operations. "Brett? What's happening with the seventy-two tablecloths? It's like—is it cotton or synthetic?" He fingers it, grimacing a little. "Michael is tight with that today." He hangs up. "Michael, can we avoid using that, or not? It's not terribly bad, but it's not great. Can you put it on the banquettes in the back or something?"

"Yes, Chef," says Lawrence, drawing out "chehhhf" with his Louisiana lilt.

"Just keep it all in one line somewhere," says Boulud, meaning tablecloths of that type should be used on *all* the tables in a row in order not to break the visual line. No detail is too small to command his attention.

Downstairs, lunch service is in full swing.

Phil, an *entremétier*, works with Fay on vegetable garnishes for the meat dishes. For the hanger steak, he reheats a confit of shallots, cooked for hours in butter with a reduction of two-thirds red wine and one-third port, salt, and pepper, which he prepared the previous afternoon, after service. The red wine is a Côteaux du Languedoc, Prieuré de St.-Jean de Bébian 1991—the restaurant's current all-purpose cooking red, a good but not extravagant wine, with some complexity, that retailed for about twelve dollars when it was released. Next to it goes a salad garnish of organic watercress from Sausalito, California. Phil has worked at Daniel since the opening. He started out on rotisserie, then worked hot apps and pasta, moving to the meat side just before the holidays. It's not his first job as a cook; he worked at Rubicon and Jardinière in San Francisco before moving to Chicago with his girlfriend, Maria. One day his former boss, Jardinière's chef-owner, Traci Des Jardins, called Phil in Chicago and told him she had sent his résumé to Daniel Boulud. Boulud called Phil and offered to try him out, and he moved to New York on two weeks' notice; Maria came a month later and went to work as Boulud's assistant, a post she filled for the first two months after the restaurant opened. (Hilary Tolman was working as Boulud's assistant at Café Boulud, and the two switched positions.) In the meantime, Phil and Maria have become engaged, and what an engagement—for the past six months they've seen each other only on Sundays.

Fay pulls a hanger steak out of a refrigerated drawer, then washes her hands. Some restaurant kitchens are hygienic, with cooks who "work clean"; many are not. The kitchen staff at Daniel is fairly fastidious about hygiene, and any time cooks touch raw meat, they must wash their hands so as not to contaminate anything else. The hanger steak is a long slab, a cut large enough for two to three portions; each cow has two of them. Although it's not the tenderest cut, hanger steak is known as the most flavorful of all the steaks; traditionally, butchers keep them for themselves, though in the past few years they've become popular bistro cuts. French menus list them as *onglets*. Fay portions it out, her long knife moving through the steak like, well, like butter.

While Fay works on a lamb saddle stuffed with spinach and tomato *coulis*, Phil prepares a potato garnish, using sliced German Butter Ball potatoes he has rinsed four or five times in water. These potatoes are somewhat waxier than Yukon Golds; rinsing them eliminates some of their starch so they will cook up nice and crisp. He dries off enough slices for a portion, tosses a knob of butter into a hot pan, waits a moment, and adds the potatoes, grinding pepper on top from a small stainless-steel Peugeot grinder he keeps balanced on the bar of the oven door. Another garnish for the lamb—tomato and red pepper compote—simmers in a huge stockpot in front of Phil. Next to that he's got leeks that have been blanched in water, two slim yellow and two orange carrots braised in chicken stock and butter. These will garnish the chicken.

Phil turns his potatoes with a sauté fork known as a *fourchette*. Although many cooks would use tongs for this job, the way Phil sees it, there's no finesse in tongs; he prefers the challenge of using the classic tool. Now he adds lightly caramelized onions and a little garlic, a handful of finely chopped parsley. Grabbing the handle of the sauté pan, he makes the contents jump. And again. And cooks them till they're golden brown. Then they are artfully stacked onto a plate; Phil puts the plate on the work area to Fay's left.

Having sautéed the hanger steak and let it rest five minutes so the juices retreat back into the meat, Fay strains a brown sauce into a tiny copper pan, then slices the meat on the bias and arranges it around Phil's potatoes. Cyrille Allannic, a French *sous-chef*, pours the sauce out onto the plate and piles watercress on top.

Fay is already on to the next plate as Allannic transfers the completed hanger steak to the tray on the pass where the rest of the order has also just landed. A runner wipes the plates and takes the tray out to the dining room.

Allannic has been with Boulud since May 1993, following him from the old Daniel to the new. Like the other French *sous-chef*, Frédéric Côte, Allannic is responsible for creating a special each day, and then supervising and plating on the hot line. Allannic plates on the meat side, Côte on the fish side.

Fay uses an electric knife to slice stuffed capon. Her regular knives are sharp, but with stuffed meats, the electric one does a neater job; the filling doesn't fall out.

Cornelius Gallagher, known as Neil, is the new *sous-chef*. An eager, slim redhead full of precise, nervous energy, Neil worked most recently at Peacock Alley, the underrated restaurant at the Waldorf-Astoria Hotel, under the visionary young French chef Laurent Gras. Before that, he worked at Bouley and Lespinasse, and he did a *stage* (a brief, unpaid working stint that every chef does in order to gain experience and learn from masters) at L'Espérance, chef Marc Meneau's famous restaurant in Burgundy, which at that time had three *Michelin* stars. In French kitchens, Gallagher was impressed by how the chefs took a recipe two or three steps further than they might in the U.S. Gallagher carries around with him a fat black binder filled with the recipes he's picked up here and there, but mostly there, in France. Today he has it open to Oysters en Gelée. On the opposite page is a list of preparations for the *garde-manger:* foie gras, vinaigrettes, rabbit terrine, gallette vin. In any other field, someone like Gallagher might be seen as suspiciously gung-ho. Here his enthusiasm is a huge asset.

"Push the service," says a cook, meaning everyone should work faster, "because someone's coming down the stairs."

The someone, it turns out, is Alex Lee.

Entering the kitchen, wearing his trademark baggy black-and-white-striped chef pants, Lee greets everyone, shaking their hands. Then he starts his rounds, tasting everyone's sauces, dishes. It's quality control. Before long, he lands at Phil's station. He samples Phil's potatoes.

"You didn't taste it!" he admonishes Phil, making a face. "Make believe you're cooking for Maria's family. It's too salty."

Up in the skybox, Lynn Heller, an editor at *Bon Appétit* magazine, is lunching with three colleagues. A white tablecloth has gone over the table; a runner has set it with china and crystal. Boulud does this now and then for particularly special VIPs, and few are more important than active members of the food press.

After schmoozing with the editors a bit, Boulud sweeps into the kitchen.

"Okay, let's go!" he says. "We're going to cook for the ladies up there."

"Two pree-fee endive, followed by two pree-fee *chapon*," shouts Alex Lee, standing at the pass. Now he shouts toward the *garde-manger*. "Hello! Do you guys have *sauce mignonette* and *sauce cocktail pour les huîtres?*" He needs sauces for a special order of oysters. "Gimme a shallot, please. Does anybody have a shallot?! *Vinaigre de vin rouge?!*"

The soup cook runs to the walk-in refrigerator on the other side of the fish station and comes back out with a large plastic jug full of red-wine vinegar. He throws together a quick cocktail sauce—a squeeze of ketchup, a dollop of horseradish, a few healthy grinds of black pepper. Of course, nothing on the menu of such a gastronomic showplace would call for a condiment as pedestrian as cocktail sauce, but Daniel is the kind of restaurant that likes to deliver whatever the guests demand. And Lee knows that unlike the French, who savor their favorite bivalves with just a squirt of lemon, when Americans see oysters, there's at least one in every crowd who will want cocktail sauce in addition to *sauce mignonette*.

In the *garde-manger*, Boulud prepares a three-tiered *plateau* for the editors in the skybox. It's widely believed that celebrity chefs do not spend much time in their own kitchens. Such is not at all the case with Daniel Boulud. Although he travels more and more, whenever he's in town, he's almost invariably in the restaurant, and during service, he spends most of that time in the kitchen. Among food cognoscenti there is a persistent belief that it's a bad idea to frequent dining establishments on the "chef's night off," but the only night off for Boulud, Lee, and the *sous-chefs* is Sunday, because the restaurant is closed on Sunday. Since the restaurant is also closed for lunch on Monday, the day line cooks alternate working Monday nights with the night line cooks, giving them an occasional five-day workweek. But Boulud is there week in, week out.

In fact, sometimes Boulud muses that it would be better for his *sous-chefs* if he *weren't* around so much—he feels more autonomy would be good for their creativity. But for Boulud it is a physical impossibility not to be there behind the pass or in his office. How could he be elsewhere? This is his *life*. He even lives, with his wife, Micky, and their ten-year-old daughter, Alix, in an apartment directly over the restaurant, part of his deal when he leased the restaurant space from Colony Capital, the company that took over and developed the old Mayfair Hotel into condominiums.

Of course, Boulud is often required to attend special events—awards presentations, gala dinners, media appearances, and the like. And the chef is active in a number of charities, including Citymeals-on-Wheels, an organization that provides hot meals to homebound elderly people; the Jewish National Fund; the March of Dimes; Lincoln Center for the Performing Arts; and others; and sometimes his presence is required behind the stove for these or other organizations. A dinner at which Boulud cooks, after all, always draws big crowds. But most days he can be found at Daniel.

On top of the pass is an assortment of canapés for the *Bon Appétit* editors. "Can you make me a little blinis?" Boulud calls to the soup cook, who shares the induction range with the hot-apps-and-pasta cook. The custom-designed six-burner induction range is the technical marvel of the kitchen, designed by Jean-Pierre Boué of Grande Cuisine Systems in Toronto. Its greatest benefit is the precision of its heating elements. The range's surface is totally smooth, the burners completely flush with the rest of its titanium-chrome/stainless-steel alloy surface, allowing for easy cleanup. And to boot, aside from the burners themselves, its other surfaces stay perfectly cool. This kitchen is noticeably less hot than most. Which is all well and good, except that at the moment, two of the burners aren't working properly.

"Smoked salmon?" asks the *garde-manger* assistant, wondering if Boulud wants some for his *plateau;* perhaps that's why he asked the soup cook for blinis.

Boulud nods, moving back to the pass. "Fire three ravioli!" he shouts.

"Make sure on the ravioli that you don't put too much tomato on it. One mine-strone, quite vegetable-y, eh? And show it to me first. A pain in the ass, Mrs. Goldstein. After that, a hanger, well-done, one chicken, white meat only, one veal medium, no leeks. She's too much of a pain. She's not going to like any-thing." Mrs. Goldstein is a regular, lunching in the dining room with her lady friends. Boulud marks up several tickets on the two middle tiers to indicate that the appropriate courses have been "fired," meaning that they've started cook-ing, or in the case of a cold dish, that they're being plated. He then slides them all the way to the right, making room for more. "Ordering three mini-soups!" he booms. "Three mini-curry soup! After that, two sole, one SOS and one tartare, no caviar, main course." SOS is kitchen shorthand for sauce on the side.

"Char, medium. Hanger, well-done," booms Boulud. "After that—okay, you're gonna make two soup and you're gonna make one for Hilary for the of-fice, too."

The hot-apps cook brings the three ravioli orders.

"A little too much tomato with the ravioli, eh?" says Boulud.

Gallagher is working on a special: sardines with Swiss chard, bacon, mush-rooms, shallots.

"Chef," says a runner to Boulud, indicating a ticket. "I think you made a mistake. I think you put three scallop and it's four."

Boulud changes the *3* on the ticket to *4* with a Sharpie and sticks it back up on the board. "Good thing you're awake this morning, eh?" he says, and then calls into the kitchen, "Ordering seven ravioli!" He moves to the phone under the bank of videos and picks it up. "Hilary, get me Jean-Pierre Boué on the phone." He picks up some papers and reads them for a moment. "Jean-Pierre? *L'induction, qu'est-ce qui se passe? On est en train de se flinguer, hein?* We're dig-ging our own graves here. What do you think the problem is?"

While he talks, he clicks a button on the video monitor, zooming in on a table. *"Je ne sais pas,"* he says to Boué. "It's not working. It worked well for a year, no problem." The black-and-white image on the video monitor isn't very clear, but Boulud can see that the party is just finishing its first course. *"Oui, on a un grave problème,"* he continues on the phone. *"C'est la folie totale."*

He hangs up as runners put up two tickets. "Ordering three ravioli, one penne with truffles, one scallop. After that, two hanger, medium-rare, one risotto, main course, one tuna, medium-rare, and a lamb, rare."

The ticket for the skybox reads:

4 char

4 crayfish

4 cheese?

Their menu is a work in progress; when Boulud puts together menus, he often decides as he goes, making changes along the way. Now his Sharpie hovers over the words *4 cheese*. Will these ladies really want a cheese course?

"The char, a flounder, and a paupiette working good on 35?" he booms.

"Yes, Chef!" comes the shout from the *poissonnier*. "Working good" means that they are where they're supposed to be in the cooking process in order to be timed to come out properly when table 35 is ready for their entrées.

"Okay," says Boulud, "I need a scallop appetizer with a penne white truffle and a pree-fee ravioli. Right now!"

Meanwhile, off to his right, David, the French *chef garde-manger*, assembles the main-course tuna tartare with no caviar. He puts a bit of caviar on top.

"No caviar, eh?" says Allannic, glancing over.

From the swinging doors by the stairs to the skybox, someone yells, "Everything okay, Alex?"

"Non!" mutters Lee. *"On est des cons."* Roughly translated: We're a bunch of assholes. He's annoyed that David got the order wrong; that osetra caviar he's scraping off is now worthless. Looking down at his hands on the counter, Lee tries to remain calm. *"Un vrai bordel,"* he says quietly. A real fucking mess. Now he looks over toward the *garde-manger*. "Could you please give me the tuna?" he says, deadpan, to David. "It's getting cold." Of course, everything in the *garde-manger* is cold, but it's not the moment to laugh at a joke.

Gallagher, who has been working in the *garde-manger* with David, comes over to Lee and says calmly, "We never got the ticket for that, that's why. We never got the ticket in the *garde-manger*." If what Gallagher says is true, then they would have heard Boulud call the order out, "One tartare, no caviar, main course," but the written instruction on the ticket never landed in their station the way it was supposed to.

"Maybe they took it away!" suggests a runner, strumming his fingers nervously.

Lee berates David again, anyway. "It's for you to follow the service," he shouts, "not for me to follow the staff!" Following the service means paying attention to the shouted orders as they come in, not relying on the paper trail.

By 2:15 things have started to heat up in the tiny pastry service kitchen. Pastry cook Ariella plates Mrs. Goldstein's desserts: coffee ice cream, with candied chestnuts all around. The serious baking, cake assembly, chocolate production, ice cream making, and so forth are accomplished downstairs in a much larger space, the pastry prep kitchen, which is adjacent to the regular prep kitchen. Beyond that is the bread bakery, which shares the pastry kitchen's ovens.

The pastry department is ruled over by Thomas Haas, the puckish German executive pastry chef, who is aided by Johnny Iuzzini, an energetic young American pastry *sous-chef*. These are Ariella's superiors. Seven or eight additional assistants fill out the team. Ariella puts Mrs. Goldstein's desserts in the window and shouts, "Pick up, please!" A runner comes and takes out the desserts.

As two more tickets come in, Haas applies the finishing touches to a glossy chocolate bombe. With a tweezers, he removes a small piece of gold leaf from a tin box and applies it to the bombe. Haas is fond of gold leaf; he uses it on quite a few desserts. "It just gives a little sparkle," he says, sparkling a little himself. "Ariella, what are you doing?"

She's building a napoleon, but Haas carefully moves it onto another plate. "I made a mistake with the orange sauce," he tells her, "but that's okay. As long as *I* made the mistake." He laughs, then claps his hands loudly. "Let's go! Eighty-five is first!" No runner appears for the moment, so he shouts again. "Pick up, please!"

In the pastry kitchen under Haas, a completely different culture reigns from that in the restaurant's hot side, where a Francophile atmosphere predominates. There are no French cooks on Haas's team. The way Ariella sees it, despite his sunny aspect and general air of walking on a cloud, Haas has a complex about the French's fabled superiority in pastry arts, and in the culinary arts in general. Hass wants to do everything not-French, just to make a point. This sets up a dynamic in the restaurant that seems odd to Ariella, since as far as she's concerned, the French way is the way to Boulud's heart. She sees the effect of his bias in the kitchen, where French people get the better positions, even if their English isn't that good. There's a presumption that if you're French, you know more. To some degree she agrees, since French cooks often start working younger. But that doesn't necessarily hold true in this type of restaurant, one that attracts top American cooks. And French cooks may be good at certain skills, but generally these don't include organizing and managing, looking at the bigger picture. As an American (she's actually a Canadian who's fluent in French, but she gets lumped in with the

Americans), Ariella feels a little like a second-class citizen. Curiously, despite his German-Austrian aesthetic and sensibilities, Ariella thinks Haas doesn't work as cleanly and well-organized as he might, either. Nor is his fly-off-the-handle temperament an asset.

Working at Daniel has not been easy for Ariella. She likes the easy, joking atmosphere of the pastry kitchen, and she appreciates Haas's charm. Still, as a woman she feels everyone is especially ready to pound her, and at times it seems as if nothing she does is right. Sometimes Haas sneaks up behind her and just goes berserk. Other days, she comes into work and whoever is in charge, Haas or Iuzzini, is just looking for trouble, looking to find fault. Today everything's going okay; no one's lashed out at her—so far.

And despite Lee's outburst a few minutes ago, the mood on the hot side seems okay, too. Boulud, while rarely jovial during service, sounds happy enough, though Ariella can't see the pass from the pastry kitchen. "Two more capon on 94?!" the chef booms at the pass. "Okay, let's go now! Rock and roll!"

Later in the afternoon, the skybox table cleared of the *Bon Appétit* editors and their lunch, Boulud stretches his legs. He's just made the rounds in the dining room, saying hello to the few diners who lingered late. Unlike his former boss, Le Cirque's Sirio Maccioni, Boulud is not a real front-of-the-house restaurateur: He's much more at home behind the pass or behind the stove. This is not to say that he's stiff or unfriendly—quite the contrary: With clients, as well as with press, Boulud is ever relaxed, affable, fluid, warm, even radiant. He smiles sweetly, genuinely seems fond of people. He becomes a different creature entirely from the hard, commanding presence with the resonant baritone the kitchen staff knows, and the change comes over him instantaneously as he pushes through the swinging door into the dining room. His is a curious brand of charisma, for while in the dining room, Boulud is attractive and quite charming, hardly intimidating; he's approachable, easy to talk to. In the kitchen, however, commanding his brigade, he's something else: a powerful, magnetic, riveting general prone to fits of choler. The chef worries about his temper; he's been working lately on controlling his outbursts.

Since he makes his dining room rounds rather late in the afternoons and evenings, after the room has cleared out somewhat, many customers never lay eyes on Boulud. But unlike at Le Cirque, where tables were close together and the scene was the thing, at Daniel the chef's presence in the dining room isn't as important. The bottom line is that people come here for the food and to be coddled by the staff.

Although the Grimes review was seven months ago and Boulud professes not to dwell on it, its effect still resonates. Those in the restaurant who are close to Boulud, such as Brett Traussi, operations manager for the Dinex Group, say that it's "all he thinks about." And Lili Lynton, Dinex's business consultant, still refers to Daniel as a "four-star" restaurant—not because she's forgotten Grimes's review, but because in her mind, that's what it is.

Several months after Grimes critiqued Daniel, he reviewed David Bouley's relatively casual downtown restaurant Bouley Bakery, giving it four stars. For the first time since Ruth Reichl gave three stars to Honmura An, a Japanese soba restaurant, in her second review as *Times* critic back in 1993 ("A noodle house?" came the hue and cry), the idea of what the stars mean—or should mean—has become an issue on the New York dining scene. People have started to wonder what Grimes's stars actually represent. Does he have an agenda? If so, what could it be?

Boulud speculates that Grimes will review Bouley's newly opened Austrian restaurant, Danube, before long, giving it four stars just to infuriate the New York food world, and could take down an important restaurant such as Le Cirque or Le Bernardin just to rule the roost. Perhaps then he'll revisit Daniel, but not before then. Boulud reflects that Le Bernardin owners Maguy Le Coze and Eric Ripert have recently removed several tables in anticipation of a visit from Grimes, a costly way to make the room feel more comfortable to a critic. Taking out a single table at Daniel would cost Boulud a cool hundred thousand dollars per year.

Boulud's public nonchalance about receiving only three stars from the *Times* is quite convincing. He's a master of image, so polished, lively, and natural at the hands of a journalist or before the camera that even his publicist marvels that he's never had media training. And Boulud doesn't concede frustration, even when pressed. He's too savvy, and too much of a class act to indulge in bellyaching or complaining. But when *really* pressed, Boulud lets on that even though he would dearly love a fourth star, he's actually after even bigger game: He would like Daniel to become the Le Pavillon of his time, a world-renowned French restaurant that will reign supreme over New York dining for decades. No doubt this goal is genuine; still, one can't help but feel that he's flashing it to deflect attention from—or even belittle—the prize that he should have but doesn't: the fourth star.

Not that his modest origins would have predicted such grand ambition. Born in the village of Saint-Pierre de Chandieu, twenty miles from Lyons, Boulud was raised on his paternal grandmother's farm as the third of five children, with two older sisters and two younger brothers. He describes his mother as very hardworking, very tolerant, and very generous, sometimes very emotional, yet good at handling stress. The perfect daughter-in-law, Boulud's mother got along famously with the elder Madame Boulud. "Passionate and hardworking" is the way Boulud describes his father. When Boulud was a child, Boulud *père* wasn't the type of man to spend his free time in cafés and bars with his friends; he preferred to be at home with his children as much as possible. He did have a sense of civic duty, however; he volunteered as a fireman and also did work for the town hall. One needn't look far to see his parents' influences, especially their hardworking natures, on Daniel Boulud.

Like everyone of their generation in France, Boulud's parents were accustomed to living through the food shortages of World War II, yet their privations didn't render them bitter or stingy; it was important to both of them that the family live in relative comfort, that a sense of joy pervade the household, and that the children have the things they wanted. "Even television!" Boulud recalls, still smiling at the thought.

Although he did not really learn to cook as a child, he and his siblings regularly helped his mother in the kitchen.

Boulud has trouble answering, though, when asked when he first knew he had a special talent. He dances around the question, reluctant even to admit that he *has* a special talent. "It doesn't matter if you're fourteen or you're forty," he says, "I don't take that for granted. They tell me I do, and that makes me very happy, but you don't believe it." When pressed, he still maintains his modesty. "For me," he says, "I think the talent comes along with the work, and I know some very talented chefs who have never been successful; perhaps they didn't have the drive or the instinct." To be successful in this business, he explains, one has to be willing to take risks, "and never look back to see whether you were right or wrong."

Boulud took his first job as an apprentice at Nandron. As a teenager, he was a little wild, very independent. An apprentice must be a follower, a role it's hard to imagine Boulud playing. "I was a great follower," he says, however, "but always enjoyed being the great leader and working alongside people who lead well." That didn't prevent him from having his butt kicked—literally— by none other than Paul Bocuse. During his apprenticeship at Nandron, he was sent to the great chef's restaurant to do a two-week *stage,* as many Lyonnaise apprentices were. Bocuse, who back then was known for being intolerant of hair that was anything other than very short, took one look at the teenaged Boulud, with an unruly mop of hair and sunglasses dangling from his shirt, and said, "Go back to the *coiffeur!* And we don't allow sunglasses!" When Boulud turned to take his leave, Bocuse literally booted him out with a foot in the rear.

At the age of fifteen, Boulud earned his first professional recognition: He was a finalist in France's competition for Best Culinary Apprentice. He spent the next eight years working in Europe, first as a cook, then as *chef de partie* in various three-star restaurants in France, interspersed with stints as *sous-chef* at the Plaza Hotel in Copenhagen, and then as chef at the Copenhagen restaurant Les Etoiles. By the end of 1980, when he had returned to France as a private chef in Mougins, Boulud was becoming increasingly intrigued by the idea of coming to the United States. His curiosity had been piqued by his friend Didier Oudill, a chef at Les Prés d'Eugénie, where Boulud had worked three years before; Oudill had spent a couple of years in the U.S., dating an American girl, a dancer at the New York City Ballet; his tales of his life in New York were highly appealing. At the same time, when Boulud had worked in the various three-star restaurants in France, a world he found a bit static (though he was stimulated by Michel Guérard's avant-garde approach), he constantly came across culinary ideas that had originated in the brave New York culinary world; these American influences were very much in evidence in France at the time. Gotham's restaurants had certainly excited Oudill, and now Boulud wanted to experience the scene for himself. Not least of all was the idea of a challenge, something Boulud was hard-put to resist.

The chef's idea, however, was not to move here, just to spend a chunk of time, so when he was offered a two-year job in Washington, D.C., as private chef to Roland de Kergorlay, the European Commission's ambassador to the U.S., he jumped at the chance.

As it turned out, though, working for the ambassador was too cushy for Boulud's taste, and he was eager to leave D.C.; looking back on his time there, he recalls, "I couldn't stand it." New York City, however, held a special fascination for him. Boulud came to New York to spend a month cooking at La Côte Basque, which in the early 1980s was a magnet for young, creative chefs. He was amazed by everything: the products, the cooking, the wine, the clientele—and the fact that the restaurant was doing a tremendous number of covers at a very high level.

Despite his plans to return home upon completion of his assignment, when Boulud was offered a job as co-executive chef at the Westbury Hotel in New York City, he leapt at the chance. After two years there and two years as executive chef at Le Régence at the Plaza Athénée Hotel, he started working for Sirio Maccioni at Le Cirque as executive chef. It was 1986, and Boulud was thirty-one years old. During his six-year tenure at the hugely popular restaurant, *the* place to see and be seen in the mid-1980s and early 1990s, Boulud then began to come into his own as a chef of the very first rank.

In 1992, when Boulud decided it was time to think about opening his own restaurant, he and his wife, Micky, whom he had met in 1984 at a Chelsea jazz club, considered doing so back in Lyons. Turning to Micky's friend Lili Lynton, a graduate of Harvard Business School and former specialist in mergers and acquisitions at Lehman Brothers, and his own attorney, Tom Danziger, Boulud put together a business plan and set about raising money. They soon realized that opening a restaurant in Lyons wasn't practicable, the financial model in France being more difficult. In New York, however, such a plan was more than feasible. They agreed to seek ten investors, each of whom would ante up two hundred thousand dollars, but Lynton's then-uncle-in-law, Joel Smilow, the former chairman, CEO, and principal shareholder of Playtex (and also a Harvard M.B.A.), told Boulud he'd like to put up the entire two million dollars and be Boulud's sole partner. Boulud knew immediately after their one-hour meeting that accepting Smilow's offer was the right move. That's typical of how Boulud operates—he's very intuitive and *follows* his intuition; he never has trouble making decisions. Negotiations for the space, meanwhile, were conducted under the greatest secrecy; Lynton and Danziger could not reveal which well-known chef intended to occupy the space they were seeking. Boulud didn't want Sirio Maccioni to get wind of his plans before he had everything in place. After all, it might be a year or two before he found and secured a suitable site. Fortunately the hunt went rather quickly, and Boulud left Le Cirque and opened the original restaurant Daniel in the Surrey Hotel on East Seventy-sixth Street in May 1993.

It's eight o'clock on a Friday morning late in January, and Daniel Boulud is still in bed. He kisses Alix good-bye as Micky takes her off to school at the Lycée Française, a nearby school that is popular with the children of diplomats, French expats, and Upper East Side socialites. It's early still, and since Boulud was in the restaurant last night until one, he goes back to sleep.

An hour later, he's up, reading the *Times* (he has ordered only the Wednesday and Friday papers, but somehow he gets it every day) and the *Daily News*, and breakfasting on a bowl of Muesli with raisins, a glass of orange juice, and coffee. Boulud always eats the same breakfast: He likes this particular Muesli, and it's hearty enough to carry him through to three o'clock or so, which is the next time he'll have an opportunity to eat. He keeps meaning to give up coffee ("not that healthy") and take up tea, but never quite gets around to it. After breakfast he makes a few calls; he usually checks in with Hilary Tolman and his chief financial officer, Marcel Doron, to see what's going on downstairs. By ten-thirty or eleven he's on his way down a flight of stairs (twenty-five of them, he can't help but notice) that leads almost directly into the kitchen at Daniel. It actually deposits him in the corridor off the banquet kitchen; a push through the swinging door, and he's in the main kitchen. Up the stairs to the skybox, he greets Tolman, opens the closet, and puts on his whites.

The restaurant has been open a year now, and Boulud feels it is time to reassess things, looking at what works, what doesn't work.

In terms of the menu, he reflects, three-quarters of the regular clientele prefer to eat lightly, especially at lunch. Salads and lighter fare will have to be emphasized, and to that end, Boulud is considering putting together a salad cart, one that will lend visual appeal for those infamous ladies who partake of a certain midday meal. Perhaps he'll include a cold fish dish on it as well. Michael Lawrence disagrees with Boulud on the salad cart question; he worries that the concept is "too brasserie," not formal enough. But, he sighs, shaking his head, "Of course, it's Daniel's call. It's his restaurant." If Boulud decides to go through with it, naturally Lawrence will do everything in his power to make sure the idea comes off as seamlessly as possible. Although the diners who come to Daniel for special occasions are thrilled to relish the more complicated preparations, it is the regulars who form the base of the business—both here and at the Café—and it is the regulars who tend to prefer eating lighter.

Lunches, in general, are not exactly a winning proposition at this type of luxury restaurant. The restaurateur must expend the same amount on overhead for lunch as for dinner, employing the same number of kitchen staff; the preparations are just as elaborate, but the prices are necessarily lower, as few would make such a splurge at lunchtime. For the diner looking for a transcendent meal, lunching at a restaurant such as Daniel is a good idea: same food, same cooks, same beautiful room, same flawless service—all at a lower price.

The point of view of the restaurateur, however, looks quite different: Lunch is a service that must be provided for the customers, even if it's not so lucrative.

One solution to this conundrum is to increase the number of covers served at lunch, making up the reduction of revenue in volume. To bring more lunch business to the lounge, where meals have been served since the opening to accommodate the fashion for lounge dining in New York, Boulud has recently introduced a "Bouchon menu," a three-course fixed-price lunch for thirty-six dollars, complete with a glass of wine, served only in the lounge. At the moment, customers choose a soup or salad to start (minestrone with winter vegetables, cranberry beans, Parmesan, pesto, and garlic toasts, or a salad of endive, mâche, apple, and bacon, with Stilton, walnuts, and port glaze). Next they can opt for steamed Scottish salmon with lime, lemongrass, and coriander, pea leaves, fennel, and sweet onion; or free-range chicken with Meyer lemon glaze, carrots, and leeks fondants and lemon thyme Basmati rice; or ravioli of artichoke and arugula with tomato confit, olives, and shaved Parmesan. For dessert, either the *tarte du jour* or a bittersweet hot chocolate soufflé with pistachio ice cream. To drink: a glass of house white (Bourgogne Blanc, F. Jobard, 1994) or red (Château de Capitoul "La Clape" Languedoc, 1997). Besides increasing the lunch business, introducing this kind of promotion also attracts publicity, always a plus. (In fact, William Grimes had come to the restaurant during the start of the Bouchon lunch promotion and wrote a piece about it. He was recognized that afternoon, though of course no one let on.)

Boulud is also considering adding more banquettes to the dining room. These, he feels, add more conviviality to a room, and at the same time they can be elegant, more private, and more comfortable than chairs. He wants to construct tents in the corners of the dining room, forming a wine *cave* in one, a beautified camouflage for the entrance of the reservations office in another. The other two will be used for tables that can be enclosed for privacy by drawing the curtains. All very elegant, very four-star.

There are also constant improvements in service. Downstairs, in the small area between the pass and the swinging "in" and "out" doors leading to the dining room, the waiters get a lesson in carving a bird, during their break between lunch and dinner service. Ten or twelve of them, arms bent at the elbows, sleeves rolled up, wave forks and knives around in the air. A dozen chickens loll about in hotel pans (three-inch-deep rectangular metal pans) on the table before them.

"This side, same thing," says the captain who's training them, turning his attention to the right side of the chicken. "You keep your fork on the left. Giovanni, have you done one?"

"What the hell?" says Giovanni, just entering from the dining room. "It's like a personal carving station!"

After the insanely busy holiday season, the restaurant is finally calming down, and Boulud feels somewhat less pressure in the day-to-day operations. He has brought over an excellent *sous-chef*, Brad Thompson, from Café Boulud and plans to hire yet another next month or early in March. At the moment, there are four: Allannic, Gallagher, Thompson, and Frédéric Côte—two Frenchmen and two Americans. Concerned that the staff not feel national favoritism, Boulud has tried deliberately to keep the staff balanced, roughly 50 percent French and 50 percent American. Fay, the lunchtime *saucier,* is becoming a junior *sous-chef,* and Boulud may be bringing in another junior *sous-chef* as well. When the brigade is complete, he says, perhaps he'll even have a little time for himself. He smiles at the thought, but no one who knows Boulud would ever imagine that he believes it.

Two

SOIGNÉ

Friday, February 4

W HEN A PERSON decides to dine at Daniel, the first contact he or she will have is with a reservationist. To that end, Daniel takes great care in training its reservationists—as it does with all of its front-of-the-house staff.

At 8:40 A.M. Erica Cantley pulls open the heavy door to the service entrance of the restaurant Daniel on East Sixty-fifth street, fifty feet or so west of the main entrance. She greets the guard sitting in the small booth, walks down the gloomy corridor lined with crates filled with glassware and upended round tabletops that lean against the wall, opens a door on the right, and goes down a flight of stairs whose walls are paneled in textured white plastic; on the wall facing her as she descends is a huge blowup photograph of a betoqued Daniel Boulud, eyebrows raised, leaning over a copper pot and adding a pinch of the ingredient that will transform the contents into something sublime. Pascal Vittu, one of the captains, believes that everything that Boulud is about is there in that photograph: elegance, passion, sincerity. He thinks prospective employees should be shown the portrait and asked what they see. If they don't see anything, he says, they shouldn't get the job.

Through another door at the bottom, a right turn into another dull corridor, and Cantley arrives at the women's locker room. One wall is lined with lockers. Those on the right—full length—are for the lucky employees with some seniority. The rest are little cubes, barely large enough to hold a bag and a set of street clothes, certainly not large enough for winter coats, a number of which are suspended on wire hangers wherever anyone can stick them. Across from the lockers is a rubber trash can that's being used as a laundry receptacle—an apron string and the checkered leg of a pair of chef's pants stick out from underneath the lid. Below the lockers runs a row of street shoes: black boots, black boots, running shoes, brown boots, black boots, black boots.

Cantley, a slim, attractive blonde, is thirty-three years old, a little puffy-eyed still this morning; she hasn't put on her makeup yet. She doesn't care that her locker is small; neither server nor cook, she's wearing the clothes she'll work in, slim black skirt, black tailored jacket over white silk blouse, red patent-leather Prada knockoff shoes.

Cantley is the reservations manager. Today she's going to train a new reservationist. Since today the books are opening up for Saturday night, March 4—reservations are accepted exactly one month to the day in advance—it'll be a trial by fire. Saturday nights are always big. Before stuffing her bag into her locker and spinning the padlock shut, she hangs her coat on a wire hanger and suspends it from the side of the bank of lockers.

Upstairs, in the coffee station nestled underneath the skybox, Cantley brews herself a cup of hot tea. Cupping it in her hands, she walks through the empty dining room to the far corner, where up six stairs and behind a discreet, padded rose-brocade screen lies the reservations room, a makeshift office. Joanna, another reservationist, is already seated at the long desk, her black coat tossed over a pile of stackable chairs to the right of the desk. It's a small, carpeted room—little more than a closet, really—with three office chairs clustered around a single desk. Two shelves line the wall above the work area; one holds a fax machine, with a menu handy next to it. On the wall behind the reservationists is a large bulletin board and an outsized calendar of the sixty-day organizer variety.

Christina, the new hire, is waiting for Cantley. A tall, slender blonde, Christina is an aspiring opera singer; she's waiting to take classes at Juilliard in the fall. (She laments that since she's a first soprano, she'll never play Carmen, one of her favorite roles.) She shares a furnished room with a friend way up in Washington Heights; her share of the rent is $320, roughly the price a party of two would pay for a modest tasting menu at dinner. Erica greets her and Joanna, and immediately gets down to work, showing Christina the reservation books, one for each month, in oversized binders.

"Valentine's Day is booked solid," says Cantley, opening up the February book to show her. "It's a Monday. We have fifty-two people on the wait list."

At the stroke of nine o'clock, the phones—there are three of them on the desk and four installed on the back wall—begin to ring. People have been trying to call before this, no doubt, but until nine o'clock the phone system plays a recording. During the workday, if one of the reservationists can't pick up a call by the third ring, it is bounced back to the system, which informs the caller in a soothing voice, over the subdued rhythmic strains of the Pink Martini Band, of Daniel's address, the fact that men are required to wear jackets in the dining room, and that Daniel hosts private parties in its banquet room. The usual menu of options follows ("To make a reservation, press one, to confirm or cancel a reservation, press two . . ."). The voice belongs to Hilary Tolman. The message sounds so polished it might have been made in a professional recording studio. Actually, it was, nailed in three takes at Broad Street Studio in Chelsea. By the time the outgoing message is finished, one of the reservationists is usually able to pick up the call.

"Good morning, Daniel, may I help you?" says Cantley, pulling the February book toward her and opening to today's date. "I'm sorry, we are fully reserved tomorrow night. Perhaps you'd like to try Café Boulud? Okay, well, thank you for thinking of us, and we hope you'll give us a try another time."

Now a house phone rings—the hot line—and Cantley answers it. Someone in the kitchen wants to know how many covers they'll have today. "You want to know for lunch?" says Cantley. "Eighty-two in the dining room, and thirty-nine in the lounge."

The phone rings again. "Good morning, Daniel, may I help you?" says Cantley. "Certainly, what date were you interested in? Saturday, March 4?" Joanna hands her the book, open to that Saturday. "How many people in your party? Four? And what time would you like to join us? I'm afraid we don't have eight o'clock available that evening, sir, but we do have tables at six forty-five and nine. Nine o'clock? And what is the name? Okay, Mr. Schoenfeld, you're all set for four people at nine on Saturday, March 4. Your reservation number is 324, and we ask that you call us the day before to confirm."

The reader will no doubt remark that Mr. Schoenfeld was the first caller to request a table for that Saturday night, yet eight o'clock is already booked. How is this possible? In between phone calls, Cantley gets down to the business of explaining to Christina the unseemlier side of how the reservation books work. She shows her the page for Saturday, March 4. Although it seems as though this task would be pretty straightforward—filling in names, numbers of diners, and phone numbers until all the slots are filled—it's actually more complicated, for there are red pencil lines through all the slots from 7:00 to 8:30. "We can book five forty-five to six forty-five, and then nine o'clock and after," Cantley explains. The prime reservations—7:00, 7:30, 8:00, 8:30—may only be booked by Bruno Jamais, the head maître d'. Jamais has twenty-five tables at his disposal in those slots. Normally, these times are reserved for Jamais's regulars, those to whom Jamais has given a business card with his private phone line. Such is the potential reward for those who generously tip this particular maître d'.

"What do we say if they call first thing in the morning and ask why eight o'clock is already unavailable?" says Christina.

"Just say, 'I'm sorry, we don't have a seating at that time,'" answers Cantley.

Christina, whose last brief job was as a reservationist at Jean Georges, is not at all surprised by this policy. However, she adds, "At Jean Georges they always let us book a few during those hours."

"It *used* to be that we could book ten of those tables," says Cantley. "Now no more; only Bruno can book those times. However," she continues, "you do want to try to fill the restaurant. During the week if it's slow, we try to fill in the seven to eight o'clock slots." Once Jamais has given them the go-ahead, that is. "For tonight, Bruno has said to me, 'You can go ahead and book seven and eight-thirty.'" She pulls over the February book, opened to tonight, and shows Christina.

What this means, effectively, is that if someone called a month ago exactly, the first day one could make reservations for Friday, February 4, and asked for a seven o'clock reservation, one would have been told that there was no seating at seven. The reservationist would have suggested six-thirty or nine. But if one called this morning and asked for a seven o'clock reservation, there would be no problem.

Now Cantley erases a "VIP" designation next to a client's name. "I don't know why everyone keeps writing 'VIP,'" she says. "We don't use that anymore. We use 'PX.'" Cantley came up with this innocuous code when she worked at the front desk as host to stymie guests who persisted in looking over the podium at the reservation sheet and questioning why other guests had the letters VIP next to their name. PX, which doesn't mean anything to anybody, causes fewer problems.

"Good morning, Daniel. Hello, Mr. Sassoon, this is Erica. Of course; that would be our pleasure," she says, flipping to today's date. "That's for today, correct? Perfect. It's just for the two of you? Okay, we'll see you at one."

As she hangs up, she tells Christina, "When they say, 'Oh, tell Daniel we're coming,' never take a chance. Hilary is Daniel's assistant; you can tell her or you can tell us. Just so Daniel has it in his mind because he always wants to know who's here."

"For me," observes Cantley, "one of the fun things about this job has been the psychological aspect of it. You're always treading that thin line between controlling the customers and accommodating them. You can't let them stomp all over you, because you have a million customers to take care of."

The phone rings. "Good morning, Daniel," says Cantley brightly—actually smiling as she says it. In the *Front Desk Staff Manual* she prepared in advance of the restaurant's opening, she wrote, "Your tone of voice should be happy, excited and one of helpfulness and attentiveness. It helps if you smile as you speak: You actually can HEAR a smile over the phone.☺"

"I'm sorry, but Valentine's Day is fully reserved," says Cantley, pretending to shoot herself in the head. "Friday, February 11? Eleven o'clock in the dining room or six, eight, or ten in the lounge. Or lunch? And we also do serve lunch on Saturday. Okay, very well. Thank you for thinking of us, and we hope to see you sometime soon."

Hanging up, she turns to Christina.

"This is the psychology of giving good phone. We never say no. We make *them* say no."

Joanna takes a call from someone requesting a menu. She hangs up, punches a number in the fax machine, and feeds a dinner menu into the fax.

The phone rings again; Joanna answers it. "Good morning, Daniel. Oh, good morning, Mr. Fairfield. Tuesday the twenty-second for lunch? Absolutely, one o'clock. We look forward to seeing you then."

"Steven Fairfield," says Cantley to Christina. "Now, *we* know that Steven Fairfield is a big VIP here, but you don't know that. Just treat everybody's call the same."

Cantley's presence at the reservations desk today is notable in that she actually quit the restaurant last spring, after doing her part in opening it: setting up all the phone and reservations systems and training reservation and front desk personnel. She stayed long enough to make sure everything ran smoothly, and then she gave notice, with no intention of coming back. But staffing problems followed—difficulties with the reservations manager who replaced her; a hostess who walked out. So Michael Lawrence called and asked her to come back. She agreed to return, just until the end of January, on a consultant basis. Boulud is the rare kind of employer who frequently rehires ex-employees—to him, the restaurant is sort of an extended family that you can never really leave. Many of his employees revere him; some fear him a bit as well; others regard him as something of a father figure. You work hard for him, but he's there if you need him, is the popular sentiment. In any case, here it is February 4, and it doesn't look as though Cantley is going anywhere anytime soon.

At eleven o'clock Cantley suggests that Joanna go in the kitchen and get her lunch, while Cantley stays and covers the phone. When Joanna comes back with her plate, Cantley takes Christina into the kitchen. In the dining room they pass a few waiters already eating, two or three to a table.

"Family meal," as it is known, is set up on a counter just opposite the pass: Today it's a bus pan full of sautéed chicken pieces, another of rice, yet another brimming with mesclun salad. Next to that, sliced homemade bread. Cantley and Christina line up behind waiters, runners, and busboys, who heap enormous portions on Melmac plates, grabbing forks. The cooks tend to wait till after the line dies down, then set a plate on whatever small space they find at their station. Those cooks who aren't behind schedule—"in the shit"—might eat standing up, or sitting on an upturned crate. Those who are behind will probably still have their food sitting on a plate in a corner of their station as the service begins, and they'll wolf down a bite or two when they can.

Schooled in restaurant management (with a degree from the Restaurant School in Philadelphia), Cantley is a consummate front-of-the-house person: The best treatment of the customer is always in the front of her mind. Her first job out of school was at Seasons restaurant at the Bostonian hotel in Boston; she then moved to Aujourd'hui at the Four Seasons, where she was named manager at the tender age of twenty-three. She next opened Nevis at the Four Seasons, but after a time, she no longer wanted to continue climbing the corporate ladder that would eventually lead to food and beverage manager. A little at loose ends, she came to New York in 1995 to work for Boulud at the old Daniel, and she also started dabbling in writing. Her new dream was to be a food and travel writer, and she wrote several pieces as a freelancer for *Time Out New York*. After working for Boulud for a year and a half, she left to live in Paris for two years. She came back to work for Boulud in 1998, helping him open Café Boulud, and then this restaurant, where she had hoped to be service manager. It is a post that doesn't exist, but she felt—and still feels—the restaurant needs one. Instead, she has enrolled in literature courses at Columbia

University's School of General Studies; an alternate dream is to teach literature and film, and she's working on her B.A. in literature. (She's also working on a cookbook.) On the other hand, she'd like to teach restaurant service, because she had a wonderful service teacher in restaurant school who inspired her profoundly.

For the moment, however, Cantley's mind is in the reservation books. When she's finished with the call, she demonstrates her stalling technique to Christina, pretending she's on a call. "Okay, just one moment, please. Let me check our availability," she says. "You just stay with them the whole time, talking, so there's no dead air. Also, if you have the time, and it's a Friday or Saturday they're asking about, you say, 'Okay, is that for lunch or dinner?' Yes, you're buying time, but you're also planting the idea in their head that lunch is a possibility."

"If we're booked for dinner," she tells Christina, "always push lunch. It's a good selling tool. You'll always hear Daniel say this: 'Suggest lunch. Suggest lunch. Suggest lunch.' And we want to be very flexible at lunch. Never give somebody a hard time if they want one-fifteen or one-thirty. We just take whatever we can get. As Bruno would say," and now she imitates his gruff, deep voice and thick French accent, "geeve zem what zey want." Despite the fact that the profit margin is slimmer at lunch, customers who are introduced to the restaurant at lunch are likely to return for dinner.

The phones start ringing nonstop again, and Cantley and Joanna both answer calls. They communicate with each other through eye contact, as well as by repeating out loud what the customer is saying. Not only does it buy time, but also that way they won't book the same slot at the same time. As Joanna takes a reservation for March, she hears Cantley saying, "Dinner for Wednesday, February 16?" and automatically hands her the February book while she pencils something in the March book.

Cantley takes a call from the concierge at the Four Seasons hotel. Hanging up, she tells Christina, "Concierges from the Four Seasons are the best. The best, the best, the best. The ones from the Stanhope are great, too—and the Pierre, and the St. Regis. They are the best. They deserve to be treated really well. They call, and they know they're asking for ridiculous things, but sometimes there's a guest standing right there in front of them waiting for the answer, so we always go through the motions. But they're always so nice to you, that you just do that back to them. Whether it's other chefs or reservations managers or hosts or dishwashers or whatever, it's all about how *soigné* you treat them. There's a French word, it's called *soigner*, and it's what we do with our guests." *Soigner* means "to care for" or "to take good care of something or someone"; indeed, it's a word that comes up over and over at Daniel. In restaurants *soigné* is used to describe everything from the little pieces of paper the reservationists distribute to the dining room and kitchen requesting special treatment for people with birthdays to the care a line cook takes in cutting a shallot into *brunoise*.

"Not only are we people's first exposure to the restaurant," Cantley acknowledges, "sometimes they have to call many, many times before they succeed in getting a reservation at the time they want. You can get a vibe from these people. Sometimes they're really angry. If you start hearing things like, 'This is ridiculous,' you have to ask yourself, 'Who do we think we are?' You have to make them feel good. To one degree or another, the eyes of the rest of the world are on us because we're holding up this higher standard. We should probably have a little photograph of Daniel up there or something," she says, indicating the wall. "We represent him. We have to be the best."

Thursday, February 10

SIX O'CLOCK P.M., and the first orders are coming in. Frédéric Côte, one of the four *sous-chefs,* stands at the pass, looking at the reservations sheet for tonight—354 covers, lots of VIPS, including Mary Ellen Ward from *Food & Wine* magazine; Pierre Orsi, a chef from Lyons and friend of Dorie Greenspan, Boulud's collaborator on *Café Boulud Cookbook;* Ariane Daguin, owner of D'Artagnan, supplier of foie gras and other duck and poultry products to just about every restaurant east of the Rockies; Alessandro Stratta, a star chef in Las Vegas (executive chef of Renoir at the Mirage Hotel) who worked under Boulud at Le Cirque. As if that weren't enough, François Pinault, the owner of Château Latour, which produces the famous first-growth Bordeaux, is coming. No question, it's going to be quite a night. The first ticket comes in.

"Ordering, please!" says Côte. Tall, French, not exactly fat but with a girth worthy of an old-style chef, Côte has Valentino-esque dark circles under his eyes. He doesn't yet need to raise his voice (a basso profundo) since things are still quiet. Despite his size and managerial position, he's a quiet, unexcitable sort who tends to keep to himself, blending into the kitchen scenery. "One crab gelée and one risotto, followed by one sea bass and one veal." The crab gelée is shorthand for Crabe à la Pomme Verte et Céleri, Maine peeky-toe crab salad in a green apple–celery gelée with curly chicory and apple chips.

As the dinner hot-apps cook, Goichi is responsible for risottos and pastas. He jumps into action. In contrast to Côte, Goichi is a string bean of a cook, a bundle of energy. A graduate of New York Technical Institute in Long Island, Goichi worked at the New York Athletic Club before going to work in France.

Boulud is almost obsessively attentive to moving diners' meals along without long waits between courses. To that end, the server writes on the ticket the exact time the guests were seated. Since cooking risotto would normally take about twenty minutes, shortcuts are necessary. After lunch service, the day shift hot-apps cook prepares a few big pots of risotto, cooking the rice until it's just over halfway cooked. He then spreads it on sheet pans so it cools evenly. That way Goichi can finish it, cooking it in about ten minutes, and get the first course on the table without making the guest wait. Tonight's risotto features butternut squash, sage, and duck confit; it's garnished with black trumpet mushroom *coulis* and toasted shallots.

Each of the four *sous-chefs* is responsible for creating a special each day, and Alex Lee rounds out the selection with a couple of his own. In the *garde-manger*, Neil Gallagher works on his, a sardine appetizer with blood orange sauce. Gallagher loves blood oranges; to his mind, the warm sunset contained in that orange globe provides the perfect antidote for the depressing weather.

As Alex Lee comes in and starts handing out paychecks, Gallagher simmers blood orange juice on the induction range to reduce it, using a pastry brush to wash down the sides of the pot. The intense liquid is the color of his hair, red-orange. Next to him is citrus powder he made by zesting one orange, two lemons, and two limes using a micro-plane zester. These he blanched three times each in a light simple syrup, keeping them separate to retain color and flavor. He dried them overnight on parchment, ground them to a fine powder in a coffee grinder, and finally, passed them through a *tamis*.

"Ordering one langoustine," says Côte, "two *ballottine,* and two artichoke soup, followed by two sea bass, one sole, and two veal, medium-rare."

The *garde-manger* assistant pulls out two plates and paints them with sauce for the *ballottine*—a spectacular foie gras terrine wrapped in black truffle, served with a mâche and black truffle salad that commands a twenty-five-dollar supplement on the seventy-five-dollar three-course *prix fixe* dinner. It's now full-on truffle season, and truffles will fly fast and furious tonight thanks to a special section of the menu: six appetizers involving black truffles.

Now Lee steps behind the pass, and Côte takes his place plating at the fish station. "Order, please!" says Lee. "One caviar, followed by one artichoke soup, one penne, one langoustine, two mushroom soup, two *ballottine*. Caviar first, guys. Followed by one tuna, medium, two veal, medium, one chicken, one scallop, one sea bass."

German, the Ecuadorian runner who stands at the inside corner of the runner's side of the pass expediting orders, yells, "Hey, guys, pick up, hello!" German has been working here since the new Daniel opened; before that he was at Jean Georges.

"*Vas-y, vas-y,*" says Lee, taking a swig of Evian.

As he calls out another order, the soup cook tends to the blinis for the caviar order, an ounce and a half of Russian osetra for which the customer will pay $110. The *garde-manger* cooks take care of the caviar order, since it's a cold app, but they have no burner, so the soup cook always does the blinis, since he has access to the induction range. Most blinis are basically tiny yeasted buckwheat pancakes, but here at Daniel the cook whips egg whites in a KitchenAid mixer before folding them into the batter with a rubber spatula, yielding a preternaturally light, unyeasted blini. The soup cook is new, having just replaced Bertrand, a French cook who has fallen victim to a severe back problem—a malady that is the kitchen equivalent of carpal tunnel syndrome. Last week he came in and lifted a very heavy pot of wild mushroom velouté. A spasm jolted his entire body, and after service he limped up the skybox stairs and asked Tolman (whom the cooks consider to be the keeper of all kinds of assorted wisdom) if she could recommend an acupuncturist. The next morning he woke up and couldn't move, and Tolman and Toto, the steward, hopped in a cab, went to Bertrand's apartment, called an ambulance, and took him to the hospital. He wound up having surgery for a herniated disk, and will be out for four months; Boulud is keeping Bertrand's job open for him until he returns. The new soup cook, Frank, a native of Rochester, New York, graduated from the Culinary Institute of America (the famed CIA in Hyde Park), the gold standard of culinary schools, in June 1998; since then he has done a three-month *stage* in Provence at Roger Vergé's Moulin de Mougins. With a large nose and a face that still shows some youthful traces of acne, Frank stoops a little as he cooks, his face close to his work as he concentrates. He's a gentle person and a serious worker.

Gallagher, working next to Frank, throws some vegetables into his now-reduced blood orange sauce and simmers them. After that come some red concord grapes that he has peeled and seeded.

Six-forty, and they're all in a groove: busy but not out of control.

"I need two mini-soup right now," says a waiter—an attractive Asian fellow wearing smart black glasses lined in chartreuse. He's had the same prescription since he was nine, and owns twenty-five pairs of glasses. "Two mini-soup!" He turns away, but Frank already has them ready and places them on a tray.

"Two mini-soup here, table 10," says German. "Pick up over here, table 45."

Soon things heat up; Lee calls out three orders in rapid succession. The pressure's on.

"Something's wrong with 53," says German. "Position one is having the caviar. And . . ." He's confused because one customer is having more than one appetizer.

"What's the problem?" says Lee. "The guy's hungry."

Gallagher is just finishing constructing his sardine special: The sardines are layered with pipérade, roasted red and yellow peppers with merguez sausage, and garnished with radish sprouts.

"Order six covers!" yells Lee, over what has become a din. Cooks, confused about orders, chatter their dismay; runners squabble. "One lobster, two tuna, two seviche, two risotto, followed by one beef, medium, one veal, three lamb, medium-rare, and one pork. Are you finished?" shouts Lee, spinning around to face two runners who have been involved in a heated discussion over a tray. "So can I go now?" Lee wants them to take the tray, so he can move on to the next order. They just stare back. "Okay, well, shut up next time!" But checking the ticket, he sees what's wrong: The tray is missing a risotto, so he turns back to the kitchen. "Order a risotto, Goichi, on the fly!"

Now Lee turns back to the runners. "So is 63 just missing the risotto?"

"Yes, Chef," says the runner.

"How long on the risotto, Goichi?" shouts Lee.

Goichi is stirring it with a flat wooden spoon, tasting.

"Five minutes."

In the space between them, Côte plates two orders of sea bass, laying the garnishes.

"Okay," says Lee, "64, 55, 15, 52 coming out."

Now Côte leans over the plates, carefully ladling on the sauces.

"Two risotto and a lobster," shouts Lee, "and I need a rush. Give me two lobsters first." The lobster is a hot appetizer—lobster *fricassée* with cabbage, root vegetables, chives, and black truffles. Because of the "Celebration of Truffles," there are far more hot apps than usual.

The runners wipe the edges of the plates as they come out, using precut, premoistened sections of paper towels that they pull from little tin boxes on the pass. "Okay, shhhh! We have to get these appetizers out here!" says Lee.

"Sixteen veal 1-2-3, please. Chicken 4, chicken 4 on 16. Sixteen is coming up. There's a lobster on that table, it's position 3. With the two tunas. Go!"

The runners are still wiping plates.

"Start to go!" yells Lee. "Pick up!"

Now the phone rings, and Lee picks up. Boulud's wife, Micky, wants to come down and have dinner in the skybox. "When do you want to come down?" Lee asks Micky on the phone. "In five minutes?" The Bouluds' oven doesn't get used much; it's filled with soft drinks. If Lee is at all unnerved by her last-minute request in the middle of a dinner rush, he doesn't show it.

Now a runner puts his fingers into a plate full of shaved black truffle and releases a shower onto a meat dish, roasted beef tenderloin and braised short ribs in red wine with celery—one of Boulud's signature dishes. A black truffle the size of a softball sits on a plate behind Frank, half-shaved.

Several just-cooked portions of meat, chops, and tidily tied roasts rest on a warm shelf above the stove in front of Philippe, the French *saucier*. A bead of sweat runs down his face as he yanks open the oven, pokes a piece of meat, spoons some juices over, and slams the door with his knee.

"Whoa!" yells Lee, in mid-order. He sees a runner screwing up an order, putting two dishes together on a tray, even though they're intended for different tables. "Don't let him do anything!" he tells the other runners. "You're a menace!"

"You told me to keep this together!" says the runner.

"Take this out!" yells Lee, setting the dishes right. "Send the fucking food out, okay?!"

Now there's another problem. They're working on the main courses for a pre-theater table, pushing the service in order to get the guests out in time to make their curtain. But one of the diners has gotten up from the table to use the restroom in between courses, and the captain doesn't want the order fired until she's back in her seat. The runner conveys the message, but too late.

"Oh, *merde!*" says Philippe, the sweat now flying off his face.

David, the captain in charge of that table, bursts into the kitchen. Normally captains and assistant captains (as regular waiters are officially called here) do not come into the kitchen during service unless there's a problem.

"The food is in the fucking pan already," Lee tells him. "So I'm not stopping the order."

"Of course not," says David, knitting his brow. Although he has come in to stop the order, he loses his nerve when he sees the mood in the kitchen. Behind him, a busboy rolls out a huge round tabletop, propelling it toward the swinging doors leading to the waiters' stations.

"He said you said to stop the order. You've gotta use your logic," says Lee. "If there's nobody at the table, we're not gonna serve it!"

At seven-thirty tension is still running high, though there hasn't been a blowup for a few minutes. Boulud comes downstairs from the skybox, clapping his hands loudly. "Monsieur François Pinault," he shouts. "Forty-seven, two people. Let's fire some canapés." Boulud looks briefly at the tickets on the pass, then inspects a clove powder mixture that Gallagher has concocted. "Who's working with this?" he asks.

"Me, Chef," says Gallagher. He's using it to dust sweetbreads before pan-roasting them; they'll go on a salad.

"It's extremely strong," says Boulud, frowning.

"I know, Chef. I'm using very little."

"Remember," says Boulud, "the ratio is fifty to one." In other words, one part ground cloves, fifty parts Wondra flour.

"Chef," says David, the *garde-manger* cook, coming up behind Boulud. Boulud follows him to the *garde-manger*. *"Qu'est-ce que vous voulez faire pour le plateau?"* What do you want to do for the canapés?

David the captain comes back in the kitchen. "Alex," he says. "We have to do a mid-course on 49." A mid-course is a complimentary extra course. Sounds as though there has been a problem at the table.

"What happened?" asks Lee.

But he never finds out because a yell comes from near the swinging in-out doors.

"Pinault just arrived!"

Boulud takes charge of Pinault's canapés himself. *"Allez,"* he says. Let's go. "Two sardines, but don't make it too big. Do you have a little bit of verjus in the preparation?"

"Yes, Chef," says Gallagher.

"Mrs. Ming, ten canapés, please," Boulud adds, calling to the *garde-manger*. Then he moves to the pass, lets fly his imposing baritone. "Ordering, François Pinault. The big time! Two sardines, two prawn, two ravioli, two pig. Very little butter, very little cheese. Low cholesterol. *Vas-y*—rock and roll!"

Pinault is not just a garden-variety VIP proprietor of one of the five most celebrated wine châteaux in the world; he's also one of the wealthiest businessmen in France, owner of Printemps department store and Fnac super-stores, as well as one of French President Jacques Chirac's closest friends. The sixty-three-year-old billionaire was born in Brittany. His father was a humble timber trader; the son followed in his father's footsteps, building up his own timber business with an investment of less than fifteen thousand dollars. Recently he bought the auction house Christie's; last year he bought Sanofi, whose holdings include Yves St. Laurent, Oscar de la Renta, Fendi, Van Cleef & Arpels, and others. Pinault happens to be particularly important to Boulud. For one thing, Daniel's deep vertical collection of Château Latour—with selections from vintages going all the way back to 1893 ($9,714 on the wine list)—is the crown jewel in Daniel's wine cellar, with an entire page of the wine list devoted to it. And for another, Pinault has approached Boulud to open a restaurant in the new Christie's in Paris. He has told Boulud that he's ready to go; he has the location. Boulud's jocular answer has been that he can't because his managers don't speak French. Yet he hasn't completely ruled it out.

"Then I'm going to do the menu for Stratta," says Boulud, "and then I'm going to do the menu for Traga." Yet another very important, very important person.

"Ordering for Gérard," calls Boulud. "Okay, we're going to do two se-viche, then two sardine." The seviche tonight involves sea scallops, oysters, and sea urchins, with osetra caviar, pink radish, and celery leaves in a horseradish-lime oyster water. It's Daniel all over: clear, pure flavors that sound as though they'll make sense, though they're unusual in combination. Synergistic, the flavors vibrate together, creating a dish in which the whole is a thousand times greater than the sum of its parts.

"*Le seviche*," says the *garde-manger* chef, "*c'est petit, ou pas?* Is it for a tasting?"

"*Tu fais un petit* appetizer," says Boulud. "Small but not as small as a tasting." Now he goes back to his tickets. "Ordering one langoustine, a quail salad, a mushroom soup. After that, two char, medium, a lamb, medium, and a pork."

In between calling out orders, Boulud works on putting together a tasting menu for Pinault. So far he has written on the ticket:

2 sard
2 prawn
2 ravioli?
2 pig

He stares at it a moment. "Neil," he calls to Gallagher. "We're starting work on the tasting. Can we do a seviche? We have to make sure the canapés work with everything. Alex, come over here. I want to do a *riz de veau*. Let me deglaze it. It's for Pinault, okay?" He scribbles on the ticket. "We have to push. You know how he is: He wants to do in-and-out in an hour." Figuratively speaking, of course; no one can eat five courses in such a short time.

They all work at a feverish pitch, their concentration intense. It may be a day like any other, but every single day these guys cook at full throttle.

"Prepare for the *six et douze,*" calls Boulud. "Ordering ten *foie gras pour* the tasting, okay? *Après ça, dix homards avec deux Saint-Jacques, deux paupiettes, neuf* veal, and a beef. Let's go, eh?!"

A runner comes out from the dining room, bearing a big bone on a plate, a beef shank. "They want it," he says.

"To go?!" cries Lee, incredulous.

Now Boulud is working on one tasting for the chef, Alessandro Stratta, another for the foie gras queen, Ariane Daguin. "Do you have any terrine or squab left?" he calls to the *garde-manger*. "No, eh?" He turns to Lee. "Two sardines and *commencer avec le seviche.*" Then he calls to the *garde-manger* again, "Can you make me a *plateau* for seven, please?" No response. "Hello?!"

"Yes, Chef!" shouts the *garde-manger* assistant.

Lee goes over the tickets. "Four is out on 20, or no?" he yells. "Ay yi yi . . ."

"No," says Boulud. "*Les* pastas. *On va faire les macaronis . . .*" He clears his throat. "Can you bring me a glass of water?" he calls to a runner, anyone. "And a cup of coffee or something? But if I have a coffee, I might jump off the—"

"You want to have a tea?" offers a runner.

"It would be nice to have a tea, yes," he says to the runner, who goes off. Then, to himself, "It would be nice to sit down and relax with it, too."

"Mr. Pinault working?" asks a runner.

"Fire two prawn!" bellows Boulud.

"Goichi," says Lee, "you have a peeler over there?"

"No, Chef."

"I've got one," says Gallagher.

"What do you got," says Lee, "a French one or an American one?"

"A French one," says Gallagher. He looks in his hard plastic utensil case; it looks like a case for a flute, or maybe a small violin. He hands the peeler to Lee. As in all restaurants, chefs and cooks are responsible for bringing and maintaining their own knives and other equipment.

Lee uses the peeler to strip the peel off a Meyer lemon. These gorgeous cit-ruses from the West Coast have a short season. They're larger and rounder than other lemons, their thin skin is more orangey, and they smell almost like a cross between a lemon and an orange. Chefs love them for their pronounced, unusual flavor, especially in savory dishes. Lee juliennes the peel, super-fine, then juliennes some watermelon radish with pretty pink flesh. These will be garnishes for a custom-made hamachi (yellowtail) appetizer, not on the menu, for chef Alessandro Stratta. Since he worked under Boulud at Le Cirque, he merits super-VIP status.

On the speakerphone, a voice calls out, "Ariane's party of eight is here. Do you want to do the canapés in the bar?"

"It's easier to do the *plateau* at the table," replies Boulud.

"Okay," says the phone. "Then we'll do a glass of champagne at the bar first."

Now Lee makes the sauce for the hamachi: splashes of citrus juice and grape seed oil, Meyer lemon zest and all-zest (made from orange, lemon, and lime), kumquat chiffonnade. He cuts a fine chiffonnade of mint and coriander for the garnish.

Boulud lifts a small plate that's about to go out. "Shit!" he yells. "The plate is frozen!" He puts it down, and the *garde-manger* cook takes it back. "Two mini-crab!" booms Boulud.

"Chef," says German. "Thirty-three now," indicating that Pinault's next course should be fired.

"*Oui*, 33," says Daniel. "Okay, now, *oui. Oui, mais* low cholesterol. The guy had a triple bypass a year ago, so slow down." He means the *saucier* should take it easy on the fats.

"What about 16?" asks German.

"What *about* 16? What are you talking about?" says Boulud.

"I'm talking about table 16."

"You think you left it somewhere? Let's go!" he spins around.

"Penne and a *ballottine* right away!" calls Lee. "Four mini-soups went out?" It's 8:55 and the kitchen is insane with activity.

Suddenly Boulud yells at a runner who has just lifted a plate with his hand: "Don't do that again! Do not do that again! You take the tray or the highway! Okay?!"

David, the captain, comes in. "*Les chefs sont là,*" he announces. The chefs are here.

"Okay, *d'accord*," says Boulud. "Okay, we're gonna have six crab gelée, six seviche to fire. Fire two crab."

Côte heats an oversized oval plate under a salamander for a few moments and then starts saucing it.

"Okay," says Boulud, "push the main course for Pinault now."

Michael Lawrence comes into the kitchen, saying, "Chef, fire table 18."

"Everything is beautiful, Michael," says Boulud.

The runners, standing in a line in front of the trays, look like gamblers anxiously watching a roulette wheel, waiting to see what numbers will come up. A few are Chinese, but most are Ecuadorian. In fact there are fifteen Ecuadorian guys working at Daniel—"all short," says one of them, Ernesto.

"Alex," says Boulud. "Are you ready for the abalone?"

"Chef," says Lawrence, coming back in, "the Evian water did not come today, so now we're gonna have to eighty-six Evian."

"Café Boulud," answers Boulud, meaning call them and get some from there. "I need two *faisan*, three *faisan*, four *faisan*, please. Now it's four."

Chris, the *entremétier* working with Philippe, the *saucier*, is sautéing spinach, making raw leaves jump. On Philippe's other side, Fay, who is acting as *sous-chef* this evening, plates meat dishes.

"Ordering twelve," bellows Boulud. "Ordering six gelée crab, six seviche, six hamachi, six sardine, six abalone, six prawn. After that six penne, six macaroni, six *rouget*, six tuna, six beef, six veal." The tasting menu for the party of twelve consists of a first course of three appetizers each, a pasta course, a fish course, and a meat course. In typical Daniel fashion, the dishes will alternate around the table, so that six guests will have veal, and those to either side of them will have beef. From apéritifs to paying the check, they'll likely stay at the table for three hours. "Now ordering eight. They're really heating up!" Boulud laughs; miraculously, it looks as though he's almost enjoying this.

Next to the soup station, a bus pan full of cut-up lobsters, still in their shells, is balanced on the tall trash receptacle. The disembodied tails are still moving, as are the front halves, the bodies. Boulud goes to the hot-apps station and gives the pans a jump. Coming back to the pass, he brushes against the bus pan of lobsters, almost toppling it. It's a dumb place for someone to have left it, but there doesn't seem to be room for it anywhere else.

"Eh. Eh. Oh," he says.

Lee looks depressed. "Abalone's fucked up," he says.

"Why?" says Boulud.

"It's gonna be cold." The rest of the order isn't ready.

The runners chatter nervously—from where they stand, the plates are taking too long.

"It's going out right now!" Boulud yells at one, regarding an order he's waiting for.

"There's a problem, Chef," says German. The diners are getting restless, no doubt. "That's why I've been asking for a half hour now." But now, finally, the plates he's been waiting for land in front of him. "Okay!" he calls. "Pick up over here!"

"One beef shank left!" cries Philippe, the *saucier*.

"One beef shank left!" echoes German.

"Sixteen, fire!" calls Philippe the *saucier*.

"And after that, 52," says Boulud. "That's the next one, eh? And then 48. Okay, *vas-y, vas-y!*"

"Okay, guys, over here!" says German. "Pick up!" He points to the trays. "Fifty-three. Sixty-eight." He returns to his post. "Fire two risotto, Goichi, when you have time."

"Eighty-six squab!" yells Philippe the *saucier*.

David, the captain, bursts through the door, both arms in the air, looking left and right, looking murderous.

"Pick up!" yells German. "Come on, come on! I need trays here right now!" There's no one available, so he dives for a tray from the pastry station.

A stocky, green-shirted dishwasher known as Gordito (his real name is Eric) comes in, slides open the cabinet below the meat plating area, waits until Fay is finished plating an order, and as she steps aside, darts in with the clean plates. Philippe slices chicken breast with an electric knife.

"Attention!" cries Boulud in French, meaning "Watch out!" "The risotto is a little too soft! They're gonna do a red wine now on 33, okay?" He turns to a runner. "What time did this table arrive?"

"Nine thirty-five," says the runner. It's now 9:50.

Boulud calls out three orders, in rapid succession. The line cooks call out, "Yes, Chef!" "Yes, Chef!" like so many "amens."

"Pepper! Pepper! Pepper!" yells Boulud. Gallagher's there instantly with a pepper mill. "Fire the pasta, please, for 12!" Now Boulud notices Côte saucing some plates for Stratta's party and screams. "Shit! Sea bass? *J'ai dit qu'ils sont déjà passés au rouge!*" I said they're already drinking red wine! *"Aïe, aïe, aïe— c'est ma faute, mais . . ."* It's my fault, but still . . .

Lee looks at the video monitor, pushes some buttons to zoom in on a table. *"Ariane a déjà fini,"* he says. The foie gras queen is already finished.

"Ils sont fatigués?" says Daniel. Are they tired?

Philippe the *saucier* points to a ticket on the board. "Chef," he says, *"il n'y a plus de* squab." There's no more.

The hot-apps cook delivers the pasta for twelve to the pass; Boulud begins shaving truffle into his hand, very fast, and garnishes the plates. "We've gotta go fast," he says. "This pasta has to be hot!"

"Chef," says German, "we've got one more fuck-up. Twenty-five, I'm ready for what, a half hour?"

"Shut up!" yells Boulud. "One second, okay? *C'est quoi cette putain de pasta?"* What's this fucking pasta? "It's cold! *Merde!* Put it in your hand—it's cold!" Now he turns to shout at German, in measured tones: "They arrive at nine o'clock. They had a four-course meal in forty-five minutes. *C'est pas mal, non?* Get me the pasta out now—hot! Come and take my job and we'll see if you don't fuck up, eh?!"

"Okay," says Lee. "Let's get back to the service. Twenty-two. Ninety-four is out. Salad and crab gelée."

Boulud rearranges the tickets. "I just want someone to help me set this up," he tells Lee, sliding the tickets at the top all the way to the right. "Appetizer, appetizer, appetizer."

"I know," says Lee, "but I don't know what's gone out yet."

"Do you have 33 yet, or soon?" says Boulud, then he turns to German. "They don't have the mini-soup on 24. Are you sure we sent them?"

"No position?" says Philippe, regarding a meat order with a missing position number for where the order will go at the table.

"No position," says a runner. "Chef, what are the positions?"

"Number 4 is the lady," says Boulud. "The veal is for the gentleman, number 3." He looks around for Fay, whom he expects to see plating in Allannic's usual spot. "Fay, where are you?" he says irritably.

Just then she reenters the kitchen, returning from the prep kitchen.

"I was getting the vegetables," she says.

"Okay, sorry."

"I was getting the vegetables!" she repeats, perhaps a tad too defensively.

"It's over," says Lee. "He just asked you a question." He follows her to the back of the kitchen, by the walk-in. Clearly she's upset. "It's over!" he repeats. "He just asked you a question. I need you in service!"

She comes back to her station and resumes plating for Philippe.

Now Lee, back at the pass, is bothered by something written on a ticket. "Nobody sees on the ticket that there's two pigeon?" he asks German. "Are you getting me?" Wood pigeon—also known as squab—was eighty-six some time ago. In fact, a glance up at the eighty-six board, a white erasable marker board up high over the kitchen exit, says clearly: *86 squab*.

"Can I speak?" interjects Boulud.

"Eighty-six squab, eh?" yells Philippe.

"I was checking the fucking vegetables!" says Fay.

"I know," says Lee. "I don't want to hear any more about the fucking vegetables. *C'est fini.*"

"Ordering!" calls out Boulud. It's 10:05. "One mushroom soup and one penne. After that, one sole and one lamb, medium-rare."

Lee puts his arm around Fay and tells her something in her ear.

"How long on the langoustines?" she asks, trying to calm down.

No one responds.

"I asked for a new langoustine," she says.

"I have a beautiful new langoustine right here," says Lee, "and there's no problem."

The runners are lined up, waiting. Boulud is now on the phone under the video monitor.

On the hot line, Chris sautés spinach, touching it as it falls back into the pan. Satisfied, he pulls it from the heat.

Two customers enter the kitchen: the well-known chef Jean-Louis Palladin and a friend. Boulud sees them and hangs up the phone, smiling. "Let's go! *C'est pour les Gascons!*" Like Ariane Daguin, Palladin is from Gascony. He and Boulud have been friends forever; it was on a tip from Palladin that Boulud got his first job in New York. Still wearing a black leather jacket, Palladin looks as though he's just arrived to join the party. Boulud embraces them, then goes back to the pass. *"Vous avez déjà mangé?"* he asks. You guys have already eaten? They nod. Apparently they ate somewhere else before stopping by to join the Gascons.

During a little lull in the service, Lee shows Gallagher his favorite knife: a ten-and-a-half-inch Masamoto Honyaki Gyokuhakuko Yanagi. The Japanese slicer is hand-forged from thirteen layers of Shiroko steel, a Japanese high-carbon steel that, though softer than stainless steel, is known for its purity and strength. Although it's harder to maintain than stainless, one can put a much sharper edge on it. "I got it at this place on Thirty-third Street," says Lee. He likes to use it for particular slicing jobs, keeping it tucked away the rest of the time so nobody else touches it. If someone were to grab it in the heat of service and whack away at something with it, the eight-hundred-dollar knife would be ruined. Lee, in fact, has an impressive knife collection—more than a hundred. He keeps the twenty or so he uses most in a drawer in his station. His other favorites are a Victorinox chef's knife that he bought for six dollars in Switzerland in 1989 (he uses this quite often), a Chinese cleaver with a six-inch blade, a five-inch Sabatier utility knife, and a couple of small two- or three-dollar Victorinox paring knives that he replaces frequently. He also has several butcher knives from the 1930s that he's quite fond of—he loves the way the steel is worn down. He keeps another fifteen or twenty under his desk downstairs in the office and the rest at home.

Now a ticket comes in. "I need a foie gras sauté," yells Lee, "and a minestrone. Foie gras *tout de suite!*"

A shout comes up from the fish station: "Eighty-six lobster!"

Gallagher wipes down the counter, taking advantage of the short respite. He rocks back and forth in his flat, soft clogs with flexible soles, trying to loosen up.

Gratinée tripes with milk and parsley come out in a big copper pan. Boulud sticks his finger in, tastes. A line cook does, too. "I need six cups for eating it," says Boulud. The runners look confused; it's a party of twelve, the Gascons. "In between each diner. They eat from the same cup. Six tripe—it's enough."

Suddenly a heavenly aroma wafts out of the pastry service area: a little puff of butter and sugar.

David, the captain, comes in. "Thirty-nine is complaining," he says. "So is 24."

Lee looks up at the tickets. "They're both working."

Boulud leaves the pass to talk to the pastry chef. He's going to order for Daguin and the Gascons. He confers with Haas, sticking his head in through the pastry window, and then returns to the pass.

Bernard Vrod, a maître d' in his sixties who went to work at Le Cirque long before Boulud yet followed him when he left, comes into the kitchen. "What's going on with 49?" he asks.

"Coming," says Lee.

Boulud whistles, claps his hands, goes back to the pastry pickup area. *"Où sont les desserts?"* he wants to know.

And now, at this late hour of the evening (it's almost eleven), Lee has some stunning news for the kitchen. Smiling at the impossible gravity of it, he calls to the fish line: *"C'est Yamamoto qui vient."* Yamamoto, a seafood-loving regular who is known to be an imperial pain in the ass, is arriving in the dining room. "He's going to want a fish menu." One of the maître d's refers to Yamamoto as Frankenstein's monster because, he says, Boulud has turned the demanding customer into one by bending over backward so far and so often to accommodate him. Yamamoto loves consommé, and once at Café Boulud they made him a beautiful consommé with foie gras dumplings, served in a beautiful pale green Japanese bowl. He tasted it, and loved the soup, but then said, "The bowl reminds me of the early seventies. I can't eat this."

"He's coming in now?" says Fay, alarmed.

"No, not yet," says Lee.

"Come on!" shouts Fay. "Lamb garnish!"

"Coming right out!" says Chris.

David, the captain, stands waiting for an order, looking dejected. "It's been crazy all night," Lee tells him. "We haven't stopped." Lee holds up the ticket he's waiting for. *"Deux pigeons?"*

"Oui, ça arrive," says Philippe. It's coming.

As Philippe lays the plate on the tray, David starts to garnish it with truffle. Boulud is wiping the edges of the dessert plates as they come out of the pastry kitchen. He sets four plates on a tray, balances another atop them in the middle. As a runner hefts it up, it almost slides off. Then more plates come out: On each is a chocolate pyramid with two glazed chestnuts. "Just one chestnut," says Boulud, removing the extra ones. "There was too much on the plate." The pastry assistant pushes out two silver trays holding linen pouches of madeleines, and two trays of handmade chocolates, which Boulud starts to rearrange. "Try to arrange the chocolates a little better," he says, "okay?"

Finally, at 11:10, the kitchen starts to calm down and clear out. In the *garde-manger,* always the first to be done, since those are the dishes that begin the meals, the cooks are covering containers of ingredients with plastic film.

"Okay!" shouts Lee finally. "Everything's in!" Meaning the last order has been submitted.

A cheer goes up in the kitchen. An end to the evening is in sight.

Friday, February 11

THIS MORNING ERICA CANTLEY has a cold—a bad one. And despite the fact that *The Dinex Group Employee Handbook*—an eighteen-page photocopied affair—states that "anyone who is ill should call in sick," Cantley's going to try to muddle through. Working at the front desk, as she will today, she'll have no direct contact with the food. The manual says, "We expect all employees to be of good cheer when dealing with customers. This is not possible when someone is feeling miserable. Therefore, it is better to call in sick, take care of oneself and get well as soon as possible." There is a little problem today, though, and that is that Bruno Jamais, the head maître d', who usually works the front desk, is in the hospital for the week. Nothing serious, but someone has to greet the customers. Today it will be Erica, cold or no cold.

Traditionally, the maître d' is the figurehead who sets the tone for a restaurant. Accordingly, for an elegant restaurant (or one that fancies itself to be elegant, or aspires to elegance), the ideal maître d' should himself be elegant, graceful, and formal. Naturally, he should be impeccably dressed. And historically, in the American restaurants of the Continental or French or Italian stripe, he should be French or Italian. It goes almost without saying, even in the twenty-first century, that he should be a he. For most of American's restaurant history, Italian maître d's have been as desirable as French maître d's, even in French restaurants, partly because Italians have owned many excellent French restaurants, such as Le Cirque, and presided over the front of the house. Perhaps surprisingly, the maître d' is not a manager; he answers to the director of the restaurant.

Besides setting the tone for the dining room, the role of the maître d' is (or should be) to make the customer feel well taken care of. *Soigné*. Which is where Boulud has a little problem. For while Bruno Jamais takes wonderful care of his regulars—those who call him directly for reservations and help to line his pockets with gold—he couldn't give less of a shit about everyone else. Or at least that's the impression he gives. To many who dine at Daniel he fits the stereotypic image of the maître d' as arrogant and intimidating.

Physically, Bruno Jamais is straight from central casting: tall and very dark, menacingly handsome, expensively suited. Looking at him, it's difficult to say whether he's Italian or French. In fact, he's French. Before coming to the U.S. to work for Boulud, he was maître d' at Lucas Carton, the renowned *Michelin* three-star in Paris.

Jamais doesn't seem to be the slightest bit interested in putting the maître d' cliché to rest. Intimidating? Laura Begley, the style editor of *Travel + Leisure* magazine, vowed never to return to Daniel after her first visit because of the reception he gave her (she didn't reveal that she was a member of the press). Arrogant? Chef Jean-Louis Palladin once asked Boulud, "Why don't you get rid of that monster at the door?" Rude? Last spring, one of Daniel's wait staff, Danielle Desaulniers, came with her father, the well-known chef and cookbook author Marcel Desaulniers, to dine at Daniel on her night off. When she walked in, Jamais told her, "You have no business eating here." When Boulud got wind of what happened, Jamais was suspended for two weeks.

Even his name seems designed to intimidate: In French, *jamais* means "never."

In the front of the house at Daniel, there's a constant struggle. There are the hosts, hostesses, assistant maître d's, captains, and so forth, whose entire raison d'être is to make the customers happy. And then there is Jamais, not particularly well liked by much of the staff, who believes that his mission is to make his regulars happy. On top of everything else, until recently he was the only employee to take a share out of the cash tip pool without putting anything in. Brett Traussi changed that policy several months ago; now Jamais, like sommelier Jean-Luc Le Dû, participates in only the credit-card portion of the tip pool, though customers, especially his regulars, do palm him tips. Many on the staff joke about Jamais's "fleet" of Porsches, but only Jamais knows how much this "handshake" money amounts to. No doubt it's considerable.

Erica Cantley may well be the person who likes Jamais the least.

After setting herself up with some hot tea and tucking a bag of herbal cough drops discreetly into a cranny in the podium, Cantley's first order of business is going over the reservation sheets. These sheets—one for lunch and one for dinner—were prepared yesterday, generated from the reservation books used to record the reservations as they came in. "The reservation sheet is the lifeline of the restaurant," says the other employee handbook, the *Front Desk Staff Manual*. The reservation sheets indicate basic information about each party, such as the time of the reservation, number of guests, whether or not it has been confirmed, and whether there are any special requests or information. Is there a birthday or anniversary involved? These would be indicated by "HB" or "ANNIV." "PX" means the person is a VIP (again, Cantley's discreet code) and "REG" means he's a regular. "WANTS TO SEE DB" means they want to see or meet Boulud, "FOBT" indicates a friend of Brett Traussi, Dinex Group's operations manager. Other abbreviations are "HA" (house account); "PT" (pre-theater, and therefore needs to make an eight-o'clock curtain); "AT" (after theater); "BANQ" (wants to be seated at a banquette); "GLS CHAMP" (give them each a glass of champagne, compliments of

Boulud, Traussi, etc.); or "SEE DB," meaning check with Boulud to see what to do about them or how to handle their check.

As customers begin to arrive in the restaurant, front-desk staff pencils other information onto the reservations sheet. If an incomplete party arrives, the host or hostess makes a check by the name, along with the appropriate number of slashes to indicate how many in the party have arrived. The party is shown to a cocktail table, and the hostess notes at which lounge table they're waiting. Once they're seated in the dining room, she writes down their table number and the exact time they were seated.

Cantley goes down the lunch reservation sheet, reading

VIPs today:

Rod Mitchell

Shaking her head, she erases VIPs and pencils in PX. Next on the list:

Ad director of Bon App.

Nixon Jason, Hamptons Magazine—no check. See GF

GF is Georgette Farkas, director of public relations and marketing, who handles all media requests.

Sticking a couple of individually wrapped cough drops into her pocket, Cantley starts on her rounds, "doing the circulation." Descending the carpeted stairway leading down to the ladies' and men's lounges and public telephone, Cantley goes to an unmarked door at the end of the dimly lit hallway. She punches in a code on an unobtrusive three-button keypad and enters the restaurant's offices.

Large group photographs line the entryway to the offices. One shows a smiling Boulud in a group shot with a large assortment of his mentors: Paul Bocuse, Roger Vergé, Michel Guérard, Gérard Nandron, and Georges Blanc. This was taken at a charity dinner he gave honoring them last year when the restaurant had just opened. Another shows Boulud and Sylvester Stallone at the old Daniel. Alex Lee, Philippe Rispoli, Cyrille Allannic, and Johnny Iuzzini stand behind them with the brigade; Stallone's fists are raised Rocky-style. Others show Boulud with Sirio Maccioni; one of these was taken in front of the old Le Cirque, which of course was housed in this same building. Another, taken from a magazine in 1993, has the caption *"GQ* Salutes Men of Style." In it, a youthful Boulud, looking movie-star sexy, models a denim jacket.

Around the corner is the photocopier; Cantley makes ten copies of the reservation sheet. The first gets dropped on Brett Traussi's desk, situated in a small, glassed-in cubicle just opposite the photocopier. There are no windows at all on this level, since it's below ground. Michael Lawrence gets a copy on his desk, in another cubicle. Turning right into a large double bank of "offices" (actually long, adjacent desks), Cantley places one each on the desks of Alex Lee and Thomas Haas.

Now, taking a right turn out of the bank of offices, she pushes through a swinging door and finds herself in the prep kitchens. The first is the bread bakery, which is attached to the large pastry prep kitchen, where she leaves a reservation sheet on the counter. Leaving that area, she enters a larger prep kitchen: This is where all the major peeling, chopping, dicing, slicing, julienning, portioning, pasta rolling, butchering, filleting, and deboning go on. (Just behind, to the left, is another room, with burners for the simmering of huge pots of stocks and cooking of sauces, ovens for roasting, industrial mixers, and so on.) But Cantley passes straight through, to a small office at the end, the stewards' office. Inside are desks for the two stewards, Toto and Jed, who are responsible for, among other things, ordering all the ingredients for the restaurant. Cantley leaves a reservation sheet here; on Fridays she also leaves a forecast for the following week, so they'll know approximately how many covers they'll be doing and how much food to order.

Cantley takes a right up a ramp, passing the small prep area for Feast & Fêtes, the catering operation, and pushes through double swinging doors that lead to a corridor in front of the women's and men's locker rooms. Up the stairs, through another corridor, through more swinging doors, and she's in the main kitchen.

She climbs the steep stairs up to the skybox, dropping a reservation sheet on Hilary Tolman's desk, descends again, enters the kitchen, and drops one on the pass.

Now she goes out the "in" door, which is propped open when the restaurant's not involved in service, crosses the dining room, goes up to the reservations office, drops one there, and finally brings the last one back with her to the front desk.

Ten-fifty, and time to set up her station, the front desk. Cantley puts the reservation sheets in a tall leather binder, prepares the take-away menus, and begins to sharpen pencils. She actually prefers mechanical pencils to regular ones: The front desk staff is under such pressure that they're constantly breaking the lead. Now she finds a memo from Georgette Farkas about a photo shoot: twelve noon in the Banquet Room. "For NYChefs.com," says the note, "6 dishes, chef's choice."

To alert the dining room and the kitchen of VIPs and special requests, she now makes up the *"soignés"*—business-card-sized slips of paper, filled out in duplicate, with the name of the guest, time of reservation, and number in the party. Copying information from the reservation sheet onto one, she writes, "See DB." Then "HB woman," "HB man," "HB Nancy," indicating three special birthday requests. One copy of each will go to the appropriate server, and the other to either the kitchen or the pastry chef, if a dessert is involved, since the pastry kitchen will send out a special dessert to the celebrant.

Seating for the VIPs was already decided last night; Cantley starts assigning other "presets," tables that are pre-assigned, now.

The assigning of tables is an art in itself. Front desk staff is expected to know all the table numbers, as well as their relative merits. Scanning the reservation sheet, Cantley notes that there are a lot of deuces (parties of two) today: thirty-eight in total. The tables considered the best are 40, 42, 47, and 48. The four are arranged in a diamond pattern in the center of the room known as the "pool," since the area is sunken down three stairs from the entry. All twenty-two of the tables in the pool are at least pretty good; the four-tops with banquettes in each of four corners are very good, as are a few of the other tables on the left side of the diamond four. The two best deuces are probably 44 and 45, just beyond the diamond four, closer to the servers' stations, which are shielded by screens. These tables are "good" because, as Cantley puts it, "you can see and be seen." Up on the "balcony," the raised area to the left of the pool, there are ten tables, including banquettes along the wall for four four-tops. On the edge of the balcony overlooking the pool are four deuces, considered to be "good." And the worst tables? Sixty-four and 66—so near the kitchen doors you can almost feel a breeze when they swing open.

When William Grimes last came to the dining room in preparation of his review, the front desk staff only realized who he was halfway through his meal. By then it was too late to change the fact that he was seated at table 66.

Two weeks ago, Boulud sat Cantley down in the skybox late one night after service and offered her a job as assistant maître d'. This was a very tempting proposition, especially since no women hold maître d' positions in French restaurants at this level in New York. Even American men rarely fill these positions; almost all are French.

Most people in Cantley's position would have jumped at such a chance, but for Cantley, the answer's not so obvious. An amazing opportunity, yes, but she would have to work under Jamais. The deciding factor was an offer from Mario Batali, the chef-owner of Babbo and several other Manhattan Italian restaurants, to be head maître d' at Esca, a high-profile new restaurant Batali is opening with Joseph Bastianich in the theater district. Cantley has accepted Batali's offer; the restaurant will open sometime around St. Patrick's Day.

When pressed, Cantley does admit that there are aspects of his job that Jamais does well. She believes, for instance, that if Jamais had been in the restaurant the first night Grimes showed up (using an alias to make his reservation, of course), the critic never would have been plopped down at table 66. Since then, a photograph of Grimes has been procured—culled from the back of his out-of-print 1993 book, *Straight Up or On the Rocks: A Cultural History of American Drink*—and to this day it's tucked conveniently on the inside wall of the coat check, where Jeanette, the coat-check attendant, can have time to recognize him and signal the front desk, averting any future disasters. When Grimes returns—and return he will—everyone in the front of the house will be ready for him. Michael Lawrence and his team are determined that, at least from their end, Daniel will merit the fourth star.

The night of the table 66 disaster, Jamais was out on his two-week suspension for the Desaulniers affair. When it was realized that it was Grimes in the house, Boulud knew that Jamais would have detected him; he immediately called Jamais back from suspension.

And then there is the matter of packing the room: Jamais is a master at the fine art of overbooking. The trick is to fill up the room as much as possible, overbooking slightly to compensate for the inevitable no-shows (generally 20 percent of the tables on any given night) that are the bane of every restaurateur, while not overbooking so much that there is a problem seating guests in a reasonably timely fashion.

Cantley believes that it is partly Boulud's loyalty that prevents him from letting Jamais go despite a number of customers who send letters complaining about him. In fact, Boulud is so loyal to his staff in general that it's often said no one gets fired here.

One pastry cook sees it a little differently: "If they want to get rid of you," she says, "they make your life miserable so you quit. But they won't fire you."

Boulud, for his part, is well aware of Jamais's shortcomings. Sometimes the maître d' does things that absolutely rankle the chef. Still, Boulud feels that while anyone can criticize Jamais, few could do his job as well.

Against the back wall of the dining room is a huge arrangement of forsythia, armfuls of bright yellow shoots promising spring (though the forsythia in Central Park have yet to bloom). Olivier Guigni of L'Olivier Floral Atelier does all the flowers at Daniel. L'Olivier's website boasts that Guigni was "discovered by Pierre Cardin" in 1980 and that Cardin made him design director of Les Fleurs de Maxim's in Paris. He came to New York in 1986, opening a Les Fleurs de Maxim's on Madison Avenue, and serving "a clientele comprised of Manhattan A-list socialites and celebrities." Guigni opened his own Atelier in 1994 in an East Seventy-sixth Street brownstone; since then he has become known for his use of fragrant herbs and architectural greens in his spectacular arrangements. Guigni changes Daniel's arrangements once a week; he sends someone to tend them every morning. On the tables today are compact bouquets of tiger lilies and rosemary branches. On the podium is a vase of flowers that resemble asparagus—green at the tips, white-bottomed.

At 11:10, after partaking of family lunch (a little ravioli and a bright lacy salad, piled high), Cantley goes downstairs to put on her face. Since someone must be at the front desk at all times once the doors open at eleven, Joanna puts on the tailored black jacket she keeps in the reservations office for just such occasions and steps behind the podium. In a moment Michael Lawrence is there to cover, so Joanna goes back to the reservations office.

Lawrence is a great manager: serious and dedicated, yet sympathetic to the needs of his staff. Cantley refers to him as "a soldier, like me." He's also got a killer deadpan sense of humor. Born in Monroe, Louisiana, Lawrence grew up in New Orleans and went to school at Louisiana State University in Baton Rouge. His first job in New York was as a captain at Tavern on the Green, the theme park–like restaurant on the edge of Central Park. Lawrence and his coworkers there referred to Tavern as "the egg shop," because on any given Sunday they'd poach four thousand eggs. From there he went to the legendary Quilted Giraffe, then on to March, Wayne Nish's elegant Manhattan townhouse restaurant. He came to Daniel at the end of 1998, helping to open it.

Magalie, a lounge server, crosses in front of Lawrence. "Only one reservation?" she says to Lawrence. "It's been busy all week."

Lawrence shakes his head—what can you do? "What's your title?" he asks her, as an afterthought.

"I don't know!" she says. Pixie-ish, tiny and slim, with short brown hair, well-fitting black suit and tie, flat black oxfords, Magalie is French. She came here from France when her boyfriend, Jean-François Bruel, was offered a job as *sous-chef* at Café Boulud.

"Let's say manager," declares Lawrence. Magalie smiles.

A Sade CD plays softly in the lounge as Brett Traussi interviews a prospective employee at one of the side tables. "We should change the music to Billie

Holiday or something," says Lawrence to a passing captain. They've been playing so much Sade, Lawrence can't bear to hear it anymore.

Whenever someone applies for a job waiting tables, they are given a thirty-five-question written test concocted by Lawrence, with questions such as "Name five vodkas," "Name four four-star restaurants," "Name seven mushrooms," "What is the difference between Pouilly-Fuissé and Pouilly-Fumé?" and "Name two champagnes from California." (The last is a trick question: There are no champagnes from California, only sparkling wines.) Lawrence scores applicants on a scale of one to ten on appearance, wine knowledge, and points of service. The test is given to all applicants, even if they've worked at other restaurants of this caliber. Some are offended, but usually it's those who don't know the difference between Pouilly-Fuissé and Pouilly-Fumé who protest.

The revolving door whooshes around, and in walks a photographer, who approaches the podium. Lawrence tells him he'll find Georgette Farkas. "Please make yourself comfortable in the lounge and we'll offer you something to drink."

Now Cantley emerges, wearing a navy suit, hair upswept in a French twist. In five minutes, she has become glamorous. She examines her manicure: nails cut short and painted deep, classic red. Despite the fact that the *Employee Handbook* demands clear nail polish only, when Cantley trains hosts, she suggests either a French manicure, which always looks correct, or a classic red. Then there's the question of hair. What Cantley calls "downtown hair"— pieces sticking out all over the place—is a particular problem.

"Did you see the piece in the *Times* on Wednesday?" Cantley asks Lawrence. "Look what I just picked up." She collects a piece of carpet fluff from the bottom of her shoe and deposits it on the podium. "At Charlie Trotter's restaurant, he makes people put double-stick tape on their shoes to pick up carpet fluff."

"We should do that, too," says Lawrence, glancing down at his own shoes—$180 Italian Aureolos. Still, his feet hurt. Sore feet are endemic here at Daniel, as they are at all restaurants. Yesterday he ordered a new pair of English shoes—four hundred dollars, supposedly wonderful for your feet. Tara, the head bartender, wears shoes from Easy Spirit, a store that has made a sub-specialty of people who work in the restaurant business, those who seek shoes that look good and provide lots of support and extra cushioning.

It's 11:45, fifteen minutes before the first reservation. Since Cantley has taken her place behind the podium, Lawrence is doing "pre-meal." At the moment, he's polishing silverware—properly!—with a rag that is lightly damp, not wet. He's careful to polish the handles as well as the part of the implement that touches the food.

Suddenly he notices on the floor, just to the side of the dining room entrance, a small piece of equipment. "We have to get this out of here!" he says. "What is this, a drill?"

Just moments after it's whisked away, a guest pushes through the revolving door, checks her coat.

The moment that door whooshes around the first time every day, it's as if the curtain of a theater has gone up. The front of the house undergoes a perceptible change. It's showtime!

The back of the house, to extend the theater metaphor, really feels like backstage as well. But step from the kitchen through the swinging "out" door and past the screen into the dining room, or through the door off the employee powder room off the back corridor, directly into the lounge, and you're onstage once again. Any back-of-the-house staff member who does so, therefore, must be properly dressed. And his or her bearing will change. One has to *behave*, as it were.

"Good morning," the red-dressed guest says to Cantley. "I'm Mrs. Benson. I'm meeting a friend for lunch."

"Good morning, Mrs. Benson. Welcome," says Cantley. "We'll be seating in just a few minutes. Please make yourself comfortable in the lounge."

Cantley makes a slash by her name; Mrs. Benson takes a seat on a plush banquette. Now Louis Armstrong is singing "Mack the Knife."

A young man wearing a dark suit and holding an attaché case comes in. He approaches the desk, looking uncertain. "Yes," he says, "I have an appointment to see Jean-Luc Le Dû." Le Dû is the sommelier.

"Very well," says Cantley. "Please make yourself comfortable in the lounge, and we'll offer you something to drink. I'll let Jean-Luc know you're here."

A couple walks in, checks coats. "I've been here once before," the man says to the woman as they approach the podium.

"Good morning," says Cantley.

"Good morning," says the man. "Wilson."

"Just one moment, Mr. Wilson; we'll seat you right away."

The couple moves away from the podium, looking at the display of Boulud's cookbook on the table by the stairs. "Sixty-one, like *Highway 61*," says Lawrence to Cantley, sotto voce.

A few minutes later, another couple comes in, the man yammering at his companion in a voice that carries. "He talks so loudly that I think they'd better be in a corner," instructs Lawrence, softly.

Cantley notices that a number of tables have been curtained off, put out of use. "Why did they do that?" she asks Bernard Vrod, Boulud's maître d' dating back to Le Cirque. The three maître d's who work under Jamais are officially assistant maître d's. They oversee service in the dining room, rather than greeting guests at the podium. "We're not going to have enough tables."

"Why are you getting excited?" answers Vrod. "We have enough tables. We'll make them wait a little bit."

"No," says Cantley. "It's stupid to make them wait."

"What did she say?" asks Lawrence, coming back from the dining room.

"She's just a little excited," says Vrod.

Now Rod Mitchell checks in. Mitchell, the proprietor of Browne Trading Company, supplies Daniel with its caviar, smoked salmon, diver-harvested sea scallops, and other specialty seafood items. After a few moments, another man in his party of four comes in. Not noticing Mitchell, who sits at a table in the lounge, the man checks in at the podium. He's carrying a bottle of wine and a heavy-looking shoulder bag.

"Why don't you let me take that for you?" offers Cantley, referring to the heavy-looking bag.

"Actually," says the gentleman, "if you could have them brought to the table, that would be great." He hands Cantley the wine—an Aloxe-Corton—and the bag, and then notices Mitchell at his table; he joins him.

Georgette Farkas comes up the stairs and tells Cantley that she needs a table for two, and it's complimentary. Two ladies from a magazine called *Velvet*. None of them has ever heard of it.

"Can you do a *soigné?*" says Lawrence, turning to Cantley.

"We'll seat them," says Farkas, "and I'll join them after lunch."

A woman who is waiting for a table comes back to the podium. "Does Olivier do your flowers?" she asks Cantley.

"Yes, he does." The spectacular arrangements come at a cost of $150,000 per year; the seasonal decorations Olivier provides, including the potted trees out in front, cost another $60,000 per year.

"Oh," says the woman, "he does my flowers at home." Next to her name on the reservation sheet is a notation: GC—gift certificate.

Later, in the dining room, lunch service is in full swing; it's 12:40. Michael Lawrence and a waiter, Jérôme, walk out toward the podium, where Cantley's still greeting guests. Olivier, the assistant sommelier, follows them. Clearly there's a problem. The Aloxe-Corton had been delivered to Rod Mitchell's VIP four-top along with the shoulder bag, as requested, but Jérôme mistakenly opened the wine and poured for the table.

"The wine wasn't even for him!" says Lawrence. "It's for 48, but it's a gift for the gentleman."

"He said, 'Open it,' " says Jérôme.

"All I said was it goes to the table, position 4," says Lawrence.

"It's not a problem," says Olivier. "It's for Jean-Luc, the wine."

"The chef said to open it," insists Jérôme.

"I *think* it's a gift for Jean-Luc," says Olivier, not really sure now.

Cantley picks up the phone. "Jean-Luc," she says into the receiver. "Jean-Luc. Has he come in yet? Okay, I need to speak with him at the front. It's an emergency. It's Erica." She waits, no response. "Hello?" she says. "I just asked you if Jean-Luc was there, and you said yes. Well, have you seen him? He's coming in at one-thirty? Thank you very much." Now she grabs a blue phone book from one of the drawers of the podium and gets Le Dû's home number. Besides the crisis in the dining room, the young man with the twelve o'clock appointment to see him is still waiting patiently in the lounge.

Just as she has a problem with Jamais, Cantley finds plenty to criticize in Le Dû. From her perspective, Jamais and Le Dû are always standing around yakking when they should be paying attention to the guests.

In the meantime, the man who had asked Cantley to have the bottle and bag delivered to the table stands talking to Lawrence, off to the side. Apparently he was away from the table and did not witness the huge mistake involving his wine. "I'm very sorry, but the bottle was opened and drunk," says Lawrence sadly. The man puts his hand over his mouth, astonished, and leaves it there a long time as he listens to Lawrence.

"He's upset," Cantley tells Olivier. "Table 48's upset."

"But Jérôme just opened the bottle of wine," protests Olivier.

"You never open the wine without presenting it," says Cantley.

Olivier disagrees. "When somebody brings in a bottle," he says, "we don't need to show it."

Lawrence comes back to the podium. "I don't understand why the wine *was* here," he says, indicating the desk, "and the wine went to the table."

"Because the gentleman asked for the wine to be brought to the table," says Cantley. "The point is—"

"The point is why did you open the wine?" Lawrence says, turning to Jérôme.

"He is wrong, wrong, wrong," Cantley mutters.

A man in his forties enters and checks his coat. He's wearing shirtsleeves. He approaches the podium and gives Cantley his name.

"Actually, we do ask that men wear jackets," says Cantley. "We can provide you with one."

The man hesitates. "Well," he says after a moment. "I should take a jacket. No tie, right?"

"A jacket is fine," says Cantley. The man goes back to the coat check, where Jeanette, the attendant, gives him a navy blazer with brass buttons. Not the most fashionable garment, but standard enough to blend in in the dining room. Jeanette keeps one in every size from forty to fifty, as it happens about once a day that someone needs one. The jackets, purchased from a menswear company owned by Georgette Farkas's stepfather, cost just under two hundred dollars. They need to be replaced sometimes as well, for occasionally a customer forgets to return one. Usually they're too embarrassed to bring it back after that.

Once the man is out of earshot, Lawrence returns to the subject of the wine incident. "The worst part of it," he says, shaking his head slowly, "is I know that man. I have known him for twenty years." He puts his head in his hands.

"Who is he?" asks Cantley.

Lawrence tells her his name; he's the vice-president of an investment firm.

"Olivier needs to be strongly reprimanded," says Cantley.

"But Daniel told him to open it," Lawrence points out.

Cantley just shakes her head.

A lady of a certain age wearing a pink Chanel jacket enters.

Lawrence greets her, asking, "Your regular table, is that okay?"

He leads her and her companion into the dining room.

The phone rings: In the kitchen they're looking for Jean-Luc. It rings again: In the cellar they're looking for Jean-Luc. "I already called his cell phone," says Cantley into the phone. "No answer."

Now Olivier comes in from the dining room, looking for Jean-Luc. He picks up the phone. "Jean-Luc? Jean-Luc? Hello, Jean-Luc is there? No?"

"Did he leave, the guy who was waiting for him?" asks Lawrence.

Cantley chortles. "Guess so."

Olivier goes into the lounge to find out for certain. "I'm very sorry," he says to the young man when he spots him.

Lawrence comes back to the podium from the dining room. "Well, it can't get any worse today," he tells Cantley. "It has to be all uphill. On table 51, two ladies ordered a pretty expensive white wine, they looked at the bottle, approved it, let Olivier open it, and when they saw it was white, they didn't want it."

"What was it?" asks Cantley.

"A '96 Smith Haut-Lafite, a hundred and twenty-nine dollars. The lady said, 'Oh my God! I thought it was red!' So I said, 'Well, maybe you'll like it.' 'No, we'll have red,' she said."

"They're dressed kind of frumpy," recalls Cantley.

"So they ordered a Château Siran Margaux, '95."

Lawrence will sell the Smith Haut-Lafite by the glass at the bar—he hopes. Now Bernard Vrod comes out of the dining room. "Thirty-six, everything is comp?" he asks Cantley.

"No. Who said that?"

"I have a ticket," says Vrod. "The *soigné* says 'comp.' "

Cantley refers to her reservation sheet. "No," she concludes.

"No, I'm talking about 41," says Vrod, looking again at the *soigné*.

"Settle it to trade," says Cantley. "House account. No check."

Rod Mitchell's guest, the victim of the wine crisis, exits the dining room and stops at the podium. "Don't worry about the wine," he says. "Because it was a gift for me, and we really enjoyed it."

"I'm so sorry, sir, about what happened," says Lawrence. He really looks as though he wants to kill himself.

The first party leaves the dining room: It's 1:45. Five minutes later, the young man waiting for Le Dû collects his coat and goes. Olivier is still trying to find him, punching buttons on the phone. "Jean-Luc? Jean-Luc?" He then turns to Lawrence. "Maybe he smoked too much."

"That's not nice!" says Lawrence.

"He had an appointment at twelve!" says Olivier, in defense of his own jab.

Just then, a well-dressed couple in their thirties enter, check their coats. Their clothes aren't spectacular, just quietly stylish.

"They look a little glamorous," says Lawrence, sotto voce. "Here's the lucky party who gets 47—the best table in the house."

And so this lucky anonymous pair will lunch, *soigné*, luxuriously late, in the shimmering center of New York's socio-gastronomic universe.

Three

HAIL TO
THE CHEF

MANHATTAN AWAKENED THIS MORNING to an unseasonably springlike day. Not a cloud to be seen in the brilliant blue sky, and in place of the icy wind that New Yorkers have come to dread as the winter has dragged on, the breeze comes in little benign puffs that make it feel more like April than February.

Early in the afternoon, Park Avenue will be closed to traffic for a span that stretches from Sixty-third Street up to Sixty-eighth Street. Restaurant Daniel's block of East Sixty-fifth Street between Park and Madison is closed as well, blocked off by rickety NYPD blue barricades. The area crackles with police presence, provided by slouchy, bantering New York cops, enjoying their plum assignment. In about six hours, President Clinton will be arriving for dinner at Daniel.

Clinton is coming for the Democratic National Committee fund-raiser hosted by Shelby Bryan, for which arrangements were made a month ago. Seats at this dinner are setting each couple back $25,000. Lest the president chance to gaze upon an entryway that's seasonally yet unappealingly void of flora, Brett Traussi has filled the sidewalk flower boxes with extravagantly fragrant narcissus. Traussi hesitated, since they cost a small fortune, but he knows Boulud well enough to know he'd have a heart attack if he noticed empty planters in front of the restaurant with such important VIPs expected.

Secret Service officers already swarm the skybox overlooking the kitchen.

An office assistant grabs Michael Lawrence. "Michael, where are we setting up the Secret Service command post?" she wants to know. "Is it in Daniel's office or downstairs?" Unsure, Lawrence frantically tries to find Anthony Francis, the banquet director, to get his opinion. The Secret Service, however, doesn't wait for an answer: They're already setting up in the skybox, unwrapping the cord from a huge, heavy phone—the hotline—and installing it on the table used for dining in the skybox. It looks like one of those ancient "portables" used by remote troops in World War II; the cord looks umbilical. If the button is to be pushed tonight, the order will come from the skybox.

Downstairs, Jean-Luc Le Dû, wearing the long black apron of the traditional French sommelier, pushes through the swinging door with an elbow, on his way to the dining room, a couple of bottles tucked under his arm.

"What time are they supposed to close down everything?" he asks Lawrence as he passes.

"Three o'clock," says Lawrence. It's now 2:45.

In order to do background checks, the Secret Service has already collected key information—Social Security numbers and dates of birth—from all the staff who will be working tonight. Still, they'll spend all afternoon checking every inch of the building. All restaurant staff, front of the house, back of the house, office, will be required to remain inside the building for the duration of the event.

Yet remarkably, the dining room will remain open to regular dinner patrons while the DNC dinner goes on in the Bellecour Room, the banquet room just off the bar. The DNC party will begin with a cocktail reception in the lounge and then move into the banquet room for dinner.

A White House advance guy lines the staff-only corridor behind the banquet room with paper signs that say POTUS HOLD. "What does that mean?" wonders a line cook walking through. "Potus," says the advance guy, "stands for President of the United States. This is in case the president has time to make phone calls at some point this evening—we'll have to close off this whole area." The line cook looks impressed.

Downstairs in the pastry prep kitchen, Thomas Haas puts the finishing touches on the garnishes for the individual presidential chocolate soufflés: white chocolate disks, each decorated with a dark-chocolate presidential seal. A few days ago, Haas contacted the White House requesting an official presidential seal, and a staffer faxed him one right away. Haas made a silkscreen out of it and screened it onto the small white disks. No matter that President Clinton doesn't eat chocolate.

In the main prep kitchen, Neil Gallagher peels Roma tomatoes for tonight's special, while Fay preps fava beans. They won't be working on the Clinton dinner, which will be prepped downstairs and finished in the tiny banquet kitchen—large enough for no more than six or seven cooks standing elbow to elbow. Only a few special orders from the DNC party's set menu will be executed in the main kitchen.

"I love fava beans," says Gallagher, "but they're a pain in the ass." With his good posture, short red hair, small pointed noise, Gallagher moves with the precision of a woodpecker.

Fay nods at his understatement. The favas must first be shelled, then the beans have to be parboiled, and finally each must be meticulously peeled to reveal the inner bean. Ten seconds too long in the boiling water, and the beans turn to mush.

The president might be coming to dinner, but in the regular dining room it will be business as usual.

Cooks start to move upstairs from the prep kitchen, pushing metal carts loaded with blenders, bus pans filled with prepped ingredients, stainless-steel cylinders full of sauce: their daily upward migration.

Julie, in charge of hot appetizers (including pastas and risottos), isn't going up; having worked lunch, she now has to prepare pasta for tomorrow. Julie has been working at Daniel for five months, following a stint at Cena, a small, well-respected New American restaurant in Manhattan's fashionable Flatiron District that flamed out after only about a year. One day, shortly after the closing, one of her mentors from Northeast Culinary, where she had trained, called and told her Daniel was looking for a line cook; Boulud had eaten at Cena, her mentor told her, and evidently liked it. Julie faxed her résumé to Daniel and was surprised when Boulud called her personally, asking her to call his assistant to make an appointment. When Julie arrived for her meeting, Boulud wasn't in the restaurant, and she interviewed with Alex Lee. The two sat down together, and Lee looked at her résumé.

"Why do you want to work here?" Lee wanted to know. "And where in the restaurant do you think you'd like to start?"

"I'll start anywhere," said Julie. "I want to learn as much as possible." This was the truth—from where she sat, Daniel was one of the few places that still made the *ballottines* and other classic preparations she wanted to master.

Lee asked her to come in for a two-day trial, so she came in and worked with the fish guys. She got the job, starting in the *garde-manger* and moving after a couple months to hot apps.

Now she places a plastic storage container on the counter; inside are six plastic-wrapped balls of pasta dough she made at six o'clock this morning. Once rolled and cut, the pasta will be frozen overnight and used tomorrow. Despite the stigma attached to freezing anything, in fact certain preparations work better if frozen. Fresh penne is one of them.

Julie plugs in an electric pasta maker—one that looks just like the crank-powered home model made by Atlas that everyone bought and tried once in the 1980s—and begins to roll out sheets of pasta, starting with the setting on 10, the thickest. She changes the setting to progressively smaller numbers, and the dough gets rolled thinner and thinner each time it goes through. For the penne she's making, she'll take it all the way down to 0, the finest, and she'll run it through twice. In a matter of seconds, she has a sheet of pasta that is four feet long.

Across the island of cutting boards from her, David, a former instructor from the California campus of the Culinary Institute of America, slices shallots with a mandoline, wearing a latex glove to prevent the smell from staying on his hand. "Tony," he says to another cook, "you should step outside for a moment."

"Is it nice?" says Tony, not looking up from his work. Small and wiry, with a dark Hawaiian complexion and twinkly eyes, Tony is originally from Oahu. He and David work the fish station together, Tony as *chef poissonnier* and David as *entremétier,* in charge of the garnishes for Tony's fish dishes.

"Yeah," says David. David left his post in the idyllic Napa Valley in order to have the opportunity to cook at Daniel, which he considers one of the very best restaurants in the country. He started out last summer as a pastry cook—the only position available at the time—and jumped at the chance to move to the "hot side" as soon as a spot opened up.

"T-shirt weather, huh?" Tony's too busy to catch the breeze.

With a small, sharp knife, Julie cuts the long sheet of pasta lengthwise, and then across into squares.

Michael Lawrence comes in. "Did you guys see the tent?" he asks. The White House staff has assembled a huge tent directly in front of the service entrance, a hundred feet from the regular entrance of the restaurant on East Sixty-fifth Street. An enclosed passageway leads directly from the tent all the way to the service door. For security reasons, no one must be able to see the president as he steps out of his car and walks the fifteen feet or so into the restaurant.

Julie pulls out a small, ridged plastic tube roller, about six inches long. Taking a square of pasta dough, she places the tube on a corner, quickly rolls the pasta around it, and slips it off in one fluid motion, making a ribbed penne.

Toto bounds in, announcing, "Five minutes, please! I have the dogs coming in! The whole kitchen."

"Why?" shouts Haas, from the pastry kitchen, playing dumb.

" 'Cause the president is coming in," says Toto. "Guys, please. Thank you very much."

"If you have shit in your lockers," shouts one of the line cooks, "get it out now!"

"Please, guys," says Toto again. "Please. Thank you very much."

Long sheets of plastic film go over all the food: pasta, fava beans, *crosnes*, salmon—everything.

"Do we have to go outside naked," calls Fay after Toto, "or can we wear our clothes?"

Outside, the cooks lean against flower boxes, marveling at the metal detector stuck halfway out of the main entry to the restaurant. They've all had to unlock their lockers and leave them open: not a happy proposition, since lately there's been a spate of locker-room thefts. Half of them light up cigarettes. It's three-thirty, and a chance to take a breath of the deliciously springlike air.

"*Mon téléphone est* on?" says Bruno Bertin, the chef in charge of Feast & Fêtes, the catering operation. "I'm calling the CIA!"

As five minutes stretch into forty-five, the runners and busboys sitting along the railings of the planter boxes are grateful for the day's warmth; on a normal February 24, five minutes without a winter coat would be about the limit. Bruno Jamais, black-suited, tall, imposing as always, stands in front of the revolving door smoking, his nose sniffing the air.

The cooks are becoming nervous, jumpy—this delay means they're now officially "in the shit."

Finally they're all summoned to the revolving door—the guests' entrance to the restaurant—to be admitted, two at a time, after passing through the metal detector. "Empty your pockets," says a Secret Service agent, and they all oblige, silly as the exercise seems. "Our knives are in *there*," says Regina, a tall, sweet-faced, prematurely gray pastry cook, nodding toward the inside of the restaurant, "if they're looking for weapons."

In the main kitchen, the line cooks set up their *mise en place* for dinner, while the *sous-chefs* work on their specials. At 4:45, a White House photographer comes in, snapping a few shots of Gallagher as he rolls blood oranges on a cutting board, applying pressure with the heel of his hand to release the juice before he cuts them in half.

Michael Lawrence appears at the door. "Is Julio in here?" he calls, in his N'Orleans lilt. "I need people in here. The bar's not set up. I don't know what the hell you're doing! It's not a holiday!"

Gallagher grabs the secret ingredient for his tomato glaze and places it out of the view of the White House photographer. In fact this special ingredient happens to have been developed by NASA under another Democratic president. It is an ingredient few of the other chefs have even tasted, and the French guys have never heard of it. The secret ingredient is Tang. Gallagher knows better than to brag about using it; still, he likes the sweet, well, *tang* it imparts to the tomatoes.

The photographer doesn't notice the Tang. "I'm just doing this out of a personal interest," he tells Lawrence. "I've worked in restaurants all my life, and I've heard so much about this one."

Gallagher's special is *rouget* with potato scallops, inspired by a Paul Bocuse dish, Rouget Parmentier. The sauce he makes from the tomatoes will be both sweet and savory. He tastes the tomatoes, then pushes them through a china cap—a conical sieve also known as a chinois.

At five minutes after five, Boulud enters the kitchen, wearing checked slacks and a sporty black cashmere jacket, looking fit and tanned. He's just flown in from the Dominican Republic, cutting short a family vacation in order to be here for Clinton's visit. Before the president makes his entrance to the dinner, he'll be camped out in Boulud's apartment above the restaurant.

Boulud walks around the kitchen, shaking hands. Ten minutes later, as everyone completes his *mise en place*, Boulud has disappeared. The soup cook cuts foie gras into dice, garnish for a soup, dipping the knife in hot water each time to keep the foie from sticking. A few cooks—those who aren't in the shit—are eating their dinner, standing in their stations or sitting on upturned plastic crates. The dishwasher mops the floor around them.

Frédéric Côte comes in, holding a camera. *"Il est arrivé, le chef,"* David, the French *garde-manger* cook, tells him. "He looks well rested."

At 5:35, James Barron, a Metro Section reporter for the *New York Times*, comes into the kitchen, looking self-conscious in whites. He's here to cover Clinton's visit to the restaurant. Barron's presence was engineered by Georgette Farkas. Her pitch, when she called him, was "How'd you like to come and cook for the president?" So Barron will be there tonight alongside Boulud and the other cooks who will cram into the closet-sized banquet kitchen, and Boulud will let him "cook" for the president. This is a way for Farkas to get coverage for the restaurant without violating Clinton's handlers' decision to have no members of the press at the dinner. An event as major as a president's visit, after all, cannot go uncovered. Barron won't be at the dinner; he'll only be behind the scenes. From Farkas's point of view, coverage in the *Times* is so valuable she doesn't mind granting Barron an exclusive.

Banquet servers are busy preparing the Bellecour Room for the event. The visual centerpiece of the room is a gigantic ice sculpture—a huge bald eagle, flanked by pillars, with the numerals 20 over the left pillar and 00 over the right. Phil is the artist responsible; he and Goichi carved it downstairs in the prep kitchen. When Phil was in culinary school he entered a number of ice-carving competitions: They'd have fifteen minutes to carve, and the sculptures would have to last four hours. Although he worked lunch and should have left by now, he's going to stay.

"You get to meet the man?" asks one of the line cooks.

"That's why I'm hanging around," says Phil.

"You were a piece of history, huh?" the line cook muses.

"Order lobster and a foie gras sauté!" That's Lee calling out the first order at 5:50. "Followed by a bass and a beef duo medium. Make sure everyone's using spoons, no one's using their fingers!"

Toto comes around, passing out toques. They're short white caps that look like those surgeons wear; everyone hates them. The cooks frown as they put them on.

"Order crab gelée and a lobster, followed by lamb, rare, and a paupiette! Order lobster and a *rouget*—Neil, *rouget!*—followed by a sole and a veal!"

Within a few minutes, things have heated up.

"Two seviche and a frog legs, followed by two sea scallops and a pork!"

"Forty, 48, and 31," says German, expediting. "Appetizer is gone."

Gallagher plates his *rouget* special as Phil looks on: celery and leeks braised in chicken stock, enriched with *beurre monté* on the plate first, then *rouget* covered with golden scales of nickel-sized potato scallops—two fillets, side by side. He spoons a green sorrel sauce around it. Goichi hands him an herb oil made with chives, basil, and tarragon, which he dribbles in three careful pools, then he sprinkles the citrus powder over all, and adds the Tang-glazed tomato on top. A sprig of chervil completes the picture. "Bocuse made this," he tells Goichi and Phil. "This is not my idea. Bocuse got it from Fernand Point. Now, if you take something like foam, that was Adría. But potato and fish? Gimme a break. Did you know that potato used to be considered a poison?"

"What are you doing here?" the soup cook asks Phil.

"I'm here to see the president. Or at least try."

Hilary Tolman is quite slim, despite her gastronomic proclivities and the fact that she doesn't belong to a gym; she attributes her trimness to a good metabolism and the number of times she runs up and down the steep stairs of the skybox. If she has a tendency to stoop a little, it's as much a result of being stuck up in the skybox as it is of her height. In any case, her long legs are useful for showing off fashion finds such as the purple suede Prada miniskirt her sister picked up for her in Rome. She has learned, however, to be careful of what she wears and where she stands, ever since the time she noticed all the busboys on the kitchen floor looking up her dress as she stood talking to Boulud in the skybox. Tonight she doesn't particularly want to stick around to see her office taken over by the Secret Service. For her, the real perk of working here is not meeting celebrities, but getting to order off the menu every day. Tolman is a true *gourmande* with a good palate; the menu descriptions she pulls together from Boulud's and Lee's notes and those of the *sous-chefs* are small works of perfection in a realm where inaccurate descriptions and misspellings are the norm.

In any case, president or no, she has sworn she'll be out tonight by six on the dot.

"Order one beluga with veg chips, onions, no blini," calls Alex Lee downstairs at the pass. "One smoked salmon sliced thin, extra onions and crème fraîche, followed by a langoustine, no emulsion." Pointing to the ticket, he turns to the waiter who wrote it. "What the fuck is that?" Then back to the *garde-manger:* "Just a little emulsion. Followed by one frogs, one arctic char over steamed vegetables, extra vegetables, no sauce. Okay, please," he says to two chattering waiters (everyone's excited tonight), "if you don't have anything to do in the kitchen, please go in the dining room. We have to keep the noise down because I still have to run the kitchen tonight, okay?" Then he tilts his head toward a runner. "You, too. I don't want you talking in here tonight, okay?"

One of the *garde-manger* cooks is wrapping his knife in a roll, putting his stuff away. "You don't wait for the president?" says French David.

"No, I'm leaving," says the cook. Fay whacks him on the ass on his way out.

"*Il est déjà là,*" Lee tells Côte, regarding the president. He's here already. Up in Boulud's apartment. Plates are going out, quickly. "The plate's dirty!" says Lee. "You have to look every time! This one, too—you have to wipe here." The runner takes a moist cloth, wipes all the edges. "Ordering arctic mushroom crab *rouget* langoustine frog. Tuna, medium-rare, char two orders squab. Long tasting!" That's to give everyone a heads-up that one table has ordered an eight-course tasting menu.

At 6:25, Boulud comes in, looks at the tickets.

"Ordering a mushroom soup and a penne black truffle," says Lee, "followed by an arctic char and a tuna medium." David delivers a plated langoustine to a tray. "Pick up langoustine, *pas beaucoup de sauce.*"

"*Tu montes les choses qu'il faut cuisiner,*" Boulud tells David. When David prepares the president's first course, he must show the food first to the president's food security person.

"The langoustine is coming?" yells Lee.

"*C'est quoi, les rougets comme Paul Bocuse?*" Boulud asks Lee. What are they, *rougets* à la Paul Bocuse?

"Yes, but the sauce is completely different," says Lee.

"Ordering langoustine and a liver salad," booms Boulud. "After that a paupiette and a beef, medium-rare."

Gallagher has heard Boulud ask Lee something about his special. "What did he ask?" says Gallagher to Lee.

"He just said, 'What's the *rouget?*' "

"Something is wrong there," says a runner.

"It's coming up," says Lee. "Tuna, no caviar." Now David comes over, looks at the *rouget*. "Paul Bocuse," says Lee. David suggests doing oysters on the half-shell because they have a lot of them. "*Vas-y, c'est une bonne idée,*" says Lee. "Mignonette. *Vas-y.*" David goes downstairs to get some oysters.

"Ordering mushroom velouté, lobster *fricassée,* and a *rouget,* followed by salmon special, squab special medium, and a pork medium. Ordering four covers: frog, artichoke soup, crab salad, oxtail, followed by scallop no potato, two squab, one shank. Artichoke mushroom soup tasting is out?"

"*Oui, Chef!*"

David comes back in with the oysters.

"You have to make some mignonette and some cocktail sauce," Lee tells him and the other *garde-manger* cook, "because we're going to offer some oysters on the half-shell."

Michael Lawrence has just stepped in. "We got a lot of oysters in the house?" he asks.

"Okay, guys," shouts Lee. "You've got to speed up the appetizers a little." He glances over at the cook who's just made a small amount of cocktail sauce. "Make a bunch," he says. "We might sell like ten of them."

Phil decides to leave after all. As he goes, he shakes hands with Lee, who looks puzzled to see him go. "I heard the president's not coming till nine o'clock tonight," Phil says. It's not even seven o'clock yet. As excited as he was, a long day is a long day.

"Yeah," says Lee. "That's what I heard."

Now Lee goes into the *garde-manger*. "Let me see the oysters," he says.

Boulud is in the small space as well, with the two *garde-manger* cooks and Lee. He's making a chicken liver salad. "Where's the foie gras?" says Boulud.

Plates are crowding the pickup area, runners wiping plates and grabbing trays as quickly as they can. "Wait a minute!" says Lee, grabbing a plate before a runner can. "It's missing the garnish."

At about 7:40, the president's food security person, Bridgette Edwards, makes her way into the kitchen. A civilian-dressed African-American woman with a friendly smile and an easy demeanor, Edwards trained as a chef in the navy, which is said to produce the best food in the armed forces. She spent fourteen years in the military before she went to work at the White House, where she's been for two years, working for the president. Edwards watches not only for Clinton's allergies (chocolate, dairy), but as a safeguard she also observes the preparation of his food at events such as this to make sure there's no monkey business. When all the plates are finished for each course, she'll randomly pick the one that will go to the president. If someone wanted to poison him, they'd have to poison the whole lot. "Hardly worth the risk," as she points out, laughingly, "and too easy to get caught."

Although the idea of chefs in the military might seem a little odd, anyone who has worked in a restaurant kitchen knows there's something militaristic about its working dynamics. Americans tend to think of the word *chef* as meaning someone who wears a white toque and stands behind a stove. But in French, *chef* means chief—as in commander-in-chief—or boss. (To indicate a restaurant chef in French, one must say *chef de cuisine*.)

Accordingly, in a restaurant, those who rank below a particular chef are about as likely to disagree with him as a private would be to disagree with his sergeant. Neither a line cook nor a *sous-chef* contradicts the executive chef; the correct response to any request is always "Yes, Chef." And when a runner is being reprimanded at the pass, whether it's his fault or not, the response, again, is "Yes, Chef." In this case the chef might be Daniel Boulud, it might be Alex Lee, or it might be a *sous-chef* taking over the pass. When a chef-owner, having had a difficult day, succumbs to the pressure of service and takes out everything that has gone wrong thus far on the general manager who happens to walk in at the wrong moment, the general manager's duty is to listen to the chef's tirade, then answer, "Yes, Chef."

Throughout the kitchen, military metaphors are used. The team of cooks is called the *brigade*. The literal translation of *sous-chef* means "under-chief." The metaphor even extends into the dining room, where the "waiters" are officially "captains" and "assistant captains." As in the military, virtues such as punctuality and discipline are of paramount importance. And just as it is for the commander-in-chief, service is the raison d'être of a restaurant chef. A president serves his country; a chef serves his customers.

There's a quality that belongs to a certain stripe of chef, and that is that above everything else, they love to feed people. This could not be truer for Daniel Boulud. Blazing culinary artistry, the need to create, the imperative to express himself through food may be what makes Boulud tick, but it is through feeding people that he seeks his own humanity.

"At eight o'clock I'll need a *plateau* for eight," says Lee to French David.

After that an eerie quiet. Clinton will be coming soon. The only sound is that of a handheld blender whirring a sauce.

And then, at 8:15, a cry: "He's coming!"

Half of the cooks gather below the bank of video monitors; the others crowd the tiny glass window in the swinging door that leads to the corridor the president will walk through. "Can we get to the bar, or no?" says one. Those right up against the window press their noses against it.

"No way," says another. "He's coming through here. He's not taking the elevator; he's taking the stairs."

"I've already cooked for the president," says Gallagher to no one in particular.

"Il est là! Il est là!" He's here! shouts French David, jumping up and down in front of the window. "He's gone."

Lee punches buttons on the video system till he has several monitors trained on the lounge and its entry. A big blurry Clinton comes into view. *"Putain, il est grand!"* says Lee—Fuck, he's tall!—though he has already met him, at the fund-raiser out in the Hamptons in the fall of 1999.

Meanwhile, Lawrence is still trying to run the dining room. "Come on, come on! Whose drinks are these?" Lawrence has been forced to channel all the drink orders through the kitchen in order to keep the lounge area clear for the president. "Let's go!"

Now Clinton comes into clearer view on a video monitor, glad-handing his way through the lounge. Gazing into the screen, Gallagher muses, "His hands are like butter, I swear. It's like holding butter—they're so soft."

"You met him?" asks Goichi.

"Yeah," says Gallagher. "Three times."

The noise of helicopters flying overhead, remarkable to hear in this practically soundproofed kitchen. Then the racket of twenty motorcycles.

"Il t'a serré la main?" David asks Lee. Did he shake your hand?

"Oui."

"Il est bien?"

"Yeah," says Lee.

"Is he going to come back here, *ou quoi?*" asks another cook.

"Daniel's going to try to have him come back."

Now Bruno Jamais appears in the kitchen. *"C'est quoi, ce bordel?"* What is this fucking mess?

"Tu l'a salué toi?" asks Côte. Did you meet the president?

It's 8:20, and the kitchen has come to a virtual standstill, everyone either gathered around the monitors or squeezed up against the window in the swinging door to maybe catch a glimpse of the president.

"Forty-seven fire!" says Fay, snapping back to service.

"Hello," says Lee, "I need that *plateau* for eight guys here now."

Now Bawa, the nighttime head steward, comes through the kitchen. He has a grin on his face as though he's seen something really interesting. "Bawa," says Lee. "What's going on?"

"He had to go to the bathroom," says Bawa, "so I had to walk him up."

"Ordering one chicken liver," says Allannic, "one langoustine, one minestrone, one hot foie gras, followed by one beef, one pork, one sole, one scallops."

"Do you have a lemon?" Fay asks David.

David makes a face.

"I'll remember that when you need tomato confit," says Fay.

"I'll just go in the refrigerator without asking you."

Boulud storms in, goes straight to the back. *"Qu'est-ce que c'est que cette sauce?"* What's with this sauce? "It's too liquid!" He comes to the pass.

"Did he see the ice sculpture?" asks Goichi.

"He did," says a line cook. "He sat right in front of it. He said, 'Who's that good-looking Japanese cook who made it?' "

"We're about to get hit," says Lee. "At nine o'clock we're going to get a big hit."

The monitors are now trained on the banquet room, where the presidential party tucks into their first course—a lobster salad with caviar cream, avocado, artichokes, and fennel. Having finished plating and sending it out, Boulud now returns to the main kitchen.

In the banquet room, Bernard Vrod circulates, pouring wine. Clinton is the sixth president Vrod, an assistant maître d', has served. Originally from Guiscriff, a town of about two thousand people in Brittany that is about ten miles from Jean-Luc Le Dû's hometown, Vrod grew up on a dairy farm; his first job was as a pastry cook and baker. He came to the United States in 1972, when he was twenty-one, and found a job at Monk's Inn, a popular New York restaurant where the wait staff dressed as monks and served fondue. He worked pastry at night, bussed tables by day, and the owner, "a nice guy," sponsored him for a green card. At that point, he gave up pastry, tired of the long hours, and decided to go front-of-the-house all the way. He went to Florida, where he worked as a waiter in Cape Chauvron for a few years, then came back to New York, and a job at Le Cirque, where he spent the next nineteen years. There, at a time when Alain Sailhac, now dean of the French Culinary Institute, was chef, he served Richard Nixon a number of times. "He loved Dover sole," recalls Vrod. "He was a nice man." And then, in his turn, Gerald Ford ("a diffi-cult guy"), Jimmy Carter ("very low-profile"), Ronald Reagan, who was of "a different class" than the others before him, and came with more Secret Ser-vice than the others had ("He came during his presidency, late at night"), and George Bush (the father), who came just after he was elected. One time Rea-gan and Nixon came together, just before Nixon passed away.

And Bill Clinton? "He seems to be a nice guy. Tonight he's not drinking."

"Can I fire 54?" asks Allannic. "What happened at that table?"

Thomas Haas brings a couple of plated desserts to the pass to show Boulud; he squirts chocolate sauce out of a squeeze bottle onto the plates. Boulud watches for a moment. The meat *entremétier* mutters, "Oh, *il est là, ce con? Photo, photo, photo partout . . .*"

"We may not be busy," warns Lee, "but we're gonna be hit. A lot of canapés are going out there."

The door to the tiny banquet kitchen is guarded by three Secret Service agents, wires in their ears. Each time a cook or restaurant staff person wants to enter, they must tell the agents what business they have inside.

In the kitchen an assembly line of six cooks, headed by Boulud, plates the main courses for the president. James Barron, the *Times* reporter, stands next to Boulud, their shoulders touching. Both Boulud and Barron wear latex gloves; no one else does. *"Allez-hup! Vite, vite, vite!"* says Boulud tensely. He's the only one talking. His tension is of a different quality than his normal authoritativeness.

Maybe having the *Times* guy here wasn't such a great idea. That's typical Boulud: Instead of focusing on how difficult it will be to feed a president, while assuring that the kitchen can handle the main dining room as smoothly as possible amid the chaos, he readily embraces the added burden of a reporter at his side. It's not only the publicity that motivates him; Boulud can't resist a challenge—the bigger the better.

These banquets present their own problems in service, since all the plates (sixty-six tonight) have to come out at pretty much the same time. Each course, prepped as much as possible in advance, is finished and plated assem-bly line–style as fast as possible in this small service kitchen. Boulud keeps tabs on the number of plates that still need to go out for each course: polenta, veg-etable garnish, lamb on top, sauce. All the way down at the right, a cook named Joe puts polenta on an empty plate; the next cook adds the vegetables.

Another, Francis, slices the saddle of lamb; Zohar, a diminutive Israeli-born cook, arranges slices on the polenta; Barron adds two lamb chops, and Boulud sauces the plate. "Where's the polenta? Slide down," says Boulud. "Okay, give me the lamb, please. Okay, the other way." Francis tries to keep up with Boulud's plating as he slices the saddle of lamb. "You will go to Philippe. No, no, he'll do that. Faster. *Donne-moi la polenta*. Faster. *Là, là, là:* there! No, no, Zohar. *Allo,* I said seven here." Francis hurriedly cuts strings off the roasted meat.

To Boulud's left is the small service window, through which go the finished plates. "I need four," says a waiter.

"I need saddle, please," says Boulud, *"chaud, chaud, chaud."* Now he looks panicked. *"Le sel, le sel!"* Salt!

The plates are getting backed up—the saddle's not being sliced fast enough.

"I need saddle, please," Boulud repeats, a crescendo of urgency in his voice.

It's very quiet for a moment.

A waiter comes and speaks softly to Boulud. "What do you mean?" Boulud answers him. "He's not finished yet?"

"No," says the waiter.

"This is the food going out to the president right now," says Boulud, tense. "One minute. I'm waiting for the saddle. *J'ai besoin des* chops *maintenant!"* Now!

Frédéric Côte walks in with two plates of salmon. "Two fish here!" he says. Apparently two people in the dining room don't eat meat; one of them is Shelby Bryan. The plates get passed overhead to the service window. "The vegetable is coming, but I don't know where it is," says Côte.

"Who's making the pasta?" asks Boulud. "Joe, go get the pasta, please. Okay, do you know who that is going to? That goes to Shelby Bryan." Boulud continues plating. "How many more?" he asks the waiter.

"Ten," says the waiter.

Anthony Francis, the banquet director, comes in. "As soon as you're finished here, Zohar, we've run out of food downstairs." A hundred of Clinton's Secret Service and other security people are being fed there.

"Please," says Boulud. *"Carré."* Saddle.

"Carré," says Francis, "can you give it to him?"

"C'est fini now," says the waiter. "That's it."

"That's it!" says Toto.

Anthony Francis points to several extra plates. "These can go down now," he says to Zohar. "I gave them food for one hundred people, but somebody didn't get anything to eat."

In the main kitchen, the back of Clinton's head fills up one of the video monitors. His hands, down to the elbows, are periodically visible as he lifts them up from the table in gesture. None of the cooks is looking anymore, however; it's 9:10 and the kitchen's going full tilt.

"You give me the four mushroom, one artichoke?" Allannic asks the soup cook.

"We have to make another *plateau*," says Lee.

Now Boulud comes in, the president's main courses having all gone out.

"Daniel," says Lee, *"Michel Trama est là."* Trama is a chef; his restaurant, L'Aubergade, in Puymirol, near Agen in southwest France, has two *Michelin* stars.

"Oui, Michel est là. Canapé, please."

"Température du porc" at fifty-five, please," says the saucier.

"Medium," agrees the runner.

Allannic calls out, "Ordering one terrine, one sauté foie gras, two *ballottine*, one endive salad, one lobster, one *rouget*, one mushroom soup, followed by one tuna, two paupiette, two lamb, one salmon."

In the *garde-manger*, French David lets fly a big sneeze, away from the food, onto his arm.

"Cyrille," says Boulud. *"Le journalist du* New York Times, *ça marche?"* meaning, Has his food been fired? He's worked; now he'll be properly fed.

"Pas encore," says Allannic. Not yet.

"Somebody get me some oysters," says Boulud. *"De jolies huîtres."* Pretty ones. "Let's go, eh? Order two foie gras, one chicken liver, followed by one squab, one paupiette." He calls to the hot-apps cook: *"Il y a des macaronis ce soir?"*

"Oui," says Gallagher, jumping in.

"Let's go 40!" shouts Cyrille. "Thirty-five. Second course is gone. Ordering one mushroom soup, one *ballottine* . . ."

The soup cook is moving very fast. He kicks a drawer shut with his foot, plates six different dishes at once. He shaves truffles on three of them, fast and furious.

Eight plates get slid to the right of the fish station for saucing.

Boulud goes into the *garde-manger*. "Give me another liner here!" he says. He wipes a plate.

"Behind you!" calls the *garde-manger* assistant.

"*C'est qui qui a commandé* frog legs, chicken liver?" says Boulud. Who is it that ordered these? "What's going on?"

A waiter comes through, muttering something about Michel Trama; he continues beyond the pass toward the dishwashing area.

"Where are you going?" Boulud calls to him as a ticket goes up; Boulud reads it. "Alaska king crab, scallops, *c'est quoi?*"

Now Lee, noticing a problem with the plates going out, yells at the runners: "The wipes are too wet! Hello! The wipes are too wet! Look at it!" No one, it seems, gives a damn that the President of the United States is in the next room.

Jean-Luc Le Dû comes in to report on Trama's wine progress. "*Ils passent au vin rouge,*" he tells Boulud. They're moving on to red wine.

"But the penne doesn't go with red wine," Boulud tells him. "Ordering one foie gras *poêlé* and one *ballottine,* followed by one arctic char and one veal."

Suddenly everyone's crowded around the small-windowed swinging door out of the kitchen. Has Clinton made a move?

"Hey!" shouts Lee. "We need a cover on the food here!"

A busboy starts to come through with a bin of linens; he makes his way toward the POTUS HOLD hallway.

"*Non!*" shouts Daniel. "*Interdit! In-ter-dit!* Fuggedaboudit! Back up!"

"Pick up 21!" yells Thomas Haas very loudly as Lee happens to walk by the pastry pickup area.

Lee has gotten the scream right in his ear, and now he explodes: "Enough fucking noise! If you respect me, you won't yell, because you yelled right in my ear. There's a guy to pick it up right here." Although Haas is executive pastry chef, Lee's approximate counterpart on the pastry side, in fact it is Lee's kitchen, since he's executive chef, Boulud's second-in-command.

Boulud wipes the deep rim of a pasta plate. "Crab salad doing well?" he calls to the *garde-manger*. "Hello? Doing well?"

"Hot foie gras!" calls German. "Let's go! Guys!"

Allannic answers, "Foie gras!" then he looks around. "Where is 60?"

"Plating," says Fay.

"Yes, Chef!" says German. "Fifty-one is gone!"

Lee says, "Are you ready, Daniel?"

"Okay, Alex," he says, "which one is it?"

Lee fingers five or six truffles. "They're all about this big," he tells Boulud.

Lee chooses one; Boulud shaves it onto a plate of penne. "Let's go!" he says to the runner. Then he indicates a plate—"For the gentleman"—and another—"for the lady."

At 9:55, a Secret Service man comes down from Boulud's office, carrying the hotline. Now there's a mad rush of Secret Service agents toward the door.

Clinton's off to the Four Seasons to attend another event. Not one to miss a dessert, Clinton had to skip his, since it was chocolate. No matter: Haas has prepared him a special *tarte Tatin* that he'll eat in the limo on the way to his next dinner.

A stream of plates comes in from the banquet room, landing in the dish-washing area; a little sauce and a few crumbs are all that is left of Bill Clinton. He never made it into the kitchen to greet the cooks. Still, all their lives, they'll remember the night they cooked for the president.

Four

SPARKS

Tuesday, March 14

W ITH SUPER TUESDAY just one week away, much of the country talks of the presidential primary races, which have been heating up: Will it be Bradley or Gore, McCain or Bush? The strong economy has the Fed worried about inflation, a fancy problem, considering the alternative (and an amusing one in retrospect). Daniel Boulud is worried, meanwhile, about ambience in his dining room. Although it might seem that after sinking $10 million into opening a new restaurant, one would be content at least with its physical aspects, not so for Boulud: He's constantly tweaking, redoing, rethinking, updating, or otherwise changing myriad details. Partly he is motivated by his natural perfectionism. But as those close to him can attest, getting that fourth star is never far from his mind.

Lately it has been suggested to Boulud that the dining room is "cold." Consequently, curtains in raw silk have been ordered, vertically striped in warm tones of gold and copper; these will fall in soft, gathered panels along the edge of the balconies all the way around the sunken area of the dining room. They should soften lines, warm up the room. In the middle of March, Boulud finds himself overseeing the installation of the tentlike structure with a circuslike top in the back corner of the dining room nearest the kitchen; the idea occurred to him about a month earlier. The tent will provide attractive and convenient storage for the most frequently ordered red wines, thereby eliminating many trips to the cellar two floors below. There is a small temperature- and humidity-controlled wine storage area in the back of the coffee station, but they've outgrown it; this way that unit may be kept at a single, lower temperature and dedicated to white wines. But why is the cave not deeper? Boulud wonders aloud. Will it be large enough to accommodate the cheese cart as well as the wine racks?

Two days later, a large sculpture is being installed squarely in the center of the sunken "pool," and again, Boulud supervises. It's quite showy: thick interlocking circles of brushed bronze, standing as tall as a maître d'. The artist is a regular customer—Arthur Carter, the owner of the *New York Observer,* the newspaper New York's media and cultural elite depends on for its gossip and city news. Carter's name is etched prominently on the sculpture's base, larger than a banner headline.

Once the piece is in place, Boulud poses for a photo shoot for *Wine Spectator* magazine.

"We're gonna do two rolls, same as ever," chirps the ponytailed English photographer. A female assistant helps with the lights. "Smi-*ling!* Very nice," he says. "Very good, Daniel."

Boulud, dressed in crisp whites, sits on the rail that runs along the periphery of the sunken section. He's a natural—as photogenic in a still shoot as he is comfortable appearing on *Charlie Rose.*

"That's good," says the photographer, "try something like that. Shift a little bit this way."

"Like that?" says Boulud. "Do you prefer it like this?" He leans forward.

"No, I like it like that. It's more composed. A few more like that and then we're finished in here." He snaps away. "Okay, why don't you hop back up on the balcony."

Boulud obliges. "Do you want me to sit on a high-stool sort of thing?"

"No, I like it like this," says the photographer. "It's more relaxed. Okay, we're going to do half a roll sitting and half a roll standing."

Boulud rolls his shoulders, tries to loosen up, forces a laugh to help him relax.

"Take a deep breath," says the photographer. "Beautiful. Perfect. Smi*ling!* Now let's have you standing again." *Snap, snap.* "Okay," he says, "last couple of frames. Very relaxed, very casual."

• • •

Downstairs in the back of the prep kitchen, Phil cooks crayfish in a stockpot the size of an industrial washing machine; it's full of boiling court bouillon. He pulls a few out with a big strainer, breaks one, looks at the tail. It's a little translucent still: perfect. He doesn't want it cooked all the way because it will be reheated, used as a component of a veal dish, Médaillons de Veau aux Ecrevisses, Crème de Paprika à l'Oseille—roasted veal medallions with Louisiana crayfish, braised fennel, spring vegetables, and a paprika-sorrel sauce.

In fact, this month will be Phil's last working at Daniel; he and Maria gave notice last week. They'll be going up to Martha's Vineyard, and then probably to Boston, where they'll look for work. A graduate of Tufts University, Phil loves Boston. Boulud told him he'd help them out in any way he could. It's not unusual in the restaurant business for chefs to help departing or former employees to find placement in other restaurants, since they all know how important it is for young cooks to gain experience in different types of restaurants and learn what they can from chefs with a variety of styles and strengths. Still, Boulud is known to be particularly helpful, as long as the cook remains in his employ for at least a year (somewhat longer is even better); the loyalty thing is a two-way street. Some cooks take advantage by seeking a job at a restaurant such as Daniel, working a few months, and then using it as a feather in their résumé. Not Phil—he's been here since before the beginning.

Boulud's generosity revealed itself some time ago to Johnny Iuzzini, the pastry *sous-chef*. Iuzzini, who had been working for Boulud since he opened the first Daniel, quit in 1997 in order to travel the world. When he told Boulud of his plans, Boulud's greatest concern was how Iuzzini would finance his trip. To that end, the chef lent him six thousand dollars. Iuzzini visited thirteen countries in seven months, traveling through Europe and Asia; when he ran out of money halfway through, Boulud wired him four thousand dollars more. When Iuzzini returned, he went to work at Payard Bistro, under François Payard, and began to pay Boulud back by having money deducted from his paycheck each week. He considers Boulud almost a second father.

Thin and wiry, Iuzzini loves to make soufflés "on the fly." "I can make a soufflé out of anything," he's fond of saying. When the notoriously picky customer Yamamoto comes in, Iuzzini likes to offer him a soufflé. The only problem is that when the other guests see it, they all want one—which is why they can't keep soufflé on the menu. Everyone wants one, and it throws off the service.

By night—or, shall we say, by night after work, which is to say very late at night—Iuzzini is a club kid. After finishing his shift well after midnight, he'll dance his way into the wee hours. His mod look, with his short hair bleached as white as flour, belies the fact that in high school he lettered in three sports: track, football, and baseball. Back when he worked with François Payard, Iuzzini was so into club culture that he worked the door at the Sound Factory in his off hours, as well as put together guest lists for them. For this he made two thousand dollars per weekend, roughly what he makes in two weeks here at Daniel.

Just behind where Iuzzini's working in the pastry prep kitchen is the dishwashing area. Here the dishwasher Gordito, in aqua gloves that reach his elbows, washes huge stockpots, bus pans, sauté pans, in a stainless-steel triple sink.

Next to him, Phil pulls the crayfish out of the stockpot with a strainer, dropping them into a huge ice bath. He pours the court-bouillon down a drain in the floor, then places a huge colander over the drain, dumps the iced-down crayfish in, shakes out the water, then lays them out on a sheet pan. He washes off the huge gas burner with a sprayer, then wipes.

At the long island in the middle of the prep kitchen, David, the fish *entremétier*, pulls the leaves off of opal basil, then chervil, placing them in small foil containers, to be used later for garnish.

Lupe, the butcher, is responsible not only for cutting meat but for breaking down fish and other creatures as well. At his station on the corner of the island nearest the entrance, he now pulls the bones out of frogs' legs. Broad-faced, squinty-eyed, and stocky, Lupe is from Puebla, Mexico. He works hard, efficiently, and incredibly fast. He loves to cook, too: chile rellenos, flautas, tacos.

Boulud enters the prep kitchen. "What are you doing with that?" he asks Lupe. "You keep the bones, eh? Keep that part also," he says, referring to the frogs' shins, which are too skinny to bone. French kitchen, nothing wasted. These can be used in a stock.

"You can start to rinse the squid," Boulud tells a prep cook, then he shows another how to prep the chicken, pushing the meat on the drumette up the bone to make a chicken lollipop.

"Philippe, Philippe!" Boulud calls across the room. The French *saucier* is working on a panful of shank bones. "Don't waste too much. *Il n'y a plus que ça?*"

Now David preps microgreens, a mixture of salad greens and herbs so small they can hardly be called baby. They cannot be rinsed, since they bruise so easily.

Now Lupe's sink is full of enormous spotted skate wings.

Soon the cooks make their habitual move upstairs a half hour before lunch service begins.

It's almost spring. Close enough, anyway, for the minds of the chefs to be on asparagus and morels, new shoots of fiddlehead ferns, and fava beans. After a winter spent working with the haute cuisine equivalents of comfort food—meats, game, tubers, truffles—everyone's thinking green and fresh and new. It is at such moments of seasonal change (and it happens more than once a season) that Daniel Boulud wakes up in the morning and decides to change the menu. This year, the promise of warmer weather inspires in him thoughts of freshness, of the bounty of the sea, of tender greens. And, *bien sûr*, that damned fourth star.

The experience one has dining at a restaurant such as Daniel, a sensation of being transported to a perfect world, would not be possible were it not for the plethora of tiny details that no one would even think about at a more casual restaurant. Before every service, for instance, one of the two "opening" captains, who start work at ten A.M. rather than at eleven, cleans all the menu covers, spraying each with a little Windex or white vinegar, and wiping them off. He then goes to the cheese trolley and makes "clean cuts" in every cheese. The last thing you want, when you're paying seventeen dollars for four selections or twenty-one dollars for six selections, is to get a slice of Livarot that's a little rubbery on one side.

Before each lunch and dinner, a service meeting is held in the dining room, just before service begins; the entire wait staff, from maître d' to busboy, attends. At this meeting Michael Lawrence usually presides, often with the assistance of Brett Traussi, but lately, Roger Eydt, a captain who was recently promoted to assistant maître d', has been leading it. Alex Lee steps in toward the end to talk about any food issues for the day. When the menu changes, however, it is Boulud who explains the new dishes to the wait staff.

At 11:35 the meeting begins. Eydt stands in front of the new tentlike structure in the corner, alongside Boulud and Brett Traussi; the dining room staff stands facing them. Traussi hands out a typed list of the dishes on the new menu, two pages stapled together.

"You know," says Traussi, starting off the meeting, "yesterday everyone pissed me off when you were all sitting down during the meeting, and the chef came in, and everyone jumped up to attention."

That explains why today everyone is standing from the start.

"Okay," says Eydt. "Bernard, station two with Daniel and Julio; David, station three with Chris and Ricardo. Nelson, you be an extra runner floating, so you can help out on station four. And then Antonio, you do silver and glass, so we won't be shorthanded. The rest of you, as usual.

"All right. At twelve o'clock we have the parents of Tony Liu, the cook. I'll ask, but we'll probably do canapés, and I'll see what else they want to do. On 42 we have to change the tablecloth because there's a little hole."

"Let's take a marker and make a big circle on it," says Boulud. The linens have been a problem lately; small holes are appearing all too often; the linen service hasn't been noticing it, and the cloths wind up on the tables, which then must be completely reset before service. Circling it with a marker before sending it back would assure that the laundry would take care of it.

"If you clean it every day," says Toto, "the problem is it gets holes."

"The guy who made the linen said it would last two or three years," points out Boulud.

"Okay, now the menu," continues Boulud. "Also the *chariot de pâtisserie* we bought." He explains to those assembled that in addition to the regular dessert menu, they'll now be offering a selection of pastries as part of the tasting menu at lunch, and they'll also be introducing a salad cart next week. Boulud then parses the two tasting menus, five courses for sixty-nine dollars or seven courses for ninety-nine dollars. He points out that if customers opt for a cheese course, they're likely to be drinking red wine. The top part of the menu, he reminds them, with all the fish dishes, will usually call for white wine, and the bottom, where the meats and poultry dishes are, will work with red. "We're going to do this for a little while until springtime really kicks in, with the morels and the favas. Until that, it's really something between late winter and early spring. So we focus on the spring. *La fraîcheur de la mer.*" In fact, "Fraîcheur de la Mer" is a heading on the new menu. "Everybody is cleaning his boat, everybody's going to go fishing, so I think that's a good idea, too. And an emphasis on spring bounty. What's important to tell the guests is that the appetizer is the upper part on both sides. You have a couple of vegetarian dishes, and of course we also have mesclun. If it looks like somebody is looking up and down and can't find anything, you can suggest that. And the carrot soup could be vegetarian without the shrimp as well."

Boulud goes on to describe a new soup, one that appears on the menu as Soupe de Champignons des Bois, Gelée de Volaille au Foie Gras; the translation below reads "Warm wild mushroom soup with jellied chicken consommé layered with foie gras, vegetable dice, and a parsley and sweet garlic puree."

"The velouté is a chicken-based stock," he explains. "This one's not as thick as that. This is mostly a clean broth of mushroom and a very clear gelée of consommé, and there's a slice of foie gras inside and a little *brunoise* of vegetables under it. And you're going to pour the hot soup around it. It's a hot and cold soup." The vegetables are carrots, celery, and mushroom.

"It's going to be a stiff gelée?" asks Traussi.

"No," says Boulud. "It'll melt down quickly. We're going to see if it's working. It's a work in progress."

Moving down the menu, Boulud discusses the frogs' legs: Cuisses de Grenouilles à la Sariette, Crème de Fèves. "We've done this a couple of times on the special," he adds. It's classic Lyonnaise. Regarding the *crème de fèves*, a cream sauce with fava beans, he says, "It's like a sweet garlic cream. Did we get any comments on it?"

"No," says Eydt.

"Did they clean the plate?" asks Boulud.

"Yeah," says Eydt. "They love it."

"Right now," continues Boulud, "we stay with the *ballottine* of foie gras with hazelnuts; it's toasted hazelnuts, which I grind into almost a powder, and they're seasoned with toasted ginger, cardamom, a little bit of allspice to it, and then it's served with a rhubarb also, poached in a very light broth, like a *sauce gastrique* of vinegar and sugar, so it's pickled lightly. But a little sweet."

"And if they're allergic to nuts?" asks a captain.

"If they're allergic to nuts," says Boulud, "they can't have it."

This appetizer appears on the menu as "Ballottine de Foie Gras aux Noisettes, Rhubarbe Confite aux Epices—Ballottine of duck foie gras rolled in spiced hazelnuts with gelée of rhubarb confit, rhubarb coulis and upland cress." The price tag is twenty-five dollars.

"Upland cress," asks Traussi. "Is that the pepper cress?"

"It's the big-leaf cress," says Boulud. He goes on to describe the pasta—handmade penne with Oregon morels, asparagus, and black truffles, with Parmesan, and a new lamb dish, roasted loin with a lemon-Indian coriander crust, braised shoulder with spring roots and dried apricot. "He did a tasting of that, no?" Meaning did Alex Lee prepare a tasting for the servers?

"No," says Eydt.

"He will let you taste that," says Boulud. It's a perpetual problem at Daniel trying to keep the staff current in terms of having tasted all the dishes. New menu items are added so frequently, dishes that remain are often tweaked day by day, and six or seven specials appear each day. It would take Lee and the *sous-chefs* hours every day to prepare samples of these as often as they're created. While it's desirable for the wait staff to know exactly how all the food tastes, it's a physical impossibility. So the chefs do the best they can, creating dishes piecemeal for staff to taste as they're added to a new menu.

Boulud explains another dish, spit-roasted duck glazed with honey and lemongrass, gratin of ruby chard with lima beans, tomato, caramelized spring onions, and an olive *jus*. "We've done something like this a couple of times," he says.

"Do you need to take the temperature?" asks Eydt, meaning does the wait staff need to ask the customer how he or she would like it done—rare, medium, or so forth?

"Yes, of course," says Boulud. "But if they think it's going to be like a Chinese duck, it's not. Then we have the stuffed breast of chicken with a slice of foie gras inside and some seasoning, and it's with crushed fingerlings. It's very simple." On the menu it's listed as "Poulet de Ferme Farci de Foie Gras, Fèves et Morilles au Jus—organic chicken breast stuffed with foie gras, *fricassée* of fava beans, morels, asparagus, sweet onions and crushed fingerling potatoes." "But we'll also have breasts without foie gras if you want. Everything is possible if you give us time."

"Are we getting crayfish?" asks Roger.

"Today we got forty-five pounds of crayfish," says Boulud, "and they were very nice." He goes on to describe the veal dish for which Phil prepared the crayfish.

Now he runs through the cold appetizers: carrot soup; Maine peeky-toe crab seasoned with lemon juice and olive oil in a green apple–celery gelée with a julienne of celery root, curly chicory, and apple chips; and tuna tartare done a new way. "Rather than go Oriental," he explains, "I wanted to go very French with the tartare. So it's seasoned with Dijon. And then it has a *coulis* of *lentilles*, and on the top, rather than serving it with a crouton, we make seasoned bread crumbs."

"So we don't have to serve the toast with the tartare anymore?" asks a waiter.

"No, the bread crumbs give it a nice crunch. When we were making it with the wasabi before, sometimes we weren't boosting it enough with the lemon. We were getting comments. With this one, I don't think we're going to have this problem because the mustard is bringing it right up."

Risotto of lobster is next—made with lobster stock and served with shelled lobster pieces, fresh peas, fennel, and a mint *coulis*. The risotto is mounted with a lobster coral and garnished with fried mint leaves. The fennel is a dried fennel garnish. "The mint is not a minty thing," says Boulud somewhat cryptically, "but I think it's always fun to hear about the combination of peas and mint. It's very British, but it's nice for spring. We don't want to make the risotto minty—just a little bit of it."

Finishing up with the fish dishes, Boulud concludes, "So next week I'm going to Lyons, and when I come back, I want a pile of letters like this." He holds up his hand to chest-height. "Compliments. Good ones. By the way, we didn't officially announce this, but David has been with Daniel now a lot of time." He indicates David, the captain. "So David expressed an interest in being a maître d'. But I'm sure David is going to find it's difficult, too. When you start to watch everything at the same time, that's where we start to lose it. Such as the sommelier, the bread boys, and maître d's. And that's where I see the sommelier having something to do because everybody is focused. When there's one sommelier in the room, it's fine, but when there's two, with the rush—Olivier, I think you do very well with it. I need to speak with Jean-Luc about it. Socialize with the guests—I think they like it. Spend a little more time with them so they feel taken care of."

"Do you want us to do anything for Little Tony?" asks a captain, in reference to the fact that the *poissonnier*'s parents will be in the dining room today.

"Yeah, yeah," says Boulud. "We'll see what they want—a tasting menu."

It's now 12:05; guests have no doubt begun to arrive. Boulud looks over the reservation sheet.

"Okay," says Roger. "We should start seating."

"Everybody knows Mr. Carter," adds Boulud, as a parting comment. "And Mr. Carter made the sculpture. It's brushed bronze."

Everyone bites his tongue—they all hate it.

Moments later, Bernard Vrod makes the rounds of the five stations, handing out three of the slim matte black pens with the discrete gold Daniel logo to the captains, who will use them to write the tickets. The first guests are ushered in, and lunch service begins.

Up on the far gallery, a platform raised a few steps above the pool area of seating, are four of the stations; there's an additional one just inside the "out" door that leads to the kitchen. Each consists of an attractive cherrywood highboylike console, with a phone and a handy chest-height drawer that pulls out to reveal a row of slots to hold the tickets for each table in the station. Below that rests a computer with touch screen for entering charges, and to the right of that a space to place small trays or glasses or anything else. Underneath are drawers holding the various silverware (Orfé from Lyons, *n'est-ce pas?*), including all the requisite fish knives, sauce spoons, and other utensils that for a while seemed to be on the verge of extinction. To the left of each console is what's known as a *guéridon*, which literally means a table with a pedestal base, but in restaurantese means a smallish cloth-covered table on which the runners deposit the trays full of food that they bring from the kitchen.

Standing next to the *guéridons*, at the top of the steps, in full view of the guests, members of the wait staff can survey their stations. Each station is staffed by a team of four: a captain, an assistant captain, a runner, and a busboy. In addition, two to four maître d's circulate around the room, as do Olivier, the assistant sommelier, at lunch and both Olivier and Jean-Luc Le Dû at dinner.

After a party is seated, the assistant greets them, offers apéritifs, and asks their preference for bottled water—still or sparkling. More than a few guests request tap water, especially since an article in the *New York Times* decrying high mark-ups on bottled water in the city's restaurants has made it more acceptable for people to jokingly ask for "Château Giuliani." Like most of the captains and assistants, Charles, the captain on station four today, is French; he has trouble imagining ordering something other than bottled water. In France, after all, tap water is not an option in formal restaurants. Here at Daniel, a simple formula is used to price the bottled water—and all cold (nonalcoholic) beverages: The cost of the beverage (what the restaurant pays) is 20 percent of the price charged. A bottle of Evian that would wholesale for two dollars, for instance, comes with a ten-dollar price tag to the guest.

At lunchtime, as soon as guests have almost finished their apéritifs, the captain goes to the table, greets them, and presents them with the menus. At dinner the tables must be turned at least twice, so the menus come a little faster. The captain also must explain the menu, since it is more complicated.

When it looks as though the guests are ready to order, the captain returns to the table and, pad and pen in hand, takes their orders. At this point there are often questions, as there are today, when Charles approaches a table of four ladies. "I don't know," says one, ordering the three-course *prix fixe* menu. She has asked for the Maine peeky-toe crab salad to start. "Should I have the halibut or the lamb?" she asks herself, cocking her head and looking up quizzically at Charles.

"Well, if this is your first time at Daniel," he says, "you might want to try the paupiette of sea bass."

"Oh, yeah?" she says. "Is it really good?"

"It's one of Daniel's signature dishes," he says. "It is very good." Originally inspired by Paul Bocuse's Rouget en Ecailles de Pomme de Terre (rouget in potato scales), the dish dates back to Boulud's tenure at Le Cirque. The sea bass fillets are wrapped in paper-thin slices of potato, cooked *à la poêle* (in a pan) to a beautiful golden-brown, placed atop a soft, buttery bed of leeks, and sauced with a shimmering reduction of syrah. Although it sells more than any other dish—Daniel served somewhere between twenty and twenty-five thousand paupiettes last year—it's simpler than most of the other preparations, and doesn't feature the kind of spectacular vegetable garnishes that distinguish most of Daniel's fish dishes. Boulud sees beauty in its simplicity; he's still as excited to cook it as he was the day he created it in 1987. After all, the most enduring classics are often the simplest dishes. In any case, it's an easy sell for the captain—how could twenty thousand guests a year be wrong? Still, one cannot help but feel that somehow the dish doesn't quite represent the soaring heights of which the kitchen is capable.

"Okay," she says. "I'll have that." She snaps her menu shut.

"But then you're both having the exact same thing," says the lady across from her, indicating her friend on the banquette. "Why don't you get two different main courses and share them?"

The indecisive one opens her menu again. "Maybe you're right," she says, then turns to her friend on the banquette, who's nodding her assent. "Do you want to try the lamb?" she asks. That's fine with her friend. The indecisive one crinkles her nose. "Well-done?" she says. "Is that okay? Or is that terrible?"

Since her friend obviously has no intention of eating lamb well-done, she switches her order back to sea bass.

"Some wine with that?" says Charles. The ladies giggle and say no, they couldn't possibly. Two of them order iced tea. Although most of the tables at dinner order at least one bottle of wine, at lunch only about one in five tables does. At about half of the tables, no one orders wine at all, and at the remaining tables, at least one person will order wine by the glass. The French servers are also surprised by this when they first come to the U.S.—in France, such a meal would be woefully incomplete without wine, whether at lunch or dinner.

Charles thanks the ladies and goes back to his station. He punches their order into the computer: four *prix fixe* lunch. Since there's no runner in sight at the moment, he takes the handwritten ticket, which is in quadruplicate, into the kitchen himself. On it are listed their first courses, with numerals from one to four by each, indicating their position at the table, then a line, and then the main courses. He hands one copy to the *garde-manger*, so he can get started on the apps right away. The other he gives to German, the expediter, and a third to Alex Lee, who's at the pass. The fourth copy he brings back to the station and files it flat in a slot in the pull-out drawer in the console. Wilson, the dimpled, diminutive Ecuadorian busboy on the station, brings a large, flat basket of bread to the table to offer the ladies, as Julio, the team's runner, goes to the coffee station to get the two iced teas and a bottle of water. He brings the beverages back to the *guéridon*, where they are picked up by Michel, the assistant captain, who places them on a pretty little silver tray and carries them to the table. Julio returns to the kitchen, waiting at the pass for the apps to come out.

When the apps come out, Julio brings them to the *guéridon*, and Michel, who has removed the decorative charger plate from the settings and laid the proper silverware, grabs two of the plates; Charles grabs the other two, and in concert they deliver them to the table. (If the table had been a deuce, Michel, the assistant, would have brought them by himself.)

It's now Michel's job to watch the table and determine when to fire the next course. This is tricky because quite a few factors come into play. First, the assistant must determine whether the party is made up of fast or slow eaters. During the day, there are a lot of business lunches, and these people tend to want the meal to move along pretty quickly. Parties of women, on the other hand, like to talk, and conventional wisdom says that these tables move much more slowly. Japanese guests also eat more slowly—they tend to have a more reverent attitude toward the dining experience and like to relax and appreciate it. Wait staff is careful not to rush these parties for fear of offending their sensibilities. Assuming a table at lunch eats at an unremarkable speed, the assistant will generally fire the next course when the guests have about two bites left of the previous one. He tells the runner, who goes in the kitchen and tells the expediter he's ready to fire.

All this, however, can be complicated by what's going on in the kitchen—how busy it is, how many orders are working at the moment, and so on. Therefore the assistant has to weigh all that additional information into his decision. And everything can be thrown off if the assistant fires the next course and then one of the guests gets up to go to the restroom, taking too long to come back.

At dinner there is not always time for such niceties. If the kitchen isn't told to fire an order after a certain amount of time elapses, they'll fire it anyway. Therefore if a table is eating slowly, the assistant has to tell the kitchen not to fire until they hear from him; otherwise, a backup of dishes will occur—a disaster in a restaurant of this caliber, where not only must the food always be delivered at just the right temperature, but discarding any food that's gotten cold is an extremely costly proposition.

The assistant captain also surveys his station constantly to see who needs tending to—which guest might need another glass of wine, a water glass refilled, and so forth. This level of service demands that the assistant anticipate the diners' needs and answer them before the request is even voiced; at the same time, the server mustn't seem to be hovering. It's impressive to see how well Daniel's wait staff juggles this. When the plates are ready to be cleared, the assistant, perhaps along with the captain or a busboy, clears the dishes, depositing them on the *guéridon*. There, the busboy scrapes and stacks the plates, leaving them there until he or a runner makes a trip into the kitchen. And the first lesson that many servers learn is "Never go to the kitchen empty-handed."

The assistant, meanwhile, resets the silverware. In order to do this, he must know which types of fish require fish knives and which don't, which dishes call for sauce spoons, and so forth. If a guest has gotten up from the table, he picks the napkin up off the chair, refolds it, and places it on the table. (This last is one of Bernard Vrod's least favorite parts of his job, since guests sometimes blow their noses into their napkins. He's even seen one spit into it.)

In the kitchen, Tony, the *poissonnier,* works on the famous paupiettes of sea bass. He has already shaped Idaho russets into rectangular blocks, not bothering to peel them since the skin will get cut away, then soaked them in water for about twenty-four hours to get some of the starch out—otherwise they don't get crispy enough. He then slices them lengthwise, using a mandoline. After dipping the slices in clarified butter, he lays four slices on a cutting board, overlapping them a bit. He lays a rectangular chunk of sea bass on top, bisecting the potatoes, sprinkles the fish with salt, pepper, and thyme, then pulls a potato slice around the fish to wrap it, first one end, then the other, cloaking the sea bass with the slices one by one. He flips the potato-covered fish over so the seam is on the bottom and places it on a parchment-covered sheet pan. Tony has worked here for a year and three months, since the restaurant's opening. Like many cooks at Daniel, Tony is a graduate of the Culinary Institute of America. Back in Hawaii, he worked on the island of Lanai at the Lodge at Koele under chef Edwin Goto, one of Hawaii's top chefs. But craving more European influence than he could find in the islands, he came to New York, working at Lespinasse when Gray Kunz was there.

Tony's parents, who live in Hawaii, are here on vacation, their first visit to New York in fifteen years.

At twelve minutes after twelve, Alex Lee calls out the first order: "Four pree-fee soup, followed by two sea bass, one veal, and one lamb, medium-rare."

"Here we go again," says David. Ironically, while Tony is a graduate of the CIA, David, his *entremétier*, was a CIA instructor.

The chef in charge of Feast & Fêtes comes into the kitchen. "Where's Fay?" he asks. She should be at the meat station but is nowhere to be seen.

"I said, 'Bruno's coming,' " quips Phil, "and she ran away."

"Hey, Tony!" shouts Alex Lee from the pass back to the fish station. "Your parents are here? Do they eat everything?"

"Yeah, they eat everything," Tony says.

Lee picks up the phone. "Did we give them champagne yet?" he asks the captain who answers. *"Incroyable.* Tony's parents are here." Lee's such a family man that their visit honestly thrills him on Tony's behalf.

On top of the pass sits a tray with big empty plastic bottles of 7-UP and Coca-Cola. The *Wine Spectator* photographer is about to shoot more photos right there. "That looks nice," says Frédéric Côte, tossing the bottles into the trash by the soup station.

"Tony," calls Lee. "They don't drink alcohol?"

"My mom does," says Tony.

As usual, there's a barely perceptible stiffening among the cooks as Boulud enters the kitchen. The soup cook tends to a batch of blinis, tender inside and crisp on the edges, just turning golden brown in the pan. Boulud goes to the hot-apps station, where the pasta and risotto are prepared. "Where's the mint?" he asks the hot-apps cook. "Where's the pea *coulis?"* The cook hands him a stainless-steel cylinder of sauce. "No, no," says Boulud, "for the risotto. There's a pea *coulis."* The cook hands it over. "So let me show you what I want you to do with the mint." Boulud takes a small copper pot, spoons some pea *coulis* into it, and adds a little lobster stock that's sitting hot on the induction range. He adds a little mint. "Stir it so there's just a little bit of mint inside," he explains, tasting it. "So you don't find it in the first taste; you find it in the second taste. First there's a lobster risotto, and then a little bit of mint behind it."

Boulud moves on to the soup station, commenting on the blinis, then comes back to the risotto. "How much did you blanch the mint?" he asks the cook.

"Just till it turned green."

Boulud moves to the pass, picks up a ticket. "Ordering!" he calls. "Three pree-fee *ballottine,* followed by three pree-fee rabbit."

Now he moves back to the risotto; he's still bothered by something. He stirs the pea *coulis* again, tastes it. He fills a plastic container with it. *"C'est le coulis de petits pois,"* he informs Côte. *"On va faire une purée de* pea shoots *avec un peu de menthe dedans."* And now to the hot-apps cook: "We're gonna take three-quarters pea shoots and one-quarter mint, blanch it together. Make a very light *coulis."* This is the kind of tinkering and adjusting that goes on whenever there's a menu change.

"I think it's better to use pea shoots and mint puree," interjects Lee, stepping over. "We have to ask Jed to order them. It's been all stems, no leaves. *Ça n'a pas de goût.* There's no flavor. We need the real Chinese ones."

In the *garde-manger,* a row ensues: The *ballottine* is not the way it's described on the menu.

"C'est la terrine de bœuf!" yells Boulud. *"Non! J'ai dit c'est pour la pree-feex tasting."* Now he bellows up to Tolman in the skybox: "Reprint the menu!"

"Better watch the service," shouts Lee, "we have one hundred covers." That's a lot for lunch. "Ordering one tartare and a green salad, followed by one halibut and a veal."

Now the *Wine Spectator* photographer and his assistant start setting up—they're going to photograph Boulud and Lee at the pass.

"Okay," shouts Lee, "everybody has his hat? Otherwise, no picture!" Dutifully yet grumpily, the cooks put on their little hats.

"Ordering two lobster risotto," calls Lee, "followed by a scallop and a lamb, medium-rare."

Boulud moves to the hot-apps station. "Okay, lobster risotto," he says, "let's go. *Corail* . . ." He adds some coral, pours in some stock.

Lee catches the action out of the corner of his eye. "Wait a minute," he says to the hot-apps cook, "are you guys roasting that?" He's referring to the stock, and whether the ingredients have been roasted prior to being used in the stock. The hot-apps cook nods. "No, no," says Lee. "I don't want that. The risotto gets dark like that. We make just the *fond de homard* next time." The cook nods. He spoons a portion of half-cooked risotto into the pan, adding a big spoonful of stock, then places a pre-measured portion of lobster in the corner of the stock pan. He stirs the risotto with a wooden spoon, jiggling the pan handle with his other hand. Leaving it a moment, he goes back to the walk-in refrigerator just beyond the fish station, then returns, stirs, tastes.

"Ordering—parents of Tony!" shouts Lee. He turns to Tony. "You want me to send them mini–carrot soup? Come here!" Tony comes over to the pass.

"I made two carrot soup à la carte," Lee tells him. Not just any carrot soup, this is chilled carrot soup with lime and some fresh carrot juice added back in; it's silky, tangy, and vibrant, garnished with Key West shrimp and a coriander-cumin cream. Sounds good to Tony, and it is.

Now the photographer's ready, and Lee and Boulud stand on crates in the pass: They need to be high enough to be seen from the other side of the board. They've put a couple of finished plates on top of the pass, where they never go in real life, to be photographed. The photographer snaps a few.

Still on the crate, Lee shouts out an order as a ticket comes in. He looks at another ticket already on the board. *"Il n'y a rien qui sort. On est dans la merde."* Nothing's going out—they're in the shit.

At the hot-apps station, the risotto cook adds peas and lobster, then spoons in a little broth, stirring. He sticks his finger in and tastes. Boulud comes over. "More *corail,*" he says. "It should be pink."

"And the coral," interjects Lee from the pass, "you always put it in at the last second, okay?"

"Where's the *fenouil?*" asks Boulud.

"It's inside, Chef."

"So today it's a work in progress, right? Tonight we get it straight."

He stirs for another moment.

"Okay," says Boulud, "are we ready?"

"Yes, Chef."

"How many, two?" The cook nods. Boulud pulls out two pasta plates—like shallow soup plates—from below. The lobster and peas keep warm in a pan. Côte walks by, shakes the pan, tastes it, and adds a little stock.

"Pree-fee ravioli is coming, please?" says Lee, looking over his shoulder. "You have lobster inside the risotto, too?" The hot-apps cook nods.

Boulud stirs the risotto, spoons it into the plates. He then spoons the lobster and peas on top. A dishwasher comes behind the hot-apps station and replaces pans on hooks overhead. Lee comes back and tastes the risotto from the pot. Boulud spoons the green pea sauce around. *"Même le menthe, un petit peu plus, hein?"* Same with the mint, he's saying; he'd like a little bit more.

"Tartare, green salad working?" calls Lee from the pass.

"Yes, Chef!" calls the *garde-manger* cook.

Boulud places a dried mint garnish on the risotto, sends it out, then he and Lee take their place once again on the crates for more photos. Eydt comes in from the dining room, takes a gander at them standing on the crates, and cracks up.

"I just happen to be too short!" quips Boulud. The French are not known for the ability to laugh at themselves, but Boulud is not above it.

Halfway through lunch, things don't seem so funny. Lee is scooping out roasted Idaho russets for a potato stuffed with caviar for Arthur Carter, the sculptor-cum-newspaperman.

Boulud takes the potatoes, starts mashing them in a wooden *saladière*. "You have a little oil in it?" he asks.

"Pas encore," says Lee.

Boulud asks the *garde-manger* chef for grape seed oil, but he doesn't have any. Suddenly a strong aroma of cardamom wafts up.

"Qu'est-ce qui sent la cardamonne comme ça?" asks Boulud. *"Tu l'as fumée ou quoi?"* Did you smoke it, or what? But as usual, something more pressing occludes his question: "Do you have some lemon zest?" he shouts.

Now a voice comes onto the speakerphone.

"Hello, kitchen?" says the voice.

"C'est qui?" says Lee.

"Table 30, we really need to push it. They have to get back to work."

"Who is this?" asks Lee.

"Who is *this?*" asks the voice.

"This is Alex. Chef."

"This is David. Captain."

"Maître d'," corrects Lee. Both laugh.

In the dining room, Julio brings in two main courses for a deuce. It's two orders of roasted loin of lamb. One had been ordered medium and one medium-rare, and these, which are sliced on the bias, are both to the rare side of medium-rare—there's almost no difference between the two. Charles shakes his head: The kitchen screwed up. He won't blame the guests if they send it back. Nor will he volunteer to them that he knows they're not cooked as ordered, however. The way he sees his job, this is a game, and half of what he has to do is bullshit. He brings the plates to the table, sets them before the guests with a look on his face that says, Here is your lamb, exactly the way it's supposed to be. If they see anything wrong with it, they don't say a word.

Boulud comes back into the kitchen, carrying a big plastic jug: five liters of *huile de pépins de raisin*. Grape seed oil. He adjusts a few plates going out.

"Okay," says the photographer; he and his assistant have just packed up all their gear. "We're finished."

"Are you having lunch now?" asks Boulud. The photographer nods. "Good," says Boulud, and the photographer and assistant leave the kitchen.

"Okay, gentlemen!" shouts Boulud. "It's business as usual now, okay? Showtime is over!"

"Okay, Chef," says a runner.

Boulud puts on his glasses. He takes a cup of espresso that's been sitting there a half hour, sips it, looking up at the tickets. "We're doing a great tasting here," he remarks. "Seven courses." He calls them out.

Confused by a ticket, Boulud goes back into the *garde-manger* to consult with Lee. "They wrote me a *ballottine*," he says, "but which is it? Foie gras or beef? If they tell us *ballottine*, it's foie gras. Maybe it's oxtail, then." He scribbles on the ticket, puts it up, then grabs the jug of grape seed oil. "Do you have fresh lemon with a grater?" he asks the *chef garde-manger*. He pours a little grape seed oil into the potato, adds butter, grates lemon zest into it. He picks up a bag of truffles, smells it. "Where are you getting these truffles from?" he asks Lee, but again, Boulud is onto something else before Lee can answer him. It's almost obsessive, Boulud's constant questioning, and considering how often his queries go unanswered, it seems perhaps the asking itself is more important to him than actually getting answers. At the very least, it keeps everyone on their toes, which they'll have to be all the time if they're to maintain the impossibly high standards Boulud aspires to.

Côte is at the pass. Boulud adds more oil to the potatoes, this time Frantoia M. Barbera, a fruity extra-virgin olive oil from Sicily. "Are you okay with the tickets, Fred?" he asks Côte.

"*Oui.*"

"What kind of caviar did he say he wants with the potato?" asks Boulud.

The answer comes from the *garde-manger:* "Beluga."

"*Qu'est-ce qu'il mange avant, Carter?*" What's he having before that? He looks at the ticket. "Let me know when Carter is clear," he tells a runner.

"Carter is ready to go," the runner tells him.

Boulud scoops more roasted potato into the bowl. Jed, the steward, brings in a stainless-steel container of pea shoots. Boulud tastes them. "Where are they from?" he asks.

"Thirty-two and 33 are out!" shouts Lee, back at the pass.

"Do you want the soft shells, or no?" asks a cook.

Boulud's looking around for a bottle. "Hey—do you have a bottle to put the grape seed oil inside," he asks the *garde-manger,* "or do I have to find one?" He takes an oval stainless-steel platter, oils it with his fingers, places the potato shell on it, sticks it in the oven. Now he turns to the hot-apps cook, who's working on a frogs'-legs app. "With that I don't roast the fava beans," he tells him. "I don't want it to look like it's roasted."

"Daniel," says Lee, *"qui reste pour le—"* But Boulud's gone. Lee looks up to heaven.

"Hey!" shouts a runner. "Hold the frogs' legs over there!"

Boulud comes out of the walk-in. "Oil the grill very well," he instructs Tony as he passes.

"Ce matin j'ai trouvé Chuck," Lee tells Boulud back at the pass. "He washed all the sea bass. That's why they won't crisp."

A huge flame jumps up on the fish line. Boulud and Lee turn around. "Whoa," says Lee.

Before long there are problems with the tickets. "Penne!" bellows Boulud. "Give me ravioli and endive right away! Hey, German, we are doing perfect today, eh? Between you and me, it's really a beautiful lunch, eh?" This is Boulud being ironic.

"Go, go, go!" shouts Lee to the runners.

The orders aren't being picked up as quickly as they should, and Boulud hits the ceiling. "Do what I ask!" he shouts, very, very loud. "It's fucking lunchtime! *Merde!*" When Boulud is mad, he says *mer-de* in two very definite syllables: "maire-*duh!*"

A shout comes from the pastry kitchen, where things are now busy: It's 2:25, and they're getting hit. "Pick up, please!" That's Ariella, the pastry cook.

A runner comes, sticks a tray on the rails of the pastry pickup area, puts the finished plates on it, pulls the ticket. Johnny Iuzzini plates a chocolate dessert. Another runner puts two little tarts on a small silver platter, along with a basket of madeleines. He pulls the ticket. "Two coffee!" he yells to the coffee station just across the way.

A third runner dries the insides of wine decanters on a stand by the water cooler, using a cloth napkin. He rolls it like a stiff snake, inserts it into the decanter, and rotates it to dry the hard-to-reach parts of the inside.

Inside the kitchen, Tony spoons bubbling juices over a portion of halibut again and again. A branch of thyme sits atop the fish, flavoring it as it cooks. Cooks here don't take the time to chop up herbs (as most cookbooks suggest) when the same effect can be achieved more efficiently this way.

The soup cook puts away his garnishes, takes a swig of water from a plastic takeout soup container.

As the last plates come out of the kitchen, Olivier, the assistant sommelier, polishes a *cloche*.

The pastry station is still going strong, however. Ariella takes a batch of madeleines out of a small convection oven, raps the pan on the counter, and pulls each madeleine out with a flick of a finger, putting them in a napkin-lined basket. A wooden box that says *Delamain Cognac Grande Champagne* sits on the counter, holding her personal stuff—a notebook, a knife, some hair ties. Ariella has a sweet face, sad eyes, and wild light brown hair she keeps pulled back. As a Canadian, she's been plagued by problems with the INS; when her J-1 working visa expires in six months, she's not sure what she'll do. She'd actually like to make a move out of restaurant kitchens and find work at a test kitchen for a food magazine, but she's not quite sure where to begin. Ariella graduated from McGill University in Montreal; she's now twenty-five years old. She studied pastry in France at the Cordon Bleu. To date, her most unusual job has been working on the *Queen Elizabeth II*, translating menu items from English into French. Since the menu was changed every day and couldn't be wholly planned in advance, they needed a translator on board. The wonderful part was that there was actually very little work for her to do each day; the rest of the time she'd get to relax and see the world.

Phil comes out of his station on the hot line and looks into the pastry window. "Can I move into your apartment?" Ariella asks him. Housing is a problem for cooks. With the long, tiring hours they work, living nearby is very desirable, but rents in Manhattan have skyrocketed in the past few years, putting them out of reach. As a result, many live in Queens or Brooklyn, a subway ride away that is at best tedious and at worst long. Phil's apartment is within walking distance—Seventy-eighth Street and York Avenue.

"Tony's friend from Hawaii already took it," says Phil. "Or he applied for it, anyhow."

"Do you know where you're going?" asks Ariella.

"Maybe Boston or D.C. Away from New York. If we move to D.C., we'll live in Virginia. The point is moving away from the city."

"When's your last day again?"

"April 8," says Phil. "Three weeks."

"Can I come and visit you wherever you go?" asks Iuzzini.

"We're going to Martha's Vineyard over the summer," says Phil.

"Phil," says Iuzzini, "we're hungry!"

Phil goes back to his station to make them something to eat.

Tony's parents come into the kitchen, shyly, having finished their lunch. His father, graying a little, wears glasses. His mother has a cherubic face; she wears earrings that look like small fans. They both look very Hawaiian. Tony's father shakes hands with the *garde-manger* cooks, who stick their arms through the canapé plating area.

As they continue toward the center of the pickup area, Lee comes out from behind the pass to shake their hands. "Thank you so much for the plant!" he says. They've brought him a small kaffir lime tree from Hawaii, and not only is he genuinely touched, but he's thrilled at the addition it will make to his garden in Port Jefferson, Long Island. Lee is an avid gardener who grows thirty varieties of heirloom tomatoes (he loves his Brandywines, Cherokee Purples, Georgia Streaks, Amanda Oranges, and Wild Mexicans), herbs from lovage and bronze fennel to nepitella (a type of catnip that tastes like a cross between oregano, mint, and thyme) and rose geranium (which he loves to infuse in a chilled strawberry soup), as well as flowers galore. He also has a fig tree that his godmother gave him—it was from a piece of root that she took off a tree that a neighbor brought from Italy. Although many who try to grow fig trees in climates that are too unlike the Mediterranean go to extreme measures to protect them from the winter—bagging them in plastic for the season, bending them down and tying them, and so forth—Lee has done nothing special, and his tree is flourishing. Ditto for his lavender bush, which he claims "thrives on neglect."

Kaffir lime produces gorgeous aromatic leaves that are a key ingredient in southeast Asian cooking. They're very difficult to come by fresh, and Lee will make great use of them. "I love that!" he tells them. "It smells beautiful!" He puts down the tray he's just carried up from the downstairs prep kitchen. On it are potatoes, a can of Thai coconut milk, two carrots, a bulb of fennel, green peppers, lemongrass, leeks. It's three o'clock, and he's already starting his prep for dinner. Other dinner cooks start bringing ingredients up as well. There is no discernible break between the two shifts.

"You're much younger than I thought," says Tony's mother. "He talks so much about you!"

Meanwhile, Tony's father has picked up the can of coconut milk. He smiles: It's an ingredient he knows from home, and he's a little surprised to see it here.

"I'm glad you came today," says Lee. "Tony is very talented and does very, very well." Now he turns to Frédéric Côte. "Fred, *dis bonjour.*" Côte and Allannic both shake Tony's parents' hands.

"Everything was delicious," says Tony's mother. "The sea bass especially."

"That was Tony who made that!" says Lee.

Just next to where they're talking, Phil brings a plate to the pastry window. "Mashed potato and a little rabbit with carrots," he announces. "A little tongue-in-cheek there." There are two spoons in it; Ariella and Iuzzini share it.

Tony comes out and brings his parents all the way into the kitchen. "I work over there," he says.

His mother points to one of the large windows by his station. "Oh, that's that window you were telling us about!" Windows, of course, are a rarity in Manhattan restaurant kitchens, but Tony has two.

"Meet Phil," says Tony.

"Did you have a good lunch?" asks Phil, shaking their hands.

"Everything was so good," says his father.

"And the short ribs," adds his mother, "I couldn't believe it!"

Open boxes of chocolate-covered macadamia nuts they've brought now line the pickup area. All who walk by—cooks, runners, waiters, busboys—taste them.

After Tony's parents leave, Lee turns his attention to a huge clear plastic bag of fiddlehead ferns—the first decent ones of the season. Seeing them makes him think of morels, which, like other early spring mushrooms, are really good in risotto. So are ramps.

Lee's approach to creating dishes is to start with a traditional marriage of ingredients. When he talks to young cooks, he often mentions the classic combination of tomato and basil. Why not mint? he'll say. Mint is the same family as basil. He also likes to take classic flavor combinations and use them as elements of a larger dish—endives and oranges, for instance. Often he just sees something beautiful and it inspires him to cook something. Fiddleheads, today, make him think of simmering them with some shallots, butter, thyme, and stock. Maybe he'll use this as a garnish—or perhaps in a stew of asparagus, morels, and fiddleheads, which, once again, could all work together in a risotto.

Often he creates the dishes first at home. The restaurant world is divided into cooks who would rather do anything other than cook on their day off, and those who would prefer nothing to cooking. At his house in Port Jefferson, Lee cooks almost every Sunday for his wife, Lori, and toddler son, Dylan, either visiting a nearby farm in season, or picking vegetables and herbs from his garden.

But Lee is a rare case—he's not just a chef with great technique and ency-clopedic knowledge; he's one who can look into the soul of an ingredient and release it into a dish. It is this quality that separates the extraordinary chefs from those who are merely excellent. And that is why, when he suddenly de-cides, in the middle of service, to cook up even something as plain as spaghetti with olive oil, garlic, and a little anchovy, tossed in a pretty confetti of beauti-fully chopped parsley, there is nothing like it in the world.

Boulud comes through and sticks his hand into the bag of fiddleheads. He picks one out, breaks it, smells it, tastes it. They're good when they're tight and plump. "These are a little better than they were," he says.

In the *garde-manger*, the dinner cooks pre-plate canapés. Stacks of trays are filled with tiny bowls cradling mini-portions of tuna confit with thyme, rose-mary, basil, and oregano. Another holds tiny toasted croutons with herbed goat cheese. A third is lined with smoked salmon with citrus crème fraîche and cucumbers.

Robbie, the dinner *chef garde-manger,* made the tuna confit at 11:15 this morning. Robbie's been working here two months. Before that, the graduate of New York Restaurant School worked at Aureole and Windows on the World. This kitchen seems positively luxurious to him compared with the dif-ficult working conditions at Aureole, with its tiny kitchen.

Neil Gallagher poaches pieces of rhubarb in port wine with bay leaf; as they're done, he removes them with a spoon. The heady aroma of bay leaf rises up.

"What on earth are you doing?" Robbie shouts from the *garde-manger*. His assistant is peeling paper-thin slices of beets off a sheet pan, laying them di-rectly on the counter. "That's really sanitary!" says Robbie.

By four o'clock there's no one left in the dining room and lounge, except on one back banquette on the upper level of the cherrywood-paneled lounge, where an elegant black gentleman, swathed in gorgeous white and green and brown African fabrics, sits alone, sipping a 1937 Calvados. With the lunch he enjoyed in the dining room, he ordered two bottles of 1964 Château Latour— $1,036 each on Daniel's wine list—asking for one of the bottles to go.

Just on the other side of the door to the banquet room, the managers' meet-ing is about to begin. These meetings are supposed to be weekly, but they don't always come off as planned.

Daniel Boulud, Brett Traussi, Roger Eydt, Bruno Jamais, Hilary Tolman,

Georgette Farkas, Alex Lee, Jean-Luc Le Dû, Bernard Vrod the mâitre d', and Anthony Francis, the banquet director, sit around a dressed table set with water glasses. As the meeting is about to start, Toto comes and takes Boulud's coffee order—regular coffee, rather than his usual espresso.

"Who's missing?" says Boulud. "Jed is not coming? Okay, when was the last meeting? It was February 17." Almost a month ago. "Michael is off this week. Sunday I'm leaving for another week plus, maybe almost two. When are you leaving, Roger?"

"One week from tomorrow," says Eydt. The difference is he won't be coming back—he's leaving to open a new restaurant in Connecticut.

"The last thing I want to hear is problems when I'm not here. This is a very free enterprise. Meaning when there is a lot of work, everyone pitches in. But when there isn't a lot of work, I don't want anybody to relax. That's the hardest part. If anyone has any spare time, it should be for the benefit of making this place better."

Next, Boulud addresses the beverage budget.

Le Dû and Jamais both comment on losses in the bar—someone's pouring drinks and not ringing them up.

"What you need to do," says Boulud, "is to watch a little bit the bartender. Because what am I doing all day long in the kitchen? I watch the cooks cook. That's what you have to do in the bar because they're controlling the budget—the beverage budget. So if anyone sees something, they should report it to Brett. They offer a drink and put it into 'spillage.' If Bruno is offering a glass of champagne to somebody, there still has to be a check."

"They should have a ticket for every drink they sell," agrees Jamais.

"It's so simple to ring up a check," says Traussi. It's just 'Absolut vodka—print.' "

Next Boulud suggests additional training for the reservationists. "Right now from the front desk the tickets still arrive late," he says. "When it says 'See DB' or this or that, we need to know where they come from. If I make the reservation, I try to write a full description."

"They're all saying, 'I'm a friend of Daniel,' " says Jamais.

"It's kind of a guessing game," complains Lee.

"With Open Table," says Traussi, "it will be more clear." Open Table is a computerized reservations system Traussi and Boulud have decided to implement; if it works as planned, it will radically simplify keeping track of a wealth of information about customers—everything from what they ate on their last visit to whether they're a journalist or a friend of one of the *sous-chefs*. Further down the road, customers will even be able to reserve a table on-line. The program will automatically print out *soignés*. The best thing about it is that the on-screen layout will look exactly like the reservation book.

"What bothered me last night," says Jamais, "was two people from *Vanity Fair*." Apparently, in his estimation they didn't necessarily deserve VIP treatment.

"I always call the magazine and find out if it's an advertising guy or what," Farkas points out. Advertising people wouldn't be afforded the same high status as writers or editors.

Nonetheless, Boulud takes Jamais to task, rather angrily, for mistreating guests, as he did with these particular guests last night. "You don't just say, 'Go to the bar,' " he tells Jamais.

"I don't say, 'Go to the bar,' " answers the maître d', somewhat testily. "I brought them over there myself."

Boulud doesn't buy it. "I want you to show those people into the bar!" he insists, raising his voice. "You grab the waitress, and you tell her what to expect. You say, 'I'm sure Daniel wants to do something really special for them.' *C'est pas* 'Sit in the bar,' let them wait half an hour, and I happen to walk through." Boulud is now furious, his face red, the tendons in his neck taut. From his point of view, this is a real front-of-the-house failure, letting VIPs wait forever in the lounge without, say, being treated to a glass of champagne.

"We don't know how long they're going to be," argues Jamais. His use of the present tense implies this won't be the last time this happens. When he sends a party to the lounge to wait for a table, it could just as easily be for five minutes.

"It doesn't matter," says Boulud. "You don't just drop them in the corner."

"They should have drinks and canapés when they sit down," Jamais avers, suddenly reversing his opinion in what looks like a ploy to deflect blame.

"It's the reservations girls," says Boulud, taking the bait. In other words, the reservationists should be doing a better job of figuring out who the VIPs are. "And the bar waiters. That's a big one. That's what happened last night. The bar and the lounge have to be watched all the time."

"We're not doing the ratings right now with the maître d's," reflects Boulud. "The maître d's should have a scorecard so they rate the evenings." Curiously, his ire at Jamais has evaporated, and the blame for the incident has been projected onto other (anonymous) front-of-the-house staff. Many front-of-the-house employees wonder why Boulud tolerates such behavior on Jamais's part. The truth is, Boulud is more than a little bothered by it.

Next subject is staff tastings. "We said we were going to do tastings for the captains and assistants," says Boulud. "We should do a few today, and tomorrow a few more."

"What time is convenient?" asks Lee.

"Six o'clock," says Eydt. "Or between six and six-twenty."

"Let's do tomorrow at twelve-thirty," suggests Lee. "I'll keep a list in my drawer of all the dishes. For me the dream is to take a captain and put him in the kitchen for a dinner shift, see what it's like."

"A chef should be at the door once, to see," retorts Jamais. "I'd like to see Alex at the door one night to see how many he would smack."

This is typical front-of-the-house vs. back-of-the-house conflict: Each side thinks the other has it easier.

"I've had some comments about the English-language skills of the busboys," says Farkas, changing the subject.

"That's a problem," says Boulud. "With the French or Spanish?"

But obviously the answer does not lie in language tutorials, which would be completely impracticable.

"We have to keep the runners away from the table," says Traussi. He recounts an incident that took place at lunch today, when a runner picked up a soup course in the kitchen. Normally he should have placed it on the *guéridon* for the captain or assistant to pick up and bring to the table. But they were serving dessert to another table, and the runner brought the soup to the table. The runners, Traussi points out, are only supposed to go back and forth from the kitchen to the *guéridon*, but not to the table. For one thing, they're not trained to communicate with the guests, but more important, they must be constantly available at the pass so the plates don't sit before going out.

"Sometimes the *guéridon*'s full," Lee points out. "They're cleaning tables."

"When you start to do the tasting menu and you get hit," says Boulud, "it's very hard to have the captain and the assistant ready for you all that time."

"But the runner never waits that table," says Traussi. "Never."

The busboy, however, is another story: He is supposed to bring bread, clear plates, and so forth. The problem won't be solved today.

"Okay, the cheese cart and the salads," says Boulud, moving on. "This week we are repairing the cheese cart, and after that we're going to do a trolley with some very nice salads."

"And we can hang some sausages on the sculpture there!" says Vrod. No one laughs at the joke.

"You want a better heater for the carving," recalls Boulud, referring to the setup used for several dishes that must be kept warm as the captain carves tableside. "What do you want, a burner?"

"You want the butane?" asks Traussi. "Like Le Cirque? Now you can buy a server *cloche* that the stove sits inside."

"It's very nice," adds Lee.

"So maybe you can buy one, eh?" says Boulud.

Boulud looks at his notes. "I have a note here about the cheese," he says. "What's going on?"

As part of the complete French-dining experience, Daniel, of course, offers a cheese course at the end of the meal. One of the captains, Pascal Vittu, is in charge of buying and caring for the cheeses, a variety of the best and rarest available.

Brett says, "We were busting Pascal's chops because there was no blue cheese that night when he was off."

"When they bring it in at the end of the night, the cooks eat a lot of the cheeses," says Bruno.

"There's one or two chubby ones we have to watch!" jokes Boulud. This is good-natured; he's trying to lighten up the accusatory tone of the proceedings. Although he's the first to yell when things aren't going as they should, his ability to defuse conflicts among the staff is one of the things that make him a great boss. "The only cook who would take it is me sometimes. So it's not a real problem. What is a real problem," he says, "is to make a reservation at Daniel when you're a large party. On a Monday night, when we get a party of ten, we're not going to say no."

"Then when the party of ten comes on a Friday night," says Lee, "it's a problem."

"We have to have a policy," says Daniel, "that Thursday, Friday, Saturday, we don't take large parties. Period. Eight."

"Eight," repeats Jamais.

"Whatever the policy is," says Traussi, "when you call Jean Georges and ask for nine, they say no. And you come away saying, 'They're rude.' "

"If you say yes, you're nuts," says Jamais. "If you say no, you're wrong."

Traussi points out that a woman came in with a party of ten, and rather than ordering a set menu or a tasting menu, they ordered à la carte. Not surprisingly, the food was slow in coming.

"We have to say with the big ones, only one party of ten and one party of eight, and after that we limit it to six," decides Boulud. "And we have to say to them, 'Are you interested in having a set menu? We'll offer you a free extra course.' We make them feel that we really want them to be happy, so we offer something.' "

"Today I authorized a party of fourteen for Mrs. Brown, who comes every day for lunch," says Traussi. "She's here five days a week. What are you gonna do?"

After a discussion of management vacation schedules, Boulud moves on to the next subject. "I had things about discipline in the kitchen," he says. "We have to make sure to stay disciplined. And that also concerns the front of the house, the busboys and the runners sometimes. We get disturbed very easily, and it can get very difficult for the cooks to focus. I would really dream of a noiseless kitchen."

"We'll have to get a new chef, then," says Jamais.

"I want to get music in the kitchen, too," says Boulud. "I want to put in the small Bose. I'm in my kitchen sometimes and the noise is unbelievable. Yesterday *j'ai gueulé parce qu'ils ont cassé quatre assiettes.*" I yelled because they broke four plates. "The commotion comes often because of—"

"Sometimes there's ten people talking in the kitchen," interjects Lee. "I try to get people not to talk in there."

"Okay, maybe everyone should have an idea of your travel plans," says Farkas to Boulud, wrapping things up. "You depart Sunday evening for Lyons, and you have two promotional dinners."

"That restaurant got two stars," says Boulud, referring to Rotonde, a restaurant where he'll be doing an event. "On Thursday they're having the whole national press of France. *Gourmet* magazine is going to do a story following Daniel to Lyons, celebrating my birthday."

"And then a few days in Chile," says Traussi, "at Santa Rita winery."

"Alex will be joining me," says Boulud. "And during that week, Brad will be starting. So Brad will be here, but Cyrille will be—"

"So when Alex is out of the kitchen, who's in charge?" asks Traussi.

"Cyrille," says Boulud.

"Five days," says Lee. "It's the first time we'll both be out at the same time."

"It's taken us seven years to achieve!" says Boulud.

And on that note, the assembled proceed to taste a number of champagnes to decide what will be the new house pour.

Monday, March 20

THE VERNAL EQUINOX, the first day of spring. In five days it will be Boulud's birthday. Those who give credence to astrology will find it noteworthy that Boulud is a double-Aries, as he and his wife, Micky, learned several years ago, when they had an astrologer friend do a chart for Boulud. In other words, when he was born on March 25, 1955, both the sun and the moon were in the sign of Aries, the first sign of the Zodiac, symbolizing the ram, with all its primal energy, along with a strong consciousness of the self as differentiated from others in the world. "Thus the Aries individual," writes the respected astrologist Alan Oken, ". . . must give his own life-energy so that Mankind may be recharged by the force of life which the Ram embodies." The slice of mankind that is lucky enough to dine at Daniel is certainly recharged by Boulud's exalted contribution.

Skeptics may giggle or even guffaw, but plugging Boulud's date, place, and time of birth, March 25, 1955, at nine A.M. in Lyons, France, into an on-line service that provides instant astrological charts along with their interpretation couldn't paint a more striking picture of Daniel Boulud. "You like to be the chief—or go it alone," it says, and it gets even more uncannily Boulud-like from there.

But one doesn't have to be an astrologer to see that Boulud is a dedicated workaholic, as many of his brigade must be in order to endure this life. For they don't only endure it, they love it; they thrive on it. Some of them complain about the hours, but few seem really to mind; rather, one has the impression that they wouldn't know what to do with themselves if they weren't cooking. Anyone who has ever been a workaholic knows about the life-giving electric buzz that such an environment brings; even if it's not reasonable or healthy, it's addictive. Boulud is different only in the sense that Daniel is *his* baby. He does know how to have fun, losing himself, for instance, in eighteen holes of golf. And he loves rock and roll: One of the biggest thrills of his life was getting to go backstage at a U2 concert and meeting Bono. The rock star actually remembered having dined at the old Daniel! But to Boulud, there are very few things in life more exhilarating than being behind the pass. Can it be, too, that immersing himself in work is a way of holding his emotions at bay? That, after all, is the specialty of the workaholic.

Normally for Boulud's birthday, Micky throws him a party, but this year, as he turns forty-five, the chef is doing something different. As he mentioned at the managers' meeting, the day after tomorrow, he'll fly to Lyons with

Philippe Rispoli (the Feast & Fêtes chef), Frédéric Côte, and Rémy Fünfrock (executive pastry chef at Café Boulud), all of whom, like Boulud, are natives of Lyons. Boulud has been invited by Philippe Gauvreau, chef at Rotonde, the *Michelin* two-star restaurant at Lyons's Casino Le Lyon Vert, to cook a gala dinner for two hundred people as part of a program in which he invited ex-Lyonnais chefs to come back to their hometown and cook.

The day of Boulud's departure is Wednesday—always an interesting day in the food business, since that's when the *Times* dining section appears. And on this Wednesday, Grimes has reviewed Chanterelle—David and Karen Waltuck's elegant TriBeCa restaurant, which has held four stars continuously since shortly after it opened in 1987. The assessment—a downgrade to three stars—is quickly apparent to any savvy reader, since the review's not on the first page of the food section. "After twenty years," writes Grimes in the review, "the dazzling newcomer of yesteryear radiates a soft glow, while restaurants like Jean Georges, Bouley Bakery, and Daniel throw off showers of sparks." Although Boulud doesn't indulge in such speculation, the discerning reader can't fail to notice that Grimes is placing Daniel in the company of two four-stars. Could the critic be revising his opinion of Daniel?

The next day, Boulud, Rispoli, Côte, and Fünfrock arrive in Lyons. Going on the little sleep they managed to catch on the plane the night before, they proceed to the Casino to prepare the gala dinner. This is the first time in twenty-six years that Boulud has returned to Lyons to cook, and it moves him beyond words. Among the guests are Paul Bocuse, Michel Troisgros (chef at the legendary Troisgros in Roanne), Pierre Orsi (chef at his eponymous restaurant in Lyons), and Gérard Nandron, Boulud's mentor. It is, he feels, the greatest honor of his career; he dedicates the evening to Nandron. At the end of the ten-course service, the luminary-filled crowd rises to give Boulud a standing ovation. Later he'll say of the dinner, "I think I threw a good show."

Two days later, Boulud celebrates his actual birthday at a friend's restaurant in nearby Bourgoin-Jallieu, surrounded by family and friends. Even after all the exhilaration of the past few days, it's not easy turning forty-five; Boulud finds it harder than forty, the most difficult birthday so far. Yes, his homecoming performance for the Lyonnais chefs meant the world to him. But now he has to face the music: In culinary terms, he's at the height of his powers. Yet could he have missed his moment in the eyes of the critic whose judgment matters most?

Five

IN THE WEEDS

I T'S JUST BEFORE NOON, and Julie, the hot-apps and pasta cook, having just returned from visiting her boyfriend in Austin, Texas, wipes down her station in preparation for lunch service. "Somebody got an extra squeeze bottle?" she says.

"What?" says David, the fish *entremétier.*

"My squeeze bottle was stolen; let's just put it that way." She grabs a bottle of Colavita extra-virgin olive oil—the current regular-use olive oil—pours a slick into each of two pans, heats them up, and adds a medium dice of yellow and green zucchini, a big spoonful of each, into each pan, along with a branch of thyme. She tosses the cubes of squash in the air—one pan, then the other. This will be for the risotto with scallops, chanterelles, and zucchini; she'll probably have to do two more pans of them during service.

David is using the poaching liquid in which he cooked some radishes to make a sauce for today's salmon special—Roasted Salmon with Slow-Roasted Vidalia Onions, Braised Radishes, Olive Oil, and a Lemon Emulsion. He has roasted the onions (although they're red—Bermuda, rather than Vidalia) with veal *jus* for about an hour and a half, until they're meltingly sweet and tender. They sit on a sheet pan lined with Silpat—a silicon-coated baking liner that professional cooks use for roasting all kinds of vegetables. David doesn't understand why home cooks don't use them more, since they're available in housewares stores. (Perhaps it's the twenty-five-dollar price tag per liner.)

Now Julie makes the garlic cream for the frogs' legs. She has removed the germ from each garlic clove and blanched them three times, changing the water each time. Then she covered them in cream and cooked them until they were very soft, and now she purees them. That done, she turns to sautéing yellow-foot chanterelles for the risotto. To clean them, she had to soak them twice in water, then she used her hands to squeeze out the water and put them on layers of paper towel to dry. She loves these mushrooms, and has even foraged for them; she insists she could smell their characteristic maple syrup smell before she spotted them. Black trumpet mushrooms and black chanterelles are cleaned the same way. Morels, on the other hand, must be washed five times, though they needn't be wrung out since they don't absorb much water. They do, however, tend to rot easily.

"Chef," says Tony the *poissonnier* to Frédéric Côte, "I made a horseradish oil, but it's not that good." He wrinkles his nose. "In fact, it tastes terrible."

At that moment Alex Lee, just returned from his trip to Chile with Boulud, walks into the kitchen. Confounding all anxieties, everything was fine here while they were gone. Boulud and Lee cooked a wine-tasting dinner at a restaurant in Santiago for the winery Viña Santa Rita and a lunch the following day. Lee was very disappointed with the products, especially considering Chile's congenial climate; he was chagrined to have to use flavorless hydroponic tomatoes. In his absence, other cooks' junk has accumulated at his station, the space just under the video monitors. "I don't want anything up here," he announces. "It's my station and I want it to be respected."

On the far side of the pass, a runner folds napkins in the pickup area. He lays out a thick square and pulls each corner into the center, making a smaller square, flattening the creases with his fingers. He turns it over and folds in the corners again, creating a form that is a thicker version of a child's "cootie-catcher." He pounds each side with the side of his fist, then pulls up four flaps from the bottom, resulting in a linen flower that will cradle the freshly baked madeleines that go out to every table at the end of the meal. Another runner does the same in the pastry pickup area.

Now Lee brings in a two-foot clear plastic bag, knotted at the top, full of baby anguilla, tiny, wormlike Spanish eels. Each one is a little fatter than a strand of spaghetti. They came from Rod Mitchell of Browne Trading Company. Lee can still taste them as he ate them in Spain—sautéed with garlic, olive oil, hot pepper, lemon, and parsley. Lee plunks the wobbly bag down on the cool surface of the induction range. "Julie," he says, "can you boil me some water with a little white vinegar in it?"

The bag of eels falls to the floor, *plop*. As Frank picks it up, Lee notices the apples Frank is caramelizing on the range. He scowls. "Take your time and caramelize them nicely," he admonishes, removing them from the burner.

Damien, a new French *garde-manger* cook, has poured the baby eels into a big wooden *saladier* in the meantime. "Put your hand in," he tells Kevin, his partner. Like Lee, Kevin did a *stage* at Martín Berasateguí in San Sebastian, as well as at El Bullí, Ferran Adrià's outrageous house of surreal cuisine just outside Barcelona—the restaurant that's on everyone's lips this year. Clearly, he's seen a few anguilla in his time. Kevin's hand goes in and he feels the slimy eels wiggle against his skin.

Lee tastes Frank's soups. "This needs salt," he says of one.

Now Lee moves on to the sauces at the meat station. Dan, the current lunchtime *saucier*, watches, waits. His eyelashes are thick and long, black. He has beautiful, shapely hands. His girlfriend is Ariella, the pastry assistant. "The chicken *jus*," says Lee, "make it a little lighter." He tastes a fifth, and a sixth, then tosses the spoon into the cylinder of water to the left of the meat station.

"The sauces are pretty consistent. Did you soak these in cognac?" he asks, referring to the dried cherries in the *poivre* sauce.

"Yeah," says Dan.

"Did you cook them out? This is really good. Consistent. Very good. Seriously."

Dan blinks his thick eyelashes. He can't believe what he's hearing. "Thank you, Chef," he says.

"When you leave here, you'll be able to *make* this sauce," says Lee. That's Lee's understated way of praising Dan for having mastered a difficult sauce, a skill that will serve Dan well on his next job. And since Dan has been working here since the opening, Lee wouldn't be surprised if he left soon. Dan just blinks. Praise around here is so unusual that he doesn't know quite how to respond.

Lee turns to the pass and calls out an order—a nine-top. The *soigné* says "Reed Exhibition Hall. See Brett, four course menu." The party is here for the Fancy Food Show, held annually at Javitz Convention Center.

Julie picks up the phone. "David?" she says, using the French pronunciation to distinguish French David, the *garde-manger* cook, from American David, the fish *entremétier*. "I have some tomatoes in the oven down there. Can you just take them out and put them in a container for me? Thank you."

Downstairs the dinner cooks have already started their prep. Julie returns to her station and peels the skin off of cooked peas. It's painstaking work. The peas are very starchy this early in the season—not sweet, as they'll soon be— so she'll add a little powdered sugar to the sauce she's making with them.

"Order one risotto and one carrot soup," calls Frédéric Côte, "followed by one beef duo and one sea bass."

Tony slices white mushrooms, *zip zip zip,* on a plastic mandoline. One of his fingers is bandaged; he cut it a few days ago doing just this. "It's like a mad dog," Chris said of the mandoline when it happened. "Once it tastes blood, it can't get enough."

Frank puts his cucumber soup through a china cap.

"Ordering one carrot soup, two *ballottine,* followed by one duck, medium, two beef. *Ballottine* is gone on 51?"

"Yes," says a runner.

"*Vas-y,* " says Côte. "*Accélérez.* We have a hundred covers for lunch."

Tony takes a pan out of the oven where an order of paupiette was finishing. A cloud of smoke puffs out. He squints, holds back his head.

"Risotto and frog legs, how long?" says Lee.

"Right now," says Julie.

"Two carrot soup and a *ballottine,* how long?"

"Working!" yells Kevin.

"Order two asparagus, one SOS," booms Côte.

"Behind you," says Frank, moving in with a bowl of soup.

"Julie," calls Kevin from the *garde-manger,* "going ahead." He's finishing the first of eight plates.

Lee is holding a small *saladier* with chunks of pineapple in the bottom. He uses a huge long knife to dig some cottage cheese out of a container and dumps it in with the fruit, keeping one eye on Frank, who's still working on the caramelized apples. Unlike all the others, who must partake of "family meal," Lee eats what he wants, and today this will be his light lunch. "The apple has too much fat," Lee says. "So after the service today I'll show you how to do it." He spins around to the *garde-manger.* "Okay, guys! I need asparagus right now!"

"Fire 47 and 49 the main course," says German.

"Wake up, Islam," says Lee to one of the runners. "Let's go! Five asparagus, one SOS, coming?"

"Yes, Chef!" says Kevin.

"Order eight mini–carrot soup, three crab salad, one beet salad, four penne, followed by eight bass à la carte."

Kevin puts the asparagus in the pickup area. "One SOS right here!" he says.

Lee eats his cottage cheese, taking huge bites while looking at the tickets. "Order eight mini-soup!" he says between mouthfuls. "Three crab salad, one beet salad, four penne, followed by eight bass à la carte." All of a sudden, everyone's moving—fast. "Fire 55!" yells Lee.

"One toast, please!" says Kevin. "I need some blinis, please, Frank." Kevin pulls out a three-tiered *plateau* and a large tin of sevruga. "The toast is burning!" he yells.

"Frank!" says Kevin, "you got the blinis coming, man? I need those blinis, *please!*" Frank pulls out the squeeze bottle full of blini batter, puts oil in a hot pan, squeezes blini shapes onto the pan.

"What's that risotto there?" Lee asks Julie.

"I made a little too much," she answers.

"You can't be like that! I told you it's *calculated*—we make it the same every time! You know better than that! The same amount of lobster, the tablespoon. Black truffle juice. It has to be the same every time!"

"Phone, Alex!" yells Kevin.

"Yeah, what do you want?" he barks into the receiver. "Can I talk to you after lunch? Okay." He hangs up, spoons risotto into a plate. "Order tartare and a risotto, followed by a halibut and a bass."

Côte has six huge plates lined up. Lee takes a slotted fish spatula and puts two disks of red onion on each. Côte places the sautéed salmon on top. Lee spoons translucent cooked radishes, some still blushing pink, next to the onions, and more on top.

"Order a pree-fee asparagus and a pree-fee tartare, followed by two pree-fee skate!"

"Yes!" shout the cooks in unison.

"Order a crab salad and one mushroom soup, followed by one loup and one bass!"

"YESSS!"

An apple garnish goes on top of the salmon: a thin disk with a julienne design in a tight tic-tac-toe pattern. Lee hands it to a runner. "This is a medium," he says. "Medium position four on table 61. Finish your table."

For Frank, whose soups and apples had drawn Lee's disapproval, it's shaping up to be a bad day. He's having trouble keeping up, and looks like he might throw in the side-towel at any moment. He looks miserable. For Julie, things aren't much better.

"You have to add stock to it!" Lee tells her, regarding her risotto. "It has to be perfect! Come on!" She adds and stirs. Lee watches, then pulls the plate from her. "Let's go!" he says, disgusted. "We're gonna redo the fucking plate. Shit!"

The temperature may be cool in the *garde-manger,* but the pressure's on. Damien piles microgreens on a plate with his fingers, then eats a little of it. He looks like a goat. The work he does, however, is meticulous; the plates done at this station are more like painting than anything else, difficult to do too quickly. *Plateaux* hang from hooks over his head on a double stainless-steel rod. Now Damien splits quail with a tiny knife—microsurgery. Delicately he debones the leg. Next he slices a *ballottine,* right through the plastic film it's wrapped in. It looks like a fat sausage.

On the meat line, Dan has meat going in several pans—duck breast, lamb loins. He pulls two garlic cloves, still in their peel, from a cranny behind him. He smashes them with his palm, tosses them in a pan. With his fingers, he picks up a veal loin tied with string from the pan in which it's cooking. He looks at it, puts it down on another side to brown, spoons duck *jus* over the duck breast in another pan.

"Order one tuna tartare," says Allannic, "one hot foie gras, and one mini-soup, followed by two crab salad main course and one lamb, medium rare." No mention is made of who the order is for: Ethel Kennedy. She loves foie gras. One wonders if these young cooks would even know who she is.

Bernard Vrod stands waiting for a *plateau* for Mrs. Kennedy's table. He has served her many times before, and Rose Kennedy, too. Once when Ted Kennedy's son Ted Jr. came in, Vrod told him proudly, "I served your grand-mother!"

Dan slices a foie, generously salts it, and grinds lots of black pepper on it. He flips it into a pan. Just a moment later, he pulls up an edge with a spoon to look under, then flips it over. Another moment and it's finished.

"Gimme the foie gras," says Lee. "Bernard, forget about the fucking *plateau.*" They're in the weeds in the *garde-manger.* Kevin does a little skipping slide to grab something behind Damien.

"Where the hell is 30?" says Lee.

"Thirty, sir, is the tasting," says a runner.

"Thirty-one is out," says Lee. "Oh! Forty-five? Fifty-two?"

"Fifty-two or 36!" says German.

"No, 52," says Lee. Vrod and another waiter are still trying to figure out what to do about the missing *plateau.* "If you gave me the order for the *plateau,*" Lee tells the other waiter, "this never would have happened." He spins around and looks at Frank. "You have nothing to do?" he says. "Don't do *mise en place* during service. Unless you need it for the service. There's a lot to do—look at the board over there. You have to follow the service!" Frank goes to help Julie. Lee drops his pen cap. While he's bent to the floor to pick it up, he drops his elbows to the floor, stretching. Frank puts two risotto plates on trays.

Bruno Jamais sidles in, hungry. "Do you have some chicken for Bruno?" Lee asks Dan. "Some hanger steak?" Then to Julie, "Did you taste the seasoning in the risotto?"

"Yes, I did, Chef."

It's crucial that the various cooks taste their dishes and make any appropriate adjustments, especially adding salt or pepper or correcting an overly seasoned sauce. Over- or undersalting is the most common mistake in any restaurant—after all, although a master chef may have created and perfected a sauce, more than likely someone just starting out in his or her career will be preparing it. To a restaurant reaching for that fourth star, such an error can be grievous. Still, under the pressure of a busy service, it's easy to slip up. Since Julie's not working at her best today, Lee's reminder to her is expedient. On the other hand, it's so basic that it's almost insulting.

Brad Thompson, the *sous-chef* who came two months ago from Café Boulud, works at the long stainless-steel-countertop island that serves as the main workspace in the prep kitchen. A muscular six-foot-two, with a shaved head and light red Van Dyke beard, Thompson is striking; handsome, even. He's not, however, a refined-looking guy; in fact, he's a dead ringer for Mr. Clean. But he does have a great palate, great skill—and a great appetite. The thirty-one-year-old became interested in food in, as he puts it, "a roundabout way." During his Hartford, Connecticut, childhood, his mother was not a particularly good cook, and he was completely uninterested in cooking. His grandfather, however, would take him to restaurants, allowing him to order anything he wanted on the condition that he'd eat it all. This suited the young Thompson just fine: He loved to eat. At one of these outings, he ate so much he threw up. He loved most everything, though he wasn't overly fond of vegetables.

When he was in college in upstate New York at the University of Rochester, Thompson needed a job, and a friend suggested restaurant work. He found a job at a Tony Roma's doing prep, peeling potatoes, scrubbing pots. One day the police came in and arrested the grill cook, so Thompson jumped in and took over. It didn't take long for him to realize that he had a knack for working the grill in a busy restaurant. Soon he took a second job at a T.G.I. Friday's just across the back alley; the two restaurants shared a Dumpster, around which cooks from both restaurants took their cigarette breaks, and a number of guys worked in both kitchens, working the lunch shift at one and the dinner shift at the other. At T.G.I. Friday's, Thompson began to bloom, developing organizational skills that impressed his employers enough for them to send him around the state doing store openings. After a year, he decided to leave school, and the company agreed to transfer him back home to Connecticut. There, in Farmington, he got his first job in a "real restaurant," Max e Mia. Eager to soak up all the knowledge and skills he could, he hounded his chef with endless questions, prompting him to suggest that Thompson buy a copy of *Larousse Gastronomique* and start reading. Thompson soon became completely absorbed in the world of food and cooking, and his chef transferred him to his flagship restaurant in Hartford.

One day in 1992, a friend told Thompson about an event at the James Beard House in New York City at which Vincent Guérithault, a French chef with a renowned restaurant in Scottsdale, Arizona, would be cooking. Thompson didn't have the means to attend the event, but on his friend's advice, he volunteered to aid Guérithault in the kitchen, alongside the Beard House's usual assortment of culinary student volunteers. By the end of the evening, Thompson had so impressed the chef that Guérithault offered him a job in Scottsdale at Guérithault-on-Camelback. After working there two years, Thompson moved to the Phoenician resort, also in Scottsdale, where he worked under chef Alessandro Stratta (now a celebrity chef in Las Vegas).

Stratta, who had worked under Daniel Boulud at Le Cirque, had long been trying to convince Boulud to visit Arizona. When Thompson had been working for Stratta for just over three years, Boulud finally went to the resort to cook for an event, and Thompson, who had been hearing about him forever, asked him if he might be able to do a brief *stage* with him in New York at some point. Boulud was very open. A month later, Thompson flew east to attend a wedding in New Jersey, and he made an appointment with Boulud at the old Daniel, taking a hotel room in Manhattan for one night in order to meet him. Boulud sat with him for an hour and a half, talking about food and Thompson's background; Boulud also happened to mention his intentions of opening Café Boulud. The point of the meeting, however, was quite unclear; in any case, it didn't seem to Thompson to be a job interview. Thompson recalls wanting to ask Boulud if he could dine there that night, but feeling too awkward.

Thompson returned to Arizona and his job, and one Sunday, Stratta called him at home and asked him to come in. "Please, Chef," replied Thompson, "I really need a day off." But Stratta insisted. When Thompson arrived, Stratta broke the news: Boulud wanted to hire Thompson as *sous-chef*. Stratta told Thompson that as much as he valued him, he felt it was an opportunity Thompson shouldn't pass up. Of course, the decision was Thompson's, and he was welcome to stay if he liked. Perhaps he'd like to go home and think it over. "No," said Thompson. "I've already decided." He began working for Boulud at the old Daniel, and then came on as *sous-chef* when Boulud closed it and opened Café Boulud.

Wednesday, April 19

IT'S ELEVEN A.M., and Thompson prepares brook trout for a special on the long island that serves as the primary workspace. With the cleaned trout opened up like a book before him, he lays a neat row of cooked chard, onion, and tomato confit onto first one fish, then the next, and the next, and the next. Now he'll wrap them in cured bacon, sliced from a slab. A number of types of bacon are kept in the downstairs walk-in: country bacon, pancetta, fresh slab, cured slab, and smoked slab, which is smoked in an actual smokehouse. This last, of course, would be overpowering with fish; the relatively mild cured is used instead. The bacon will keep the filling inside, melting to fuse the whole package shut; the flavor of the bacon will be retained in the fish. Thompson lays two parallel sets of bacon strips on his board, with an inch-wide space between them. He lays a fish on top and wraps the bacon around the top and bottom portions, leaving the fish's midriff exposed. The wrapped fish go onto parchment-lined sheetpans.

"What's the crayfish situation?" Thompson asks Chris, the lunchtime *entremétier* for the meat station.

"Jed says we have enough for the week," says Chris.

Scott, the *garde-manger* cook, is training to work the fish station. He nods toward the trout Thompson is preparing. "I actually had that at the Café," he says, "and they wrapped the whole thing, even the middle. It looked real nice." Scott has perpetual bed-head.

"It's a lot of bacon, though," says Thompson. "I remember we used to do it that way over there. But this will be nice. It gives it some nice stripes. I can cut here and here," he says, pointing to two places where the fish will be cut on the bias after it's cooked, "and then it'll be two nice pieces."

"And the stuffing is spiced tuna?" asks Scott.

"Tuna confit," says Thompson. "Yesterday it was wrapped all the way around, and we didn't like the way it looked. There was too much going on."

Scott picks up a sad-looking rutabaga a few feet from Thompson. "This is shit," he says, tossing it back on the cutting board; he walks away.

"We have matzoh!" shouts Michael Lawrence upstairs. Today is Passover, and as ever, Lawrence wants to be prepared for any eventuality. Last year a couple who comes frequently to the restaurant happened to come on Passover, and they asked for matzoh, so they could comply with the Jewish restriction against eating leavened bread during the holiday. The waiter heard the request and went to Lawrence, who told the waiter to tell them yes, of course we have matzoh. He then sent someone around the corner to buy some. As it turned out, none of the local groceries had it—they were all sold out. Lawrence isn't about to make the same mistake this year.

The kitchen, too, is trying to be prepared today, but the tactic backfires. "You guys have to learn to cook!" yells Lee a few minutes after noon, as service starts to heat up. "You don't cook mushrooms three or four hours before service! You don't cook artichokes and put them in lemon juice if you're not going to cook them right away!" He turns to David, the fish *entremétier*. "Peel the salsify right before service, so it's fresh."

While *mise en place*—having all the ingredients prepared as much as possible before service—is absolutely essential to cooks, the better a restaurant is, the more things will be cooked *à la minute*. There's certainly a balance, but it's not always easy for less-experienced cooks to know exactly what can be done ahead of time without sacrificing freshness.

Thompson has taken over at the pass. "Order of pree-fee ravioli and two pree-fee tartare, followed by three pree-fee lamb, medium-rare," he calls.

In the *garde-manger*, Damien builds a hut out of asparagus, white and green, crossing the spears on top of each other, at perpendicular angles.

"Two asparagus and a crab," says Thompson. "You got two mushroom soup and a pea soup. The pea soup is à la carte, okay?"

Tony is shelling a gigantic container of cooked peas into a small plastic container. They're already out of the pods; now he carefully peels the outer membrane from each. It's garnish for the risotto and for the pea soup.

"So two raviolis," says Thompson, "54 and 55."

"Yes, Chef!"

"Order of pree-fee asparagus, penne, followed by two pree-fee lamb, medium-rare."

Boulud enters; it's 12:35. Thompson tells him that a friend of Boulud's had called wanting to know if he would play golf on Sunday. Suddenly Boulud spins around to face Frank. Something is bothering him. The bacon garnish for the five-pea soup is not right. "Let it dry in towels," says Boulud. "It has to be extremely dry and well cooked, but not burnt." Boulud pulls it down from the shelf and looks closer, fingering it. "It's good, but you want that to be very, very crispy. Dry it. Put it on a bunch of paper towels."

Lee comes over and weighs in. "When it's hot," he offers, "you drain it very well. You start early in the morning, and after that you put it on the paper and it should be perfect."

"Then you let it cook again," says Boulud. "And after that, you put cheese-cloth on the sheet pan. You lay it flat. You put the bacon on it and let it dry again. Otherwise you don't have enough crispiness and toastiness."

Daniel, a tall, dark, bearded American waiter, catches Boulud's attention. "What are the nine herbs in the ravioli?" he asks Boulud. The dish is called nine-herb ravioli.

"It's a signature dish," says Boulud. "It's in my cookbook. Parsley, chervil, tarragon, dill . . ." He looks to Lee for assistance, but he's elsewhere. "Basil, watercress, sage. And then after that, greens—spinach, chard." He's annoyed that a waiter who's been here some time doesn't know what's in a signature dish.

Frank, meanwhile, lays the bacon in the sheet pan, his lips pressed together. Lee shows up at his side again. "I explained this before," says Lee.

"I know," says Frank, chastened.

At the fish station, Tony plates Thompson's trout special. Cooked trouts come off the hot pan. He heaps the vegetable garnish—cèpes and morels, roasted fingerling potatoes, ramps, and pearl onions with a port wine glaze on the plate—then props up two pieces of fish, cut all the way through its double thickness, up against them.

"Who cut the trout?" asks Boulud. It was Scott, new to the station. "Try to cut it on the bias," Boulud tells him. "Because the head is on a bias." Boulud reaches over and tastes one of the peas Tony's been shelling. "They're good, these peas, even though they're big," he says.

Lee walks by and glances at the peas. "*Ils sont tros gros*," he comments, not having heard Boulud's remark. "They're too big. They're not even sweet."

"Cook the fish all over," Boulud tells Tony. "How is the garnish for the trout? Is it well seasoned?"

"Scott's training," says Thompson. "Because he's going to be the morning fish guy."

"Yeah, yeah," says Boulud. That explains why he hasn't gotten the hang of it yet. There's been so much turnover in the kitchen lately that it's hard for Boulud to keep track of who's where. Business has continued to boom as spring has set in, and although the much-discussed salad cart never materialized, Boulud hasn't stopped brainstorming, refining, rethinking. He doesn't talk about the fourth star, at least not in front of the interloper clad in whites who constantly scribbles in her notebook from behind the pass, but the fact that he's in the restaurant for twelve hours every day, watching, commanding, tasting, cooking, correcting, adjusting, shouting, and cursing, is testament to the fact that he cares deeply about the quality of what's going out on every single plate. In most restaurants, this simply wouldn't be the case.

Lee is at the soup station, delivering the promised lesson in caramelizing apples. He squirts some oil in a pan, swirls it around. "This is the best way to caramelize apples," he says. "They have to be uniform. When they're not cut the same, they caramelize at different times."

"Professor Silver?" asks Boulud.

Silver is a regular who once announced that he doesn't like any of Daniel's desserts, adding, "I wish you could do an apple tart." Since then, every time he comes in, they have to make him a *tarte aux pommes*—a fairly labor-intensive proposition and a real pain in the neck during the press of service.

There's a real divide among American chefs when it comes to accommodating customer requests. Thomas Keller, for instance, the star chef of Napa Valley's French Laundry, is known for doing things his way, period. If the customer doesn't like it, so be it. But Boulud's philosophy is to give his customers what they want, within reason of course. In reality, the restaurant's regulars are so important to the business that he sometimes gives them what they want even if it's *not* particularly reasonable.

"VIP," confirms Lee.

"Once you get nice caramelization all around, you turn it down a little," he continues. "You go get the apple, and I'll show you how to turn it, too." Lee seems to have eyes on several places on his head, and now he turns to David. "You don't cook the vegetables that way!" he says. "Look at the potato!"

"Professor Silver says to say hello to you," says Daniel the waiter.

"Hello to him," says Boulud. "Did he get the *plateau?* He's been here awhile. His was the first ticket in the kitchen."

"Don't you see that you left a ravioli in the pan after it's cooking?" Lee says to Julie. "Yes or no? You have time to cook in two different pots, you know." He means that the different orders should be fired separately. "During a rush it's going to go fast. You can do it."

The runners are all lined up, waiting.

"Trout is very delicate," Lee reminds Scott.

"Ordering one asparagus and one mushroom soup," says Thompson, "followed by one duck and one lamb, medium-rare. Forty-four just went out. Fifty-four is coming right now. Everything's fired."

"Okay," says Boulud. "Two lobster salad." He goes to a vegetable mixture on the induction range, tastes it, then goes back and looks at a ticket that just came in.

"All right, 54," says Thompson. "Order three pree-fee asparagus, one pree-fee ravioli, one pree-fee lamb, one pree-fee trout. We have one mushroom soup first."

Boulud, Lee, and Thompson all have their heads over the vegetable mélange. Boulud picks up a little of it with a spoon, looking at it. *"Alors, tomate?"* he says.

Scott shows Boulud the trout, cut on a bias. The string is still on.

"Once the trout is cooked," says Boulud, "you must remove the string."

"No, it's *burnt!*" comes a yell from the soup station. "It's *not* okay!" shouts Lee. "When you cook bacon at home, do you make it that dark? Fuck that!"

Looking at the *soignés,* Boulud realizes Tony DiDio, an important wine distributor and a PX regular, is coming for lunch, and two sets of journalists are coming as well. He picks up the phone and speaks with Lawrence. "As soon as they arrive," he says of one of the parties of journalists, "sit them down. Where are you gonna seat them? Okay, 53? No, 53's no good. *Mais non*— you're not gonna put two men side by side on the banquette. Give me 47. No, 42." There's a pause. "Who are you gonna keep it for? *Mais non.* Tony DiDio. You put Tony DiDio on forty-something. Okay?" The forty-something tables are those in the center of the pool, the best in the house. Another *soigné* says, "Christian Dior. 8 people. PX des. tasting. No check per F&F."

Boulud distributes the vegetable mélange on two plates.

"Order three tuna, one crab, one asparagus, followed by three bass, one penne, one halibut," says Thompson.

"Qu'est-ce qu'il veut, Professor Silver?" asks Boulud.

"Should we do something?" says Lee.

Boulud squeezes a lemon on the vegetables.

"Yeah," says Lee. "Get some porcini," he tells Thompson. "We'll do a little thing."

Boulud places shrimp atop the vegetables; Lee helps. Microgreens go on top. The dish looks like spring itself. Boulud takes some *pistou*, drizzles it around the periphery.

Frank places strips of bacon, paper toweling between them, on a plate. He shows them to Lee. To his great relief, this time it makes the grade. Other than a passing glance, none of the other cooks seem to have taken the slightest interest in Frank's unfolding drama; they're all concerned with their own abilities to cook well and keep up with the service.

Boulud is on the phone again. "Cynthia Penney and Andrew Dornenburg are here," he announces. "They just got here." It's 1:05. Andrew Dornenburg is coauthor, with his wife, Karen Page, of three chef-related books. The most recent, *Becoming a Chef*, was published two years ago. They're now working on a book called *Chef's Night Out*, for which they're interviewing chefs across the country to find out where they like to eat when they're not working. As with their other books, they have interviewed Boulud for this one. Dornenburg spent years working as a chef as well. Cynthia Penney, for her part, is an American journalist who's writing a piece for the British magazine *Waitrose Food Illustrated*. After she and Dornenburg have lunch, she'll interview Boulud.

"There's no more mâche in the house?" says Boulud into the phone now, talking to Jed downstairs. "And can you give me some more lentils?"

Lawrence stands at the pass.

"What did you do?" Boulud asks him, meaning where did you seat Penney and Dornenburg.

"There was no reservation," says Lawrence.

"Forty-two right away," says Boulud. "Don't tell them there was no reservation." Forty-two is a four-top in the center of the pool, one of the four very best tables.

Thompson is on the phone. "Hello! Hello!" he yells. "Send someone up with some mâche right away!"

"Give me the phone," says Boulud, concerned because the other table of journalists has arrived. "Hello! *Les journalistes*, you're gonna put them on 12 now because I don't want them to see 42. Keep them away from them. And you have anybody on 10 or 20? Where's Michael? Are you gonna put somebody on

10 or 20? On 16? Because there's a problem." He throws down his side-towel and storms out toward the dining room.

Boulud is back in a flash. "Okay," he says, "can I have a *plateau* for two people right away, with spoons and everything? And then fire another *plateau* right away after that."

Boulud goes and has words with Lawrence. This is ridiculous—it's not even a busy lunch, and the service is all screwed up. "It's only thirty-nine people!" Boulud tells him. "Every captain has five to seven tables to take care of, and no more. Am I right?"

"Yehhhs, Chehhhf," Lawrence drawls.

"Otherwise they run like chickens without their heads, you know? Okay, *on y va!*" Let's go! *"Pas de problème."* Now he turns to a runner. "If you work here, I want to make sure you have a role to play for the well-being of the service. Otherwise . . . I just want to make sure you get the *plateau*, get the champagne, let's go, this and that."

"Tony DiDio, I have the champagne already," says the runner.

Boulud waves his arms, snaps his fingers. "Boom, boom! Let's go! So let's make sure we have a *plateau* on 42 and 35." He yells in to the *garde-manger*. "Next time I want something super nice. Tony DiDio, four people, *plateau* for four." Boulud is enraged. First they screwed up the journalists' reservations, and then the stupid business with the seating. And only thirty-nine covers—it should be easy.

Lee places two small dishes of risotto on a tray. "Professor Silver," he says. "It's a white asparagus and porcini risotto."

"Chef, fire 40, please," says a runner.

Lee picks up the phone. "Hello. Hello. Neil, can you come up? Neil, we need you up here. Toto, can you call Jed? Can somebody ask him if he ordered scallops, please? *Mais qu'est-ce qu'il fait, lui?*"

"Okay, one tartare and one ravioli working good?" asks Boulud.

Neil is there in an instant, a big spoon dangling off his hip, held in place by his apron string.

"I don't know why we accepted this," says Lee, holding up a piece of mâche with his fingers. *"C'est de la merde."* It's from France, and it's shit.

"Il faut acheter de la mâche américaine," says Boulud. We should be buying American mâche. So, the four terrines, *ça marche, ou pas?"*

"Eight terrines," says Lee from the far side of the kitchen. "Neil is doing them."

Neil has eight little square plates lined up, each divided into four squares.

• • •

One twenty-five P.M., and everybody's quiet, working. Boulud looks at the tickets. "Okay," he says, "you got 48, eh? Okay, now we have one asparagus, one pea soup working good?"

"Yes, Chef," says Frank.

"Forty-seven is the journalists," says a runner.

"It says 54 here," says Boulud. "What? Forty-seven?" He picks up the phone. "Hello?" And slams it down. "Did you understand that I didn't want 47 next to 52? There's three. The other one's from London *Food Illustrated.* There's three, all of which we didn't have reservations for. They told me that 47 had to be out of there very fast."

A hostess from the front desk runs in. "I just checked myself, Chef. It's 47."

"So give me the terrine, then." They're gorgeous, mosaic-like terrines on the small square plates.

"Can I get a *plateau* for two, please?" says Thompson. "Table 12."

"Okay," says Boulud. "So this is 47. No, no."

"Listen to me," says Thompson to a runner. "Thirty and then 55."

"The terrine's gone?" says Boulud. "Okay, please, let's go. Forty-seven right now. Listen to me—47 first. This one and this one. The beef for the man and the rabbit for the lady. *Alors, avec le lapin:* pleurote mushrooms and foie gras. And the other one with artichoke. Now 47. Let's go here—47. The two journalists."

At the same time as this insanity, there are dozens of main courses going out.

"Thirty!" yells Thompson, pointing. "Go! Starting to go!"

Lee spins around, yells at the runners. "What's going on?"

"Tony DiDio, *il est où, lui?*" says Boulud. He still hasn't been told where DiDio's been seated. "Two tartare, please!"

Lee yells at the fish cook: "The fish is overcooked and this one is raw!" He pulls it off the plate, changes it for another one. "Everything is overcooked!"

"I want to know," booms Boulud, loud and deep—he means business. "Tony DiDio, what's going on—if we're going to do a menu or not."

"Ordering a crab salad and a ravioli for the journalists!" calls Lee. "Gimme a terrine! Gimme a mini-soup, please!"

Thompson glares at a runner. "What are you waiting here for?" he bellows.

Brett Traussi appears. "Go and tell me," Boulud says to him. "Tony DiDio is sitting on 53, and I need to know." Traussi goes into the dining room, and Boulud touches a plate. "Right here," he tells a runner, "this is table 12. No, 11." Now he stops long enough to criticize the *haricots verts* Allannic is plating. *"Ils sont tout mœlleux!"* he says. They're mushy. "They soak up the sauce."

"Chef," says a runner.

"Yes, I know you're waiting for a scallop over here," says Thompson. "It's coming right now."

"Who is making the two anchovies for the tasting?" asks Boulud. "Frank, you're making it? Okay, let's go! Send it out when they're ready. How long is it going to be for the ravioli tasting? We've got to get that table out!" He points to a cook who miraculously seems to have a free hand. "Work with him on the fish, because we're not gonna get the fish out otherwise. Okay, listen to me! Number two, you have the asparagus?"

"Julie, fire 41!" shouts Dan.

"Yes!" she responds.

"Où sont les anchois?" says Boulud.

Jean-Luc Le Dû pushes into the kitchen. "Chef! Chef!" he says. *"Cinquante-deux, ils connaissent vachement bien les vins, ils sont français—"*

"I'm sorry," says Boulud, frighteningly polite and calm, turning back toward the kitchen, "but I'm expecting two scallops and a veal."

"Yes, Chef!" call the fish cook and *saucier*.

"I hope they're together," says Boulud. "That's all I have to say." Now he wipes the edges of a plate of asparagus. He can see right away that they're overcooked. "Who cooked the asparagus?" It was Kevin. "So you wake up when you cook it," says Boulud. "Did you see what you did? Don't be ashamed to put a timer around your neck. You set it for four minutes—*ding!*—you come back. There's no way you can overcook it." If Kevin is humiliated, he doesn't show it.

Le Dû comes back in, excited. *"Le cinquante-deux, c'est l'ami de Philippe Rispoli. Parce que le mec il en connait, un maximum, hein?"* At 52, he says, is seated a friend of Philippe Rispoli, the Feast & Fêtes chef. The guy knows a lot about wine.

"Il est vieux?" asks Daniel. Is he old?

"Non, il est jeune."

Boulud picks up the phone. "Philippe! Philippe! Fifty-two, do you know who it is? Are they your friends?" Michael Lawrence appears on the other side of the pass. "Michael, who took the order on 52? They didn't write anything on there."

"You got the *soigné*," says Lawrence. "It's friends of Rispoli."

"We never got the *soigné* for that. Michael, I really do not want to repeat myself."

"It's my fault, Chef," says Lawrence, dutifully.

"Especially when your things were not covered top notch on the front desk. How many girls on the phones in reservations?"

"Two."

"Do you see me cutting down my staff in the kitchen?"

"I'm sorry, Chef."

Philippe Rispoli comes up from down in the prep kitchen. He and Boulud stare at the video monitor. They can see a woman.

"Elle est mignonne, hein?" She's cute, says Rispoli. She's so blurry, in truth, he can barely tell she's female.

Boulud is now on the other side of the pass. He pokes a piece of meat. *"C'est cru, là.* That's raw. That's not even rare." It goes back to the *saucier*.

Rispoli is on the phone. "He's French or American? He's French?" He can't figure out who these people could be.

"Please tell Michael or the captain on table 10, so that he follows up with the dessert and everything," says Boulud. "And with table 42 and 47 as well. I'm gonna order the desserts right now, but tell the captain to follow."

"C'est des amis," Rispoli tells Boulud. He's figured out that they are indeed friends.

It's 2:10, and the action is slowing down. One would think that anyone who didn't get yelled at today must feel fortunate. But Thompson remembers a similar day last year at Café Boulud, when at the end of the debacle, one of the cooks came up to him and asked sadly, "How come no one yelled at me today, Chef?" That cook worried that he wasn't important enough to be noticed.

Boulud climbs the stairs to the skybox, opens his closet, changes into a clean jacket, accented with royal blue piping. A crisp, white apron goes around his waist—immaculate, elegant. Downstairs, Frank takes out another pan of bacon, lines a second pan with paper towels. The runners stand at the pass, clowning around.

A half hour later, Boulud, in his pristine whites, goes into the dining room and takes a seat with Cynthia Penney and Andrew Dornenburg, who sit back in their comfortable chairs, wholly satisfied with their amazing meal. A basket of madeleines, a silver tray of chocolates, and coffee are on the table. Boulud looks fresh, his eyes twinkle.

In three months Penney's article will appear in the July issue of *Waitrose*

Food Illustrated. "Cynthia Penney asks a bunch of New Yorkers to name the things that give the city its appeal," the header will read. Philippe de Montebello, the director of the Metropolitan Museum of Art, will point to his museum's Greek Gallery; clothing designer Cynthia Rowley likes parasailing past the Statue of Liberty; Mario Batali confesses to a penchant for sneaking out in his chef's whites to Gray's Papaya, a hot dog stand a block away from his restaurant, Babbo. As for Boulud, "In July, I love the local tomatoes," Penney will quote him as saying. "Sometimes I take my Jeep down to Union Square Greenmarket at about eight A.M. Very often I choose the produce, but I trust the farmers, so they often make a selection and keep it on the back of the truck for us."

Well, sort of. In fact, it's Jed and Thompson who actually go.

By the end of the month, there's a note on the door of the locker room:

MEMORANDUM
FRIDAY *4/28*
TO: *All Staff*
FROM: *DB*
SUBJECT: *The week of the James Beard Awards*

A reminder: Please keep in mind that the James Beard Award week is coming up [May 3–10] and that even more journalists, chefs, food critics, and general VIPs will be coming than usual.

   The kitchen should be ready with special offerings, reservationists should be careful not to overbook, service should remain polished and efficient and the front of the house should be as gracious and welcoming as I know it has the capacity to be!

   I want to ensure that the restaurant remains civilized, elegant and up to the standards of excellence for which we are renowned.

On the first day of Beard Week, Georgette Farkas can be seen limping around on a cane, having broken her toe when her stiletto heel caught in one of the holes in the rubber safety floor mat in the downstairs prep kitchen. David, the fish *entremétier*, has given notice; he'll soon be attending business school at the University of Pittsburgh. His undergraduate degree was in hotel and restaurant management from the University of Missouri; eventually he wants to go into hotel management. Julie, the hot-apps cook, is gone—she's moving to Texas to join her boyfriend. Tony, the fish cook, is gone, quit, skedaddled. He's surfing in Costa Rica for a month, and then—who knows? On Tony's last day, Neil Gallagher was wondering what to do with some extra pig's blood, when he hit upon the perfect use for it. He filled a bucket with it, and he and a couple of the guys stuffed Tony into the bucket; he was folded in half, his legs sticking out. When he got out, covered with blood, they doused him with flour. It was the least Gallagher could do for his pal, who was an intern at Lespinasse when Gallagher worked there.

Scott, who used to work David's position, has taken Tony's position. David is around for two more weeks.

Christian, a young Danish cook who has been here two months, is working Julie's position on hot apps, sautéing mushrooms for risotto in a nonstick pan. "Don't sauté mushrooms in that kind of pan," says Lee, walking by. "Use a regular pan."

Allannic grinds apricot powder, pressing on the top of an electric coffee grinder. The apricots have been drying for a week. The sweet-tart aroma of a thousand apricots wafts up, mouthwatering, as Allannic spreads each batch of the powder on a sheet pan. He'll use this for the lamb, just to dust around the plate. At Daniel it is far from uncommon for hours of work to go into a single element out of dozens on a plate—and with this one, many people won't even taste it.

David peels the stems of fresh porcini mushrooms, while Scott uses scissors to cut the fins off a Dover sole with the ease of a child cutting paper dolls. Sole is not on the menu, but for VIPs who request it they serve the fish whole.

At 12:15 the first order goes out: risotto and pea soup.

Boulud shows David how to properly prep the porcini—trimming the lower edge of the cap, then cleaning them well with a damp towel. This lesson despite the fact that David will only be around two more weeks. "If you think there's too much soil in it," says Boulud, "you clean them with a little mushroom brush."

Scott dusts Wondra flour onto a skate fillet—the barley flour in Wondra makes it brown nice and crisply—and places it in a pan with sizzling butter.

Boulud enters the walk-in refrigerator just behind the fish station and comes back out again holding a sheet pan of porcini, uncovered. "Who did that here?" he asks, loudly.

"It was left over from the weekend," says David. It's a weak excuse for the sloppy storage of expensive ingredients.

After it's been cooking about three minutes, Scott checks under the skate with a flexible fish spatula. He flips it, spooning browning butter over it. He looks under a sea bass paupiette, which is getting golden. Boulud flips it when he walks by.

"Okay, guys!" yells Lee. "I need the floor clean here! You're gonna get everything off the floor!"

"You need a good spoon to work with risotto," Boulud tells Christian. "That's the last time I say that." He goes to the phone, calls for Toto to repair the door of the walk-in. Then he shouts across the kitchen, moving back toward the walk-in, "First thing you have to do in the morning here is you look at the shelf," meaning the shelf of the walk-in. "When I come at twelve and I look at the shelf and I see stuff like that, I wonder what the hell is going on here. Okay, you take everything and you start fresh. *C'est l'idée.* That's the first thing to do in the morning is to inspect everything in the refrigerator up here. Same thing in the fish station, okay? The first thing you do in the morning." By this point, he's standing inside the walk-in, getting madder and madder. Lee joins him, along with several cooks, and he continues to yell. Although it may not seem that serious, such sloppiness is completely anathema to the kind of well-oiled machine Daniel needs to be. Worse, it could be a symptom of malaise among the cooks.

Bruno Jamais brings in a couple to see Boulud, who's still in the fridge.

"Allo, Chef!" calls Jamais.

Lee, back at the pass, shakes hands with the couple. He goes back to get Boulud.

With a big smile, Boulud comes to shake their hands in front of the pastry pickup area. His Jekyll-and-Hyde transformation is remarkable.

At the pass, Kevin shows Lee a ticket. "Journalist?" he asks.

"Yeah," says Lee. "Make nice."

Bernard Vrod comes in. "Ariane Daguin," he says to Lee.

"Elle est là?" She's here? It's the foie gras queen.

"Avec CNN," says Vrod.

Lee rolls his eyes. It can't be. "Don't tell Daniel," he says. He turns to Kevin. "What did you put on the *plateau?*"

"A little lobster," he says, "some terrine—"

"I told you: No fucking terrine on the *plateau!*" shouts Lee. "You know we like to start the tasting with the terrine! That's the way it's always been! What the fuck are you doing? Bravo!"

"What's his name?" a runner asks Frank, pointing to the hot-apps cook.

"Christian," says Frank.

"Christian!" says the runner. "Fire two penne tasting and two risotto!" No one is expediting, neither German on the runners' side nor any chef. Frank grabs some finished fish plates and puts them on the trays.

Côte comes back. *"Que s'est-il passé avec les VIP là?"* he asks. What happened with those VIPs?

A huge crash is heard from the dishwashing area, but no one even blinks. Scott plates an order of salmon, Côte adds the garnish.

Michael Lawrence appears at the pass. "Alex!" he says. "Teitelbaum's in a hurry today!"

"Ravioli and asparagus salad on the fly, guys!" cries Lee. He turns to Kevin. "I don't want to see terrine on the *plateau* anymore. 'Cause you fucked me today." And then to Christian: "Can you stay tonight? Because David's sick. He's like this," and Lee retches. "Can you do me this favor? I have somebody working on *mise en place* already." This won't be easy for Christian, since he's new on the station and having a hard time. Yesterday he was admonished for overcooking the risotto. Today, unbeknownst to the chefs, it's undercooked, and almost inedibly salty. From the point of view of the *sous-chefs*, it's a tricky business, criticizing the work of a new cook, because there's always the danger that he might overreact and have an even harder time of it.

Lee picks up the phone. "Hello, Neil? You think you can come up for a few minutes?"

Gallagher is up almost before Lee puts down the phone.

"Can you take the pass for me?" asks Lee.

Gallagher pulls a microphone from the right-hand wall. It's rarely been used before. He calls out an order. It's startlingly loud.

Boulud comes in. "Why did we send canapés on a *plate?*" he asks Kevin. Kevin mumbles a response. "I don't give a fucking damn!" says Boulud. We serve everything on *plateaux*, okay? It doesn't make sense—you have two plates on the table instead of one *plateau*. Does that make sense?"

"Yes."

"Well, use your head, then!"

Neil calls out another order on the microphone.

"Not too loud, please," says Boulud. "Everyone can hear." He turns back to Kevin. "Who did you send that to?" he asks.

"Journalists," says Kevin.

The phone rings. Boulud picks it up, tries to sort out the canapé crisis.

"Do you have the *rouget* for me?" Lee yells to the fish station. "The *rouget?*"

"Forty-seven!" shouts Boulud.

"I need a sliced tomato confit, please!" belts Lee.

Daniel the waiter comes in, concerned about Teitelbaum's table. "They have to be out by two-thirty," he says.

"Okay, then we'll make sure they're out by two-thirty," says Boulud. "Cyrille! Cyrille! Hello! Fifteen minutes! Can I have some people from downstairs?"

"Who do you want?" calls Lee from the *garde-manger*. "There's no one down there. Scott, can I have that *rouget?*"

Meanwhile, Toto has appeared, and he's trying to tell someone—anyone—that French David, the dinner hot-apps cook, is sick. *"Il est malade!"* he tells Allannic. For a cook to admit being sick, he must be *really* sick.

Someone's appetizer was screwed up, and a runner waits, unsure of what to do about it. "Alex is making another appetizer for them," Boulud tells them.

"Can I get a tomato confit?!" calls Lee. "Get me heavy cream! Tapenade!" And then he yells at the top of his lungs to the two bickering *garde-manger* cooks, "Both you guys calm down, okay?! *C'est fini.* Okay? *Merde.* You guys try and work together, okay?"

"We got the risotto on 61, are you sure?" Boulud asks Ernesto, a runner.

"Yes," says Ernesto.

"He sent it out?"

"I did," says Ernesto.

"Fifty-six, did you get out the *ballottine?*"

"Yes, Chef."

"So every time you take something, you tell me. Okay?"

"Yes, sir," says Ernesto.

"Don't take anything without telling me, okay?"

"Yes, sir. Fifty-three is going. I take 53, Chef. The appetizers." Ernesto runs with it, shaking out a kink in his leg.

Lawrence pops in again—and he's rarely the bearer of good news. "Alex," he says. "Guys. I don't have any canapés on 42. They've already ordered. I need to give them something."

"Who are they?" asks Kevin.

"VIP, 4," says Lawrence.

"Fire two frog legs right away!" calls Boulud. "For Ariane!"

"I've got to get something to the table," says Lawrence. "It's been twenty minutes." In the *garde-manger*, they're arranging a *plateau*.

"Pick up!" yells Lawrence when they're finished.

Vrod comes in from the dining room, looks at the *plateau*. "What are you doing with that? Don't put any crab on it! No crab."

Now a runner comes in from the dining room, holding two asparagus salads. "What are you doing with that?" Lawrence asks him. "Chef, I have two, 42 and 47. But I don't understand what's going on with 44."

"Did he take it?" asks Boulud. "I want to know what he did with the asparagus."

"Forty-seven," says Lawrence.

"And 44?" asks Boulud. "And 44?!"

Lawrence runs after him.

The runner comes back in. "Chef," he says, "I need one mini-soup on 44 as well."

"No," says Boulud, "because I gave them three mini-soup before."

A waiter runs in. "No mini-soup!"

"Mr. Teitelbaum wants his soup right now," says Lawrence.

"When they pick up the food from Mr. Teitelbaum, they should know to fire the main course right away," says Boulud.

"They did," says Lawrence.

"Oh, yeah," says Boulud, sarcastic. "Right."

By two-thirty, service is starting to wind down on the hot side, as a heavenly sweet aroma wafts up from the pastry area.

"Chef," asks Daniel the waiter, "what's the dessert you've chosen for 35?"

"It should have already been served," says Boulud. "They have to leave at two-thirty." He leaves the pass, goes to the pastry window. "We have a table of nine people where you can do nine fruit and nine chocolate, *si tu veux*," Boulud tells Iuzzini. In French, *si tu veux* literally means "if you want," but it often means "I want." This is for table 30, restaurateurs from six restaurants in Canada, mostly Montreal. Boulud doesn't know them. "They went to Palladin yesterday," says Boulud. "They had eleven desserts. If they can do eleven, we can do thirty-five."

Six

CLEAN

I N *DOWN AND OUT IN PARIS AND LONDON,* George Orwell
wrote voluptuously and voluminously about the filth to be
found in restaurant kitchens in Paris. Based on the writer's real-
life experiences, the Paris half of the book is a fictional account of the life of a
plongeur (dishwasher), working first in a tony Paris hotel and then in a chic
restaurant. "It is not a figure of speech, it is a mere statement of fact to say that
a French cook will spit in the soup—that is, if he is not going to drink it himself," Orwell wrote.

> *He is an artist, but his art is not cleanliness. To a certain extent he is even
> dirty because he is an artist, for food, to look smart, needs dirty treatment.
> When a steak, for instance, is brought up for the head cook's inspection, he
> does not handle it with a fork. He picks it up with his fingers and slaps it
> down, runs his thumb round the dish and licks it to taste the gravy, runs it
> round and licks again, then steps back and contemplates the piece of meat
> like an artist judging a picture, then presses it lovingly into place with his
> fat, pink fingers, every one of which he has licked a hundred times that
> morning. When he is satisfied, he takes a cloth and wipes his fingerprints
> from the dish, and hands it to the waiter. . . . Whenever one pays more than,
> say, ten francs for a dish of meat in Paris, one may be certain that it has been
> fingered in this manner. In very cheap restaurants it is different; there, the*

*same trouble is not taken over the food, and it is just forked out of the pan
and flung onto a plate, without handling. Roughly speaking, the more one
pays for food, the more sweat and spittle one is obliged to eat with it.*

Unlike the kitchens that Orwell describes, with inches of grime on the floor
and vermin in every corner, the kitchen at Daniel is clean, very clean. It is
clean not only when it has just been cleaned (the floor, for instance, is washed
several times during the day); in general, it looks—well, clean enough to eat
from. At Daniel a huge premium is placed on "working clean"; it's one of the
virtues that Alex Lee and the other *sous-chefs* look for when evaluating a potential new cook as he or she "trails" prior to being hired. A closely related
virtue, organization, is terribly important as well. Line cooks are expected to
have their *mise en place* done completely in advance of service; they must be
perfectly well organized in order to keep up with the frenetic pace. No one has
time to stop and look for something, and unless everything is in order, that's
impossible.

Fortunately, our government has installed checks on hygiene in places such
as restaurant kitchens. City health departments regulate cleanliness and food
safety in such workplaces, and in locales that do a good job with enforcement,
kitchens that don't comply with regulations do get closed down. As a culture,
we have become more germ-phobic (which is the dark side of food safety-
conscious), and accordingly, city health departments have made the results of
these inspections increasingly accessible to the public. In Los Angeles, for instance, a letter grade (A through F) is assigned to each restaurant and may be
posted in public view. The New York City Department of Health posts brief
summaries of inspection reports on its website for anyone to see.

At Daniel cooks are conscientious about cleaning their work surfaces and
knives, washing their hands after touching a protein or using the restroom, and
so forth.

As required by law, signs in the various employees' restrooms and over the
kitchen washbasins say:

WASH YOUR HANDS WHENEVER YOU
Use the restroom
Use a handkerchief or tissue
Touch any soiled object or surface, soiled clothing, washrag, etc.
Handle raw food

Inevitably, though, things come to pass that aren't exactly, well, appetizing.

Cooks do sneeze during service. Normally they turn away from the food and avoid sneezing into their hands. One cannot help but think, though, that a few of those little microbes just might land on the food.

And despite the recommendations of the hand-washing sign posted in the employee restrooms, there is simply no way that a cook washes his hands every time he touches his hair or face. The fish cook's nose itches, and he's got six orders to fire in the next three minutes. Does he wash his hand after he scratches his nose? Maybe not.

Specifically, it is the New York City Department of Health that enforces hygiene and food-safety issues in restaurants throughout the five boroughs; it does so through its department of Environmental Health Services. Every restaurant in the city is inspected approximately once a year—that is, unless there are violations or noncompliance that would inspire more frequent visits. Restaurants that do not comply with the EHS regulations may be shut down until compliance is achieved, or they may be issued violations, in certain circumstances; these may result in a reinspection two weeks later, and then every two weeks until compliance is met.

One would like to think that three- and four-star restaurants would be above such concerns as passing a health department inspection. But a quick glance at the New York City Department of Health website at the time of this writing turns up allegations (and they are only allegations until heard before a tribunal) of Class A (the most egregious) violations concerning food safety at Alain Ducasse at the Essex House, Jean Georges, Lespinasse, Danube, and Bouley Bakery. How dire are these particular allegations? For the moment, let's just say that none of the violations would prevent this writer from dining—most happily—in any of these establishments. Still, they all appear with an asterisk on the written report, indicating a "Public Health Hazard that must be corrected immediately."

For any restaurant, a visit from the health department is stressful for the simple reason that no matter how clean the restaurant, and no matter how hygiene-minded the staff, it is virtually impossible to comply fully with every regulation.

Sauces, for example, must be tasted. Although one or two chefs have been known to use plastic spoons of the picnic variety to taste sauces and soups, filling a pocket with them to make the tasting rounds, then tossing them away each time something is tasted, most chefs will tell you that plastic spoons are most unpleasant to use for tasting, since the sauces bead up on them. Many cooks use stainless or silver spoons to taste. At Daniel, as in most kitchens, a cylindrical stainless-steel receptacle containing water is used to hold spoons—one can be found on every station on the hot line. When a cook tastes something, he or she drops the used spoon into the water, where it stays until it's time to taste something else. Despite the fact that the water in these cylinders is (at least theoretically) changed every half hour or so, if a health department inspector saw them, it would be what's known as a Class B violation, specifically number 9E, "Sanitized equipment or utensil, including in-use food dispensing utensil, improperly used or stored." A minor infraction, to be sure. But four or more such Class B, C, and D violations—known as "general violations"—found on an inspection visit result in a health department hearing and fines. These are not as serious as Class A violations: Four or more of these result in a reinspection, usually about two weeks later.

Fingers may be the most practical for tasting and testing. Cooks have notoriously high pain thresholds, and their skin tends to be insensitive to heat, so in general they have no problem plunging a digit into scalding liquid. This doesn't present a real food-safety problem if the food is not finished cooking. But fingers are also used to taste food that will not be cooked more before it is served. The best way to judge the doneness of a piece of meat, for instance, is to touch it, which is why cooks are taught to judge "temperature," or doneness, by feel. Using an instant-read thermometer may be more accurate, but nothing beats the sense of touch for quickness and ease. Rare, for instance, feels like the flesh between one's thumb and forefinger when the hand is relaxed. Medium-rare feels like the same flesh when the thumb and forefinger stretch out slightly to form a V. Experienced cooks have internalized such measures and can poke meat in their sleep.

But finger-poking happens to be a Class A violation, falling under the heading "Food Protection: Contamination by Worker"; it's number 5B: "Food worker does not use proper utensil to eliminate bare hand contact with food that will not receive adequate additional heat treatment." It's this infraction for which Alain Ducasse and Danube will be cited. (For chronology's sake, Alain Ducasse will not open until the summer of 2000; Danube's alleged violation is from an inspection that will occur in January 2001.)

And it's hard to imagine a restaurant of *any* kind that doesn't violate Class B violation number 9F: "Wiping cloths dirty or not stored in sanitizing solution." At Daniel you may not see dirty wiping cloths lying about, but like cooks everywhere, Daniel's cooks use side-towels (that hang perpetually over the apron strings around their waists) for everything from wiping down counters to holding burning-hot skillet handles. The *saucier* and *garde-manger* cooks use wet side-towels to wipe down their stations and they *might* store these in sanitizing solution, but usually they're kept in warm, soapy water.

Still, the employees of Daniel try very, very hard to comply with not only Department of Health regulations, but a general sense of hygiene, cleanliness, and safe food practices. The dishwasher itself is a wonder to see. Made by Hobart, it looks more like a car wash than a kitchen appliance. During its two-minute cycle, it washes at 160 degrees Fahrenheit and rinses at 180 degrees; a garbage disposal is built into the bottom of it. The stemware is washed first thing in the morning, when the water is cleanest, and then it's all washed again just before service, so the glasses sparkle perfectly.

But the interests of food safety and the aims of its police don't always jibe with those of the gourmand. Take cheese, for example.

"*C'est un privilège*," says Pascal Vittu, solemnly, chin raised, looking down his nose. Pascal, a thirty-two-year-old captain, is speaking about his favorite subject in the world. Its selection of cheese is one of the things that sets Daniel apart from just about every other restaurant in town, and Pascal, in addition to his role as captain, is also Daniel's cheese sommelier. There are only a handful of restaurants in New York that have cheese trolleys in the same league as Daniel's: Jean Georges, Lespinasse, Alain Ducasse, Gramercy Tavern, and Picholine. For Pascal, it's not good enough to simply offer a chèvre, a Comté, a Livarot—he seeks out the finest cheeses from artisanal and farmstead cheese-makers and top *affineurs* around the world.

But Pascal is worried. Because as every cheese lover knows, the cheeses with the most character are made from unpasteurized milk. These are the cheeses with the most complexity, the most intrigue. And lately, the issue of pasteurization and cheese has been the source of tremendous controversy, for the FDA considers cheeses made from raw milk to be unsafe for consumption unless they're aged for at least sixty days. And now the agency is even considering banning *all* unpasteurized cheeses. It's already bad enough that Pascal can't get Epoisse—someone in France died from listeriosis after eating an infected Epoisse. The raw-milk issue poses a particular problem with goat cheeses, many of which are best very young and fresh; these must be pasteurized. Fortunately for Pascal and the cheese-loving patrons of Daniel, a few unpasteurized chèvres do manage to squeak through.

But even if some delicious contraband raw-milk cheese happens to find its way into the restaurant despite the strict importation laws, New York City Department of Health regulations list "Unpasteurized milk or milk product present" as a Class A violation.

Pascal is tall and slim, his light brown head balanced on a thin neck. His almond eyes point downward at the edges and are rung by deep circles—the result, perhaps, of too many double-shifts for too many years. He looks like a Doonesbury cartoon. Or a mortician. Some of the staff jokingly call him Lurch.

Raised on a farm near Toulouse in southern France, Pascal had a childhood duty to walk five miles after school to the dairy farm to pick up the eggs and milk. But to him it wasn't a hardship, *"C'était un privilège"*—again, the privilege mantra. Just out of Ecole Hôtelière in Toulouse, Pascal took a job as busboy at Les Trois Marches in Versailles back in 1987; it was there that he, to use his words, discovered his profession. No matter that his 1,900-franc rent ate up half of his salary (for unlike in the United States, wait staff in France is salaried, a service charge built into the price of menu items; customers will often leave an additional *pourboire*, but it's usually just a token). In any case, waiters in France, even in top restaurants, don't make anything near what they can earn at a top American restaurant like Daniel. Trois Marches featured seventy-five cheeses on its cart, and soon the busboy was allowed to take charge of the house-smoked salmon (which they smoked in the garden behind the restaurant) as well as—ah, bliss!—the cheeses.

After spending a year and a half in Versailles, Pascal went southwest to Pauillac, where he spent three years as a waiter at the Relais & Châteaux Cordeillan-Bages. In January 1992 he moved to England, where he went to work first at Le Manoir Aux Quat' Saisons, Raymond Blanc's *Michelin* two-star in Oxford, and then at Pied à Terre in London, as headwaiter.

His two-plus years in England had a profound effect on Pascal; today he talks about experiencing what he calls an *ouverture*—an opening up. "I saw a world that was more vast," he explains. "I realized now that there wasn't only France."

But on learning that his mother was ill in the spring of 1994, Pascal returned to France, working a season at La Terrace, a two-star in Juan Les Pins in the Côte d'Azur, and saving up enough money to stop working for five months to be with his parents. By the next spring, he was installed in Paris at the two-star Amphycles as maître d'hôtel.

Pascal struck up a friendship with another maître d', Laurent, at the three-star Arpège, who told him, after knowing Pascal for a few months, that Pascal should leave France. "You have blinders on here," his friend told him in 1996. "You have to go see something else." Laurent called his friend Michel, who was working at Bouley (the original, now closed), and asked if he could put Pascal up. Although Michel was just about to leave for France to attend to his visa, he told Pascal he would be welcome to stay at the apartment he shared with his girlfriend, who also worked at Bouley.

When Michel returned from France a few days later, he and Pascal had dinner at Park Bistro. Michel told Pascal that Bouley wasn't doing visas for anyone since he planned to close his restaurant soon, but that the person to watch was Daniel Boulud.

Pascal made an appointment to see Boulud for a five-minute meeting on a Tuesday, and they proceeded to talk about food for two hours. All of a sudden, Boulud looked at his watch, realized he was late, and rushed off, saying, "Speak with my assistant, Georgette." That would be Georgette Farkas, of course. On Wednesday Farkas had all the papers to do a visa. Pascal spent a week "having a good time" and sightseeing in Manhattan, and thirteen days after he arrived in the United States, he started to work for Boulud.

Pascal can't imagine returning to France to live. Here, in the United States, he has what he refers to (always in English, even if he's speaking French at the moment) as "freedom of expression." And how does Pascal express himself? Through cheese. After spending one year as a front waiter at the old Daniel, Pascal became captain. Then one day in 1997, Boulud said to him something like, "You know, Pascal, I'm very happy about my restaurant, but I don't have any cheese." That was a slight exaggeration—at that time he had five or six cheeses, which were presented on a plate that came out of the kitchen. Pascal and Boulud put together a little basket, and soon they were designing a cheese cart. Before long, in addition to his share of the pooled tips, Pascal had a nominal supplemental salary for taking care of the cheeses.

Today Pascal buys cheese twice a week, purchasing for Daniel, Café Boulud, and Feast & Fêtes from three cheese shops scattered around Manhattan. Because he believes that Steve Jenkins, the cheesemonger for Fairway Market on the Upper West Side, was the first in New York to offer farmstead cheeses, he has a soft spot for Fairway. From Ideal, on the Upper East Side, he likes to buy triple creams, such as Pierre Robert, Brillat-Savarin, Chaource, and Gratte-Paille, as well as hard cheeses. But his cheesemonger of preference is Murray's Cheese Shop on Bleecker Street in Greenwich Village, owned by

Rob Kaufelt since 1991. (Within a year, though, Pascal will have stopped shopping at Fairway and Ideal, relying solely on Murray's for all his cheeses.) "Robert goes deeper and deeper into each appellation than any of the others," says Pascal. When Kaufelt was starting out, Pascal explains, he would be content to bring in, say, a Pont-l'Evêque. Now he searches for a range of Pont-L'Evêques, from a decent, affordable one made by an industrial producer (as mass production is referred to in cheesedom) to a *fermier* or farmstead example made in small lots entirely of milk raised at the dairy where the cheese was made, and several in between.

Cheese production is divided into two parts: There is the cheesemaker—the *fromager*—who actually makes the cheese from the milk, and then there is the *affineur*. It is the *affineur*'s job to age and cure the cheese, bathing the rind, if necessary, keeping it at the proper humidity, and so forth. *Affineurs,* most of whom are in France and Italy, buy their cheeses from different producers and then use their skill to age them, which is an art in itself; the best *affineurs* turn out formidable cheeses.

It's a Monday morning—no lunch service today—and Pascal ambles west along Bleecker Street to the corner of Cornelia Street and into Murray's. Hundreds of cheeses fill up the cases of this tiny shop; a little paper sign stuck into each tells what it is—Saint-Nectaire, Chabichou, Manchego, Livarot, Berkshire Blue. On the left are rows of dried salamis and olives, and on the back wall good bread, *cornichons,* olive oil, anchovies. On top of the cheese cases are displays of featured cheeses, American farmstead selections on the left, a mountain range of tender, shaggy pyramid-shaped chèvres on the right.

"Do you need me today?" Rob Kaufelt asks him, after greeting him. "Or Valérie?" But Kaufelt already knows the answer, since it's always Valérie Montbarbon who helps him. Valérie greets Pascal, and they kiss on both cheeks; she's French, after all, from Toulon. He follows her past the counter into a small back room: This is where the serious buying goes down. The room is a temperature- and humidity-controlled environment, a sort of large walk-in. The walls are lined with shelves holding all manner of cheese: Along one side are stacked wooden palettes of chèvres, a sheet of thin paper protecting the top of each; next to that is a gigantic farmstead Cheddar, more than a foot tall.

Valérie starts showing Pascal cheeses, beginning with a Pouligny Saint-Pierre, a pyramid-shaped chèvre. *"C'est un peu jeune,"* she confides; their business is conducted entirely in French. She finds another Pouligny that is more aged; Pascal takes five of them. He then asks if she has a Chavignol. She hands

him one, which he takes in his hands, feeling it with his fingers. He brings it up
to his nose, inhaling deeply: It smells fresh, like milk. Pascal loves this, buying
cheese: He loves handling it, smelling it, just being around it, and it's written
all over his face. This one is lovely; exactly the way it should smell at this age,
five or six weeks of affinage. *"J'en veux bien quatre,"* he says. I'll take four. And
after that some Selles-sur-Cher—he's making his way through the goat
cheeses of the Loire Valley. These, incidentally, are not the same cheeses offered from the case out front to civilians; here in back are the really special
farmstead and artisanal cheeses with tiny productions, those that Murray's re-
serves for important restaurant clients such as Daniel. Valérie moves next into
cheeses from Corsica, sliding a Fleur du Maquis out from a rack. It's about
four inches in diameter and two and a half inches high, drum-shaped, and covered with a fine mold, along with rosemary, savory, a few juniper berries, and
a few tiny red chili peppers. Now a supple Robiola from Italy, and then Pascal
asks about Livarot and Pont-l'Evêque. These, Valérie tells him, will be from
the case outside; she returns with three of the former, four of the latter, and a
Tomme de Savoie. "Ah," says Valérie as she pulls out the Tomme de Savoie.
"Il est craqué." She gets another. When cheeses are cracked, they can get little
infections known as *picures,* which can cause an ammonia-like smell; usually
this happens in the shipping, so even the very best cheeses, cured by the top
affineurs, can fall victim to it. The second one is good; it smells the way it
should, like dust, like the cellar. Saint-Nectaire, Comté, Tomme d'Abon-
dance—a large, flat, round mountain cheese from Haute-Savoie with a wonderful odor of hazelnuts. Remarkably, it takes five hundred liters of milk to
make one. A pock-marked two-year-old mimolette looks like the moon; another, a year younger, looks like a cantaloupe, but a little smoother. Pascal
takes the moon, *bien sûr.* Then on to sheep cheeses.

The whole transaction is over in twenty minutes. A peck on either cheek,
and Pascal is out of there. Although money was not discussed—Pascal does so
much business with Valérie he knows the prices for everything he's bought
today—he figures he spent four or five hundred dollars. In any case, he spends
a total of about a thousand dollars per week for the two restaurants and the
catering operation.

But Pascal wonders how long he'll be able to do this, since the USDA has
proposed regulations that would ban both the importation of and the domestic
sale of any unpasteurized cheese. As far as he's concerned, such regulations
would be a draconian measure that would address something that isn't even a
problem, especially considering that listeria is frequently found in mass-

produced packaged lunch meats, and even pasteurized packaged cheese products. For Pascal, there are much more common—and at the same time, much graver—food-safety issues that should be addressed. For instance, in France, when a consumer buys meat or cheese or any other food product in a shop, there is always a cashier, whose only job is to handle money. That way you never have someone touching money, with all its legions of bacteria, many of which can cause food-borne illness, and then touching food, the way we do in the U.S. That, Pascal believes, would be worth regulating. In the meantime, if all the character is regulated out of cheese, how will he express himself?

Wednesday, May 3

It's early afternoon, and in the downstairs prep kitchen, the dinner cooks are already hard at work doing their prep for tonight.

Lupe, with blood all over his apron, fillets *rouget*. He stands in his habitual spot at the corner of the work island closest to the door. He takes a six-inch-long fish, runs a blade along its flat side to scale it, then slices off a fillet in one continuous motion. A second motion and he cuts off the head and the second fillet. And again. And again. Six seconds per fish. Every few fish, he rinses off his knife, runs it down a steel. Next to him, using the same oversized cutting board, an assistant pulls small bones out of salmon using fish tweezers.

Neil Gallagher, who has been upstairs in lunch service, installs himself next to the assistant. He begins cutting lemongrass on the bias with a long serrated knife on a small cutting board.

Next to Gallagher, a line cook tears herb garnishes, using his fingers. Another cuts the seed sacs out of peeled plum tomatoes. The resulting "fillets" look almost like the *rouget* fillets. There's perfect silence in the prep kitchen.

Patrice, a tall, thin French fish cook, portions salmon with a squared-off knife.

Near the ice machine (a large model that resembles those found in hotel corridors), another cook removes crab meat from its shells with the point of a paring knife, dropping it into a large stainless-steel bowl set in a larger bowl filled with ice. He wears latex gloves whose purpose has less to do with hygiene than with avoiding smelly hands that might impart an off-odor to other preparations.

Philippe, the French *saucier*, is at the end of the island. He's small, thin, intense-looking. Next to him is a sheet pan of squab stuffed with greens, their legs tied together with string. Their wings and hearts are in one pile, their breasts on another. He scoops crème frâiche into a shallow plastic container, adds a generous amount of salt, some cumin, fennel seed, coriander, paprika, chili powder, and honey, and whisks. This will be a "Moroccan Spice" marinade for the squab. He tastes it with his finger, whisks with the huge, long whisk. He lays the breasts in it.

Patrice absently steels his knife, staring into the distance. He resumes cutting the salmon, laying each portion skin-up on a parchment-covered sheet pan.

Philippe, having just braised the squab legs, pours the braising liquid into a rectangular pan on the floor.

"Hey, Chris," says the cook doing the crab. "Where would be the best place to go buy a bike?"

"Outside the city," says Chris.

"You want a mountain bike?" asks Bobby, a Hawaiian cook who wears a choker of puka shells. "I've got one hardly used."

"You've hardly used it?"

"You want it?" asks Bobby.

"Yeah."

Philippe now takes huge plastic bags filled with veal for sauce. He slits the plastic bags with the point of a paring knife, empties them onto the cutting board.

The cook who had been tearing the herbs now cuts zucchini, quartering them lengthwise, then cutting out the seeds.

Philippe cuts through veal bones with a powerful Hobart electric saw with a vertical blade. He pushes the bones through, one by one, *zzzzhhhhhh, zzzzzhhhh*, and drops them into a big plastic container on the floor.

A *garde-manger* cook cuts tuna—a big, gorgeous, deep red piece. Taking an enormous fillet, he cuts off the dark parts and the sinewy parts, then he cuts the deep rosy red part into dice for tartare. This is quality tuna, number-one grade, sushi quality. Today it's local, but sometimes it comes from the Gulf, or Hawaii, or the Carolina coast; in any case, it's always beautiful. Its wholesale price ranges from $11.95 to $15.95 per pound. The dice goes into a small plastic box, which is set over ice in a larger box.

Lupe's assistant trims the *rouget* fillets, tossing them onto a big pile with a casual backhand. Lupe works on prawns.

The herb and zucchini cook now chops parsley—making a soft, green mountain, perfectly dry.

Across the island, Ayamu, a Japanese cook, peels Idaho potatoes for gnocchi, then places them into a food mill. He separates eggs, straining them through his fingers, putting the yolks into a small stainless-steel bowl and the whites in a taller stainless-steel cylinder. He whisks the yolks with a fork. Then he sprinkles flour onto the counter and cranks the food mill over it. Next a sprinkle of finely chopped chives, then a couple of handfuls of flour go on top. "Laura," he says to a cooking school extern working nearby, "can I borrow some salt and pepper?" He grinds pepper onto the heap and adds salt with his fingers. Picking up a pastry blade, he starts mixing, gently, adds more flour, and pushes everything toward the center. He blends some more, then drizzles a little more flour from his palm. He makes a low mountain, pushing in a well with his fist, and into the well go the yolks. Now he starts folding it all together with a fork. He picks up the pastry blade again, scoops up from the sides, and smushes it down, rhythmically. He smushes it all together with his hands, then chops a few times with the blade, cuts it in three, and shapes each into a nice ball. He scrapes the stainless-steel counter.

The only noise in the kitchen is the high-pitched whirring of the meat blade, and the lower-pitched crunch as it goes through the bones. It's very cool: about sixty degrees.

Ayamu rolls one of the dough balls into a snake, using both palms, then quickly cuts it on the bias into short lengths—*tap tap tap* on the stainless-steel counter. He sprinkles flour on top, then puts them on a parchment-covered sheet pan.

Brad Thompson brings a large box of tiny chanterelles upstairs to clean. He intends to pickle them and cover them in oil. Many cooks complain about cleaning chanterelles—they're a pain in the neck—but Thompson secretly likes it. He'll do these during service this evening when it's not too busy; it's better than standing around. Every kind of mushroom is treated differently. With these, the stems must be peeled first with a paring knife, then they're soaked in water. Then rinsed. With the larger ones, the gills must be removed; that's where the worms like to hide, if there are any. With the scraps, he'll make a stock: They have nice flavor, and make a great sauce. Last year when Thompson worked for a few days at Alain Ducasse's restaurant in Monte Carlo, he was taken with a sauce they made by cooking chanterelles in butter and simmering them in the liquid they gave off. Then they were put into a blender and pureed, then finished with a little butter. Thompson's mouth starts to water as he remembers it. That decides it: He'll braise these in butter and chicken stock, put them in the blender, and make a sauce. At Ducasse they used theirs for risotto. . . .

The runners are cutting extra-thick paper toweling into small squares for wiping the edges of plates.

Just outside the pastry pickup area, Ariella puts a selection of desserts on a new cart that just came into use two weeks ago (unlike the ill-fated salad cart). During lunch service, guests now have the option of choosing something off the three-tiered cart, in addition to ordering from the dessert menu. The wait staff loves it because they get to eat anything left over at the end of lunch service. On the bottom are dishes of melon balls flavored with mint, pineapple, and flecks of vanilla bean; pear with anise. An apricot flan tart sits on a pedestal on the middle tier; on top is a *tarte Tatin* on a gold cardboard-lined plate.

"Make the raspberry look good," Johnny Iuzzini instructs Ariella as she arranges the garnish atop a raspberry tart.

"Yeahhhh," says Ariella.

"Yeahhhh," echoes Iuzzini.

"Yeahhhh."

Iuzzini spoons oranges infused with a light rosemary syrup into a crystal bowl. "I don't like my vegetables cooked," reflects Iuzzini. "I don't like my fruits touched. But this is what the chef likes."

Ariella slices the raspberry tart with an electric knife.

"You should use a cutting board," Iuzzini tells her.

Ariella now halves some strawberries to garnish the top of the tart. After a moment, she says, "Um, *chéri?*"

"*Oui, madame?*" says Iuzzini.

"There are too many holes in the tart. I don't think it looks nice." By *holes*, she means places where the raspberries aren't close enough together.

"Quarter the strawberries and put the quarters in the little holes," Iuzzini tells her. "Put them in with the stem on."

"Like this?"

"Cut side up," says Iuzzini.

"You're the boss," says Ariella. As pastry *sous-chef*, he's her supervisor.

"No," says Iuzzini, "I'm just a stupid pastry cook who got promoted." Now he shouts over to the runners: "I need three yellow napkins! I know you're very busy over there holding each other's penises, but . . . "

As Iuzzini folds the requested napkins, covering the top of the cart, Alex Lee comes and rubs Iuzzini's neck.

"Don't touch me!" yells Iuzzini. "I have witnesses! Sexual harassment!" Lee elbows him in the back.

"Johnny?" says Ariella. "How many pieces do you want this cut into? Ten?" It's a *tarte Tatin*.

"Eight," says Iuzzini. "Eight. Eight. Eight."

"Order one tartare, one risotto," calls Thompson, "followed by one scallop and one venison, medium-rare. Lamb and duck working good?"

"Yes, Chef!" calls Dan, the *saucier*.

All of a sudden, Michael Lawrence comes whooshing through, waving his arms frantically. "Health department is here! Health department is here!" he yells, running through the kitchen, then busting through the swinging door leading out, toward the prep kitchen.

Everyone snaps to attention. Bernard Vrod instructs a runner to wipe the faucets. Toques—the short, surgeon-type—go on everyone's heads. Like Christos of the kitchen, cooks pull long swaths of plastic film, covering meats, poultry, fish, and putting them into refrigerated units. Counters are wiped, water poured out, off-heat saucepans disappear.

When inspectors make their visits, they don't burst in through employee entrances or climb in through windows to catch unsuspecting line cooks sticking their fingers in the soup. They understand that their mission does not mandate disrupting business, so they enter, civilly, through the same door that guests use. They find a maître d' or manager—someone who seems to be in charge—or, failing that, a bartender. They show their badge and identification, explain the reason for their visit, and wait politely until they are shown into the kitchen and other areas they want to examine. Their Department of Health–issued jackets don't exactly enhance the ambiance, but *c'est comme ça*—perhaps that's why they aren't kept waiting too long.

Fay tells Dan to get rid of anything that's being held at a temperature lower than oven heat or over thirty degrees. In fact, she's right about the hot foods, which, according to the Environmental Health Service rules, must be held at or above 140 degrees Fahrenheit; for the cold foods, she's off by eight degrees, but fortunately she errs on the safe side: Cold foods must be held at or below 45 degrees Fahrenheit, except for smoked fish, which must be held below 38 degrees. Failure to do either constitutes a Class A violation, the most serious level of infraction.

"Okay!" yells Thompson as he puts on his toque. "No towels anywhere!"

The last time the health department visited Café Boulud during Thompson's tenure there, the restaurant was fined because Thompson was not wearing a toque. He found this ridiculous, since his head was shaved and couldn't possibly pose the risk of unsanitariness. However, according to one New York City Department of Health inspector, a Mr. Brisett, it is not only hairs falling into risotto that Environmental Health Services worries about, it is also sweat. Kitchens can be very hot, and in the press of service, he explains, they don't want a cook wiping his brow with the back of his hand as beads of sweat fly into the food. EHS is, however, liberal about the type of "hair restraint" that must be worn: "It doesn't matter," says Brisett, "it can be a baseball cap, anything."

Brett Traussi comes in from the dining room, taps the board at the pass for attention. "Is there any roast chicken or anything else out?" he yells. "Cover everything up!"

"We're in the middle of service," says Thompson, "so there are things that have to be out."

"No," says Traussi. "Nothing is allowed to be out."

Jed comes up, putting on a toque. He has a whole box of them for anyone who needs one.

Brett goes into the kitchen, points to the flame under the fish sauces in the warm *bain-marie*. "Full blast!" he says.

David, the maître d', brings in three Japanese customers. It's not exactly the moment.

Thompson says, "I need—"

"What do you need?" says Lawrence, back from the prep kitchen.

"Thermometer," says Thompson.

"I'll get it for you," says Lawrence.

"Order pree-fee tuna, soup, salad, followed by two pree-fee lamb, medium-rare," calls Thompson. "It's the last table, so . . . "

"Do you have everything?" Lawrence asks Iuzzini.

The inspector, Claudia Castro, a slight woman, about five-four, comes in, wearing jeans and a jacket that says NYC DEPT OF HEALTH, and in smaller letters, "Environmental Health Services." She goes into the kitchen, starts pulling open drawers, examining *bain-maries*. She looks up—she can't be more than twenty-seven years old.

Fay, who has pulled on a pair of latex gloves, yells, "How am I supposed to pick my nose?"

The inspector goes into the walk-in behind the fish station; Traussi follows her in. A little crash, as something breaks in the coffee area. At the pass, she touches some lightbulbs that are up underneath the board. Traussi unscrews one, at her request, then he introduces Alex Lee to the inspector.

Sliding tickets over on the board, Thompson watches her as she goes into the pastry service area.

In the pastry area, Iuzzini shows Castro the ice cream cabinets. Expressionless, she makes notes on a clipboard before inspecting the pastry sink. "Is this where they wash their hands?" she asks Traussi.

"This is really a production sink," answers Traussi. He points to the sink next to the water cooler. "That's where they wash their hands," he says.

Castro goes to look at it, scribbling on her clipboard, and she's gone—down to the prep kitchen.

When Castro files her report four days later, she issues four violations, including one Class B and three Class C and Class D. (Class D are the least egregious.) The Class B violations all fall under the heading of "Food Protection: Potential Contamination by Other Source," and letters D, E, and F are circled. Category D is "Food contact surface not properly maintained or not washed, rinsed and sanitized after each use and following any activity when contamination may have occurred." Surely no cross-contamination occurred—especially because Castro was in the kitchen; and in any case that's something the cooks are all pretty vigilant about. According to Inspector Brisett, that particular violation often means cutting boards that are pitted from use—a no-no. Category E is "Sanitized equipment or utensil, including in-use food dispensing utensil, improperly used or stored"—a classic: probably the spoons standing in water. And F is "Wiping cloths dirty or not stored in sanitizing solution."

The Class C and D violations are less exciting, though Castro does explicate them on the form:

CLASS C VIOLATIONS
12C. Light fixtures in serving counter and basement walk-in box noted unshielded to contain possible breakage.
12E. Lowboy refrigerators in pastry area not provided with thermometers.
12G. Wall in basement kitchen noted in disrepair.
13C. Test kit to measure concentration of sanitizer used to wash ice-cream machine not provided.

CLASS D VIOLATIONS

14C. "Wash hands" sign not posted at handwash sink in bsmt
     prep area.

14D. Resuscitation equipment not provided.

14E. Inspection report sign not posted.

15F. "No smoking" signs not posted.

   Although the violations may appear to be more numerous than four, EHS groups together all the letters within a particular number, so 12C, E, and G together count as one. And any violations grouped in number 15 involve "Distribution of Tobacco Products Through Vending Machines, Tobacco Product Regulation Act and Smoke-Free Air Act"; they are not counted in the total.

   Minor as they may be, there are a total of four violations, and so a hearing is scheduled for June 12. Not surprisingly, it is decided that rather than have Brett Traussi waste valuable time going downtown to the hearing—time that can be better spent improving the workings of the restaurant—Dinex will simply correct the violations and pay the full fine. After all, clean is one thing, and stellar is another.

Seven

COMMERCE

W HEN ONE SPENDS a great deal of time in the kitchen of an outstanding restaurant such as Daniel, one is apt to forget that one of the primary functions of any restaurant is to make money. Chefs and cooks do not approach their work as if it is merely a job; to all of them it is a way of life, and to the most dedicated of them, it's more like a calling. Walk through the swinging "out" door into the dining room, though, and it would take a concerted effort not to understand that what's going on is, indeed, commerce.

For while the management of Daniel makes a monumental effort to make guests feel *soigné,* in the minds of the waiters, the restaurant is about something else entirely: Even for those who are consummate professionals, this is still a job. At lunchtime their goal is to get through the lunch service, delivering meals as smoothly as possible; at dinner it is to turn the tables the appropriate number of times to keep pace with the reservation sheets—for a deuce, that means the guests had better be out of there in about an hour and a half.

At the end of each shift comes the reckoning. Each position is assigned a certain number of points: captains get six, assistants five, runners three and a half, and busboys two and a half. The sommelier gets four, and assistant sommelier three. Maître d's get five. The closing captain calculates the value of one point by first adding up the value of all the points on the floor during that shift, then tallying up all the tips. He then divides that total by the number of points. So if there are eighty points on the floor, the value of one point will be the value of the tips divided by eighty. These tips, however, are not distributed until the staff receive their weekly paycheck, since at Daniel, taxes are deducted from everything.

The accounting is done by the closing captain to keep everything above board and correct. Michael Lawrence keeps records on his computer using Microsoft Excel: one grid for credit-card gratuities and another for cash gratuities, and at the end of the week members of the wait staff are given a printout. Bruno Jamais and the sommeliers, who pocket quite a bit of "handshake" money, participate only in the credit-card tip pool, since their handshakes go directly into their pockets rather than into the cash pool.

Everyone on the wait staff earns the same base pay: $3.20 per hour less taxes. When a new server accepts a job at Daniel, he is always required to sign a tip declaration form, agreeing to report 18 percent of gross cash sales. Lawrence points out that it's for their own good, mindful of his own tax ordeal several years ago, when the IRS went after the dining room staff in a number of high-profile restaurants and an audit revealed that he owed $24,200. The initial amount he had underreported was far less than that, of course, but after penalties and interest were added, it represented quite a sum. He lets this serve as a cautionary tale for those who would play fast and loose with the taxman.

Of course, the key to commerce in this, or any, restaurant is how many covers can be served during a shift. The more covers served, the higher the profits for the restaurant and the higher the value of a point for the dining room staff. Ironically, the chefs (other than the chef-owner), cooks, dishwashers, and stewards who must contend with the increased workload and explosive pressure that come with a greater number of covers do not reap any additional financial reward.

Considering that there are often more people who wish to make reservations at Daniel than the restaurant can accommodate, especially on weekends, deciding where the cap on covers should be is a crucial decision, one that influences the livelihoods of many people. And it is this job that falls to Bruno Jamais.

Say it's Friday afternoon, and there are 325 reservations on the books for dinner. The phone keeps ringing in the reservation room, and there are still slots open, especially very early and late. The restaurant can handle up to 380 diners—that's about the breaking point, though Brett Traussi, for one, doesn't recommend even that many. More than that, and the service and cooking may be compromised. The reason Jamais is so good at what he does is his keen ability to overbook just enough to account for cancellations, packing the room as much as possible without putting it over the straining point. It is a very difficult business, and from Boulud's point of view, he would be hard-pressed to find someone who could do it as successfully as Jamais.

Because this, after all, is a business, one of the most important people in the restaurant is its chief financial officer, Marcel Doron. Born in Transylvania, Doron grew up speaking Romanian and Hungarian and eating spicy foods with lots of paprika. He spent seven years in Israel in his youth, then went to Germany, where he studied music for seven years, eventually becoming a concert violinist. He abandoned that career when he came to the U.S., where he attended business school, and eventually became a CPA.

Besides constantly monitoring the spending at Daniel, he also has to monitor what goes into his own mouth, for Doron loves to eat. "I love everything," he says, "that's my problem." Since starting to work for Dinex in 1993, he has gained forty pounds; he recently lost twenty-two and then gained back five. It's a constant struggle, and he doesn't have time to exercise. When he's nervous, he eats. If he has a difficult day or stays at work late and has a difficult night, he starts grabbing food, and everything tastes good. There was a time, a few months ago, when the kitchen would make him salads every day, but these days he's going for the harder stuff. To make his struggle all the more difficult, his office lies between the bread bakery and the chocolate lab.

But Doron doesn't allow his fondness for food to stand in the way of his ruling over the finances of the restaurant with an iron fist and remarkable precision. At any given moment, for instance, he knows the actual cost of one of the rolls he loves so much. This is more impressive than it sounds, for that price varies, not only according to the cost of ingredients, but also according to the season and how many are being served. As the heady yeasty scents waft into his tiny office, he thinks about the average cost of bread per cover: Back in February it was 74.7 cents. It is now May, and as they head into summer, when the restaurant is less busy and guests eat less bread, the bread cost rises—by July it will double because fewer rolls will be produced. Mark Fiorentino, the baker, and his assistant are both full-time employees, and their wages remain the same no matter how many rolls they produce. Economies of scale dictate that the labor cost per unit rises when fewer rolls are made. By September the bread costs will be back down to eighty-four cents per cover.

To arrive at this figure, Doron had to calculate Mark's earnings, including benefits. In September, the month before the study, he had made 172,000 units.

Dividing this number into Mark's compensation plus the cost of the ingredients gives Doron his unit cost.

What really interests Doron, though, is the average cost of bread over the course of a year. On a yearly basis, he wants the cost of bread per cover to average eighty-five cents. But not all bread is created equal. The ingredients for the walnut loaf, for instance, cost ninety-one cents, whereas ingredients for the rustic loaf are twenty-two cents, and for the multigrain, only seven and a half cents.

Then there is the question of waste, which of course everyone in the restaurant tries to minimize. Mark gets the number of reservations daily for the next day, and he tries to produce accordingly. For instance, if three hundred guests are expected for dinner, he'll make 240 of his signature focaccia rolls, along with about 120 olive rolls, 120 rustic rolls, and six dozen butter and salt rolls; 552 rolls in all, plus thirty-two loaves. But even when he thinks he has made the right number, the restaurant winds up with a bunch left over, and Boulud yells. Mark says, Yes, Chef, okay, Chef, I'll make fewer. And so he does, but then they don't have enough. Go figure.

People often assume that because high-end restaurants charge so much per plate, they're making a killing on every meal. And sometimes they are—but not always.

Those who work on the business end of restaurants, such as Lili Lynton, the Dinex Group's business consultant, think in terms of what is called "gross margin," a figure that represents a dish's menu price less the cost of the ingredients. At Daniel the gross margin runs at about 67 percent, which Lynton says is pretty typical. The actual cost of the food represents about 33 percent, or roughly one-third, of the price of a menu item.

To look at it another way, consider the cost of the protein element of one of Daniel's signature dishes. For the beef duo—roasted beef tenderloin and braised short ribs in red wine with celery, celery root puree, and black truffle, the meat itself (about eight and a half ounces) costs about $6.50. The rest of the ingredients would add up to about $3.50. The menu price for this item: thirty dollars.

And what does the other twenty dollars buy you?

The largest cost in the restaurant is not food, it's payroll—Daniel has between 140 and 150 employees. Laypeople tend to think wait staff doesn't cost the management anything, since the bulk of their pay comes from tips. Not so.

Beside the minimal base pay, Dinex also provides staff with individual health coverage, picking up 50 percent of the premium after three months of employment, 75 percent in the second year of employment, and full coverage after three years of service. Dinex wants permanent wait staff, and permanent wait staff needs benefits.

Next is rent. Daniel's off–Park Avenue address is among the most expensive real estate in the world.

Then there's advertising and promotion.

What Doron files under "other operating costs" makes up 15 percent of sales. Decor is a huge part of these costs. By the time it is open for a year and a half, Dinex will have spent 20 percent again of the original budget on new decorations for Daniel. The flower and plant budget alone is about $210,000 per year. Kitchen supplies, cleaning supplies, printing, telephone, utilities, equipment rental, credit-card service charges, liquor license fees, permits, repairs, uniforms, storage, legal and accounting fees, postage and messenger services, and so on fall into this category as well.

It's a complicated balancing act that Doron performs in trying to keep food costs at 33 percent. Life would be easier for him if Daniel were an Italian restaurant, for Italian cuisine has lower food costs, or if Daniel's rent were lower. He can't tell Lee to skimp on the quality of ingredients; Boulud would never accept that. However, he also realizes that no one wants to pay forty dollars for a pork dish. The way he sees it, Daniel has to remain competitive with other uptown operations. If a bistro around the corner charges twenty dollars for a steak and Daniel charges thirty, that's fine. A bistro is casual, and Daniel is grand dining. If, on the other hand, Jean Georges, a comparable type of establishment, charges twenty-five dollars for a steak and Daniel charges thirty, that's a problem. The only answer is to charge what the market can bear and the ingredients justify.

It is commonly said that restaurants make most of their money at the bar, and high-end restaurants without much bar business are presumed to have a difficult time succeeding financially. But Daniel does not want a lot of bar business, because a big bar business translates into a big bar scene. When guests at Daniel are seated in the lounge until their table is ready, they don't want to have to elbow their way to a bar stool—they want a quiet, sedate refuge in which to relax. The way Lynton sees it, the bar is a sort of buffer zone whose function is to be comfortable enough to discourage customers from leaving when they must wait for a table.

Yet Daniel is profitable—"very profitable," according to Lynton. Just how profitable, she won't say. In any case, the big bucks come from food and wine. Still, she's quick to point out that it's not run only as a business. "We're open to feed people," she says.

While money and financial concerns are obviously very important to Boulud, they do not by any means seem to be his primary or even secondary motivation as a restaurateur. The proceeds from his books, for instance, go back into the restaurant, though he'd have every right to pocket them.

Like many chefs, Boulud is a man who likes to feed people—to take care of people. It's an impulse that seems to come from rather deep inside, and there's a generosity of spirit there that goes along with it.

In any case, the last thing in the world Boulud would do is cut costs when it came to the quality of the ingredients.

To that end, rather than sending his stewards down to the Fulton Fish Market to barter, Boulud prefers to use a network of top-notch purveyors. The majority of the fish—all the cod, skate, halibut, monkfish, and peeky-toe crab, oysters, mussels, clams, and several European fish, as well as the smoked salmon and caviar—comes from Browne Trading Company, Rod Mitchell's company in Maine. A few other fish—Florida red snapper, for example—come from a different supplier, as do specialty items such as frogs' legs, which come from a source in Florida that sells nothing else. Most of the meats come from a few different farms in Pennsylvania and New York State, though Daniel does also use a few bulk purveyors. Most of the game comes from Ariane Daguin's company, D'Artagnan, for instance, and some of the meat comes from Di Bragga, a family-run business that has a good relationship with Boulud. These enterprises reserve their very best products for Daniel because, as D'Artagnan's Daguin puts it, "He is one of my best customers; he was one of my first customers, and, of course, he pays on time." Which is not necessarily the case with every restaurant of this caliber: Daguin's difficulties collecting payment from Bouley Bakery have forced her to file suit. In February 2001 an uncontested judgment will award Daguin $67,000 in the case.

Thursday, May 11

IT'S A GLOOMY day for spring, wet, gray, and heavy, but if you work downstairs at Daniel, whether in the prep kitchen, bread bakery, chocolate lab, or business offices, you'd forget the weather soon after coming to work, since all are at basement level and therefore windowless.

And there is yet another floor below this one—the "cellar." It is on this floor that the restaurant stores its supplies. Locked caged shelves hold endless bottles of condiments, dry goods, and so forth—Colavita extra-virgin olive oil in one-liter bottles and five-liter jugs, bottles of French walnut oil, sherry vinegar, red-wine vinegar, Banyuls wine vinegar, aged balsamic vinegar, domestic red *verjus* in one-liter boxes, French white *verjus* in bottles, small cellophane bags of polenta, large plastic bags of *sel gris* (gray sea salt), square boxes of Kosher salt, cylindrical boxes of sea salt, burlap bags of basmati rice, huge paper sacks of flour, boxes of couscous, boxes of green lentils from France *(les vrais lentilles du Puy, appellation d'origine contrôlée)*, cartoonishly big cans of Redpack tomato paste (six-liter, fifteen-ounce size), jars of Maille mustard, Maille cornichons, Ligurean black olive paste, green peppercorns, pickled ginger, bottles of ketchup (Heinz, of course), twenty-five bottles of Angostura bitters. Next to that is a tall refrigerated unit with clear windows that holds the cheese. To the right are five-pound bags of coffee beans (La Colombe 100 percent Arabica, Monte Carlo blend), six-pound bags of espresso beans (Moka d'Oro), teas galore in tins from Harney & Sons, plastic Ziploc bags from In Pursuit of Tea, boxes from Republic of Tea, as well as cans of black truffles from Urbani and glass tubes of saffron. All the way to the left are the pastry stores: oversize cans of cashews and pistachios from Bazzini, tubs of almond paste, cans of whole chestnuts and chestnut paste, bottles of raspberry extract, enough Valrhôna chocolate to supply heaven for the next three months, tubs of cocoa butter, boxes of Minute Rice, jumbo Turkish apricots, dark brown and confectioners' sugar, big cans of Libby's pumpkin puree.

A small room to the side contains all the linens—tablecloths, napkins, and the like, as well as chef pants, jackets, aprons, and side-towels—all of which are sometimes piled in a hopeless jumble. Mauricio, a steward, takes care of all these linens, bundling the chef outfits into packages of three, all in the proper sizes, for each cook. Like all the other rooms down here, this one is kept locked.

Next to the linen room is the wine cellar. Its lack of windows may make it a little claustrophobic, but there is no place that Jean-Luc Le Dû would rather spend his time.

When he came to the U.S. in the mid-1980s, at the age of nineteen, Le Dû wouldn't have guessed that a restaurant basement is where he would wind up. Originally from Brittany, Le Dû was an aspiring rock musician. His first home in the U.S. was Miami, where he played guitar for a band. He stumbled into the world of wine by accident when he tasted a bottle of 1964 Cheval Blanc and was utterly smitten. When he came to New York in the late 1980s and went to work as a waiter at the restaurant Bouley, his nascent interest in wine quickly turned into a passion, and Le Dû began studying wine, buying as much as he could for his personal cellar. As it happened, a serious interest in wine was shared by other waiters at Bouley, who would get together on their days off to cook and taste wines. One of them has since become sommelier at Le Bernardin, another at Aureole. Le Dû went to work at the old Daniel in 1996, starting as a captain; in early 1997 he became sommelier. That year he won first prize for the northeastern U.S. in a sommelier competition sponsored by SOPEXA, the trade organization known as Food and Wines from France; in the ensuing national competition, he took third place.

The sommelier of an important restaurant such as Daniel generally has a two-part job. One is to oversee the wine service, assist customers with their wine choices, maintain the cellar and the lists, and so forth. The other is to buy.

Le Dû loves to buy wine. He's constantly on the prowl, traveling to wine regions, going to tastings, attending auctions. At the old Daniel, Le Dû handled the job of sommelier by himself, keeping about 350 wines on the list, and between five and six thousand bottles in the cellar.

Here he has an assistant, Olivier. Le Dû prefers staying in the cellar buying and selling to working in the dining room, an activity he leaves largely to Olivier, who was previously assistant sommelier at Raymond Blanc's restaurant in England, Le Manoir aux Quat' Saisons. Olivier has worked out well because even though he's not what Le Dû describes as a "wine head," he's great with the customers. "When I spoke with Olivier," Le Dû recalls of their interview, "you could feel he'd take good care of people. I was lucky."

In a typical year, Le Dû makes three trips to wine regions, usually combining vacations with work. In July he'll go to Napa for a few days, then on to Oregon for the Pinot Noir Festival, and then to Washington State. A month and a half ago, Le Dû visited Bordeaux and Burgundy to taste the 1999 vintage. (Verdict: The Burgundy is good; Bordeaux is very nice.) Happily, the prices of French wines are much lower this year. Producers lowered them by about 10 percent because of a general outcry against the ridiculously escalating prices of the previous few years. Not surprisingly, it is these two regions that are the backbone of Daniel's wine list. The seven-hundred-square-foot cellar consists of about eighteen-thousand bottles. It's well organized, having been designed by Le Dû himself, along with Brett Traussi, in advance of the restaurant opening.

Le Dû takes great pleasure in showing a guest around his cellar. Like many wine lovers, he enjoys simply looking at a great bottle, maybe stroking it a little, thinking about what's inside.

All the dessert wines are half-bottles. Nifty.

Ah, look there: several bottles of 1937 Domaine Romanée-Conti from an auction in Chicago. A couple magnums of "Cros Parantoux" 1988 from Domaine Henri Jayer. Some 1920 Château Latour. Six bottles of 1928 Cos d'Estournel—a stellar second-growth from an extraordinary vintage—purchased directly from the château. Some old Gajas from Italy. On another row, some 1983 Weinbach Gewürztraminer, and some white Burgundies from Domaine Michel Niellon—to Le Dû's mind, the best producer in Chassagne.

Le Dû keeps close track of every one of these almost eighteen-thousand bottles on his computer. Each entry lists a bin number, the number of bottles that should be there, the vineyard, the name, the cost per case.

Restaurateurs are in the habit of telling the public that they generally price wines at 250 percent of wholesale—in other words, that a bottle they purchased for $10 would be listed at $25. Assuming that the wholesale price was 70 percent of suggested retail (in fact, it ranges from 65 percent to 75 percent), that same bottle would cost $14.25 in a typical wine shop, so the restaurant's price would be 1.75 times, or 175 percent, that of retail. But the public often has the impression that the markup is higher. Here at Daniel it wouldn't be wrong: The price of every bottle is multiplied by 325 percent on average. That means that a bottle for which Le Dû paid $10 would sell for $32.50, or slightly more than 2.25 times what it would cost at retail. This is not true of every wine, but prices are set with that number in mind. An exception would be very expensive wines and rare wines, which are set at market price, depending on the scarcity of the wine. With these, sometimes the restaurant's purchase price bears no real relationship to what the wine is worth. Case in point: a 1994 Turley-Hayne zinfandel. In a retail store, it would cost between $150 and $180. On Daniel's wine list it's $218, less than 150 percent of the average retail price. But Le Dû bought them two years ago for $54 a bottle, so his markup here, while very reasonable vis-à-vis the retail price, is actually 400 percent of what he originally paid. In this case everyone wins, especially because that bottle requires no more upkeep than any other.

Restaurateurs are also in the habit of being a little bit touchy when it comes to defending their pricing of wine, protesting, for instance, that expensive glassware is needed to show off the wines—glassware that is easily broken. At

Daniel, however, Le Dû fell in love with a line of glasses made by the German company Spiegelau; these cost only approximately six dollars apiece.

In general, while diners tend to understand that highly skilled labor, and even artistry, are required to prepare the food and therefore they're willing to accept the idea of paying a high price for it, with wine, the attitude changes. After all, the cork is pulled and it's poured. Why should people pay such a premium?

What they don't think about is what it costs the restaurateur to store the wine. Wine takes up a lot of space, and in a city such as New York, rents are at a premium. Upkeep is significant. The temperature and humidity must be controlled. Financially, it's a pretty big burden to keep that much money tied up in inventory—this cellar holds almost $800,000 worth of wine. That's $800,000 that isn't earning any interest (though most of it is gaining in value). All this contributes to the cost of the wine in your glass.

That, and the fact that the controller has determined that he needs a certain profit margin on the wine.

For a restaurant like Daniel, it's quite important to have a world-class cellar, so Boulud has been very aggressive in his wine program. Which couldn't make Le Dû happier.

A delivery comes in. The delivery person, a Chinese man who speaks little English, pushes in five heavy cartons stacked on a dolly. He has brought them down from street level in the freight elevator. After Le Dû signs for it, he must decide what section it should go in. He consults his computer.

The wine is a 1994 red Bordeaux. "Check me on 8455, please," Le Dû tells David, his cellar steward. 8455 is the bin number; it appears next to the name of the wine on the wine list as well. "And look at the same time to see if there are any open spots. The cellar is getting a little cramped."

"We could issue 8455," says David.

"For five cases," says Le Dû.

"Well, we're going to have to move just a couple of sections," says David, "but we can do it."

Le Dû enters the name of the wine in the computer—Château Pavie-Macquin, and then a series of numbers: 425 12. That means he paid $425 for a case of twelve. 35.42 3.25 115.12 123. That means per bottle he paid $35.42, multiplied by 3.25 makes $115.12. But $115.12 looks less than graceful on a menu, so he rounds it up to a more elegant $123. Next is a line that reads: "Profit expressed as $ per bottle." Le Dû enters *$87.58*. No explanation necessary.

He writes on a pad: *Pavie 94. Price 123*. Later he'll enter it on Tolman's computer upstairs; it will be on the list tonight.

Later, Le Dû does a tasting in the cellar with Deirdre Ledwitz, a sales rep from Martin Scott, a top wine importer, and Jean-Noël Fourmeaux, owner (with his wife, Marketta) of Château Potelle, a California winery Ledwitz represents. They sit in folding chairs around a small table in Le Dû's tiny office at the entryway of the cellar. Ledwitz pours him a Château Potelle sauvignon blanc, a chardonnay V.G.S., and then a Potelle 1997 Old Vine zinfandel. "This is a picture of the vineyard at seven in the morning," Fourmeaux tells Le Dû, showing him a photo. "We have longer sun exposure, but we have a longer growing season." Le Dû sticks his nose all the way in the glass, inhales. Then swirls and tastes. The wine is plummy and rustic. He then pours a cab, and then a new release called Epice. "It's a field blend made by accident," Fourmeaux explains. *"Viognier, gewürz, chard. Il a le nez de gewürz, la bouche de chard."* It has the nose of a Gewürztraminer, the palate of a chardonnay. "And the finish of a viognier," he adds in English.

After he has tasted everything and Fourmeaux has excused himself to go to another meeting, Le Dû points to the chardonnay V.G.S. The initials stand for, believe it or not, "Very Good Shit." "How much is that?" asks Le Dû.

"Thirty-two," says Ledwitz, then she does some quick calculations out loud. "Three hundred seventy-six"—that's the case price—"thirty-one dollars a bottle." She points to the Epice. "And this is twelve."

"I'll take this Epice and I want to re-taste this," he says, pointing to the zinfandel. "What do you think of the sauvignon blanc?"

"I think the price is good," she says. "A hundred and four dollars. Want to take twenty?"

"I'll take two," he says.

"Three?"

"I have not the money right now," says Le Dû.

"Could you do it by the glass?"

"No."

"Pourquoi?"

"Parce que. Because it's not a spring wine."

"It'll take me a week or two," she says. "I'm holding Napa Valley Wine Company for you. I think I have ten left."

This is the game: If you want this, you've got to take that, too.

Le Dû eyes her watch. "You must be doing quite well," he says. "You're wearing the Bulgari watch. Life is good in the wine business."

"I didn't buy it," she says. "A friend bought it for me. We saw it together in the Place Vendôme."

"Does he want to be friends with me?" quips Le Dû.

"Does *she?*"

"Is she pretty?" he asks.

"She's not your type," says the rep. "She's not high upkeep."

Round one has been won by Ledwitz.

Ding! On to round two.

"Do you want Dominique Laurent?" asks the rep.

"I can get it," says Le Dû.

"How can you get it?" she asks.

"I'll bring it in myself," he says. "Or through a broker."

Ledwitz looks alarmed. "I don't know if you can do that," she says, looking him right in the eye. "We have exclusivity in the U.S."

Le Dû, it seems, has won round two.

The rep, hopping from one foot to another, as it were, punches the air a couple times, then jumps back in. "I'm just gonna warn you," she says, "there's not gonna be a '99 for us if you don't take '98. I just have to tell you that."

"Then it's not gonna be Martin Scott for us."

"Have you told that to Anne-Claude Leflaive?" Leflaive is one of the top Burgundy producers, imported by Martin Scott.

"In the end," says Le Dû, "I'm the one who's paying for the ego of all those winemakers. Whether it's in France—"

"So why don't you buy chardonnay V.G.S.?" asks the rep.

"Because I don't think it's worth thirty-one dollars. I have to sell it for too much. I like all the V.G.S."

"So no Leflaive," says the rep. "Paradigm merlot and Dehlinger chardonnay?"

"How much is the Paradigm?"

"Three hundred and sixty."

"Three-sixty? I'd like five cases, if I could."

"Five," repeats the rep. "It's really allocated. I don't know if I can give you five, but I can ask. The Dehlinger chardonnay is two hundred and forty."

"Okay," says Le Dû. "How many can I get?"

"You can probably get five."

"What about pinot noirs from Dehlinger?"

"Not yet," says the rep. "Not until the fall."

"Okay," says Le Dû.

"You need anything else?"

At the end of the encounter, it seems Ledwitz has taken the match, though it's a close one. Le Dû's jabs below the belt didn't particularly impress the judges, though his Dominique Laurent offense showed pluck. But Ledwitz's endurance earned points; playing the Leflaive trump showed finesse, and she walked away with some good sales.

It has often been observed that New York passes directly from winter to scorching summer, with hardly a day of anything resembling spring. But Monday, May 15, is a gorgeous spring morning. At the Union Square farmers' market, forty-eight blocks downtown from Daniel as the crow flies, a woman in a black skirt, oversized goggle-glasses, and a double strand of giant pearls stands in front of Maxwell's Farm regarding the "fresh-picked asparagus" promised on the sign. A guy dressed entirely in tennis-ball yellow, complete with fluorescent helmet, whizzes by on Rollerblades. Farmers wait underneath peaked white tents. It's nine A.M., a good time to shop at the market. Across Broadway, people come out of a McDonald's, having grabbed their furtive Egg McMuffins on the way to the office. Everyone's going uptown, some stopping in the corner deli for a regular joe.

Although Wednesday is the day chefs really converge on the market, on this morning, Brad Thompson emerges from the subway, checking things out. He tries to come once a week—either by himself or with Jed. As he looks around, he's a little surprised that the pickings are slimmer than usual for the time of year; he had thought there'd be a wider selection of produce in the market by now. As usual, the restaurant isn't far from Thompson's thoughts. He hasn't had a day off in a few weeks. On Saturday two new guys trained. Jed handles all the résumés and sets up guys to trail, bringing them to the attention of Alex Lee or Thompson, who give input. Thompson always looks first at the candidate's knife skills, then whether he works clean, whether he knows what he's doing. He can usually tell in a half hour whether someone's going to make it. The recruit trails for five days, then Lee or Thompson find out how much money they want. Thompson was impressed lately by a recent CIA grad. He worked clean, presented himself well, stayed busy all day. He never brought up money. When the first thing a prospective cook brings up is money, that's a sure sign to Thompson that his head's not in the right place, though no one knows better than he how hard it is for cooks because it's so expensive to live in New York. They just have to understand that for the first year or two out of school, they're just not going to make much money.

Thompson looks around to see whether there's anything he should pick up for the DreamWorks party to be held at Daniel tomorrow: five hundred people celebrating Woody Allen's new movie. Allen and Steven Spielberg are both supposed to be there. The chefs started doing some of the prep on Saturday, including making the short ribs; today they'll do the *mise en place,* cook the lobster and take it out of the shell, tomorrow they'll make the soups. Then there's the French guards—the Grenadiers de Napoléon—who are in town to promote Delta Airlines's inaugural flight of its new New York–Lyons route, and tourism to the surrounding Rhône-Alpes region. Boulud suggested to Thompson that it might be cool to feed them on the sidewalk during lunch tomorrow. For Mother's Day yesterday Boulud and other French chefs participated in a pétanque game in Central Park, as the *grenadiers* and news cameras looked on.

Thompson inspects some organic herbs, but nothing inspires a purchase today—it's still a little early in the season for the really exciting ingredients—so he heads uptown empty-handed.

The following day, the entry on the weekly schedule reads: "1:00 sidewalk picnic lunch for 60 GRENADIERS DE NAPOLEON (Rhône-Alpes promo). See DB—no reimbursement??????" In other words, Boulud intends to treat all sixty of them to lunch. Never mind that it's the same day that five hundred people are taking over the restaurant. The entire staff will be in at five P.M. to work the party tonight, which begins at nine P.M.

It's ten in the morning and a dozen *plateaux* are lined up on the pass, where a runner polishes them.

Damien peels asparagus in the *garde-manger.* Allannic cooks one huge pot of *mirepoix* and another full of tomato, onion, tripe cut into two-inch squares, lots of sliced garlic, bouquet garni.

David trims salsify.

On the pass sits a big stainless-steel cylinder of "red-wine redux" on ice; a crate of Del Cabo organic English peas, thirty pounds, product of Mexico, from Jacobs Farms/Del Cabo–Pescadero, California; and half-cooked risotto spread on a parchment-lined sheet pan. Next to that Frédéric Côte spoons black truffles out of a fourteen-ounce can from Urbani, a New York–based importer. He chops them, holding the tip of his German knife with his ring finger for the best rocking motion, then smoothes them off the knife with his finger.

German, still in street clothes—designer jeans and a shirt tucked in—polishes silver trays.

Damien ties bundles of asparagus of uniform length with white string.

Kevin spreads microgreens in a hotel pan, covering them with a few layers of paper towels. He won't wash the microgreens because they contain a lot of herbs, which break and bruise when you wash them.

Umberto, an assistant captain, folds a large doily, then places it on the dessert cart. The twenty-three-year-old from Acapulco is working an "opening" schedule. The "openings" come in at ten A.M., bringing all the china into the dining room and wiping it down with vinegar wipes; setting the tables; draping the *guéridons* with tablecloths and stocking them with wine coasters, salt and pepper sets, six-inch plates for guests who skip a course, and so on. The "guards" and "closings" come in at eleven; they're responsible for linen requisitions, resetting the dining room for dinner, wrapping up the cheese and cleaning the cheese cart, putting all the flowers in the walk-in. Umberto's last job, where he stayed nine months, was as a front waiter at Gramercy Tavern.

Now Côte makes a mayonnaise in a huge stainless-steel bowl, whisking in truffle oil with a wire whip; the olive oil he used was an extra-virgin Sinolea.

On the hot-apps side of the induction range, a medium saucepan of blood orange juice is reducing, next to five bundles of asparagus simmering in plenty of water. On the side are many more bundles of green asparagus.

It's 11:50; in ten minutes the first reservations will be seated. Frank boils sugar snap peas in a huge pot for the chilled five-pea soup with rosemary cream. *Bain-maries* full of ice await them. The five peas include these sugar snaps, snow peas, pea leaves, fava beans (okay, so they're not peas . . .), and frozen English peas, which make up about 20 percent. "They're actually better for soup," Frank explains. "When they're flash-frozen, they're sweeter than anything else."

Gordito (the dishwasher) mops the floor next to the bread station. Olivier comes around the corner, carrying a plastic crate containing a dozen full bottles. He slips on the wet floor, taking a dive. Nothing breaks—he's okay.

Five minutes later, and there's total silence as everyone finishes *mise en place*. Normally everyone's reasonably jovial at this hour, but between the sixty *grenadiers* and the five hundred VIPs at tonight's party, everyone's a tad edgy.

Outside on the sidewalk in front of the restaurant, preparations are under way for the *grenadiers'* picnic. "They're all French," says Brett Traussi to David, the maître d', "so we should put out ashtrays. And I was going to steal six flower arrangements from the restaurant, and then we have to skirt these garbage cans."

It's amazing the transformations restaurant people achieve with the most banal tools. White linen is wrapped around garbage cans for a *soigné* look. Cheap, round, chest-high plastic occasional tables are draped with tablecloths that sweep the ground, conferring instant elegance (these tables are perfect height for a walk-around party). Eight-foot-long folding tables are covered to the ground, hiding cheap metal legs. On top of them, upside-down stockpots, covered with white cloth, give the table height for presentation.

Six bottles of white wine (Alois Lageder Benefizium Porer Pinot Grigio Alto Aldige 1998) and seven bottles of red (Tardieu-Laurent Les Grands Augustins Vin de Pays d'Oc 1998) stand next to dozens of plastic wineglasses; there are plates, napkins, and so forth. Big bottles of Evian are on ice.

"You've got the tarts, right?" says maître d' David.

"We have some sliced meats," says Traussi, "so you probably need some platters."

A passerby looks on with interest. "You just let us know what time, and we'll be here," he says.

"We'll let you know," says David.

Back in the kitchen, Boulud has arrived. "Go downstairs for the five hundred," he tells Thompson. "I'll do the pass."

"*Tu veux toujours les* bamboo mats *pour les* sushi?" Lee asks Boulud. Do you still want the bamboo mats for the sushi?

Boulud nods, then turns back to Thompson. "Anything low on lunch?" he asks.

"No," says Thompson. "Everything's fine. We've got plenty of everything."

"So what did he say?" Lee asks Neil Gallagher. "Does he want you up here or down there?"

"Here, I think," says Gallagher.

"Hamachi," says Boulud. "Let's go. We've got five hundred coming tonight. I think we should make a citrus—"

"But you don't want to make it too far ahead," Lee interjects. "I'll do it. I've got some good soy sauce."

"Ten lime, five lemon, five orange," says Boulud. *"Basilic, un peu, aussi?"* A little basil?

"Basilic, cilantro," says Lee.

"Après ça," says Boulud.

"Zest and juice," says Gallagher.

"Not a lot of zest," says Lee. "And some grated ginger."

"Ginger," says Boulud, "we've got one cup of soy sauce. Lemongrass."

"Je ne sais pas," says Lee. "Lemongrass will be strong. We'll do the marinade and then use it tonight."

"What else?" says Boulud. "Some chiles?"

"Actually," says Lee, "you know what you do? See if the guy has some sambal downstairs. It's really good. And some olive oil."

"Put some sugar in it, maybe," says Boulud.

"We'll definitely need it," agrees Lee. "It'll be too acidic."

"What we should do is slice that fish. Or chop it maybe?"

"You could chop it," says Lee, "but if it's chopped, it's gonna be a pile of chopped hamachi. It's not gonna be a lot."

Boulud is confident enough in his own talent to work comfortably with someone as gifted as Lee. That's part of his genius as a chef: that he knows exactly whom to listen to (not that there are many around him who would dare to contradict him). And his respect for Lee is colossal; Boulud believes that Lee has the magic touch. All things being equal between certain chefs— knowledge, technique, experience, and so forth—there are still some who simply shimmer with talent, and anything they cook will be delicious. Part of it is infallible intuition; palate comes into play as well. Boulud shares the trait with his gifted protégé.

Behind them, Frank breaks an eared soup cup. *"Pardon,* Chef," he says.

"Twenty dollars each," says Boulud, not even turning around. Then to Lee: "If we cut it in dice, it'll be a little better. And then after that we do the leftover tuna. Three raw fish: hamachi, tuna, salmon. Three tartare things, non?"

"Salmon?" says Lee.

"Why not?" says Boulud. "What time are we dressing up the plates?"

"It depends," says Lee. "Some things don't look nice if they're done too far ahead."

Downstairs, Zohar, the Israeli banquet cook, purees pea soup in an enormous stockpot on the floor, using a Dynamic SMX6000 "hand blender." It's 115 volts and 600 watts, and it reaches to her hip. It looks like a jackhammer and makes almost as much noise. A big splash of heavy cream goes in, a few grinds of pepper, and a few drops of—gasp—green food coloring.

Thomas Haas walks by and points to some frogs' legs that Lupe is prepping. "This is bad," he says. An anti-French remark is coming, no doubt; a frog joke. "In Germany you would go to jail for that."

Outside in the fresh air of Sixty-fifth Street, things are shaping up. The table nearest the restaurant entrance has turned into a spectacular buffet: a silver tureen of radishes, beautifully scored, along with a small dish of salt with a sign that says FLEUR DE SEL, sweet butter piped into little ramekins, compound butters, complete with signs: BEURRE CORNICHON, BEURRE MOUTARDE, BEURRE ECHALOTTE. A basket of the restaurant's signature bread, focaccia. Pasta salad with fat shrimp. A big wooden bowl full of curried chicken salad decorated with a purple cluster of chive blossoms and chervil. Braised artichoke hearts. Caprese salad of tomato, mozzarella, and basil. Smoked salmon garnished with lime. Sliced meats. Baskets of rolls. Philippe Rispoli arranges the serving dishes for maximum effect. Bundles of raw white and green asparagus serve as the perfect seasonal decoration, tied with elegant narrow ribbons imprinted with DANIEL BOULUD DANIEL BOULUD DANIEL BOULUD and balanced in pots of geraniums, along with shiny peppers of yellow and red, long purple eggplants, squashes. The large glass awning over the entrance shields this all from the sun. Desserts have appeared on a table all the way to the right, near the employee entrance: fruit salad, apple tart, pistachio tart, chocolate tart, lemon tart. This is Boulud's idea of a "casual picnic."

"The problem is that the *grenadiers* got a lot of press yesterday on TV," says Traussi, "so I don't think they'll get a lot of press today." Still, Traussi knows as well as anyone that although Boulud enjoys press coverage, that's not why he's doing this. The reason is simple: Boulud loves to feed people, and these guys are from Lyons. For most people, such hospitality would be extraordinary. For Boulud, *c'est normal.*

Two restaurant patrons, an elderly man and a younger woman, approach the entrance. "How are you?" the gentleman says to David.

"Good," says David.

"What's going on here?" he asks.

"A party."

A cook comes out with a large bowl of *pommes sarladaises*.

"*Plus gros, non?*" says Philippe. Perhaps it should be bigger.

"*Qu'est-ce que tu veux?*" says the cook, meaning, roughly, Give me a break. He places the *pommes* over a Bunsen burner.

A tall woman walks by with a bull terrier clenching a tennis ball in its mouth.

Traussi can't help but think about the laws they're violating: health department, liquor laws, Bureau of Traffic. When Boulud came up with this idea, Traussi was on vacation, or else he would have had something to say about it.

"Do you know what else we need?" says David. "I forgot the salt and pepper."

"Just the little ones?" asks a runner.

"Yeah," says David.

Bruno Jamais comes out the revolving door periodically, just to see what's going on. Across the street a guy on the third floor of a run-down townhouse leans on his elbow, looking out the window. Next door, scaffolding covers the facade of another townhouse; construction has been going on there for what seems like forever, much to Boulud's chagrin.

Michael Lawrence comes out, looks things over. "Shouldn't we have an espresso spoon in here?" he asks, regarding the regular teaspoon in the *fleur de sel*.

"No, they like a lot of salt, those people in France," says David.

"Mmm, that's my favorite," says Lawrence. "Our chicken salad."

"So where do we sign up for lunch?" says a passerby. Everyone's a comedian.

"Shouldn't there be some balsamic vinegar for the salad?" asks David, ignoring the passerby. "There's only olive oil."

A cop starts toward them from Park Avenue. Just what Traussi has been dreading.

"Uh-oh," says David. "Here comes the fuzz."

"Is this the party for the U.N.?" says the officer as he approaches.

"No," says David, cool. "It's a charity benefit."

"So it has nothing to do with the U.N.?"

David shakes his head. Doesn't a New York cop know he's twenty blocks and several avenues away from the U.N.?

The cop walks away, looking confused.

Jed sticks his head out the service door. A guy with a dolly stacked with boxes of mushrooms comes walking down Park Avenue, making the right onto Sixty-fifth Street. He backs into the receiving door.

"What's this for?" asks a guy walking down the street as he heads toward the buffet.

"It's for you!" says Edouard, an office intern from France.

"Really?" says the guy.

Edouard works for Anthony Francis, the head of banquets, in his office. But to earn extra money, he also works helping out serving banquets and even cooking with Philippe Rispoli. He would have loved to learn to cook, doing a kitchen internship instead, but his friends who are doing that have parents who can send them money. Edouard's parents are both writers and don't have the means, so he's working in service instead. Edouard's mother is from Martinique and his father is from France, and he spent five months a year in Martinique until he was twelve. The summer before last he worked at Paul Bocuse.

At one-thirty, a taxi pulls up, and four *grenadiers* jump out. One puts his hat on a tall side-table. The trunk pops open; it's full of more hats. They go onto the heads of the *grenadiers;* swords go into sheaths at their sides.

Bernard Vrod comes out of the restaurant, hands on hips, to regard the scene.

A woman passes by. "Oh, look at this!" she exclaims. She pats Vrod's arm as she walks by—obviously a regular.

"How are you?" he says. "Good to see you!"

One *grenadier* runs up and smells the hydrangea, dramatically.

German, who has just been promoted from expediter to assistant captain, stands at attention next to one of the serving tables. Another *grenadier* notices him and can't bear not to crack a joke inspired by German's military posture. *"C'est moi qui suis le grenadier,"* he yells gleefully, *"et c'est toi qui es le garçon!"* Part of the joke is that one would never call a waiter *garçon* in this type of establishment. German takes it in stride. *"Tu comprends le français?"*

"Non," says German.

Georgette comes out and greets the *grenadiers,* smiling warmly. Now a tour bus pulls up, full of *grenadiers.* Across the street, five ragged construction workers eat boxed lunches on the stoop, asbestos masks on their heads.

"I thought I had seen it all," says Vrod as the *grenadiers* step off the bus. They're quite a sight with their elaborate soldier costumes, tall hats, sabers.

Ariella, stepping out for some air on a short break, takes in the sight. She had no idea this was going on. "Did Daniel *hire* these people?" she asks, stunned.

"No," says Vrod.

"Who *are* they?" she asks.

"We're feeding them," says Vrod.

"Is this like primitive France or something?" she asks.

The *grenadiers* salute as they disembark the bus. Eight guards line up along either side of the entryway to the restaurant. Some of them are women in period garb. Some have musical instruments. Some are dressed as nobility. The bus driver opens the luggage compartment in the belly of the bus, revealing more musical instruments.

In the kitchen, Boulud works the pass, heedless of what's going on outside. "A paupiette right now," he says. "Give me a lobster risotto with a lobster salad. Give me a paupiette right away, okay? For table 61. You can fire two paupiette together—two."

He goes to the meat station. Cyrille Allannic plates lamb on the pass. "Hello," says Allannic. "Medium-rare, medium."

"Okay, risotto, tartare gone?" says Boulud.

"Working! Working!" call the hot-apps and *garde-manger* cooks.

"Tartare and a crab tasting, please!" calls Boulud, and he hands the pass over to Allannic.

Soon the *grenadiers* line up across the street, playing a march, as Boulud appears outside. The construction workers look on, baffled, as Boulud stands in the middle of Sixty-fifth Street, nodding his approval, Napoléon inspecting the troops. When they're finished playing, he goes down the line, greeting each one in turn.

After the *grenadiers* go into the restaurant and march around the dining room, much to the amusement of the lunch guests, it's 2:05, and they come back out for their own lunch. One of them yells out, *"Bon appétit!"* and they fall hungrily upon the food.

Eight

WANDERLUST

NEW YORK CITY has its own seasons; rather than following the almanac, summer is framed on one side by Memorial Day and on the other by Labor Day. Between these holiday weekends, offices curtail their workweek to summer hours, which for many—just about everyone in the publishing business, for instance—means half days on Friday. Come Friday afternoon, everyone's on their way out of town, up the Hudson, down the coast, or—for a large part of Daniel's clientele in particular—eastward to the Hamptons. The slack that is created by vacationing New Yorkers, though, is more than taken up by visitors to New York City.

It's the first week of June, and Boulud has a good deal of travel on his agenda for the summer. First stop is Brazil, where he'll teach a cooking class at a culinary school, judge a professional cooking competition, visit the central market in São Paulo, lunch with chefs, friends, and press, and attend a twentieth-anniversary gala dinner given by *Vogue* Brazil. Early next month he'll go to Jackson Hole, Wyoming, to cook at a benefit for the Grand Teton Music Festival; at the end of July, he'll go to France for two weeks, where he'll join his wife, Micky, and daughter, Alix, who will be there for a month and a half. Georgette Farkas is skeptical about these plans. "He'll never stay away that long," she predicts.

No question that Boulud has had to make tremendous sacrifices in his personal life in order to achieve what he has. The long hours that he spends in the restaurant leave little time for his wife and daughter. The sacrifice that sometimes feels the most significant to him, however, is not being able to travel as much as he'd like. China, India, Japan—all these destinations hold powerful allure for Boulud, who's never visited them. He dreams of playing midnight golf in Iceland. Still, if pressed, Boulud would say he has gotten more than he has given up. Being in the restaurant every night, surrounded by people and immersed in that world, happens to be the greatest pleasure in his life. He feels fortunate that Micky is so tolerant and independent; still, if he were home every night, he doubts their marriage would have lasted. It's not that he wouldn't be able to spend that much time with Micky (or she with him); rather that he has never conceived of a life as a "normal" husband, working until six or seven, coming home, and then, what, cooking together? Such a picture of conventional domesticity just isn't Boulud. Plus, he sees the distance between them as helpful in their relationship.

For her part, when Micky met Boulud in 1984, she had no idea what the life of a chef was about. She was born in Lausanne, Switzerland, to a French mother and an American filmmaker father, who created documentaries for the International Rescue Committee. Micky's father moved the family to Princeton, New Jersey, when she was a year old, and then a few years later to New York City, where he switched gears and took a position as a banker with First Boston. Micky's mother stayed home and cared for her and her two sisters; the girls attended the Fleming School, an erstwhile French school in Manhattan. When she was seven or eight, her parents divorced, and her mother moved Micky and her sisters back to Lausanne. Micky finished her schooling there, including university, earning a master's degree in clinical psychology. After working for a year in Geneva, counseling inmates of a prison for juvenile delinquents, she moved for a year to Paris, where she practiced family and couples therapy. When she was twenty-five, she moved back to New York City to do some advanced training at the Ackerman Institute for Family Therapy, intending to return to Lausanne, where a job awaited her. It was then, having a late dinner one night with her family and a few friends at a little jazz boîte-restaurant called Chelsea Place, a spot frequented late at night by chefs after service, that she met Boulud. One of the friends at her table was the chef for the French ambassador in New York; he knew Boulud from the diplomatic circuit. Micky knew right away that she would marry Boulud.

At that time, Boulud was a *sous-chef* at the Westbury, and Micky undertook to learn something about his world. To that end, she enrolled in a course in restaurant management at the New School and promptly got a job as a hostess at the Four Seasons. When Boulud left the Westbury to help open Le Régence, the restaurant at the Plaza Athénée, Micky understood that he'd be fairly inaccessible for some time, so she went off traveling throughout Asia with a girlfriend for six months. When she returned, she and Boulud decided to get married.

In the early years of their marriage, Micky found herself alone much of the time. And Boulud was obviously happy being at work. Micky realized she had better involve herself in Boulud's world if this was to work. She and Boulud started a food newsletter, of which she took the reins, and then she helped him write his first cookbook. In October 1989, Alix was born. When Boulud opened the first Daniel in 1993, Micky became very involved, especially with the interior design, which was being overseen by her step-grandmother. Micky started putting in more and more hours, helping out wherever needed—filling in sometimes as hostess once the restaurant opened—but after six months, the demands of caring for a small child while working became untenable, and Micky left the restaurant in order to care for Alix full-time.

Now with Alix in school, Micky has been doing quite a bit of volunteer work. (Lately she's been working for the Women's Commission for Women and Children Refugees—coincidentally, a part of the International Rescue Committee.) It has never been easy being married to Boulud, and it's not getting any easier: Workaholism is a progressive disease. Yet Micky is resigned. As she sees it, Boulud is a great artist. He's on a mission, and the most important thing in his life is the restaurant. For Micky the restaurant does not come first, but she's been able to accept that for him it does. Is it good? Is it bad? Micky doesn't know. She just knows that this is the way it is. Although it is not the kind of life or the kind of marriage she imagined for herself, she is willing to accept that there's another way to live a life than that which she had envisioned. "If you marry an astronaut or a guy who has a circus, you have to live in a different way," she reflects. And she knows, too, that if she gives Boulud her full support, he'll be able to achieve that much more. His sense of humor makes it tolerable, and his need to create, to make people happy, makes it feel worthwhile. If Boulud were the kind of chef who was driven primarily by ego or money or power, she couldn't stick with it. But that's not Boulud. So she puts up with the absences.

Nor is the staff of Daniel immune to wanderlust. Like many cooks, Fay has planned a working vacation—but hers will be paid for by Boulud, who had the idea a few months ago to start a scholarship fund of sorts to send cooks abroad to cook and eat. Boulud, who celebrates his twentieth year in New York this year, as well as his thirtieth year of cooking professionally, has had the idea to throw a huge ten-course dinner with thirty dishes, using the proceeds to fund the cooks-abroad program. He tried to organize the dinner this spring, but it got so big he's moved it to the end of September. Boulud sees lots of potential talent in Fay and has selected her as the first recipient, even though he hasn't yet filled the coffers of the fund.

But wanderlust also takes forms other than yearning for vacation: Lots of staff members are quitting. Besides a small exodus of line cooks, the pastry chef, Thomas Haas, will also be leaving at the end of the summer. His departure was decided last November, in fact. He has long wanted to start his own business, as well as spend more time with his family. Boulud, however, wanted a three-year commitment from him, so it was mutually decided Haas would leave in August, when he'll move to Vancouver with his wife and two children.

In a way, this kind of staff turnover is to be expected: Cooks below the position of *sous-chef* typically stay at a restaurant no more than a year to eighteen months—just long enough to learn a great deal from the chef. Even though a cook could include the job on his résumé if he stayed only a few months, if he stays longer, the chef will feel he's given him a respectable amount of time, and both parties will be satisfied. Since Daniel has been open well beyond the one-year mark, the normal cycle of turnover is now kicking in.

But what's going on here goes beyond normal attrition. Chez Daniel, a problem of morale has been developing in the kitchen. When Boulud was first putting together the team for this restaurant, there was a tremendous sense of excitement, a feeling among the cooks that they would have the opportunity to do something that had never been done before. The feeling was that there would be an amazing synergism that would pull the level of the food up above the simply marvelous into the consistently transcendent. It's been eighteen months since Daniel opened, and at least from the point of view of some of the cooks who have been here from the start, that synergy has so far proved elusive. It's not the best of circumstances for a restaurant that's trying to assert its rightful position as a four-star establishment.

Many of the line cooks have become resentful of the *sous-chefs*, complaining that they don't work hard enough. And the French *sous-chefs* have been singled out for particularly vehement derision. They're just coasting along, the line cooks grumble, spending their afternoons watching TV in the skybox while their subordinates break their necks.

Rather than put up with it, many cooks have bolted. They won't have trouble finding work elsewhere; since New York is in the throes of a restaurant boom the likes of which haven't been seen since the mid-1980s, cooks with the experience of having worked at Daniel will have their pick of positions. By the same token, it is not easy for Boulud to keep Daniel staffed with the best cooks or wait staff. With so many new restaurants in town, there is simply not enough skilled help to go around.

The result of the exodus and the attendant influx of less-experienced cooks is an atmosphere of tension that some of the cooks find it hard to put up with. Vociferous outbursts have long been the norm here, but lately the yelling is getting even worse. Why should they tolerate all this, the cooks remaining on the brigade ask themselves and one another, when there are so many opportunities—and perhaps more money—in other restaurants?

And so, a couple of weeks ago, despite Boulud's tremendously generous offer to send Fay to France, she decided that for her, it is also time to move on. Fueling her decision is her frustration with the *sous-chefs*, whose poor work ethics, she feels, have a deleterious effect on the rest of the brigade, which needs leadership by example. She sat down with Boulud and explained that she wouldn't be able to accept the trip, since she was giving her notice. Boulud, however, wouldn't hear of her not going, quitting or no. True, he might never see her again, but he appreciated her hard work, her contribution to the restaurant. And besides, something told him that at some point she'd be back.

Wednesday, June 7

IT'S 5:40, AND everyone's upstairs, finishing their *mise en place*. The waiters are setting up as well. "I got like three job offers today," says one to Pascal.

Five minutes later, the first order comes in. "One carrot soup, one lobster risotto," calls Gallagher, "followed by two bass." Lee is out of the restaurant today.

Joe, a diminutive twenty-one-year-old extern from Johnston & Wales, the Rhode Island cooking school, who has been working the soup station for three days, goes to work on the chilled carrot soup. Joe used to work in Rhode Island with a *sous-chef* who used to work for Boulud. He couldn't be more excited to be here. Unlike many of the line cooks who never cooked before they enrolled in culinary school, Joe has been cooking since he was thirteen. As a latchkey kid, Joe made dinner for his family every weeknight.

The fact that many of the line cooks are relative newcomers to the craft sometimes shows in their work. On occasion they make mistakes that a practiced home cook probably wouldn't: adding vegetables to oil that is far too hot, for instance, and then continuing to sauté them anyway. Even those who excel at turning out the specific preparations their station requires, many of which are far more complicated than what a home cook would attempt, don't necessarily have the same feel for cooking that someone who grew up cooking by a mother's side might. But catching mistakes is what *sous-chefs* are for. On most days, they're on top of it, but now and then botched garnishes do go out to the dining room.

"Order a beet salad and a frog legs, followed by a bass and a beef, medium-rare," calls Gallagher.

Bobby, working the hot-apps station, makes lobster risotto, stirring it with a metal spoon. When it's almost done, in goes more butter. He tastes it, tosses the spoon into the cylinder of water. He takes another spoon, jiggles the pan as he stirs. He spoons the risotto onto a plate, arranging pieces of lobster on top. With a hand-blender he whirs a green *coulis* till it's frothy; an aroma of mint and peas wafts up. He spoons the *coulis* around the risotto.

Scott, the *poissonnier*, puts two orders of potato-wrapped bass in a pan. Over the fire it goes, and as he taps down the fish, a big flame jumps out. The leek garnish is already on the plate, which he sauces, almost lovingly: It's still early, after all. The fish, now beautifully browned, goes on top. After two months on this station, Scott works it well.

Brad Thompson walks through, tasting sauces and garnishes.

"Bobby," he says, stopping at the soup station, tasting the chilled cucumber soup.

"Yes, Chef?"

"It's a little bit salty. Did you add a little bit of milk to it?"

"Yes."

"Did you make that today?" he asks, pointing to a crab and avocado gazpacho with basil and crisp spring vegetables.

"Yeah," says Bobby.

Thompson tastes it. "More fennel," he says. "And it's a little salty, too." Thompson is far more diligent than the other *sous-chefs* at this quality-control part of relating to the cooks; he approaches this part of his job much like Alex Lee does: He's more teacher than taskmaster. Thompson dreams of opening his own restaurant one day, an authentic Cajun place in New York, and one has the impression not only that he'll achieve that dream, but also that he'll be the kind of chef whom cooks love to work for.

Like Thompson, many of the line cooks yearn to have their own restaurants (who wouldn't want to be the boss in this culture?), but the best most of them can hope for, if they don't burn out from overwork and stress, is to rise to the level of *sous-chef* at a good restaurant or perhaps one day *chef de cuisine* or executive chef.

Still, few of them seem to harbor the fantasy of becoming a superstar chef. Most realize that few people are blessed with the qualities necessary, the attributes they see in Boulud—not only formidable technique and creativity, but also business acumen, managerial skills, leadership abilities, charisma, and inexhaustible drive. Not to mention skills that seem impossible to learn. Told he must plan a four-course dinner for sixty people, for instance, for $125 per person, Boulud can instantly conjure a menu that will not only thrill guests, but also work within the appropriate structure for food costs.

Tonight the reservation sheet lists Wendy Wasserstein. Next to her name it says, "She is a friend of M. Lynton." That would be Michael Lynton, Lili Lynton's brother, president of AOL International, formerly the chairman and CEO of the Penguin Group (publishers), and before that the head of Hollywood Pictures, a division of Disney. In fact, it was Michael Lynton who introduced his close friend Micky Boulud to his sister back in the early 1980s. It seems unlikely that many of the cooks know that Wasserstein happens to be a Pulitzer Prize–winning playwright.

Two weeks ago the restaurant started using Open Table, a computerized reservation service. Open Table provides hardware and software that allows Daniel to keep track of its customers, including such information as what guests ordered last time they visited, whether they prefer a banquette or a table in the pool, and so forth. Eventually diners will be able to reserve tables online through the service.

Hans Kaufman is slotted for ten P.M.; the note says, "Used to be a chef at Palio. Would like to say hello to DB." In fact, Kaufman was executive chef at Palio, one of Manhattan's toniest Italian restaurants, for many years.

Faith Popcorn will dine here tonight as well. Her *soigné* says she's a regular; she's also the country's best-known trend-spotter and author of the bestselling book *The Popcorn Report*.

Gallagher simmers morels and truffles in chicken stock, adds cream. The resulting sauce pulls away from the side of the pan a little. The heady scent of truffles comes up. He shakes the pan, sticks in his finger, tastes.

Suddenly Boulud is in the kitchen with two guests. He looks at Gallagher's panful of goodies, forgetting which special it could be for.

"Where'd that come from?" he asks Gallagher.

"*Le micro*," says Gallagher—the microwave.

Boulud's face falls, and then he realizes Gallagher's ribbing him. "*Faut pas déconner*," he says. Don't even joke about it.

A few minutes later, the morel mixture has gone on top of handmade penne, topped with a zucchini blossom, tied with a scallion. The zucchini blossom is stuffed with chopped zucchini, onion, garlic, thyme, parsley, eggs, Parmesan, mascarpone.

"Clean the plate," says Boulud.

"Are you ready for the consommé?" asks Bobby.

"Yeah," says Thompson. "Just put it in a tureen with some herbs. A little chervil and chives and celery leaves."

Frédéric Côte drinks from a glass bottle of Evian.

"This is the consommé for 53," says a runner.

"*Vamanos, vamanos*," says Thompson. "Ordering two tartare, one pea soup, two gazpacho, followed by one sole, two squash blossoms, one monkfish."

"German," says Gallagher, "you've got five apps and four people on the table."

"Yeah, that's right," says German. The table ordered an extra app.

"Get a VIP for five ladies," says Thompson.

Boulud comes back in, having just gone out to the dining room. "I hope I'm gonna get my brain blown away," he says, "because instead of waiting for the fucking customers, we should have gotten a *plateau* ready." The five-top of VIPs is already seated, and Boulud can't stand the idea that they'll have to wait for their canapés.

Thompson calls out an order, then wonders about a table doing a tasting. "I would like to see the sommelier," he says, "to know what kind of menu I'm going to do with them."

"*Attention là*, please, Brad," say Boulud.

"*Oui*," says Thompson.

"It's six-twenty—when can I have the terrine? The *ballottine?*" Boulud goes into the *garde-manger* to check things out.

"Okay," says a runner. "Sixty-five is up."

"How long on the beet salad?" calls Bobby.

"*Girolles,* fava," says French David to Boulud, who tastes the sauce he's made.

David ladles a little chicken stock into a saucepan, spoons in morels and batons of truffle, adds a shot of olive oil, a little truffle juice. Then a big blob of soft butter.

"Order penne, beet salad, followed by a sole and a pork," says Thompson.

David adds just-cooked penne to the pan, more soft butter, chopped chives, and shakes it over the flame. Tastes. Adds salt and pepper. Two zucchini blossoms go on top, and it's ready, served in a big bowl, not a soup plate.

Hilary Tolman's on her way out—Wednesday is the night she works late; it's almost seven. She rubs Thompson's back, pecks his cheek, and goes. The tension level is high.

"*Il y a des courgettes là-bas ou pas?*" asks Boulud.

"Yes," says Thompson.

"Show me, then, *vite fait.*"

Thompson goes downstairs, brings back up a box of zucchini blossoms. Boulud cuts one off of the small green zucchini still attached to it. "We can keep the other part," he says. "Toss it in pasta with the truffle. We're gonna make this one with olive oil, a little bit of Parmesan, a little bit of *jus de poulet* around. And the zucchini blossom fried."

"Can you put on some water for blanching?" Thompson says to Bobby. "As long as they have the zucchini attached, the blossoms are nice. If we can get them from the market, we can get them with the zucchini all the time." He goes to work, cutting off the blossoms, leaving about an inch and a half of zucchini attached.

Boulud makes penne with slivers of zucchini.

"Where's the zucchini we washed?" asks Bobby.

"I didn't wash them yet," says Thompson.

"Where are they?" asks Boulud.

"They're in the refrigerator, Chef," says Thompson, setting out an order of risotto. "*Cloche! Cloche! Cloche,* please!" In a flash, a runner is there with a dome-shaped cover for the risotto.

Boulud now sautés some pretty zucchini disks, only about three-quarters of an inch in diameter, adds oil, pepper, tosses them a few times. Then he tosses the penne, adds Parmesan, stirs, adds zucchini, tosses again. Tosses in morels, truffles, zucchini blossoms on top, this time fried. Bobby takes it, wipes the plate. Boulud whistles, stopping an order, goes back to the plate and drizzles olive oil. "The *courgettes* are way overcooked," he announces.

Boulud now calls out, "Order two tasting. One mini-pea, one mini-carrot; one oxtail, one *ballottine;* one tartare, one crab gazpacho; one bass, one halibut, followed by one beef, medium-rare, one lamb, medium-rare. Ordering a risotto and one carrot soup, no shrimp, followed by one beef, medium-rare, and one pork. Order two mini-soup, after that two foie gras and two veal."

Thompson wipes down the pasta station. There's a loud sizzling noise from zucchini central. French David squints into the smoke. Boulud comes right over as David continues to sauté. Boulud wipes down the top of the induction range. The pasta's cooking in a big stockpot fitted with two parallel cylindrical pasta inserts, side by side. David does the scallions.

"David, can you give me a plate, please?" asks Bobby.

Côte plates glazed, spit-roasted duck with cherries, raspberries, blueberries, and mâche on top that looks thick, like mistletoe. He drizzles sauce around.

"Vas-y, vas-y!" Boulud yells to a runner. *"Arrête tes conneries!"* Stop your bullshit!

Scott looks up from the fish station, bemused.

"C'est ton bulot, non?" says Boulud. Even when the chef reminds him that his job is at stake, the runner remains unflustered, which is typical. In a way, that's what makes them good runners. If Boulud yelling at them doesn't throw them, nothing will.

A runner points to a bowl of carrot soup that's about to go out. "Some lime zest, *s'il vous plaît?"* he says to Bobby.

"Yes, Chef," says Bobby to the runner.

"Don't forget, okay?" says the runner.

Boulud asks Thompson to make him a light batter.

"Do you have any eggs over here?" Thompson asks the *garde-manger.* "Joe! Go down and get me two eggs, please."

"Fifty-six is clear, or not?" Boulud asks Thompson; then he goes to the video monitor to check.

"Order 56," says German, "I'm not ready for it."

"Ça va," says Boulud. *"Cinquante-six j'en veux pas."*

"Don't touch the fucking plate!" German says.

Pascal comes in. "Forty-seven, I don't have the fish, *hein?"*

"Yes, yes," says Boulud. "I know. The other one went out; that one's coming. Okay, excuse me! Let me recap what's going on." Now he explodes. *"Will you give me the halibut right now or tout est terminé!* Let's go!"

Philippe, the *saucier,* cuts two slices off of a coriander-seed crust flavored with lemon—it's hard, like a block—and places it on a portion of loin of lamb.

"The foie gras on 96?" says Boulud. "What's going on? Where's Michael—is he here?" He goes to the phone. "Hello, hello? Get me Michael—I want him in the kitchen."

"I think Michael is off, Chef," says German.

The meat with the coriander crust comes out of the oven; Philippe slices it with an electric knife. Little particles of crust jump off with the vibrations of the knife, doing a little dance.

"Be sure to get a time," Boulud is telling a runner. "There was no time on 96. Try to break a sweat tonight, because I'm busy, so I hope you are."

Now Allannic plates the rosy slices of coriander-crusted meat alongside some braised shoulder of lamb with spring roots and dried apricot.

"Okay, pick up here," says German. "Ninety-five."

"So right now I'm getting a frog and two risotto," says Boulud, "and then I'm getting another frog with the penne. I don't know in what order you want to give me them, but don't give me everything together."

Philippe is working in a real groove. He strews salt, grinds pepper on three portions of meat, lays them in a medium-sized pan, butted right up against each other. (Whoever said "Don't crowd the pan" hasn't cooked here.) As he cuts more coriander crust, he leans his body weight—he's pretty thin—onto the knife, since the crust is so hard. He turns over the meat in the pan with a deft movement of the tongs, slices the coriander-crust meat on the bias, then uses his tongs to place the lid on a pot, turns and wipes down the counter, checks pan, turns meat. He moves like a well-oiled machine. He pulls a spoon out of water, scoops up some butter, and drops it in a pan. Next to him, Allannic continues to plate small works of art: the dark ocher of a sauce, the rosy meat, the garnishes, then *whoosh!* the plates disappear under *cloches.*

Philippe turns the meat with the tongs, presses one with his finger, slips the tongs over the oven rail. "I don't need 25 now," he tells the *entremétier.* "Twenty-three and 28 together, then 36." He slices some squab with the electric knife; it goes on top of a savoy cabbage confit with foie gras.

"I'm waiting for a dish," Pascal announces.

"Order risotto, split, followed by monkfish, split," says Thompson. "Split" means that two people are sharing one order; this one's for the bar.

Philippe drags some butter around a pan. At his knees, down to the left, are all the vegetable garnishes, kept in a drawer. As the meats come off the heat, he places them on a rack above the stove. He clears his cutting board of crumbs, giving it a sweep with his big knife. A bearded cook is doing the vegetables: He squirts oil on some greens, his nose very close to the pan.

Allannic plates garnishes, in preparation for the meat: unctuous purple endives on two, and on another, peas, beautiful slender carrots, perfect lettuce on top, with disks of yellow squash. Philippe plates truffled chicken breast. Allannic lays asparagus next to the endive, then chanterelles; hen goes on top, then more asparagus and mushroom.

It's eight o'clock, and the kitchen's in full swing now; in a good rhythm; busy, concentrated, quiet.

Thompson calls out an order.

"Is 63 fired?" asks German.

"Everything's fired," says Thompson, calmly.

Now there's a little lull. Côte meticulously unfolds and refolds his side-towel, wipes down the counters. Boulud and Thompson reorganize the tickets. Côte swigs his bottle of Evian. David clowns around with Bobby.

Magalie, the lounge server, gives a ticket to Thompson.

"Baked potatoes take forty-five minutes," he tells her, looking at the ticket. She shrugs. "Can you go get some small potatoes for me?" Thompson asks a cook. "Small. They're going to take a long time." He turns to a runner. "It's going to be an hour for that table," he says.

"It's okay," says the runner.

Thompson hands the ticket to Boulud. "One hour, I told him," says Thompson.

"What time is he coming?" asks Boulud.

"Now," says Thompson. "It's already fired. They want it steak house–style with sour cream."

"The guy lives in the building," says Boulud. "He can have anything he wants. I know him." Then he calls out an order.

Thompson gives the spuds to Joe. "Wrap them in foil," he tells him, "and pour salt on the tray."

"Order two tuna," calls Boulud, "two lettuce, tomato, onion with goat cheese, chopped up so they don't have to chew it, SOS. One hot pea soup, two beets, one risotto, three monkfish, one sole, one bass. They're real Florida people."

"Can you make two mini-soups, please?" calls Thompson. "I want to send two mini-soups to 95 since they're gonna have such a long wait."

A pan comes flying off of Philippe's range with a clatter. He manages to grab it before it hits the floor, and scoot it back on, all in one motion. He looks up to see if Boulud is looking. He is. The moment passes.

"There will be four mini-terrine on 42," says Boulud. "Okay, the risotto is coming over, German." He looks over the ticket with the special request for the chopped salad. *"Il n'a pas de dents?"* he mutters to himself. The guy doesn't have any teeth? It reminds him of the country club out on Long Island where he plays golf on Sundays—the old guys all wait on line for the salad buffet, carefully choose their ingredients, and watch delightedly as the whole thing gets chopped up before their eyes.

"Ten, 44, 33, fire, fire, fire!" says Thompson. "Order two beet salad, risotto, followed by three bass."

"Where is 45?" asks Boulud. He picks up the phone, looks at the video monitor. "Hello? Yeah, what's going on with 45 now? Ah, *anniversaire de mariage.*"

The chopped salad comes out of the *garde-manger;* it looks like a mountain.

"Table 12, let's give him something else," says Boulud. "Bernard, *c'est qui qui a commandé le douze?"*

Thompson starts to unwrap the potatoes from the foil; then he rewraps them; they're halfway done. The *garde-manger* cook arranges a beet salad: yellow upon red slices in a circle, fleshlike. The yellow slices are almost translucent.

"Can I fire the middle course, or did you want to do something else for 90?" asks Thompson.

Boulud pulls the ticket, looks at it.

A busboy comes in from the dining room, bringing a tray full of used bottles back. He picks up a half-finished bottle of Evian, takes a long drink from it, then tosses it. The glasses go on trays into dishwashing, along with a stack of plates.

"You fired the toast for 45?" yells Boulud.

"Huh?" says a runner.

"The toast for 45, you have it?! Please, we have to have a little more discipline the way we take orders." Now Boulud's having a big problem with an order. A waiter comes in, and Boulud yells at him. "The first thing you do, you put the number of the table; the last thing you do, you put the time. It's not difficult!" Now he yells into the kitchen. "You have the caramel seasoning? You have the caramel seasoning of the foie gras, you know where it is? In five minutes we're firing a frog and a sardine."

The 86 board says "SARDINE."

Thomas Haas comes in with a plated dessert the color of yams. He shows it to Boulud. Côte puts down a plate of bacon-wrapped trout. The trout falls off the plate, but he doesn't see it; he's moving too fast.

"Look, look!" says a runner.

"Oh, shit!" says Côte.

Boulud starts yelling about the baked potato—where is it? Why wasn't it fired?

"I did it!" says Thompson. "It's done!"

In the back, chickens turn on the spit—a vertical rotisserie—turning this way and that. Thompson puts them on plates, slices off the tops, two big pieces of meat. He plates the potatoes, plain, with a small dish of chives and a dish of sour cream. Sad. Who comes to Daniel to eat that? Philippe pulls the strings off of osso bucco.

"Let's go—12, 94, 65!" says Thompson.

The sardine dish comes out of the *garde-manger*, the fish stacked up chunkily. The sardines taste very fresh and delicate, not at all what you think of when you think of sardines. There's almost a lack of salt and acid until you taste a bite along with the garnish: Underneath the fish there's a little sharp stripe of mustard, a little pile of salty baby herbs—tatsoi and lemon basil salad, pickled baby porcini. Altogether, it's a marvelous balance of flavors and textures, a dish that sings.

Nine-thirty now, and another lull. Boulud goes up to the skybox. The moment he leaves, David starts clowning again, playing mouth trumpet, throwing things, moving around the kitchen. Côte and Allannic chat idly. Everyone moves less stiffly.

"Ordering risotto, asparagus soup," calls Thompson, "followed by one beef and one osso bucco. Ordering foie gras, one gazpacho, one tartare, followed by one squab, one bass, and one beef." Two more orders come in rapid succession.

Allannic throws something across the island at David. Even serious Philippe cracks a smile, jokes with Côte. There's general merriment.

"Can I get the mini-soup to complete the table?" says German.

"Oh, will you stop crying?" says Thompson.

German goes into the dining room.

"Eighty-six monkfish!" yells Gallagher.

But the gleefulness doesn't last long; Boulud comes back in, checks on some small appetizers, then goes back out to the dining room. "This is the table Daniel was asking about," says Thompson, pointing to the small apps. "He's out talking to them right now."

David comes over and looks at the order. *"Chaque fois c'est foutu."* It's screwed up every time.

"Oui," says Thompson.

Boulud comes back in, followed by Le Dû.

"Can I send it?" asks Thompson.

"Yes," says Boulud. "Right away." He turns to Le Dû. *"Pour les vins, ça commence avec la terrine."* He describes the dishes he'll be doing, then makes some wine suggestions.

By 10:15, everyone's once again moving at lightning speed—the energy level and mood has once again totally changed; jocularity has given way to passionate intensity.

"Order three mini-soup," calls Boulud, "after that one *ballottine*, one risotto, one tartare, followed by one monkfish, one sole." He looks at the *soigné*. "Petro's lawyer? *N'importe quoi.* With another tartare, sardine and crab salad, gazpacho tasting. Where's Brad now?"

"Bathroom," says Roy, the *garde-manger* cook.

"Okay."

Gallagher steps in to help Boulud. When Thompson comes back in, Boulud is at the hot-apps station, having a hard time.

"C'est une poêle de merde!" he says. David takes away the offending pan. "AAARGH!" yells Boulud. *"Ah putain de merde d'induction!"* There's a burning smell; potatoes are sticking. Everyone looks up.

"Okay, the first one that has to go is 95," says Thompson.

"Yeah, here," says Boulud.

"Then start 63."

"There's not enough frog in there," says Boulud to David. "Give me some more frog in the cassoulette."

Now the 86 board says "SARDINE, MONKFISH, SQUAB."

"I wanted to see them," says Boulud. "One mini-frog, one penne. Oh, I don't know anything anymore. Shit. German."

"Yes, Chef?"

Boulud calls out a tasting menu, then turns back to German. "You tell Jean-Luc and you tell the captain and you tell everybody about the tasting. You got it, eh? Make sure very small portions on this, eh? On the crab and the sardine, very small."

"And there's one beluga?" asks German. "Before everything, no?"

"Yes. Oh, and why don't they start with the foie gras?"

The meat station is now very crazy.

"Eighty-six frog legs!" yells Gallagher.

"Quand tu la donnes, tu dis ce que c'est," Allannic tells Philippe. When you give it, tell me what it is. He turns to Thompson. "Twenty-five is plated, okay?"

"I said 15 and then 20," says Thompson.

"Let's reheat everything, replate everything," says Boulud. "Now I have two tables fucked up!"

"It's on the table," says a waiter.

"Bring it to me! They're gonna wait fifteen minutes, we're gonna redo the whole table. So this time we're gonna have it fucking straight, okay? Philippe, how come 34 is not done yet? Okay, what's going on there?!"

Now Boulud gets into it with Thompson over the tickets. He's about as mad as he ever gets. In a matter of minutes, the tension in the kitchen has become almost unbearable.

"Let's recap, let's recap," says Boulud. "Try to make those tabs to be perfect, okay?! And calm down. If you see too many tables come in, you just stop. Okay, which are you making?"

"Twenty-five," says Philippe.

"Okay. Duo of beef, medium-well, and a bass and—61? Forty-one is on the run? We're getting very late on this one. Nine fifty-two—it's going to be ten fifty-two by the time it goes. We're fifteen minutes behind on this one."

Olivier comes in. "I need water glasses," he tells two busboys, who are polishing glasses. "Emergency, guys. Emergency water glasses."

"Okay," says Boulud, "we have a big table on 63. Be careful, eh? How long ago did you serve 53?"

Bernard Vrod comes in. "Do you remember a Sicilian girl who worked at Daniel?" he asks. "Brad, figure it out. Diana?" They all go to the video to check her out.

"Eleven o'clock, let's go, please!" yells Boulud a few moments later. "Tasting menu on 47 now. After that we're gonna fire a tray of soup, no meat, no seafood."

"Okay, German," says Thompson. "Sixty-three and we have the fish coming for 53."

There's no response.

"Let's go! I need a runner here!" says Thompson. "Please, please! Take 63 first. Start to go with 63. Please, I have seven plates here!"

"Ordering hot foie gras," calls Boulud. *Stop selling the frogs' legs!* Eh? It's *over!*"

A runner adds it to the 86 board.

"Pascal!" calls Boulud, but he's not there. "There's no more frog legs!" he yells to another waiter. "Do you understand?"

A waiter comes in with a plate, points to the potato garnish. "It was cold," he says.

"It went to the table *cold?*" says Boulud, turning to Philippe. "Chef! When you put mashed potato in a cassoulette, make sure it is warm!"

Thompson leans over to Gallagher. "This is my home," he says softly. "This is my love." At moments like these, they're not thinking about the fact that a hot dish doesn't go out cold in a four-star restaurant; they're just thinking about how to lead their charges through such a stressful service.

Suddenly there's an ear-splitting whistle—it's Boulud.

"Cut it out, okay?" he yells at a waiter. "Please just keep going back and forth. When there's no frog, you have to go back and forth, saying 'No frog.' Now I'm waiting for Pascal to come back and tell me what he wants instead of frogs."

Le Dû comes through, in a huff, arguing with Umberto.

Philippe stands some meat up on its sides in the pan.

"How many foie gras do you have in the pan?" asks Boulud.

"Three," says Philippe.

"Very good." He turns to German. "Did you send something to the girl?" That would be the Sicilian girl who used to work at the original Daniel. German says yes. "Okay, good—we gave you the app on 37."

"Go for it, Chef," says German. "Fire!"

"Go for it!" says Boulud.

Zohar comes back—she's been catering a benefit for Schneider Children's Medical Center. She hands Boulud a commemorative chef's jacket they gave her for him—*DANIEL BOULUD* is stitched in front. "Did you apologize for me that I wasn't there?" he asks.

She shakes her head. "I was plating dessert," she says, looking a little sorry.

Boulud drapes the jacket around her, grasping her shoulders. "It's for you," he tells her, looking at her squarely. "Thank you, Zohar. You are the best cook I have ever had."

If only the rest of the brigade felt half as good.

Wednesday, June 14

DOWNSTAIRS IN THE pastry prep kitchen, visions of summer fruits dance in Thomas Haas's head as he makes an apricot *tarte Tatin*. No matter that the apricots here aren't as sweet as they are in Europe: Last night he drizzled maple syrup on them, then roasted them very slowly in the oven overnight, intensifying their flavor. Now he makes a caramel in a very deep, slope-sided sauté pan, melting sugar until it's a deep honey color, then adding butter. The apricots go in the pan over the caramel, and he covers them with foil so the steam will stay in for the first half of the baking time. Into the oven it goes; the puff pastry that will cradle it bakes separately.

Ariella helps a new assistant bake several almond cakes.

Twenty minutes into the baking of the *Tatin*, the foil comes off. "Ariella," says Haas, "put it on a sheet pan so the air circulates underneath it."

Since her J-1 visa will be up at the end of the summer, Ariella's been looking around for something else to do—perhaps working in a test kitchen at a magazine, maybe eventually doing some writing. She's getting a little tired of the power trips, tired of hearing the familiar refrains: "If you don't like it here, go somewhere else." "We can live without you." "Don't think you're so great." She knows her place—she's just a cook—so she keeps her head down and works, but sometimes she feels bitter about not being adequately recompensed for working such long hours. Ariella tries to console herself with the thought that she's done a good job, but sometimes she wishes someone would *tell* her she's done a good job. In the restaurant world, you work really hard and someone else takes all the credit.

Still, Daniel has not been a bad place for Ariella, all told. She has learned a lot and also feels she's grown up a lot, become more mentally tough.

Haas turns his attention to preparing a chocolate spray decoration for an orange chocolate cake. He chops up equal amounts of cocoa butter and Valrhôna milk chocolate, putting the pieces into a glass bowl, which goes into a microwave. Is it necessary to use Valrhôna chocolate for a spray? "When you work in a restaurant with an unlimited budget," he says with a gleam in his eye, "anything is possible."

Roger, another American pastry cook, cuts rhubarb into half-inch pieces. "Before June 16," Haas tells him, "you always have to peel your rhubarb." Using a paring knife, the cook pulls the strings off of the long red stalks.

On a far counter, with a rhythmic *chop chop chop*, a bread prep cook cuts olives in half for baker Mark's olive bread. So far he's filled his eight-quart container up to the six-quart mark.

The chocolate comes out of the microwave; Haas swirls it around, adding a touch of red food coloring. "This gives a beautiful touch to it," he announces.

Now Ariella makes little squares for the champagne truffle cake. *Sablé* goes on the bottom, then a chocolate *feuilleton*, then chocolate sacher, dark chocolate, and white sponge biscuit. Haas sticks his finger in it, tastes, then uses a blowtorch to heat the metal ring that encircles a cold chocolate cake; the heat helps him as he lifts the ring off to unmold it. He inspects the sides.

Jacqueline, yet another pastry cook, spreads raspberry jam on a six-inch circle of *sablé* that sits on a white cardboard circle. She places coconut and chocolate biscuit on top of the jam, and a metal pastry ring goes around the whole thing. Now she lays in some pastry cream with visible flecks of vanilla bean, smoothing it with a small offset spatula.

Twenty minutes later, Haas opens the door to the convection oven; it whines down. He pokes at the apricot *tarte Tatin* with his finger and replaces the foil, which the air from the convection oven has blown off. (The convection oven is good for most things they do in pastry, but not everything.) He places a sheet pan on top to hold the foil in place, and closes the door.

Haas takes a minute to show Jacqueline a letter he's received, on stationery that says "Palm Gardens Nursing Home," from Brooklyn. It's from an administrator there named Thomas Haas, who ate in the restaurant and noticed Haas's name on the menu. "Dear Thomas," Haas reads. "Always good to see someone with a great name. I understand you're a wonderful pastry chef. Hope to have an acquaintance someday." Haas laughs delightedly, then sails it into the circular file.

On the far side of the pastry prep, Regina dips small, perfect mint leaves in egg wash, then sugar, placing them on a Silpat sheet to dry. Regina came to Daniel a year ago in May, just after finishing cooking school at Peter Kump's, here in New York City. Her husband's a lawyer, and she's older than many of the cooks. Regina's family had a bakery on Long Island, where she grew up, and she always loved making pastry; before cooking school, she worked as a cake decorator. She thought she knew everything there was to know about pastry once she went through the program at Peter Kump's, where she completed the full culinary program (not just pastry) but found she was wrong. But this is where you learn it all—working with a great pastry chef. And Thomas is a wonderful teacher.

It's 11:35, and Ariella has gone upstairs to prepare for service. The *tarte Tatin* comes out, and Haas pulls off the foil. A heavenly apricot smell wafts up. The top of the *tarte* is a little soupy-looking, so he puts it back in the oven to let the liquid evaporate.

Sam, a tall, Asian-American pastry cook—also older—regards a plastic-wrapped block of chocolate that sits on the floor. He whacks it three times with a heavy cleaver, trying to break it up.

Now Haas goes to work on a new creation. He explains to Sonya, another pastry cook, what he wants: first a *sablé* shell, then crème brûlée. Sugar will be sprinkled over the crème brûlée, a blowtorch used to caramelize it, then apricots will go over it, along with a glaze. He was doing something like it with the rhubarb tart, and people loved it.

"Which apricots do you want me to use?" asks Sonya. She's from Mexico City, with high cheekbones, hair pulled up in a chignon, and fair olive skin accentuated by two well-placed beauty marks.

"You ask too many questions," says Haas lightly. "So, Sonya, after you are done with what you're doing, you can take a little puff pastry, cut it out, put it on a Silpat on a sheet pan with another Silpat on top. Bring it to room temperature about fifteen minutes, then cook it."

"Are we doing the fig tart?" asks Regina.

"No," says Haas, "we don't do it." Now he puts up a huge Plexiglas shield in preparation for spraying chocolate over a cake. "When Daniel hired me," he quips, "he said, 'Maybe this guy can save me some money using German engineering techniques.' " This is a joke; the setup looks decidedly low-tech. He peels a layer of chocolate off the shield from the last time it was used. The chocolate that comes off is shiny as a mirror.

Now Sonya presses a large pastry ring into the puff pastry.

Haas looks at a recipe binder open on the counter for a pastry he wants Regina to make. Perhaps the greatest difference between the pastry side of the restaurant and the hot side is the necessary precision involved in pastry.

"I think we need eight thousand grams of flour," says Haas, and then he starts calculating out loud to get two-thirds of the recipe. "Two thousand, four thousand, five thousand. It's five thousand if you do sixty-six percent."

"Two-thirds," affirms Regina.

"Two-thirds, yeah," says Haas. "So we need one thousand one hundred thirty grams of cream, four hundred fifty grams of *sirop de sucre inverti*, and one thousand four hundred thirty-three grams of seventy-five percent." Seventy-five percent refers to chocolate with a cocoa content of 75 percent;

sirop de sucre inverti is invert sugar, a liquid form of sugar, made up of equal parts of glucose and fructose. Sweeter than granulated sugar, it also prevents graininess in fondants. "That's sixty-six percent of two thousand one hundred fifty, four hundred grams butter, that's one hundred thirty, two hundred sixty-five, and two hundred. Three hundred grams framboise liqueur." Haas does all these conversions incredibly quickly in his head. The pastry kitchen's recipes differ from home cookbook recipes in that they are merely lists of ingredients; the pastry cook must know what to do with them.

"Chef, do you need anything now?" asks Sonya, preparing to eat her lunch.

"No, just have your lunch and then I'm going to spray this cake and then we start cutting all the chocolates in the back. We might cut them here because it seems to be very full back there."

"Chef," asks Sonya, "in what oven should we put the puff pastry?"

"Convection," says Haas. "As soon as the tarts are out we fire them."

Haas pours his melted chocolate into a plastic reservoir on a large spray gun, which is plugged into a wall outlet. He tests it on the Plexiglas shield. This cake he's decorating is a test for the National Pastry Team Competition, to be held in Beaver Creek, Colorado; it begins in eight days, on June 22. He'll be flying out there to compete on a team with Rémy Fünfrock, pastry chef at Café Boulud. The theme this year is "toys."

"Oh, two things," he says, pulling on latex gloves, "before I forget. Try not to keep a mess under here." He indicates the storage area under the island where he's working. Then he nods toward some beans one of the cooks is using as weights for a tart crust. "Better than beans is rice. Rice doesn't smell."

Haas takes a cake out of the oven, places it in front of the shield, and applies a fine spray of chocolate over it.

Two days later, Michael Lawrence comes in to work to find a small disaster: The automatic answering system for reservations has malfunctioned. No one figures it out until nine-thirty, so customers who called before nine o'clock got no recording, and those who call after have to listen to ringing until the reservationists pick up. As he and Leslie Lopez, the reservations manager who replaced Erica Cantley, try to fix it, they accidentally erase the outgoing message. They record another one, using Leslie's voice. By ten-thirty the mess is resolved.

Boulud is out of the country, in Brazil for a week. For most of the staff, this means everything feels a little looser. Now that summer is upon them, the chef less in evidence, things will be a little easier. Lawrence, however, prefers it when Boulud is in the house. When he's not, Lawrence has to crack the whip constantly. It's not that his staff is lazy or that they slack off when the chef is away; it's rather that Boulud's charismatic presence always creates a kind of buzz, an electric current that zaps everyone into performing at the top of their game. Lawrence still marvels at Boulud's charisma and its power to pull a team together; he's never seen anything like it—not at March, not even at the Quilted Giraffe.

Much of Lawrence's job, besides managing the front-of-the-house staff, is making sure that everything stays up to the high standards Boulud has set. Lately, in addition to polishing the service and making countless adjustments to the decor, Lawrence has been rethinking the *mise en place* in the bar, including reconfiguring the refrigerator, all with the aim of streamlining, making things more efficient. The bar has become busier and busier lately, and with the arrival of warm weather, Boulud has decided that he wants to start serving drinks on the terrace in front of the restaurant, an enterprise that will begin next week. Meanwhile, the lounge has been getting more and more requests for "walk-ins"—that is, diners without reservations who want to dine in the lounge. At the moment, there are only six or seven tables for that purpose, and Lawrence has a problem with adequate staffing as well. He really feels a crunch as a result of the restaurant boom—there aren't enough qualified people to go around. Still, turnover, which is on a slightly shorter cycle in the front of the house than in the kitchen, is starting to settle down, eighteen months after opening. At the moment, he's happy with about 95 percent of his staff, not bad considering the market.

But the terrace is a problem. Although they'll start by serving only drinks, the idea has been to eventually serve food there as well. Yet unlike East Seventy-sixth Street, the site of Café Boulud, Sixty-fifth Street is a major crosstown thoroughfare. Who's going to want to sit there with all the noise and exhaust, Lawrence wonders, not to mention the interminable construction across the street? The proposition will require one waiter and one busboy, which means he'll have to hire someone else. And there will be logistical problems, depending on what they wind up serving out there. For starters, the terrace is a long way from the kitchen. They've talked about setting up a *mise en place* inside one of the side doors because you can't go through the revolving door with more than one plate. Perhaps, on the other hand, they'll go through the service entrance. He'll have to play it by ear.

The phone rings in the bar; Lawrence answers it. It's Boulud, calling from São Paulo, checking in. When he's out of town, he keeps in close touch with the restaurant, calling key staff people every day; Michael usually hears from him at least daily, but he sometimes calls six or seven times in a single day. "What's happening?" is what he always asks when he calls, and often he'll come out with a question totally out of the blue to Lawrence, such as "What kind of wine are they drinking on table 50?" The ever-patient Lawrence always replies with, "I don't know offhand, Chef, but if you'll hold on a second, I'll find out."

Today Lawrence has something to report to Boulud. "We had a comment about the service being cold and haughty," he says, "and it was Pascal. I've talked to him, but I think you should sit down with him. He needs to change his attitude with the guests sometimes. And a lot of the complaint letters we've gotten involve him."

Daniel receives, on the average, two or three complaint letters a month; they're handled by Hilary Tolman. They might be about anything from the way a guest was treated at the front desk to something they say they found in their food. Tolman feels that about half the letters she receives are without basis, that behind them is just someone trying to get a free meal. She answers all the letters, however, apologizing for the real or perceived misstep or slight, and giving unhappy customers her direct phone number. Although she's surprised that anyone would want to return if they were that unhappy, this way if they do wish to give the restaurant another chance, she can make the reservation for them and make sure they're given extra care. In about half the cases, Tolman agrees that the complaint was justified (perhaps because the server confirms it), and she makes some sort of amends. In about 20 percent of the cases, Tolman is actually mortified by what happened. For instance, earlier this year, a waiter dropped a big chunk of the two-thousand-dollar-per-pound truffle he was shaving onto a guest's plate, and he reached in with his fingers to retrieve it. ("I couldn't help it," the waiter later told Tolman. "All I could see was all that money falling into his plate!") Tolman invited the guest back to Daniel for a meal on the house.

It's late June, and two blocks away from the restaurant, Central Park is so extravagantly leafy that it's almost hard to remember spring, though it officially ended only days ago. Thompson and Jed have just come in from the farmers' market, hauling big white plastic garbage bags filled with produce: One holds nettles, parsley, basil, red spring onions the size of scallions, potatoes, sour cherries, more herbs. Early summer—this is the time everyone starts to get really excited about ingredients. They also bought oyster mushrooms, which Jed lays on clear plastic trays, and a variety of berries: purple mulberries, white mulberries, wild cherries, raspberries. Some of these they'll use for pastry, others for sautéed foie gras.

Tim Stark, a farmer in Pennsylvania who has become something of a celebrity (if such a thing as a celebrity farmer is possible) thanks to his heirloom tomatoes, is now growing microsalad for Daniel; they have a bag of that, too.

Thompson goes into the pastry kitchen, looking for cherry pitters. Johnny Iuzzini is eating his lunch. "Jean-Georges was at the market," Thompson tells him. "I'm gonna tell Daniel."

"Tell him Ducasse was there, too," says Iuzzini.

There is, in fact, a degree of healthy competition between these chefs.

According to Lili Lynton, Boulud's decision to open such an ambitious new restaurant was in no small part in reaction to Vongerichten's having opened Jean Georges. And recently, when Lufthansa Airlines approached Boulud to design menus and dishes for its first-class service, Boulud acceded. Would he have agreed had Vongerichten not already been involved in the same program?

Nevertheless, whatever Boulud's motivation in reopening Daniel in such grand fashion, if Boulud and Vongerichten insist on keeping up their competition, that can only benefit New York's diners. Wisely Boulud has not succumbed to the temptation of opening restaurants around the world or of going Las Vegas, as Vongerichten has. Whatever the financial rewards that would bring, many in the food business now feel Vongerichten has spread himself too thin to maintain the highest possible quality. Ducasse, in the meantime, who has by now opened six restaurants and one country inn, has been boasting around the world that he has no trouble being in two places at once—and he has managed to be the first chef to garner three *Michelin* stars simultaneously in his two eponymous restaurants, one in Monte Carlo and the other in Paris. The food world is now atwitter with the news that he's opening another in New York at the end of the summer.

Ariella comes through with an empty cart, having brought all her stuff upstairs for service.

"Tonight's the night," Iuzzini tells Thompson. "I'm going to write Theresa a letter and say either she has to marry me right now and have my children, or I can't deal with it." Three months ago he met his girlfriend, a waiflike Puerto Rican beauty who works at a cosmetics counter at Bergdorf-Goodman. Obviously, he's more than smitten.

Haas, for his part, has returned from the National Pastry Team competition at Beaver Creek, not exactly victorious, but not completely demoralized, either. He would have preferred first place, with its fifty-thousand-dollar prize, but his team came in fourth, winning five thousand dollars.

But there's even bigger news: William Grimes was in on Monday night with three other people. His presence sent a frisson through the ranks. Shouts of "What do we have in the house?" ricocheted around the kitchen as the chefs scrambled to whip up something formidable for the critic. Still, as much as they would have loved to create a spectacular last-minute special for him, to do so would be impossible without letting on that they knew it was he. It was essential to pretend they didn't know he was there.

Two days later, everyone's still talking about Grimes's visit. Could a review be imminent? It hardly seems likely, so soon after the first—after all, it hasn't even been thirteen months; Le Bernardin hasn't been reviewed in *years*. But if not, what would Grimes be doing here?

Friday, July 7

SUMMER HAS BEGUN officially, and warm weather's bounty enlivens the downstairs prep kitchen. Cloistered as they are, however, the cooks at Daniel barely know the sky, the trees, the sun, the seashore, the way New York City's nine-to-fivers do, with long, lazy weekends stretching out ahead of them. No such luxury in the restaurant business, least of all at Daniel, where lunch prep is in full swing. It's eleven o'clock.

David dismembers live lobsters, pulling them apart with his hands and a knife. The body parts still twitch in their bus pan.

Thompson pulls small cavaillon melons from wooden crates, peels them. Their heady smell overpowers the clean-smelling, very fresh cod fillets that lie on a tray next to them. At least Thompson managed to get away to New Orleans for the Fourth of July weekend, eating like a king the whole time, which was the point of the trip.

On the other side of Thompson lies a sheet pan of unctuous roasted baby eggplants. Zebra-striped mackerel, three or four inches long, are lined up in yet another sheet pan next to a plastic crate of razor clams. A cook pokes a finger into one, and part of a clam jumps out. Now he pours them into a plastic pan that fits into the sink. He jerks the hose off of a reel on the west wall and rinses them.

Upstairs, twenty minutes into the lunch service, Frédéric Côte calls, "Ordering one pree-fee haricot salad, three pree-fee ravioli, followed by one pree-fee salmon, one pree-fee skate, two pree-fee lamb." He points to a tray of paper-thin roasted tomatoes in the *garde-manger*. "This is garbage, eh?" Côte tells an American *garde-manger* cook. "They're black. They should be red. Garbage." His stove-side manner leaves a little to be desired.

Now Alex Lee comes in, and he's not pleased, either. "Make sure before we go home the kitchen is clean, because the kitchen was a big piece of shit downstairs. The walk-ins have to be clean, the tables have to be clean before you go." He nods toward a cook who's just given notice. "I'm glad that guy's leaving, too—he doesn't want to fucking work. Where's Charlie?" he asks, referring to a new cook.

"He's downstairs getting the good olive oil," says the *garde-manger* cook.

"Why didn't you have it already?"

Charlie comes in, holding a bottle of olive oil.

"I want you up here," says Lee. "We've got a busy lunch."

"Okay, Chef."

If there is one person who has not been afflicted by wanderlust, it's Lee. His friends in other restaurants constantly ask him why he's still with Boulud, why he doesn't leave, do his own thing. Actually, Lee gets job offers almost every week. But despite the fact that Daniel can be a very difficult place to work, Lee says he loves what he's doing here. (Several of the cooks, however, intimate that compared with a year ago, Lee's heart is no longer in it. They feel he longs to spend more time with his family.) In any case, Lee points out that Boulud gives him the opportunity to cook the food he wants to cook, he can buy the ingredients he wants, which is fairly unusual, and he feels the complete confidence that Boulud has in him. Lee also enjoys nurturing his staff, teaching them, and watching them grow, though he doesn't have as much time to do this as he'd like. One day, perhaps in a small restaurant of his own, he'll be able to focus more on developing his staff's talents.

Leslie, the new daytime hot-apps cook, sauces ravioli bowls, making circles using the bottom of a ladle. She came last week from Café Boulud, where she worked the same station for the past year and a half. Leslie doesn't like changing jobs, so as transitions go, this one has been good for her. Charlie comes to help her in pasta—he'll be working between pasta and *garde-manger* today, wherever it's busy.

"*Café con leche?*" Lee asks an observer. Dressed in whites, the Spanish chef standing against the bulletin board beside the pass is second-in-command at Zalacaín, a renowned restaurant in Madrid. The chef nods, and Lee orders one for him. They don't have the same kind of turnover problem at Zalacaín—he's worked there twenty years, *"una vida."*

Côte spoons a *pistou* of parti-colored summer vegetables—*haricots verts,* tiny cherry tomatoes, yellow corn—on a plate. Lee comes by, puts a spoon in, tastes. Salmon goes on top.

"Alex, can you call down for frog legs?" says Leslie.

Lee gets on the phone. *"Necesito rana,"* he says. "Frogs' legs. You don't have it? None? None in the house? Shit! We should tell him to order it. Jed? Jed?" Now he belts out for all to hear: "Eighty-six frogs' legs!" Then back into the phone; Jed has come on. "You don't have frogs? Shit! You guys gotta tell me. I've got a VIP Feast and Fêtes. Okay, you guys gotta tell me before the service, before we start."

Côte lays a fillet of golden-brown skate onto a plate that's just been garnished with a ring of chanterelles. Inside, the fish is stuffed with more chanterelles, crispy onions, creamy spinach, and a red-wine bordelaise sauce. *"J'aime bien ça,"* Lee tells him. "I tasted it yesterday." Then he's back on the phone. "Hello, Jed? Is there anything I can offer instead of the frog legs?" He calls to a runner with an answer for the captain whose table had tried to order them: "Tell him we can offer sea scallops instead of the frog."

"Chef," replies the runner, "did you say we were—"

"Please go take care of that first!" yells Lee; the runner goes out. "You guys stay on the service, okay? I had to pick up a tray to go into the dining room because there were no fuckin' runners. All right? The lobster salad, fire."

The runner comes back. "Chef, order gazpacho instead!"

Lee picks up the phone again. "Hello, Jed? There isn't one pot washer up here. Not one of them. I don't know what the fuck they're doing."

Michael Lawrence comes in. "So we don't have frog legs, after they ordered them," he says. "And last night there were no morels."

"Morels are finished," says Lee. "I told them at the beginning of service."

"You told them? Well, we should change the menu."

"We changed the menu," Allannic pipes in.

"Tell Hilary tonight that she needs to," says Lee. He notices a soup that's just landed on a tray, ready to go out, but its garnish is messed up. "What's this? It looks like nothing."

"Oh, Chef," says Frank, "you knocked it over."

"Please arrange it so it looks nice," says Lee.

Frank does. It goes back on the tray.

"Tell your guys to wake up, too," Lee tells Lawrence, "because there wasn't one runner in here. We're in the shit here." Lawrence is on his way back out to the dining room, shaking his head. "What are you shaking your head for?" yells Lee. "You have a problem?"

Now Lee gets on the phone again. "Hello," he says, "I need Jed. What do you have tonight? Give me a list of what mushrooms we can offer because we have to change the menu. You have enough chanterelles? Because we have to eighty-six the morels." Two tickets come in, and he calls out, "Ordering mesclun and *ballottine,* followed by two monkfish. Ordering one carrot soup followed by two carpaccio."

Now he turns his attention to making a *pissaladière*—he has to develop one to accompany the new version of tuna tartare. "I want to bring up the anchovies. We're going to marinate them now," he says. Again he picks up the phone. "Mark *le boulanger,* please. Hi, Mark. You know how you make a *pissaladière?* It's basically like a pizza dough. I'm gonna make you some onions because we need some *pissaladières* for the new menu. I'll talk to you about it." He pushes some buttons. "Hello, Jed? Do we have Vidalia onions now? Could you send me up like eight of them? We're gonna try a *pissaladière* for the new menu. Roy's actually bringing up anchovies, so if you want to bring it to him . . ."

Roy brings up the anchovies in a hotel pan.

"I need three hotel pans," says Lee. Two fish dishes land on trays. "Okay, monkfish position five, salmon position one."

Lawrence comes back in. "Alex, table 95," he says. "Hilary's sister is in a rush."

"When you order something special, it takes longer," says Lee. "Fillet of lamb takes fifteen, twenty minutes. If they want to order that in a hurry, they shouldn't eat that here. You know how to cook. You know what it takes to cook something right." Then he yells, over the kitchen din: "Hey, listen! Follow the service, all right?" Now he turns to Côte and asks him to cook some onions.

"Caramélisé?" says Côte.

"Gently *caramélisé,* " says Lee.

Côte smiles. *"C'est la cuisine qui chante. La cuisine du midi!"* He tells Lee how he likes to prepare dough for *pissaladière:* He lets it rise three times, then "breaks it." It doesn't rise as much in the end as it normally would, but it's more *moelleux,* tender. "Onions, garlic, anchovies," says Côte, smiling, *"c'est la cuisine qui chante!"*

Marcel Doron, the CFO, comes up from downstairs and orders skate for his lunch.

"You eat that?" says Lee. "Let me know how you like it because we're gonna do it for the new menu." Then he turns to the menu; he starts to make changes—"creamy morels" becomes "bluefoot mushrooms."

Downstairs, Brad Thompson is prepping the large white fungus that looks almost like an oyster mushroom. Some of them are shaded periwinkle blue at the base—hence the name "bluefoot."

The night cooks do their prep for dinner. Fay works on veal saddle, which she has poached in chicken stock and *mirepoix*. She lays the meat on plastic film. Jed tastes it. "It tastes like anchovies," he says.

"I hope those anchovies don't taste like anchovies," she tells him, "or we're really in the shit."

Jed makes an unpleasant face. Today everything tastes like anchovies. And every day lately, they're in the shit. Normally at this time of year, restaurants are somewhat slower, but business has continued to be brisk so far this summer at Daniel.

Fay pokes the roll with the point of her knife, presses out the air.

"David?" says the speakerphone.

"Oui?" says David.

"Tu as les planches pour les cerises?" Do you have the boards for the cherries?

"La plage? Tu vas à la plage?" You're going to the beach? puns Thompson, trying to confuse everyone.

There are, in fact, frogs' legs; Lupe is prepping them. A big plastic hotel pan holds frogs that have already had their torsos removed. From the waist down, they're about six inches long. Lupe snips with scissors at their knees, then cuts off the thighs. He drops the calves into a pan, the thighs on a sheet—three purposeful snips, the visceral sound of scissors going through little bones.

Upstairs it's 2:05, and Frank's station has slowed down. He slices onions for the *pissaladières*.

"Hello—one risotto and two bass, pree-fee, how long?" calls Lee. "Go, go, go—it's a tasting!"

"Yes, Chef," says Leslie.

Lee asks the *garde-manger* chef if he has any more of the *ricotta salata* he's been using for the string bean salad, a warm salad of *haricots verts*, corn, basil, olives, tomatoes, and *ricotta salata*, all glossed with good, fruity olive oil. He does. Lee takes a thin square, lays it over green-flecked pasta in an oval copper pan. Then he, Allannic, and Côte discuss Boulud's travels—the chef is now in California.

"*Il a mangé à* French Laundry," says Allannic. He had dinner at the famed Napa Valley restaurant.

"*Il a bien mangé?*" asks Côte.

"*Oui.*"

"*Comment tu sais?*" asks Côte, suddenly looking slightly suspicious. Why is Allannic in such close contact with the chef while he's away? Allannic is acting as though he were there with Boulud.

Allannic throws him a puzzled look: Why does Côte bother asking him such a question?

It's three-thirty, and up in the skybox, Michael Lawrence is going over the menu with Tolman. "You need a degree from Harvard to read our fucking menu," he says. "We have to change the dessert menu," he adds. "They're asking for mango. Can we just put 'a selection of macerated fruits'?"

Frank comes up, sticks his head around the corner to Tolman's desk. "Special tonight for soup is different—they've changed it to yellow beet borscht," he says. "Chef asked me to come up and tell you."

Now Côte comes up. "*Tu as le* Larousse Gastronomique?" he asks.

"*Tu l'as ramené,*" she says. He finds it, takes it from the shelf.

Tolman is making menu changes, inputting them on her computer.

Côte puts the book back. "Okay," he says, "thank you very much."

Tolman picks up the phone and calls downstairs to Rica Buxbaum, Allannic's wife, who runs Boulud's website and maintains his recipe database. "Rica," she says, "is your husband there?" When Allannic comes on the line, she asks him about his special for tonight. Then she looks down at her menu notes. "Oh, 'medley,' " she says. "We haven't used that for a while." She crosses it out; writes "casserole." " 'Medley' sounds a little too two-star," she tells Lawrence.

Downstairs, the waiters and cooks devour the remains of the pastry cart, picking up tarts with their fingers, stuffing them into their mouths. It takes about thirty seconds for the cart to be wiped out.

The next Monday, Boulud has returned from his California trip. As dinner service gets under way, he finishes up some calls in the skybox.

In the kitchen below him, over the pass, someone has taped up a cut-out ad for NEW MR. CLEAN ANTIBACTERIAL; below is written "Chef Bradford—for hire." Thompson really does look like Mr. Clean.

Thompson smirks when he sees it. "I have a hoop earring at home," he says.

"Hey," says Gallagher. "Did you go to CIA? Do you know Marcus Famington?"

"I know Chef Famington," says Frank.

"He's outside," says Gallagher.

By 6:10, there are four tickets up already; Gallagher is expediting.

Boulud steps in, looking tanned, refreshed. "Order two mini-soups, followed by one crab, one haricot salad, after that one skate, one bass." Boulud grabs Fay around the shoulders. *"Ça va toi?"* he asks her.

"Hello," she says.

"The four terrine are gone, right?" says Gallagher.

"Whose table is that?" asks Boulud.

"Fifty-four, Chef," says a runner.

Fay has two pans going. In one, two pieces of meat stand on their sides, browning; in the other, two lie flat, their first sides browning. She adds a dollop of butter. There's a palpable tension in there: The party is over. Boulud is back.

The Spanish chef snips herbs with scissors. If he were at home at his restaurant, he'd be in charge of dishes like oxtail in a rice crêpe with truffles, or lasagne with clams and *brandade*. Zalacaín was the first restaurant in Spain to garner three stars in the *Michelin* guide. (Today it has one.)

"Two oxtail, pree-fee, followed by two lamb, medium-rare," calls Lee.

Fay's working hard already. But nothing is 86, and she's in a good groove.

"Table 48, please," says Boulud. "Two *ballottine là*. Two beet salad, I mean."

A tall waiter comes in, hands Boulud a plate. "The guy told me there's a hair in his plate," he says. He sounds skeptical.

Boulud removes a hair, puts it to the side of the plate. He and Lee examine it. "Give me another *ballottine* tasting, please," says Boulud. He seems sure the hair didn't come from the kitchen.

The waiter goes back into the dining room to see what the customer's hair looks like. He returns. *"Il a les cheveux courts, normaux,"* he says. Normal, short hair.

Boulud now walks by Frank, who reaches out to shake his hand. Boulud takes a silver spoon, tastes his risotto. Then he goes to the *garde-manger.* *"Aïe, aïe, aïe,"* he says. "Don't cut the terrine like that."

Tonight David's wearing a toque—the medium-high, pleated kind—and so is the fish cook. "That's a good-looking hat," Frank tells him.

"We're gonna get you one with a propeller on it," says Gallagher. Fay and the *garde-manger* cook wear the short Nehru kind. Fay's little ponytail sticks out of hers.

Boulud is pleased to see the cooks wearing toques; he wishes his brigade would always wear them. The cooks hate the short kind, and the tall kind are always bumping into the lights. He and Lee frequently argue about it, Lee standing up for the cooks. In France everyone wears them, no questions asked, Boulud contends. Perhaps, Lee counters, but they'd have to be laundered three times per week. Well, says Boulud, in France they make one last all week. The *sous-chefs* flat-out refuse to wear them; for them it's a matter of pride. At Jean Georges they wear them, Boulud points out. Yes, says Lee, because there's an open kitchen that's visible from Broadway. And so forth.

Pascal comes into the kitchen. *"Les gens veulent un petit changement sur le menu,"* he says. His table wants a small change to their tasting menu.

"Pascal, tu m'emmerdes," says Lee, meaning, You bug the shit out of me. "And I need the garnish for the caviar."

"Who's got the fucking garnish for the caviar?" Boulud wants to know.

"What table is the caviar for?" asks Lee.

"Table 53, Chef," says the runner.

"Ordering a tartare, langoustine, and after that a salmon and a halibut," calls Boulud.

Olivier comes through, holding wine bottles. He adjusts his head to the left, the right, as he passes through. He always looks as though his collar is too tight.

"Gazpacho and tuna on 44 gone?" calls Boulud.

"No, Chef," says the runner.

A sauté pan clatters to the floor. The meat garnish cook picks it up and tosses it to dishwashing. Next to him cooked carrots, spinach, peaches, red currants glisten on a paper towel on an oval metal platter.

"Aïe, aïe, aïe," says Côte.

"Pick up a bass and a halibut, pree-fee," calls Lee.

Thomas Haas brings a new dessert into the kitchen to show Boulud and Lee: fresh peaches with peach gelée with a lemon-thyme *bavaroise* and almond quenelle, a vanilla mini-quenelle, and lemon-thyme-infused peach sauce. The peach is pure and ripe, gorgeous. Jean-Luc Le Dû comes in with a spoon to taste it.

"*Je suis dans la merde!*" yells Lee. "Get out of the kitchen, please! *Merde.*" Lee turns around, doesn't see the dessert. "Thomas, what happened to the dessert?"

A runner's starting out the swinging door with a full tray.

"No, no, no, no, no," calls Boulud in a basso profundo.

"No?" says the runner.

"Come back, please," says Boulud. "Anchovy should replace the crab. You see the tomato on the side there? Is that the way we give it to them?" The garnish has fallen off. The new plate comes, with the anchovy. "Anchovy replace the crab, all right?"

"Right, Chef." He goes.

"Listen, William, can I fire 47 or 63?"

William, the tallest runner—or, shall we say, the only tall runner—is the new expediter, since German has become a waiter. William wears shiny braces on his teeth.

"Forty-seven is okay," says William.

"Sixty-three?" asks Lee.

"Go ahead," says William. "Forty-seven is out, Chef."

Boulud tastes the dessert.

"On 54, they ordered three halibuts and two bass," says William.

"What?" says Lee.

"On 54," says Boulud.

"And on 63 they want an à la carte portion."

Boulud fixes the tickets. "Ordering two langoustine and after that two veal special," he calls.

Now Haas brings in a raspberry dessert. He cuts a bite, brings it to Boulud.

"I'd love to taste that," says Lee, "but I don't know if I want to eat it."

They all watch for Boulud's reaction. He concentrates, moving it around his mouth.

"A little too much *bavaroise*," he says, finally. "What is it?"

"You let the raspberry infuse into the anglaise," says Haas.

"You cook the raspberry?" asks Boulud.

"Yes." Haas waits, but no verdict is forthcoming.

"Ordering two foie gras," says Lee, using the mike now, "followed by one squab, medium-rare, one monkfeeesh."

Back in the pastry area, Haas assembles a dessert that's a mini-version of his sprayed-chocolate confection from the pastry competition: chocolate-hazelnut cake with orange. He puts it in the window. "Pick up, please!" he yells, shrilly.

"Where's the loup?" asks Boulud. *"Ça va pas là? Oh!"*

Pans flash at the fish station. Boulud pulls back two plates as a runner lifts up the *cloches* already there. "Follow the service, eh?" says Boulud. And then he sees something he really doesn't like. "Fucking shit. Now we have to redo everything. Can I have some scallion green? I saw some nice green scallion—now, what is this shit here?" He picks apart the dish, touches some overcooked fish. "We have to start from scratch," he announces.

"I'll start from scratch," says Gallagher. He pounds his fish on the stainless-steel counter. "Fuckin' shit."

"Hello," says Boulud. "We have to redo this whole table now." Although the rest of the order is fine, it will be cold if it waits for the fish order to be re-cooked.

Gallagher starts plating.

"Sixty-four, Chef," says William.

"I'm asking for this table now," says Boulud. "What is it?"

"Sixty-three and 60."

"What is this?" says Boulud, looking at three other plates. "This is shit. This is garbage. I don't want it." They take the three plates away.

"Hello," says Lee. "Put it over here and give it to the pastry." He doesn't want it thrown away; let Haas and his crew eat it.

"What is the next table coming up?" calls Boulud. "We need a fucking ticket for 60." But he gets no response. Now he bellows, and his voice is starting to sound hoarse. "Yes or no?" He picks up the phone. "Hello. How are you? Who? What? I don't know about it. Oh, my God. How was it?"

Lee yells from the *garde-manger*—the runners are babbling too much. "Shut up over there," he says. "Watch it, because *je suis énervé.*"

Now it's quiet, except for the sound of Fay slicing with her electric knife.

"Okay, *d'accord*," says Boulud into the phone. He hangs up, wipes the edge of a plate. A parade of runners and busboys are coming in and out, picking up, going to the dining room, coming back with finished plates, picking up. "Three cucumber soup going well?" calls Boulud.

"Yes, Chef!"

"Three hot foie gras *poêlé* going well?"

"Yes, Chef!"

David has to dash out of his station to get more chanterelles downstairs. As he barrels down the stairs, he bumps smack into Jacqueline, the pastry cook, who's on her way up, leaving for the day. There's a butterfly embroidered on her blue silk pants.

" 'Excuse me' is the word," she says. "Jerk."

David comes back up with a tray of chanterelles. A busboy is carrying a basketful of baked goods.

"Do you know what that is?" Boulud asks Thompson.

"Yes, Chef," says Thompson.

"Cheese *gougère.*"

"Gimme two napkins!" yells Lee, loud. A runner runs up with them. "I need two plates for these," Lee adds, softly.

"Pick up!" screeches Haas from the pastry window.

"Shut up," mutters Lee, under his breath. "What's going on 32, where are you?"

"I just sent two *ballottine,*" says William.

"Hello," says Lee. "Two foie gras sauté on 51 is out?"

"Oui, Chef."

"Fifty-two is out?"

"Oui, Chef."

"Sixty-two is out?"

"Oui, Chef."

"Fire 51 and 61 and 62!" yells Fay.

"Back in a flash," says Boulud. He and Lee go into the banquet room to check on a wine dinner in progress there. A moment of quiet.

Fay rises up on her toes to put a plate under the heat. She moves the pan back with her tongs, drops the tongs on the oven rail. "Two hen, please!" she says. "Two hen tasting!"

But the relative peace doesn't last long. By 7:35 the runners are all lined up, waiting for plates, and Boulud and Lee are back, going through the tickets on the board.

"How long on 56?" asks Boulud.

"Fifty minutes, sir," says William.

"You want to fire 10?" Lee asks Ernesto, who nods. "But Daniel says it's too fast," adds Lee.

"Forty-eight, Cyrille," says Boulud, putting down a plate. "Don't fucking move the plate! What are you waiting for? Thirty-two. It's not finished?"

"No, it's 54," says Allannic. "Let's go."

William puts one of the orders of hen on another tray. "Two hens, follow him," he says. "Fifty-four."

"I'm missing a foie gras," says a waiter.

"*Merde*," says Lee.

A waiter brings back two plates of bass. "They're not ready," he says.

"They're not ready?" says Boulud, furious. "I gave them fifteen minutes."

"I didn't say to fire it," says the waiter.

Boulud puts his hands on the waiter's shoulders, his pitch rising as he talks. "If we wait every time we fire, then we're in the shit. So we anticipate sometimes. If you don't take the initiative, we go."

In the bread room, two busboys pile rolls into a basket. One falls on the floor; it gets tossed back into the basket.

An hour later, there are scores of orders working. All is quiet, concentrated. No one talks.

The bearded waiter, Daniel, comes in. "Order super-rush," he says. "They have to be out in one hour; they have to catch a plane."

"Langoustine is not a super-rush dish," says Boulud. "How long did they wait?"

"Seven forty-five reservation," says David, the maître d'. It's now eight-thirty.

Now Bernard Vrod comes in. "Johnny, emergency," he tells Iuzzini. "We need a soup." That would be a dessert soup, strawberry with elderflower and mascarpone sorbet.

"How many?" says Iuzzini.

"One."

Jed and Thompson are furiously stirring risotto in a huge pot at the end of the hot line—it's the second course for the wine dinner.

"Are we ready, or what?" Lee asks them.

"Yeah, one minute," says Thompson. "Clear this off—we're gonna do it right here."

"Oh, shit," says Fay. "What am I plating?" She's doing the wrong meat. On top of everything else, she's had to pee for the past two hours.

"William, can I have a *saucière*, please?" asks Thompson. William passes a sauce boat through. "They want the sauce on the side."

"Where are you going?" says Lee to a runner who's going out with a loaded tray.

"Fifty-four, Chef," says William.

"What about 56?"

"Going in a minute, Chef."

"You know what else?" says Fay to Chris. "I forgot my socks today. Isn't that gross? First time."

It's ten o'clock before Fay gets to step out to the restroom.

It's been hellish, but she'll be out of here soon.

The next day, Georgette Farkas receives a call from John Tierney, the *New York Times* reporter who writes "The Big City" column in the Metro Section. In France farmers and others have been destroying McDonald's outlets as a protest, as Americans try to foist beef from cows fed with bovine growth hormone on the European market. Tierney has the idea to do a fun piece, interviewing the city's top French chefs about their opinions of McDonald's. Farkas sets up a phone interview for Tierney with Boulud.

Although this year he's been so consumed with putting the restaurant solidly on its feet and into four-star shape that he hasn't had as much time as he'd like to create new dishes (he's largely left that in the able hands of Alex Lee and the *sous-chefs*), Boulud has for some time been pondering the idea of the hamburger. Long a fan of the iconic American sandwich, he has had the idea to create his own version of it, more flavorful, of course, than the original; more Daniel.

Tierney's call inspires Boulud, and he tells the reporter that he will create a burger especially for him. He goes about concocting a burger: He forms a beef patty around a slice of foie gras, coating the whole thing with lots of truffles. It's superb. The only problem is he'd have to sell it for thirty-five or forty dollars, an impossible proposition even in this go-go economic climate. A braised short rib burger is his next thought. And Boulud loves cheeseburgers, but he doesn't want the cheese to be on the meat. He has Mark the baker make up some buns with a little Parmesan and Gruyère sprinkled over them, along with sesame and poppy seeds. That's good. He toasts the buns, spreads them with butter, hot mustard, and horseradish, layers on curly chicory and tomato confit, then a roasted burger filled with boneless short ribs. A knockout! A week later, he serves it to Tierney.

When the article is published on the front page of the Metro Section on July 18, with a headline that says FRENCH CHEFS CAST AN EYE ON LE BIG MAC, Boulud's genius is vividly apparent. After Tierney's tongue-in-cheek introduction about the globalization of cuisine and its effect on "culturally oppressed diners," he interviews chefs, asking them to contemplate McDonald's cuisine.

Lespinasse's Christian Delouvrier is first up. "Ketchup is not that bad," is his assessment. "When you eat a good hamburger that's cooked properly, it's delicious." Le Bernardin's Eric Ripert weighs in with "To stop at McDonald's is amusing to me. About twice a year I go. I get the fries and the Coke, and take a ton of ketchup and mayonnaise with the hamburger." Last is Boulud, who tells Tierney a story about sneaking a McDonald's meal at a Washington airport. "There is no shame in going to McDonald's," Tierney quotes him as saying. "The food is predictable. You go there twenty years later, and it tastes the same."

Then why, Tierney wants to know, "are the McDonald's bashers so popular in France?"

"The French are jealous," Boulud concludes. "The hamburger may be the most successful snack in the world. The French wish they could have invented McDonald's."

Now, this is a brilliant piece of thinking, for not only is it possibly true, but it also, naturally, wins American hearts and minds, along with piquing Tierney's interest. "Then Mr. Boulud made an extraordinary gesture to bring Americans and French together at the peace table," Tierney writes. "The revered chef from Lyons offered to create a burger." Boulud invited Tierney to have lunch in the skybox, where he fed him his perfected "DB Burger." And Tierney was so charmed that he spent the last third of the column raving about how magnificent it was. "Call me a traitor," he ends the article, "but globalization suddenly seemed sublime."

This is classic Boulud. Not content to toss off the same kind of run-of-the-mill phone interview that his colleagues apparently did, he lured the *Times* reporter into the skybox, one of most privileged places for food-lovers in the land, and did what he does best: He fed him. The result: less than four column inches for Delouvrier and Ripert together, more than seven column inches for Boulud. Boulud managed, in his charming way, to turn an article about what French chefs think of McDonald's into much bigger news: Daniel Boulud creates a hamburger.

In the meantime, there's been no sign of Grimes since his visit last month. If he had been considering a review, it looks as though, for the moment at least, it's not happening. Perhaps what drove him uptown and through Daniel's revolving door for that unlikely visit was nothing more than a little summertime wanderlust.

Nine

BALANCE

A T DANIEL, the inevitable friction between the front of the house and the back of the house has grown. This conflict is present in every restaurant from the day it opens. Even after their years of schooling and training, cooks are paid between eight-fifty and twelve dollars an hour, with two hours of overtime "built in" daily, plus a sixth time-and-a-half day every other week. Some resent the fact that at a maximum of $39,000 (and as little as $27,625) many cooks earn less than busboys, who gross about $37,500 a year, including tips. Starting pay for *sous-chefs* is $50,000—less than what runners make (their pay averages around $52,500 a year with tips). The cooks generally don't bother hiding their disdain for the wait staff; many convey an air of superiority. Naturally, the wait staff doesn't appreciate the disrespect. It's the choice of the cooks, after all, to work in the kitchen; no one's twisting their arms. And besides, wait staff works longer hours, nor does it get yearly bonuses, as the kitchen staff does.

Given that great divide, there isn't too much socializing between the front and back of the house.

In fact, things can get downright nasty, with the chefs screaming at the wait staff. Charles, a captain, actually considers this a good thing. When things are very tense and there's lots of screaming and yelling, it forces him to focus more, and that makes it easier for him to do the best job possible.

Contrary to what the cooks might think, waiting tables is not the easiest gig in town. Bernard Vrod is fond of pointing out that if the most stressful job in the world is that of an air traffic controller, the second is that of a waiter. Customers ask to create their own tasting menu, or request a particular dish, but with a different sauce. "That's what gives us an ulcer," says Vrod. Boulud has given the directive that guests can have anything they want. That's all well and good, but if you're a captain, try asking the chef for something special on a night when the cooks are doing 380 covers, three journalists are in the dining room, and the kitchen's in the shit. It's the restaurant equivalent to stepping into the firing line of the artillery. In such a situation, any captain with an instinct for survival will note the request, go into the kitchen, pretend to ask the chef, then come back and tell the guest it's just not possible.

Nor is front-of-the-house work at Daniel the highest paid in New York. Although it's certainly competitive, some of the wait staff complain that with so many people on the floor, everyone's share of the tip pool is smaller.

It's a Thursday morning during the first week of August. Boulud is in France, on vacation with Micky and Alix. The summer has been cool and rainy, a little depressing, even considering that the alternative would be steamy and sticky. While most of America has been revved up by the presidential race—the Republican Party nominated George W. Bush as its candidate last week, and the Democratic Convention will be held next week in Los Angeles—New Yorkers find solace for the gloomy summer in baseball (both the Yankees and the Mets have been rocking) and in the continuing bull market. The past six weeks have seen a seemingly endless string of restaurant openings—so much glitz, so many hot chefs, so much hype. Who can keep up? Even so, it seems as though the weekends have all been wet, putting a damper on the plans of beach lovers and grill aficionados; New Yorkers can become rather childish about their summers. Perhaps it's a result of all that workaholism during the rest of the year.

At the end of the staff meeting in advance of service, Pascal, the cheese steward, explains the current cheese selection to German and two runners. L'Abbaye de Tamié from Savoie, L'Abbaye de Citeaux from Burgundy, Maroilles, Brin d'Amour, Champs de Mars.

"What's this one?" asks a runner.

"Morbier," says Pascal.

"Where's this one from?" asks the other runner.

"Corsica," says Pascal.

"Can you tell me this one again?" asks German, taking notes. If he's called upon to explain the offerings to a guest, he must seem to know them like the back of his hand.

"That's the Maroilles," says Pascal.

The cool weather is affecting diners' appetite for cheese: They're hungry for it, which is unusual for summertime.

Ariella arranges pastries on the cart. Today is her twenty-sixth birthday, and Iuzzini has brought her a huge bouquet of gorgeous long-stemmed roses—lavender, pink, apricot, red. She has started to panic about her visa problem—her J-1 expires September 5, so she'll either have to find another job where they'll sponsor her, or she'll have to leave Daniel and find some kind of freelance work for which a working visa won't be necessary. Her boyfriend Dan, the long-eyelashed *saucier*, quit last month to take a job as *sous-chef* at Mercer Kitchen, one of Jean-Georges Vongerichten's restaurants.

As for Iuzzini, he's about to go on vacation in the Dominican Republic with twenty-two of his closest relatives. He's not taking Theresa, though; he's not ready to mix girlfriend with family. When he comes back, he plans to start taking tap-dance classes again. That's autumn for you.

There is a review of Alain Ducasse's new restaurant in the Essex House in today's *New York Post*. The headline says LAUGH-RIOT—TILL THE CHECK ARRIVES.

"I don't even know if it's worth reading," says Allannic, but he does anyway.

Lee has taken the Spanish chef out to a farewell lunch at Cello, Chef Laurent Tourondel's small, elegant French restaurant in a nearby townhouse.

"Ordering, please," says a runner.

Cyrille looks up at the ticket. "Order one beet salad, one tartare, followed by one swordfish, no chorizo, one lamb, medium-rare."

Bruno Jamais comes in and grabs the Ducasse review.

"*Attends, je lis, je lis,*" says Allannic. Everyone in the kitchen respects Ducasse profoundly, yet while no one wishes him ill, one senses a perverse streak of delight in a negative review.

Thomas Haas will be leaving at the end of the week. Boulud spoke with Iuzzini about the job of executive pastry chef but stopped short of offering him the position. As much respect as Boulud has for Iuzzini—who's still only twenty-five years old—Boulud doesn't feel he's quite ready to handle the whole thing by himself yet. Although Iuzzini can certainly handle the production end of things, Boulud feels that in order to head up the pastry department of a restaurant at this level, a pastry chef should have worked in half a dozen of the best pastry kitchens in France. Iuzzini doesn't have that experience. Instead, Boulud has hired a pastry chef from France, Alain Poitier, and put Iuzzini in charge until Poitier arrives at the end of September.

Brad Thompson is now working on banquets. He had asked Boulud if he could do banquets exclusively, but Boulud wants him available to pinch-hit in the kitchen. Thompson says he prefers the independence of taking charge of the banquets, but one can't help but feel that he would rather be in charge of a busy kitchen. Perhaps he'd rather work independently than play third or fourth fiddle. The big chef has also been on a diet, not to lose weight, but to eat more healthfully. If he's good all week, avoiding fried and fatty foods, including his favorites, Popeyes fried chicken and Johnny Rockets hamburgers, he lets himself eat whatever he wants on Sundays. And what he wants is Popeyes chicken and Johnny Rockets hamburgers.

Jed's going up to Vermont this weekend, to his family's farm.

"Bring me some maple syrup," says Thompson.

"You already have some," says Jed. "I'm just gonna fish all weekend. Sunday morning, before you're up, I'm just going to drop my line in and sit there all day." Jed's father hunts partridge and grouse, which he raises for that purpose.

"What does he do?" asks Thompson. "Put 'em in a cage and gas 'em?"

"Yeah," says Jed. "That's what he does."

Ten days later, Fay is getting ready to say good-bye; Alex Lee is on vacation. Boulud returned from France yesterday. Just as New York will soon be getting back to work, his autumnal challenge will be whipping the staff out of its dog-day complacency and into solid four-star brilliance. Can he do it with all the staff attrition? AZ, a new Asian fusion restaurant in the Flatiron District with a kitchen headed up by Patricia Yeo, a relative unknown who trained with Bobby Flay, just got a three-star review from Grimes. Everyone devours the Wednesday reviews, Boulud included, and he makes a mental note to try this place out. Although Boulud has too much class to complain, his brigade reels at the injustice: How can an upstart with so little experience possibly merit the same rating as Daniel?

Boulud sits at the table in the skybox, making calls, catching up. Tolman is about to go on vacation to Cape Cod. She was supposed to go to Asia as well, but that part of her trip was canceled when family plans fell through.

Boulud calls Jed. "What did you tell me about some cooks starting on the twenty-first of August?" he asks him. He scribbles notes as Jed answers. "How do you spell Freelock? Give me a phrase on what he has done. Um-hm. And Alex hired him? He spoke to him? He got a reference from the chef and everything? And how much is he getting paid, do you know? A *stagiaire* from Lausanne? I was told we had a cook starting."

"Daniel," says Tolman. "Daniel."

"He worked where? How long?"

"Daniel."

"It was only *open* two months." He looks up at Tolman.

"Can you talk to Mrs. Vandenberg now?" He nods, barely. "He'll be right with you," says Tolman into the phone. The woman waiting to speak to him is a banquet client.

"Okay," says Boulud to Jed. "Let's get organized for mostly externs and young graduates, and I'll take care of the *chef de partie.*"

Neil Gallagher has just returned from his vacation in Spain, where he spent a few days working at El Bullí, Ferran Adría's Catalan restaurant that has been getting so much press in the United States this year. Adría actually let him videotape in the unconventional kitchen. Gallagher bounds up to the skybox to give Boulud a copy of the videotape.

"Freelock," as it turns out, is a young cook named Ryan Freelove, an entry-level cook from Florida. They'll probably start him in the *garde-manger.* As the pay for such a position is slim, Jed jokingly refers to him as "Freelabor." There are two other new hires in the kitchen: Tim Dover, an amiable, dimpled Scottish cook, also for the *garde-manger,* and Robert Martin, the goateed night hot-apps cook.

In the kitchen, Fay and her partner Chris do their *mise en place,* Fay with a giant bandaged digit. A few mornings ago she was cutting short ribs down in the prep kitchen and the knife slipped. When she saw the "meat" of her finger, she got dizzy and came upstairs. "You're green, you're green!" Chris said to her. The tetanus shot, she says, hurt more than the cut. Still, she finds it embarrassing, cutting herself. You get to a certain point and you think you're beyond that. She needed five stitches, which came out yesterday.

"I'm starting kick-boxing," she tells Chris. "Though I probably can't afford it." She's also starting a new job at Peacock Alley. Jean-Georges Vongerichten offered her a job as *sous-chef,* and she went in to trail there but decided she wasn't interested. At Peacock Alley she'll be *tournant,* working various stations as needed and earning $30,000 for a thirty-five-hour week.

The restaurant is closed for lunch, and there's no banquet stuff; that's all han-dled by a separate kitchen in the hotel. It is also closed for the entire month of August; she'll start when they reopen in September. Although her new salary represents a cut in pay, the forty thousand dollars she makes now is for a sixty-hour week, twelve months a year. Vongerichten offered her fifty thousand dol-lars to come in as *sous-chef*—more than she makes here as *saucier,* and commensurate with the starting salary for *sous-chefs* at Daniel.

"What's the 'classic' tonight?" she asks Chris.

"Pork belly," says Chris.

There are forty-four covers for lunch today, very slow. That's to be ex-pected in August.

"Ordering one cold soup, one gazpacho, followed by one monkfish, one striped bass," says Allannic. He then goes to work on a Tupperware drum filled with heirloom tomatoes—three green-striped zebra, one huge golden-yellow with roads etched in, two big purplish red guys, five walnut-shaped red ones, two smallish, round ones, five small purply-green-brick-red ones, three peach-skinned yellow ones—cutting out the stem ends carefully with a small, curved turning knife.

Roger, yet another new *garde-manger* cook, arranges five shrimp on a plate, tails in the air. String beans sit in a *saladier.* He grinds pepper on them, gives a squirt of vinegar, tosses them with his fingers, heaps them between the shrimp. Dressed baby arugula is mounded on top, also with fingers; it looks like laun-dry. Mandarin sections go between the shrimps, frizzled fried shallots go on top. He drizzles sauce around with the squirt bottle, puts the plate on the pass. Next, the *ballottine.*

"Have you ever done the *ballotine?*" asks the soup cook.

"With forty-four covers, if I need help, I need to look for another job," Roger says, not smiling. He runs water at his sink, lets it get very hot, and runs a knife under it before slicing the *ballottine.*

Gallagher appears. "We missed you yesterday," he tells William, the expe-diter who was out sick.

"Oh, yeah," says William.

"It was a real *bordel,*" says Gallagher. Between a Spanish wine dinner and Boulud having just gotten back from France, it was no party. "Ordering one tuna," he calls, "one bean salad, one tomato soup no cilantro, followed by one monkfish, one pree-fee cod, one crab cake main course."

Tolman comes and speaks quietly to Gallagher. She's always discreet when she orders her lunch, but to an outsider it looks almost nefarious. "Roger?"

asks Gallagher as Tolman heads back up the stairs. "Can I have just a big vegetable salad?"

"Fire 54!" shouts Fay.

"What?" says Kevin, from the fish station.

"Fifty-four!"

Cyrille Allannic puts the heirloom tomatoes, still whole, on a flat, round
Chinese-looking strainer. He uses the utensil to hold the tomatoes down in
boiling water for fifteen seconds, then he drops them, skins loosened, into a tall
stainless-steel container of ice water. A ticket comes up and he moves to the
pass. "Ordering two mini-soup, followed by one zucchini main course and one
seafood salad."

Gallagher, wearing gloves, preps a big hotel pan full of red and yellow
peppers. He slices them bottom to top, punches out the stem ends, cuts around
the inside, putting usable scraps in one *saladier,* seeds and pith in another. He
cuts the pepper, laying it open and flat, his knife staying parallel to the cutting
board. All around, there's an economy of motion, fluidity. Class. The flat
sheets of red pepper go in one bowl, yellow in another.

"Want some help, Patrice?" calls Fay to the fish station. Patrice shakes his
head.

"Roger, you made that salad for Hilary, right?" asks Gallagher.

Fay slices chicken breasts with the electric knife.

After calling out a few more orders, Gallagher juliennes the peppers. He
shaves off some of the bumpy flesh on the inside to get a uniform thickness:
soigné.

Bernard Vrod comes in from the dining room. "Neil," he says, "best crab
cake he ever had!"

Gallagher looks up. "The crab cake?" He juliennes, very fast, then turns to
sauce a plate for a meat order. These guys may be turning out some of the
most stupendous food in the world, but that doesn't mean they have time to
bask in praise. Gallagher's busy spooning the vegetable garnish onto the plate.
"Jesus, Chris, you're good," he says, looking at the *entremétier*'s vegetables.

"I'm just good at reheatin' stuff," says Chris.

The sliced chicken breasts go on top.

Chris, who once worked a union job at the Righa Royal, as Fay will at Peacock Alley at the Waldorf, tells her about the drug testing you have to go
through for the hotel union employees. "It's weird," he says of the testing center near Rockefeller Center. "There's a little picture of poop. And there's a big
clock. They give you a glove and a tongue depressor."

Gallagher chimes in that he went to a drug-testing center near Second Avenue and Forty-seventh Street when he got a job at Peacock Alley.

"A woman did my physical," says Chris, trimming baby turnips. "It was like an alien abduction. You have to stand naked."

"Order three pree-fee tomato soup," calls Gallagher, "three pree-fee mushroom risotto, one pree-fee bean salad, followed by two skate, one bean salad main course, and five lamb, medium-rare."

"Pree-fee?" says Fay. "Five lamb pree-fee?"

Gallagher nods. The tomatoes, which Allannic has peeled by now, glisten on a sheet pan lined with paper towels.

It's 1:50, very slow. Boulud is still upstairs.

Fay works on the lamb.

"You're going out to eat with like seven people," marvels Chris, "and you say, 'I'll have the lamb.' 'Yeah, I'll have the lamb.' 'I'll have the lamb.' 'I'll have the lamb.' It's ridiculous."

All the lamb fillets are going in two big pans, which Fay fires right away on the flame. She flips them a minute later. Lamb smoke fills the station, goes up into the efficient exhaust system. She pulls them off, arranges them on a round screen to rest. That accomplished, she turns to Chris. "Do you need something else done?" she asks Chris. Fay is a true team player.

"No," he says, working on the vegetable garnishes—cranberry beans, arugula, tomato confit, artichokes, and a black-olive *jus*.

"Patrice is crazy!" shouts Kevin. "Patrice thinks the chorizo that we got last week that was cured is spoiled."

"It smells like fruit," says Chris. "Like fucked-up rotten fruit."

"It's not the chorizo that smells," insists Kevin. He's prepping baby spinach leaves, aided by a dishwasher. The fish station has a charcoal grill next to the flat top. Kevin's pans come off the stove as they're finished and, once the contents are removed, go into a bus pan on the floor on a plastic crate, ready to go to dishwashing.

Twenty-eight-year-old Kevin is originally from Santa Fe, New Mexico, from a restaurant family—they owned the well-known La Tertulia ("the gathering place") for twenty-seven years. After attending the CIA, he did *stages* at the *Michelin* three-stars El Bullí and Georges Blanc, before returning to the U.S. to work at Commander's Palace in New Orleans. Kevin came to New York eight months ago, after his parents sold La Tertulia, and a month later, he started working at Daniel, in the *garde-manger*. His younger brother was a back waiter at Café Boulud; now he's working as a waiter at La Madeleine.

Their dream is to open up a restaurant together, with Kevin behind the stove and his brother in the front of the house. They've got it all planned out—it's to be Spanish- and French-leaning Mediterranean with an adjacent tapas bar, in St. Louis, where he and his brother both went to college (at St. Louis University). The way Kevin figures it, St. Louis is where Chicago was ten years ago in terms of the food business. Better to be a big fish in a small pond.

"Quieres algo más?" asks the dishwasher.

Kevin shakes his head.

Philippe, the nighttime *saucier,* comes through now and does a heavy-footed flamenco as he enters the walk-in.

Chris, meanwhile, finishes up his garnishes, adding chopped tomatoes to a big pan of cranberry beans, and then some arugula, toss toss toss. Fay slices the lamb, which she has briefly reheated, on the bias with the electric knife, arranging it on steel platters. It's perfect: red in the center, rosy pink all around. Her dream is one day to buy a house in Brooklyn and open a restaurant there.

"Look," says Chris. "Fennelstick is eating your lamb!" Fennelstick is Patrice—so-called because he's a tall stalk of a man.

"You have the tossed salad, Chris?" asks Fay. "Is it seasoned?"

"Yes." Now he and Neil plate the lamb. First cranberry beans, then lamb on top. Neil squeezes good olive oil over the lamb, arranges the arugula salad over it.

A runner touches the plate. "Awww!" he cries, recoiling from the heat.

"You guys are getting weak, man," says Chris. "You can't take the heat."

The lamb goes out at 2:10, as Patrice finishes an order of skate, with a beautiful baby herb salad on top.

By 2:12 there are no more tickets in the kitchen. Sam, the pastry assistant, finishes two plates in the pastry area—a raspberry pyramid on a meringue lattice.

The last week of August, the banquet room closes for renovations—a year and eight months after the restaurant opened. Work is also done in the lounge: The lighting is redesigned, making it warmer, and seats are replaced. In the banquet room, chairs are redone; new, more modern paintings hung; and a high-tech projection screen installed, one that's hidden but comes down with the push of a button—useful for luncheon presentations and the like.

Boulud and his partner Joel Smilow also announce this week that they have sold their interest in Payard Pâtisserie & Bistro. They had been thinking of cutting Chef François Payard loose for the past six months or so, since the relationship has not been symbiotic. Although financially the partnership, in which Payard owned 30 percent, was satisfactory to Dinex, the company felt Payard didn't take management direction from them, nor did he contribute to the group creatively. As Lili Lynton puts it, "No relationship in which we just earn a lot of money is fine." This one lacked balance.

In the meantime, Alain Ducasse is all anyone in New York's food world can talk about. His restaurant is being reviewed everywhere. When Ducasse prepared to open it, he scorned the traditional route of hiring a publicist to ease communication with the American food press. All requests for information had to go through his assistant, who told journalists that Mr. Ducasse wanted to handle all requests for information personally. Journalists, even under the press of a deadline, were told to send a fax to Mr. Ducasse and wait for an answer, even for basic information such as the opening date, the name of the chef, and so on—details that are normally covered in a press release. The Essex House's publicity department seemed completely incapable of handling pre-opening inquiries. An announcement was made that the restaurant would accept names for a waiting list, and a special phone number for this purpose was sent to clients who had eaten at Ducasse's establishments in France and Monte Carlo, as well as the food press. By the time the restaurant opened, the waiting list was 2,700 names long—or so said Ducasse's organization. And the prices made a meal at Daniel seem like a bargain.

The public, of course, saw none of this: What they did see was an endless barrage of negative press once the restaurant opened in July. *Fortune* magazine ran a headline that said ISHTAR: THE RESTAURANT. "Dante, have we got news for you: There's now a new circle of hell," wrote Rebecca Ascher-Walsh. "At Alain Ducasse at the Essex House, you'll see grownups spitting food into napkins, you'll bite into bread so burned you'd think Freddy Krueger were running the kitchen. . . ." And it got worse from there. A few days later, William Grimes wrote what he insisted was not a review (since Alain Ducasse had only been open two weeks when he visited it, and Grimes went only once), but rather a "sneak preview." In it he dwelt more on the rituals—getting a reservation, the stainless-steel carrier of half a dozen mineral waters from which to choose, the wax-sealed wine list, the warming cart used when diners must leave the table, *verveine* tea snipped off a live plant, a silver implement "with medical implications" for which he could only guess a use, the proffering of a selection of pens for signing the bill. Only a few lines were devoted to the food, one of which referred to a "viciously acidic" sauce. Next Gael Greene stuck her fork into Ducasse in a *New York* magazine review early in August.

Rumors of staffing problems abounded, and regular folks who ate there—that is, the regular folks who could cough up five hundred dollars or more for dinner for two—complained about it on Internet bulletin boards. Suddenly the place went from impossible to get in to no problem. To top it off, Alain Ducasse was closed on weekends and served lunch only twice a week. This would be dining on Ducasse's terms, which New Yorkers resented. And he was rarely spotted in the restaurant, which they resented even more. No one—but no one—is too good for Manhattanites. Yet Ducasse seemed to be.

And so, for other New York chefs, Alain Ducasse has become a living (if not living in New York) cautionary tale. The most respected chef in the world, the only one who boasts eight—count 'em, eight—*Michelin* stars, and here he is being raked over the coals, again and again and again, by journalists and civilians alike. It's enough to scare a chef out of his whites.

There has also been a subtle subtext of anti-French sentiment in all of this. Frenchman Alain Ducasse blows into town, dares to charge us three hundred dollars a person—*and he doesn't even speak English!* Who does he think he is?

But Boulud has his own problems. Besides the friction between the front of the house and the back of the house, morale in the kitchen continues to sag. Cooks who were attracted to the idea of working here because of Boulud's reputation for having spent plenty of time working closely with the cooks at the old Daniel have been disappointed. Certainly he works cheek-to-jowl with them during service, but he's so busy running the big operation that he doesn't have the time to guide them through their *mise en place*. Many therefore feel cheated out of the experience of learning directly from the chef.

For his part, Boulud has very much wanted to keep a balance in the ratio of French to American chefs in the kitchen, but it's difficult to manage that balance there, just as it is in the dining room. As Traussi points out, the easiest people to hire are French people because they're used to meeting demands. Daniel sponsors workers all the time, helping them get their work visas; most have J-1s, training visas. Still, the balance in the kitchen seems to be tilting more toward Americans, which Boulud isn't entirely comfortable with.

In the front of the house, the opposite is true—most of the maître d's, captains, and assistants are French, while the runners and busboys are mostly Ecuadorian. And with the captains, there's another problem of balance as well: If they put seven captains on the schedule, they're stretched a little thinner than would be ideal. If they put on an eighth, none of them would make the kind of living they need to for Daniel to be competitive on the marketplace and attract the top people. If they had six captains, they'd all have to work six days, so they put seven on, allowing each a five-day workweek.

And then there's that annoying matter of the fourth star. Although Boulud still downplays his preoccupation with getting it, those close to him contest his coolness. "I think it's the focus of Daniel's existence," is the way Brett Traussi puts it. "I don't think he cares about anything else." The *sous-chefs* are well aware of its importance to their chef. The Wednesday-morning analysis of Grimes's review has become a ritual, and the discussion is usually not pretty. Even if they don't talk much about the fourth star as a goal, it's never far from anyone's mind; it's a given. All of the cooks have more than a little at stake vis-à-vis the restaurant's star status, whether it's the right to include experience in a four-star establishment on their résumé or a wish that their painstaking, back-breaking work be recognized for what it is: arguably the best in the country.

Labor Day comes and goes, a bookend marking the unofficial end of summer in the city. It may be hot (finally!), but New Yorkers have had their fourteen weeks of laxity, and now everyone's ready to get back to business. The stock market is surging. The Democratic Party has chosen Al Gore as its candidate in the presidential election, and the campaign is in full swing. Restaurant openings, which slowed a little during August with no press around to cover them, have picked up once again. It's *the season;* autumn every year is when New York City really comes alive.

Take the first Monday after Labor Day, for instance. Monday is known as a slow restaurant night, but tonight Daniel is packed. Although there is only a modest number of covers in the dining room, there's also a party celebrating *Bon Appétit* magazine's annual awards in the Bellecour Room ("80 people," says the schedule posted on the bulletin board in the kitchen, listing all the week's events, "DB must speak, super VIP"). But Boulud, Georgette Farkas, and Jean-Luc Le Dû have cooked up a fine way to fill the restaurant on a handful of Monday nights: a series of special wine dinners, each themed to a particular region, with foods to match. "Invitations" to attend are sent by e-mail only, quick and easy, with no printing or mailing costs. They are a great way to promote the restaurant, too.

On the eastern balcony of the dining room, cleverly screened off from the rest of the dining room, one of these wine dinners is just getting under way. Le Dû serves glasses of white wine off a long table at the head of the room to guests who have paid five hundred dollars a head to attend an evening featuring wines of the Rhône Valley, matched with five courses. All the evening's wines are lined up on the table. Le Dû and Georgette Farkas chat easily with guests as they file in; everyone stands around enjoying glasses of Saint-Joseph "Deschant," Domaine Chapoutier 1997 and Crozes Hermitage, Domaine Alain Graillot 1998, as waiters pass canapés: tender *vol-au-vent* of creamy spinach, crayfish, and chanterelles; tartlets of crab and vegetables *basquaise* with bacon; summer tomato, anchovies, and *ricotta salata;* red mullet *escabèche.*

After a few minutes, Farkas shows everyone to their assigned seats—forty-six in all. Most people have come in pairs, though there are a few parties of four. Along the wall, a long communal table seats six on a side, everyone in pairs. Introductions are made all around: Bob Grimes, a longtime friend of Boulud's and vice-chairman of Citymeals-on-Wheels, has come with his friend Ed Matthews (since his wife doesn't care for these dining extravaganzas); in addition, there are two jovial, heavyset dot-com guys; a twinkly-eyed, long-bearded Russian wine collector, accompanied by his tall, birdlike wife. He seems vaguely amused by everything, and she looks bored. The rest of the tables are deuces and four-tops.

Farkas stands at the front and makes a little speech welcoming everyone. The weather is just cooling down, she says, and Daniel is now in the mood to cook for fall. Since Lyons is his home, he's enthralled with the idea of this particular wine dinner, matching dishes from Lyons with wines from the Rhône.

Outside, however, the weather is not particularly autumnal, nor, as it turns out, are the dishes particularly Rhônish. Never mind, though—they're spectacular. First, a neat slab of duck foie gras terrine with caramelized apples and a fig and purple plum chutney with port. Le Dû stands up to introduce the first wine, a Condrieu "Les Ayguets" Vendange Tardive, Domaine Cuilleron 1998. He shouts over the din of conversation. Everyone's already having a jolly time, and the evening has barely started. "In the late eighteenth and nineteenth centuries," Le Dû shouts, and the clatter of plates and chatter of happy guests drown out the story of the wine. "This is eighty percent rousanne and twenty percent marsanne," he manages to get in before he's completely overwhelmed. No matter; the late-harvest Condrieu—very rare for the appellation—is unparalleled; viscous-golden, with an intriguing floral note in the nose—gentian! It's velvety, well balanced, rich and complex, and the flavors linger on and on in the mouth. With the velvety foie gras and its contrasting bright yet deep fruit flavors, a brilliant match.

Pistou of summer vegetables follows, with clams, prawns, and a saffron cream, matched with an Hermitage Blanc, Domaine Jean-Louis Chave 1997.

White Hermitage is fairly rare, always exciting to try, but the consensus at the long table is that this one's over-oaked.

Then a pancetta-wrapped Montauk tuna with black truffle, chanterelles, and a potato-parsley puree. The black truffle does something magical to the tuna, and the juxtaposition of textures is marvelous. The wine, a Châteauneuf-du-Pape 1990 from Château de Beaucastel, is stunning—an inspired choice with the tuna, from the most accomplished producer of Châteauneuf.

Succulent roasted squab is next, its breast deeply rich and earthy, meaty and rare, along with a stuffed leg with braised Savoy cabbage, young root vegetables, and black trumpets—punctuated brightly by wild huckleberries (incorrectly translated as *"myrtilles sauvages"*—wild blueberries—but who's counting?). The wine with this course is the movie star of the bunch: "La Landonne," one of the three most prized wines of the Rhône, a Côte Rôtie from Guigal, 1988 (the other two stars are "La Mouline" and "La Turque," from the same producer). Le Dû, still shouting over the revelry, tells the story of how the two slopes of Côte Rôtie—la Côte Brune and la Côte Blonde—were named after two sisters, one of whom was a tomboy. "So today we have the tomboy wine," he says. Le Dû, along with all present, raves about the wine, though to at least one palate present the wine is closed; that is, it's in a phase in which the flavors and aromas become dormant, a natural part of the evolution of any great red wine, and in fact not surprising in a twelve-year-old La Landonne. If anyone else notices this, however, no one mentions it.

The last course, a chilled pyramid of blackberry sorbet filled with pistachio nougat, is matched with a very unusual wine, an Hermitage *vin de paille,* Domaine Chapoutier 1996. It's a wine made from grapes that have been dried into raisins on straw mats (*paille* means "straw"), concentrating the sugar to produce a very intense, sweet, raisiny-tasting dessert wine. The wine is interesting, but not stunning, and it clashes a little with the blackberry and pistachio flavors of the dessert. It's an odd denouement to an incredible evening.

Boulud never gets a chance to come in and say hello to these guests; he was too crazed with the super-VIP *Bon Appétit* party in the banquet room, which went, in the end, swimmingly well.

Wednesday, September 13

DOWNSTAIRS, IN A display case emblazoned with the legend DANIEL IN THE NEWS—and yes, there's enough to keep it filled—is a big spread in today's *New York Post* about the best chefs in New York. Ten critics, including Ruth Reichl, Robert Sietsema, critic for the *Village Voice*, John Mariani, and a handful of *Post* critics, have been asked to choose their favorite. Featured first, with a big picture, is Daniel Boulud, John Mariani's choice.

It's 6:35, and there's already a lot of smoke on the meat side of the kitchen. Philippe has four pans going; three hold medallions tied into neat rounds, another a chop. He pulls one of the pans off the stove, sticks it on the oven shelf, turns the medallions with tongs, shoves the pan in, and closes the door with his foot.

"Two risotto gazpacho working?" yells Alex Lee.

"Yes!" from the hot-apps station.

"Yes!" from soup.

Lee spies Pascal eating off to the side. "Pascal, *mange pas pendant le service. Merde,* " Lee tells him.

Pascal raises up his hand, palm up, a gesture of *merde* to you, too, pal.

"Si tu fais ça, tout le monde vont manger pendant le service." Lee says it gently: If you eat during service, everyone else will want to, too. "One risotto borscht," Lee calls, then turns to the runners, who are staring at him. "Okay, you guys try to follow the service and do your job. You don't know how long you'll keep it!" He smiles. "Imagine you're a mason. If one piece doesn't work, you change that piece." The runners smile. It's actually a light moment. Lee plays his role as boss, and being the heavy is part of the game. He doesn't really mind it, but truly being stern is not in his nature.

"Pascal, sents pas les fleurs non plus," Lee adds. Don't smell the flowers, either. Now Lee's making fun of himself. "Ordering one tomato soup no crab and one crab, the pree-fee size, for Micky."

A new runner, Dominic, an American guy, stands out among the Ecuadorians. He's the same height—that is, not tall—with a medium build, round face, and slicked reddish hair. He's sweating profusely.

"You been taking salt?" Lee asks him.

"Yeah," says Dominic. "I'm not sweating anymore."

If there's one person who acts as a liaison between the front of the house and the back of the house, that would be Alex Lee. Lee takes an interest in *every* aspect of the restaurant. Not only does he facilitate communication between Boulud and the entire staff, but he actually runs the restaurant as if it were his own.

At 7:10 Boulud walks in and all chitchat stops. Côte stands a paupiette on its end over a drain, lets the fat roll off, and then plates it.

Lee finishes a frogs' legs dish he's just created, with parsley and garlic, black trumpet mushrooms, walnuts, and a sauce made with three types of pumpkin. The frogs' legs, sautéed, are perfectly tender, golden brown on the outside. The inspiration came from thinking about classic frog leg preparations: cream sauce; *persillade,* which involves parsley and garlic; and Provençale; all this in conjunction with late-summer/early-fall ingredients—walnuts, pumpkins, black trumpets. The result is pure Alex Lee brilliance, sumptuously capturing the exact moment of the season.

"Fire two more ravioli," calls Lee. "Two tunas and a risotto."

Food & Wine editor Nancy Ellen Ward is at table 55; they want to do an eight-course tasting menu with wines. There's also a *soigné* for the owner of a restaurant called Tandoor. "House acct. 3 regs," says another, and "Press." Another says "DB's trainer, with parents. VIP treatment, please. See DB comp!" But that's not all—there's "See JL wine broker with winemaker," "lifestyle editor of *Forbes,*" two happy birthday, one happy anniversary, two more regulars, and two banquet clients.

At 9:15 is Andrew Wylie, one of the most important literary agents in town. In the world! Two hundred and forty-five covers all told. Not full capacity by any stretch, but not bad for a Wednesday night. The season's just beginning, and with it, a higher ratio of New Yorkers to out-of-towners.

A sign above the swinging "in" and "out" doors announces LA LOTERIE DES CARTES VERTES 2002—Green Card Lottery 2002. Working visas are a constant problem for the many foreign-born cooks and wait staff. Although Dinex helps the staff attain the appropriate visas, winning a green card through the annual lottery would instantly put an end to the troublesome issue, and it would also give the winner the freedom to seek employment elsewhere.

"Ça va!" yells Boulud to Bobby in the *garde-manger.* "You're putting too much of that! It's a little condiment, it's not a garnish, okay?" He's referring to the ginger confit Bobby's putting on an order of sautéed foie gras with figs and baby grapes.

"Yes, Chef," says Bobby.

Now Bobby plates a *ballottine,* concentrating.

"Less is more," says Boulud. Then uh-oh, he walks into the *garde-manger.* Tim, the bedimpled Scottish *garde-manger* cook new to the job, looks on as he works. "When you do the *ballottine,*" says Boulud, "the film has to go in one direction. Look at this—it's shit." He points to the plastic film that keeps the *ballottine* in place as it sets; it's all twisted.

"Order frog and risotto followed by striped bass and squab," calls Lee.

Thompson has been working on the tasting menu for the *Food & Wine* editor, including a smaller version of lobster risotto. "Chef, when I do a small one like this, do you want the coral cream also?" he asks.

"Do they want a lot of food?" asks Boulud.

"I'll find out," says the captain who's waiting on them.

"No, *ça va*," says Boulud. "I can do five courses plus cheese or six courses without cheese."

Le Dû figures out the wines with Boulud, then Boulud gives the ticket to Philippe.

When the third of five or six courses has gone out, Boulud, Lee, and Thompson consult again, then Boulud looks up at the tickets. "Let's go, give it to me, those two duos," he says. "Ordering one foie gras, one lobster risotto, one lamb, medium-rare. Table 16's gotta go."

"Yes, Chef," says a runner.

"We have string beans, if you want," says Boulud to David, the maître d'.

David goes back out to the dining room, then returns. "They don't want it," he says hoarsely.

"Are you losing your voice?" asks Boulud.

"Yeah."

"You were screaming at the Giants game on Sunday."

David smiles; Boulud bellows out a long order.

"Five *rouget*, one tuna," calls Lee. "Let's pick it up!" Then he turns to the *garde-manger;* they're falling behind. "Hello!"

"Yes, Chef," says the *garde-manger* cook.

"Ordering one pree-fee corn, one pree-fee tomato, followed by one pree-fee tuna, one pree-fee *rouget!* I really need someone in *garde-manger* to get those guys out of the shit there."

Bruno Jamais lumbers in, looks around, walks out again.

"Is Michael here?" says Boulud; he picks up the phone. "I want to see Michael in here." He turns back to the kitchen. "Okay, a corn and a tomato."

Gallagher deposits two plates on a tray; Boulud examines them. *"La caille est trop cuite, et le foie gras n'est pas assez cuit,"* he announces. The quail is over-cooked, the foie gras undercooked. He sends them back to Philippe. Then turns to William. "On 21 I'm changing things," he says, "so I have to explain to you again."

A ticket goes up. "Ordering another caviar to share, one blinis. Ordering a tomato bean salad. Ordering two tartare heirloom salad and after that a paupiette and a lamb, medium-rare."

"Give me that soup," says Boulud. "We are really in the shit."

By 8:55 the kitchen has reached a fever pitch. "Let's go!" shouts Boulud. "It's been fifteen minutes for that table! Then I need a tomato soup and a tartare. Ravioli main course working good?"

"Working!" yells the hot-apps cook.

"It's fifteen minutes!" repeats Boulud. "Seventeen minutes, actually."

Now Gallagher does some vegetarian plates for a party in the banquet room—special orders during banquets are done in the main kitchen. A cornucopia of late-summer vegetables is artfully arranged on each plate. Gallagher spoons a gorgeous, pale frothy cream sauce around the periphery.

"Here's a main-course ravioli," says Damien, now on hot apps. He wears a "beard" that is a short vertical line from his lower lip to his chin; a short cap is his toque.

"Okay, listen to me," says Boulud to the lineup of runners, pointing to various plates. "Table 30. Table 61. Table 48 gets scallop in the middle, okay?"

"Two risotto and a tartare," calls Lee.

"Order a tartare and a gazpacho, and after that a lamb, medium, and a swordfish. Order a pree-fee bass and a pree-fee lamb for the bar." He calls out two more orders in rapid succession. "You got 36 soup, *hein?* You got 56 appetizer, *hein?* One no anchovy, Bobby, *hein?*"

"Where's the barley?" a runner asks Philippe. There's a garnish missing for the lamb.

"Je l'ai donné, je l'ai donné," says Philippe. It went out on another tray to the wrong table.

"The barley went out to the wrong table," Boulud tells a runner. "Can you check it out?"

"Fucking shit," says Philippe under his breath. Although it's tense, no one is really pissed.

"That's beef?" says Boulud as a meat dish lands on a tray. "Give me the potato and hit the deck."

Gallagher puts up four more tickets in the meat station. The meat *entremétier* suddenly drops to the floor and does five push-ups. Then he washes his hands. No one even notices.

"Order two beluga caviar followed by two beef, one medium-rare, one medium," calls Lee.

Umberto comes in with a full tray, tries to get Lee's attention. "Sixty-four's not ready," he says. They all look at it.

"Did you jump table in the front?" Boulud asks Philippe.

"No, Chef," says Philippe.

"So 15 and 45 are done, eh? What did you do with the table?" Boulud asks the runner.

"The table was cleared, but the person got up to go to the bathroom, and they came back," he says. "So it's fine, Chef." The waiters would never put plates on a table from which a diner was missing. The runner starts back for the dining room with the tray of plates.

"Hey!" Boulud calls. "Come here!"

The runner comes back.

"The table is not cleared!" says Boulud.

Michael Lawrence comes in. "Fifty-four is not cleared," he says "but German said to leave the food on the *guéridon*. I don't care."

Now German comes in. "What are you pissed at?" he asks Lawrence.

"I'm pissed that you pulled it in and the table wasn't cleared and you left it at the station."

German starts to protest.

"I don't care! You do your job right, and don't worry about the rest, okay?"

Johnny Iuzzini comes in, hair freshly dyed blue-black, goatee shaved off. He wanted to go black from platinum; he didn't realize the color he chose was blue-black. But that's okay; it's just hair. Iuzzini celebrated his twenty-sixth birthday last week, and he's wiped out. Since Thomas Haas left, he's been working from six-thirty in the morning to eleven-thirty at night. Still, he's glad Haas is gone. Iuzzini always felt he was too arrogant and liked to play people against each other. Once he and Haas got into an argument, and Iuzzini told him, "Thomas, I've been here a lot longer than you, and I'm going to stay a lot longer than you." Haas, says Iuzzini, knew he was right.

Iuzzini, meanwhile, couldn't be happier with his team—they're tight. The reason they work so well, he believes, is that he comes in first thing in the morning and stays till last thing at night. He's not pleased, however, that the new executive pastry chef will be bringing along a new pastry *sous-chef* as well. Still, he concedes he probably wasn't ready to take the job on for real and in the meantime he'd hate to let Boulud down—or himself. He looks into the kitchen and sees that things aren't going that great here either: Half of the cooks are new.

Lawrence brushes past him, and Iuzzini hands him a twenty-dollar bill. "I found this in the locker room," Iuzzini says. "I believe in karma and shit, so I can't keep it."

Lawrence looks dubious, grins. He pretends to pocket it.

"No, really," says Iuzzini. "But if no one claims it, I want it."

"No one's gonna claim it," says Lawrence. "Everything in there just gets stolen anyway." It's true: There's a kleptomaniac in the house. Someone has been not only breaking into lockers, but also stealing pants on hangers around the locker room—even swiping dirty T-shirts.

Brad Thompson comes through the swinging door from the banquet kitchen with Celia, an office worker who's helping Thompson with the menus for Boulud's Lufthansa project; she lives with Scott, the fish cook. Thompson and Boulud are scheduled to leave for Germany in a couple days to meet with the Lufthansa people; Thompson's looking forward to getting out of the country. He and Boulud have also been working closely putting together dishes for a company that plans to sell flash-frozen *sous-vide* meals over the Internet. (*Sous-vide* is a vacuum-packing technology that's popular in France, where high-quality frozen entrées are very respectable.)

Thompson goes into the kitchen. In a moment he comes back out.

"We're not going," he tells Celia.

"To Germany?" she says. She looks crushed on Thompson's behalf.

"Because of what's going on in there." What's going on, as usual lately, is that they're in the shit. Too many new cooks, too many covers.

"He knew it would be busy when he made the plans," says Celia.

"Yeah, but it's different when he's in the middle of it."

"But he has to go!" says Celia.

"They're gonna be pissed," says Brad. "They've paid for first-class tickets."

Thompson is clearly disappointed. He really wanted to go. True, he wouldn't get to see much of Germany in less than two days. But still.

Boulud's plan was to go to France for two days for his brother's wedding, and then spend two days in Germany. If he's not showing up at his brother's wedding, the situation here must be serious. Hostilities among the staff are manageable; still, the ongoing turnover is troublesome at a time when the restaurant is packed every night. Boulud leaving the country now could spell real trouble. The Germans, one hopes, won't take it personally.

Ten Chefs, Twenty Years, Thirty Dishes

I T'S FRIDAY MORNING, September 22, one day into autumn according to the almanac, and Jed has just returned from the farmers' market. He doesn't normally go on Fridays, but preparations are already under way for Boulud's long-awaited extravaganza celebrating his thirty years as a chef and twenty years cooking in America. Monday's dinner, *"20 Ans en Amérique"*—Twenty Years in America—will be the feast of a lifetime: thirty dishes in ten courses prepared by ten chefs from Daniel and Café Boulud. It didn't take long to sell out eighty places at five hundred dollars a pop. Each one of Daniel's chefs will present his three dishes together in one course. It's a chance for them to really stretch, show their stuff. They've been planning for weeks, and now the shopping and prepping begins. All ten chefs have visions of their preparations running through their heads.

And what better time of year than the cusp of summer and fall; it's still warm enough to relish the cool tang of a marinated raw fish or a chilled shell-fish soup, but thoughts of those in the kitchen are turning also to chestnuts, *cèpes*, huckleberries and figs, game, roasted meats.

As usual, Jed is thinking about ingredients. This morning he has picked up elderberries at the market, and tri-star strawberries. In years past, strawberry season would have been long finished, but these tri-stars, relative newcomers on the market, are sweet and flavorful well into the fall—nothing like the giant insipid foam-rubber specimens that pass for out-of-season strawberries in the supermarket.

Jed thinks about what provisions he'll need to order for each of the dishes, ticking down a list in his mind. Frédéric Côte is doing foie gras three ways, one of which involves *cèpes*. Here they got lucky, he thinks; they've got beautiful cèpes from France all of a sudden. For Alex Lee's raw fish course, he'll have to get Thai snapper. Hamachi is no problem; that'll come from New Zealand, phenomenal, and tuna as usual. Lee is also doing an oyster and sea urchin velouté. Urchin season in Maine started a couple of weeks ago; Rod Mitchell of Browne Trading Company has divers he works with up there; the urchins are just a little small. His divers don't like to work on Sunday, but Jed will have to let him know they'll have to. White truffles have started, but they're only so-so. They have a couple in the house; Andrew Carmellini, the executive chef at Café Boulud, can use them for his lasagne/gnocchi/risotto course. Sea scallops, for Neil Gallagher, they'll get live Monday morning from Cape Cod Bay in Massachusetts; since it's illegal to ship out live scallops from Maine, they won't get them from Browne Trading. Langoustine and lobster they'll get fresh. Neil's lobsters will be Canadian hard-shells. For Brad Thompson's striped bass three ways, the bass will be wild, probably from Long Island. Cyrille Allannic is doing an epigram of veal from the farm: Tripe, they got a beautiful one yesterday, fresh and white (not frozen like usual); for the whole leg, Jed contacted Four Story Hill, the Pennsylvania farm that supplies all the restaurant's veal, two weeks ago. Jean-François Bruel, the *sous-chef* at Café Boulud, is doing Scottish game. Now's the season, and Jean-François should already have the grouse; the venison for his course is actually from Millbok Farm in upstate New York. They normally kill once a week, but then they do it once more weekly for Daniel and Jean Georges, sending a delivery twice a week. The chestnuts that go with the venison are from Tim Stark, known throughout the state as the Tomato Guy since a *New York* magazine article about how he supplies all the top chefs ran last year. Tim has long sold his tomatoes at the Union Square Greenmarket, but these days he can barely keep up with the demands of the restaurants. In the autumn, he supplies Daniel with a hundred pounds of chestnuts a week. Johnny Iuzzini will need figs and plums—the black mission figs are very nice right now, and a farmer at Union Square had some beautiful Italian plums.

"Do you have any bones?" Joe, the soup-cook extern, asks.

"We had eighty pounds of pheasant bones yesterday," says Jed.

"Those are almost over," says another cook.

Okay, then, bones. Now Jed will go talk to each chef and see if there's anything he hasn't thought of that they might need. What else? he thinks. The market will get nice California Brussels sprouts; broccoli, the late, late summer, early fall things. Watermelon radish. Huckleberries—they come from Oregon; the purveyor's getting them tomorrow, Jed will get them Monday.

Downstairs, Brad Thompson starts working on his striped bass dishes for Monday. Since sea bass is such a versatile fish, Thompson thought it would be nice to show all the different ways of cooking it. Despite running jokes about how Thompson will give the guests overly large portions, he's planned on one ounce per preparation, so that's only three ounces of fish per person for his course. He'll take the skin off and make nice squares; these he'll wrap in lettuce leaves with black truffles, carrot, and celery leaf, and steam them. For the second dish, he'll bake the bass in *casuelas*—individual earthenware pots—with chorizo, cockles, peppers, and parsley. And finally he'll roast a large sea bass whole, removing the bones first and tying it up with herbs. He'll present it whole: It should be beautiful.

In the end, Thompson had wound up going to Germany—he left Sunday night and just came back on Tuesday. He spent the whole day tasting with the Lufthansa people; Boulud missed that, and his brother's wedding, too. After the return flight, Thompson came directly to the restaurant from the airport. In three or four weeks, he'll go back to Germany for the final presentation. If everything's fine, production of the in-flight meals will start at the end of December.

In the meantime, the banquet business has been so busy that Thompson hasn't had a day off in weeks. On top of everything else, his lease is about to expire, and he has to find a new apartment. He'd like to find a girlfriend, too. But who can meet anyone when you have to work seven days a week? Not to mention she has to love every kind of food.

At least Thompson has his vacation to look forward to (even if it is a working vacation): On October 15, he'll leave for France, where he'll be the guest chef on a bicycle tour of Burgundy. It's a great gig: He'll be responsible for cooking two dinners in châteaux along the eight-night route, and he gets to bring along a guest. He has invited his mom, and his dad will come along, too.

Upstairs, at eleven o'clock, Dominic, the sweaty runner, comes in, sweating. Dominic is twenty-three years old, a graduate of Reed College in Portland, Oregon—a philosophy major, in fact, with a passion for logic and the philosophy of mathematics. He's worked at Morgan Jennty in Queens, the Hard

Rock Cafe in Miami, Jardinière in San Francisco. Dominic doesn't particularly like working at Daniel. Everyplace else he's worked, employees decide in conjunction with the restaurant on what to declare in taxes; here he loses five to six hundred per paycheck, so a $1,300 weekly gross might come out to $750 net. He's also bothered by what he sees as inefficiency. Having so many people on the floor, he says, breeds laziness, "especially among the French," and of course the tips have to be divided among a lot of people. Nowhere else that he's worked have the tips been pooled. Dominic doesn't intend to make a career out of restaurant work, however; he plans to get a job with Merrill Lynch.

At 11:15 the family meal comes out. A busboy, muttering, puts out sandwiches on homemade white bread, *frites*, salad, *"Soave, soave, soave,"* he says. Everyone lines up as he puts out the food.

Upstairs in the skybox, Boulud, in his whites, is in a meeting.

"Marc, good morning," says Kevin, picking up a plate. "How are you?"

Marc is the meat *entremétier;* this is his second week. He's fresh from a stint at Peacock Alley; before that he worked at Quilty's and Jack's Fifth.

Young Joe is in his station, taking good care of his soups. Pieces of paper taped over the station remind him of the recipes:

CURRY SAFFRON CAULIFLOWER SOUP
small dice caulif, ckd
start mussles, save ckg liq. + shells (cln well)
blanched scallions, thinly sliced
curry oil
saffron poached apple discs, no skin and core
whipped cream with chopped cilantro, season and do not
    overwhip
whole cilantro leaves

APPLE CHESTNUT SOUP
caramelized turned apples
braised chestnuts
foie gras
whole celery leaves
ch. chives

PHEASANT CONSOMMÉ
brunoise celery root, ckd

brunoise carrot, ckd
julienne pheasant
sauté blk tr mush
quenelle of chicken livers + pheasant meat
braised chestnuts
chopped chives
f.g. dice
pheasant jus

He grabs a pinch of salt with his fingers, salts the curry soup, then stirs it, lovingly.

"Who took my paper towels?" asks one of the cooks. Like plastic film and side-towels, they're a hot commodity. No one confesses.

French David ladles melted butter over paupiettes of black sea bass, already wearing their raw potato wrappers. He slides them into a refrigerated cabinet.

The cook calls out the first order at 12:02: "Two green salad with tomato and onions, followed by one lobster and one halibut main course."

Five minutes later, the salads go out, topped with curly microgreens.

Frédéric Côte browns pieces of fennel in a deep pot, turning them with tongs. Patrice puts a sauce through a china cap, pressing it with the back of a spoon. Joe separates eggs, passing the yolks back and forth between a shell in either hand. Everyone's moving fast, but relaxed—the efficient last-minute prep of a busy lunch. Leslie, the hot-apps cook, comes back to her station with a Styrofoam cup of coffee and a roll—she didn't have time to eat. Joe now makes his blini batter, whipping it vigorously in a large, stainless-steel bowl.

"How do you call downstairs?" Marc says.

"Push 1-4-7," says Joe.

Marc does, talks into the phone. "Bobby. Bobby. Dude—where's my pepper mill? My pepper mill. Whereabouts. In the cabinet?" He hangs up, goes to find it.

"Don't lend anything to Bobby," says Joe, pouring his blini batter into a squeeze bottle. "Not a pen, not a spatula—nothing." He doesn't spill a drop.

Marc finds the black plastic pepper mill, comes back to the phone and calls again. "Yeah, I found it. Holy shit, dude—it's totally melted." A cook flips through *Gourmet* magazine that was sitting next to the phone.

"David, can you fire this for me?" asks William, handing him a ticket. "Ordering, please!"

The other cook calls out the order: "One pree-fee tomato, one pree-fee ravioli, followed by one pree-fee bass and one pree-fee beef." Now Côte steps up and calls out an order over the microphone.

Alex Lee comes in at 12:20. He has a photo album filled with pictures of his garden in Port Washington. In one, his two-year-old son, Dylan, is picking heirloom tomatoes, surrounded by riotously gorgeous flowers.

Hilary Tolman comes down from the skybox and whispers something in Lee's ear.

"Order a pumpkin soup for Hilary!" Lee shouts. "She's sick! Sick VIP!" And then he turns to the brigade, serious. "Okay, we're gonna be in the shit today—eighty covers." Although that's only a fraction of what they do during dinner, at lunch all the guests come at roughly the same time, one seating only.

Joe flips his blinis, using a spoon.

Lee calls to the cook at the far end of the station, "Hey, you gotta watch your *mise en place*. We're very busy tonight—like three hundred and fifty!"

David arranges an order of roasted halibut with *cèpes* on the plate with salsify and country bacon, over a butternut squash–parsley puree, puts it on a tray. The almost unlikely but stunning combination of the delicate halibut with the earthy *cèpes* gives new meaning to the phrase surf 'n' turf.

Lee completes the sheet listing the night's specials. Each *sous-chef* writes in his dish, but Lee fills in the gaps. *"Le jus, c'est quoi?"* he asks Allannic.

"Jus de cèpes," says Allannic.

Now Lee turns to Côte. *"On fait quoi avec le foie gras que j'ai fait?"* he asks him. "Apples, or what?"

"Figues sautées jardines," says Côte.

"And the crabs, *c'est quoi, les* peeky-toe crabs, for the monkfish?"

"Bah oui," says Côte. But of course.

Jean-Pierre, a maître d' known as J.P., comes in. "These people were here last night," he tells Lee, "so I thought maybe we'd send a little middle course? But I don't want to call him." Meaning Boulud.

"We'll see how they do with their salad and foie gras. If not, we can do a dessert." The foie gras is sautéed, with a quince, apple, and pear compote, toasted walnuts, and frisée with a port and cinnamon sauce.

Lee goes back to work on the specials list: "Monkfish like the old menu," he writes, "and crab cake but not blue crab. Guinea hen with porcini, corn, bacon, white asparagus, roasted potato, porcini *jus*. Pork belly like always." Tolman will make the dishes sound mellifluously appetizing when she writes them up on the final menu.

"Okay, guys," Lee calls out, "watch your service today. Eighty covers, gonna go very fast."

Downstairs, preparations for the 20 Years dinner are taking on epic proportions. At Lupe's station a huge box half the size of a refrigerator, fitted inside with a Styrofoam box, holds half a veal. Boulud stands admiring it with Jed and Thompson. Lupe's sink is filled with Dover sole.

"They used to cut it in half," says Boulud, regarding the veal.

"Yeah," says Jed. "Now they do quarters."

Thompson goes back to what he was doing—quail, but not for Monday; this is for a party tonight. He pulls a tiny wishbone half an inch long out of the quail. Once they're boned, he'll stuff them with foie gras wrapped in spinach leaves and fig wrapped in prosciutto.

Lupe finishes up the sole he's been filleting, reaches for another.

"Look at him," says Gallagher, walking by. "He's so fast."

Lupe cuts off the head, slices down the middle, fillet, fillet, flip, fillet, fillet, and tosses the bones. And again.

Jed flops the veal onto the counter opposite him. "Okay, Lupe," he says, "you have half." Jed pokes it. "It's too fresh," he says. "It was just killed." A leg hangs off of the counter.

Thompson looks over at them. "Where's my fuckin' pigs, man?" he says to Jed. As if he didn't have enough to do for Monday, he's roasting pigs at a tailgate party at the Giants game on Sunday. Jed will be there, too, as will Brett Traussi, a number of the cooks, and a bunch of purveyors. He also has a party for sixty-five people in the banquet room on Saturday night.

"Pigs are coming, man. Brad, you okay, or what?" says Jed.

"No." By Thompson's side is a prep list for the Saturday party:

> FRI
> cook terrine
> tomato confit jars
> radish diced
> dill
> cook chanterelles
> baby tom confit
> truffle sauce
> slice truffles
> wrap tuna (Fri + Sat)

stuff quail
quail jus
turnips
chard
parsley puree
parsley fried

SAT
Lob salad:
cook 25 lobs
clean + portion
dressing
artichokes 100 pc
turn potatoes (250)
roast artich (250)
cipollini (250)
parsley
chix jus
crab gm station
tie beef
shallots caramelized
pot puree sauce

Thompson turns to a young prep cook to his right, who's finishing prepping some cabbage. "Okay, when you're done with that," he says, "we have to start cutting potatoes." An almost imperceptible look of annoyance flickers across the cook's face. Thompson doesn't miss it. "Ah, *putain*, yeah, that's right," Thompson adds.

Lupe steels a knife eighteen times, really fast, then goes back to work on the sole. "I can do salmon even faster," he tells Gallagher.

"I do salmon in one minute," says Gallagher.

Lupe does the last sole. He puts the fish frames in a container under the sink, then hefts the tray of sole up over his head, depositing it a few places over on the central island. He washes his knife and steel, then wipes down his cutting board. And cleans it some more. He picks up the board, wipes the counter underneath. There's a damp cloth underneath the board to keep it from slipping.

Kevin and the fish cook prep broccoli rabe, whacking off several inches from the bottoms of the stems and pulling off the big leaves.

Alex Lee comes through, noticing the broccoli rabe. "We should save the bottoms for the family meal," he says. Then he looks around. "It's really crowded in here. Someone might want to go work in the banquet kitchen. Brad doesn't need it. You might get more done."

He's right: Despite the generous size of the prep kitchens, when the cooks are all working in their spots—six or eight around the central island, and others at the counters that line the walls—there's barely room for anyone to pass between them. They all work practically back-to-back. Every time someone comes through on their way to the offices, the pastry prep area, the bread bakery, or the back room of the prep kitchen, everyone has to move aside to let them by—a real annoyance when you're working under time pressure.

Tim, the dimpled cook from Scotland who has been at Daniel for three months, preps sea urchins, which he's a little surprised to see. At home such creatures are considered fish bait. Using scissors, he cuts around the central opening, dumping the runny guts into a pan. The roe—the edible part—stays in sacs in the shell; these go into a big bowl that has some purple slime in it, too. Tim has been in the U.S. for seven months, the prior four spent in a restaurant in Maine. That place was more about making money than doing nice food, so he's thrilled to be here. The funny thing is they did two hundred covers up there—half of what they can do here, where the quality is so much higher. At the restaurant where he worked in Scotland, they did forty covers—everything was *à la minute*. Tim is twenty-five; he's been working in kitchens since he was seventeen. Like many of Daniel's cooks, he lives in Astoria, Queens, where a growing colony of French restaurant workers has recently established itself. Although it's in another borough, across the East River, it's a short and easy subway ride away.

Jed hauls in a carton holding two baby pigs—they stay in the middle of the floor.

Lupe, meanwhile, has cut the shank off the veal hindquarter. Cyrille Allannic comes in, sees it, shrugs: He wanted it whole. *Rien à faire*. "Lupe," he says, "you bone this here."

"You need the other half, or no?" Jed asks Allannic.

"And the sweetbreads and everything else is there in the fridge?" Allannic asks him.

"Yeah," says Jed, "I got those, too."

Lupe strokes the fat from the veal leg with the blade of his knife. "Cyrille, Cyrille," he says. "You wanna take off all these bones? Only the meat you want it nice and everything?"

Allannic stares at it.

"Or you want it like a big lamb with the bone?"

"I don't know," says Allannic. "I have to ask Daniel."

Yes, this is a party honoring Boulud—his chefs meeting a huge challenge, strutting their stuff. But he, nevertheless, is the chef.

Thompson, who has been laying slices of truffle onto deep, red pieces of tuna, suddenly puts his hands into the air.

"What do you want?" asks Lupe.

"One towel, that's all I want. One fucking towel."

Lupe, still thinking about the veal, calls over to Philippe. "Make chops, Philippe? You want to make veal chops and the veal saddle?"

"I don't know," says the *saucier*. "Let's see what he wants to do about the saddle." He, of course, being Boulud.

Thompson now lays the truffle-layered tuna onto slices of pancetta. This is for pancetta-wrapped tuna with black truffle, chanterelles, and a potato-parsley puree—a dish that works really well for banquets because he can sear the tuna ahead of time, then flash it in the oven to heat it before serving.

Lupe doesn't stand around waiting for an answer about the veal; he starts on something else. He hefts a baby lamb onto the cutting board, cuts it at the waist, cuts off the head. He opens the chest and abdominal cavity, removing the lungs and other organs, putting them on a big piece of paper next to the head. With a cleaver, he now hacks through the rib cage. To complete the butchering, he alternates between the cleaver and the small knife he uses for fish—he takes out the rack, cuts off the shoulders and legs. Three minutes flat, the whole thing. Then he does another, going at the waist with the cleaver. This time he leaves the legs attached.

Now Thompson tries another strategy with his tuna—he puts the truffles directly on the pancetta, then lays the tuna over. For Thompson, part of being a good cook is finding the best and most efficient way to do any job, and he'll tinker until he's satisfied that it can't be done any more smartly. He slices truffles on his plastic mandoline.

Allannic comes back with news about the leg of veal. "Keep the bone," he says. "Leave it inside. He wants me to reattach it. So you just clear a little bit of the fat, leave the bones, take the fat. Arrange a little bit here"—and he shows him what he means—"and take out some of this here. And then we'll attach it." Allannic actually intends to sew the hoof back on. It's just for presentation, so it should work. Lupe wrestles with the foot, bending his knees as he puts it back in place.

Using a huge needle and cotton string, Allannic and Lupe perform the reconstructive surgery on the veal.

AGAINST ALL ODDS, and despite the tremendous pressure on ten chefs with limited time and limited space to pull off this evening what is undoubtedly the most ambitious meal to be held so far this millennium (if not the last), everyone's in a good mood this afternoon. Over the weekend, Daniel won a couple of big prizes at the *Time Out New York* Awards—Boulud won the award for Best Chef in New York City and Daniel won for Best French Restaurant. So what if it doesn't have four stars in the *New York Times*—William Grimes isn't the only palate in town that matters.

Ariella, the pastry cook, has left. She landed a job at the well-known restaurant Alison on Dominick as executive pastry chef. Not only is the title a huge step up, but she also has been told that the restaurant will take care of her visa problem.

Yesterday was the Giants game, and the tailgater with the baby pig roast came off famously, attended by ten Daniel staff members and ten purveyors. But today Thompson is running behind his own self-imposed schedule. He looks at the clock: It's four-thirty. "Holy shit," he says. "I don't know if I'm going to make it."

The prep area is busy again. Across the island, Gallagher is laying delicate slices of crystallized almonds on a Silpat sheet to dry.

Ayamu, a line cook who now works with Thompson on banquets, helps the *sous-chef* with his striped bass dishes. He spreads out a piece of lettuce, arranges a small piece of fish on top, along with a slice of truffle, and seals the package up. It's tidy and compact, the size of a piece of sushi.

"Brad," says Gallagher, "what time does the first course go out tonight?"

"Seven-thirty, they sit down," says Thompson. "Probably the first course will go out at a quarter to eight."

"We're out of here what, at two?" asks Gallagher.

"Yeah, probably. I'm leaving after my course."

"You're going out tonight?"

"No way," says Thompson. "I'm working lunch dinner, lunch dinner, lunch dinner."

A young cook slices hamachi very thin, slightly overlapping two slices on plastic film pulled taut over a sheet pan. He brushes oil on each with a pastry brush.

Jed brings a container of silken tofu to Bruno Bertin for tonight's second course, the Soupes Glacées de Coquillage—chilled shellfish soups. Bertin spent time teaching French cooking at the Cordon Bleu in Japan, and Japanese food influenced him tremendously during his five years there. The silken tofu is for a shrimp nage with squid, tofu, squid ink dumplings, and shiso. On October 13, a couple weeks from today, Bertin will mark his second anniversary in the U.S. "I want to change the menu tonight to read 'Bruno: Two Years en Amérique,'" he says. By his side, a *stagiaire* cuts shiso leaves into a fine julienne. The shiso, with its intense minty-floral flavor, will impart to the nage a beguiling note.

Upstairs, in the corridor leading from the service entrance to the back of the house, long tables covered with paper cloths hold dishes, white porcelain trays in different shapes, eared cups, and so on. Eight banquet waiters stand around polishing glasses. Under the tables, plastic bins labeled FIRST COURSE, SECOND COURSE, THIRD COURSE hold tonight's wines.

"Okay," says Anthony Francis, the banquet director, "we've still got about another thousand glasses to be polished." It's not hyperbole: Twenty different wines will be served tonight—two with each course—from a Gewürztraminer Vendange Tardive, Domaine Trimbach 1997 to a Corton Charlemagne, Domaine Bonneau du Martray 1997 to a Dashe Zinfandel "Todd Brothers Ranch," Alexander Valley 1997 to a Quinta de la Rosa Vintage Port 1996. Multiplied by eighty people, that's sixteen hundred glasses.

In the main kitchen, on the pass, Alex Lee has a plate of his homegrown lavender, prepped into tiny beautiful buds. Next to that, a dish of fennel seeds, also homegrown: A bite into one releases a tiny explosion of licorice flavor.

Across the way, family meal has already been set out. A small, stocky waiter heaps a tremendous amount of rice onto his plate—carbo-loading for the onslaught tonight. Pascal piles chicken onto his.

In the kitchen, Marc presses puree through a drum-shaped tamis into a huge pot. He looks like a young Sam Waterston.

Tim shows Lee a new batch of urchins. A horrid smell wafts up: putrid tidepool.

"Are these okay?" he asks.

"No!" says Lee, recoiling.

"Can we use them for something?" says Tim.

"Throw them away!" says Lee.

At six o'clock Boulud comes in. *"Fais gaffe aux marques des doigts,"* he tells Frédéric Côte, who's plating one of his foie gras dishes. Be careful of fingerprints.

"Ils arrivent à sept heures," he tells Allannic. "And at seven-thirty they're seated."

Allannic looks at the menu to try to figure out when his course—the seventh—will be served. He guesses 10:15.

Boulud goes out into the corridor to check on things. "We need a cabinet from downstairs to put the sterno in," he says.

Perhaps there's a chef somewhere in the world who, in Boulud's place tonight, would relax and let his ten super-talented *sous-chefs* simply cook for him. If anyone deserves it, it's Daniel Boulud. But that's not in the cards. Because it's not in his nature. Boulud is a chef, and he has to, well, be a chef. It's known in the business that on the occasions when Boulud cooks at events with his fellow star chefs, it is he who takes charge of the kitchen, right from the start. The other chefs always defer to Boulud, even Alain Ducasse, Charlie Trotter, Jean-Georges Vongerichten, and the like.

He walks down the stairs to the prep kitchen. "It's my two years in America," Bertin is saying when Boulud gets to his prep area. "Everyone has to do something nice for me." Boulud steps into the station and checks out Bertin's stuff, most of which is already on a cart, ready to go upstairs, since Bertin's course is second. *"J'ai un super tofu,"* Bertin tells him.

Boulud tastes it. *"On est déjà dans la merde, hein?"* he says. One begins to have the impression that no one here really feels right *unless* they're in the shit. *"C'est assez salé?"* Boulud asks him, regarding the tofu. Is it salted enough? "Maybe a little *fleur de sel*. It's very bland, tofu."

Bertin's *stagiaire* coats mussels in *panné anglaise*, "like Chicken McNuggets," says Bertin. This will lend toothsome interest to the reduction of mussel *jus* stirred into a curried cream of cauliflower and apple soup; coriander will impart an exotic nuance.

Boulud now walks through the prep kitchen. Gallagher is prepping cipollini for a Savoy cabbage, bacon, and chanterelle galette to accompany his langoustines. He has cut the tiny squat onions in half and roasted them— they're gorgeous little rounds, their inner concentric circles roasted a deep honey-brown. Behind them is blanched Savoy cabbage. Now he spoons confectioners' sugar into a small strainer, holds it over thinly sliced lemons, and as he taps the strainer lightly with the edge of a fish spatula—*tap tap tap tap*—the powdered sugar rains lightly down upon them. Next to Gallagher, there's a tall rack, useful for holding lots of prepped ingredients on sheet pans. It's empty. "You gonna take this?" Gallagher asks Bertin. "If not, I'm taking it." A split second goes by in which Bertin doesn't answer. "Okay," says Gallagher, "I'm taking it." He starts putting his sheet pans of prepped ingredients in it: tips of asparagus sprinkled with grated Parmesan, langoustines with frozen brioche sliced paper-thin.

Alex Lee shows Gallagher the first plate for his own course, explaining all the elements: hamachi with golden osetra, leeks and caramelized lemon. Then he goes back upstairs.

By 6:20 the pastry kitchen is being scrubbed top to bottom. Johnny Iuzzini has finished all his pastry work—everything else will have to wait until just before his course is up. He stands on a counter, soapy brush in hand, cleaning the ceiling. Another cook kneels on another counter, cleaning the upper shelves.

There's still much work to be done for the rest of the chefs, though, and the prep kitchen remains a hotbed of quiet, concentrated activity.

Remarkably, the main dining room is open tonight for regular diners as well—service up there has already started—though they've kept the covers down to a reasonable minimum to accommodate all the extra craziness that is the result of the *"20 Ans en Amérique"* dinner.

It's 7:05, and the plating has begun. A cloth-covered table has been set up, running the length of the corridor between the banquet kitchen and the main kitchen. Square, white porcelain plates are set up, two deep, all along the length of the table. Since the table isn't large enough to accommodate all the plates that will be needed, some of them are still stacked in square towers.

Frédéric Côte's foie gras course is first—and Côte begins squirting big C-shapes of black truffle vinaigrette onto the plates from a squeeze bottle. Two more cooks come over, and Côte shows them how he wants the squirted sauces to look: Each end of the C is to be crossed with smaller lines, one out of balsamic reduction and the other of a mustard sauce.

Jean-Luc Le Dû comes over to discuss the wines with Côte: a Savennières "Bécherelle," Domaine de la Coulée de Serrant and the Gewürztraminer Vendange Tardive, Domaine Trimbach, both 1997. The two cooks continue piping the sauces onto the plates.

By seven-thirty the piped plates have all been moved into the tiny banquet kitchen, held by an ingenious rack with slots on all four sides. When it's empty, it takes up little space, but when it's full, as it is now, the plates radiate all the way around, held securely by their edges. Côte, aided by several other cooks, starts plating the Foie Gras en Trois Façons, in the form of three terrines in colorful earth tones: Poule-au-Pot en Gelée with Herbs; Oxtail, Artichokes, and Porcini with Black Truffle; and Braised Rabbit in Red Wine with Lentils and Carrot.

In the meantime, small Japanese-looking bowls, rough brown porcelain on the outside and glazed a brilliant green on the inside, stand on dainty feet on sheet pans lined with paper. These will hold Bertin's shrimp nage with squid, tofu, squid ink dumplings, and shiso.

"Combien pour les soupes?" says Bertin. "I have eighty covers."

"Sounds like they need eighty-five," says a cook.

Another cook comes by and looks at the small bowls. "Man, those are nice," he says.

Boulud comes up next to Bertin to check the numbers.

Finally, at 7:35, Michael Lawrence comes back. "Chef," he announces, "we're opening the door."

Boulud holds up one of the footed bowls. "Michael," he says, "I need twenty like this."

"Chef," says Lawrence, "I don't think we have twenty."

"We have them," says Toto. "We have them downstairs."

Anyone inside the kitchen, seeing the kind of food the guests are about to experience, might imagine a veritable stampede once the doors are open. But this is Daniel, and the genteel crowd outside in the lounge must finish up their conversations, sip their champagne, and drift oh so nonchalantly through those inviting double doors of the Bellecour Room.

Once seated, the guests open the large menus in their trademark burnished tomato-soup-colored covers, bound with silky, knotted golden cords. "20 Ans en Amérique," it reads along the inside top. "A Gourmand Feast of 30 dishes served in 10 courses by 10 Chefs with 20 wines Commemorating Daniel's 30 years of cooking and 20 years as a Chef in America." And in smaller type underneath: "Dinner proceeds will sponsor a travel-study program enabling young cooks to apprentice under Europe's finest chefs." The courses, along with the names of the chef responsible for each and the accompanying wines, take up both sides of the menu, and at the bottom Jean-Luc Le Dû is listed as sommelier and Mark Fiorentino as *boulanger*. An insert lists twelve wine importers and distributors, plus one California winery, plus Olivier Guini, *L'Olivier*, the florist, and thanks them for their "generous contributions to this evening's festivities."

It's not until 8:15 that the first plates go out, carried two at a time by the able wait staff. Frédéric Côte's three takes on foie gras leads the procession of dishes. In this course, Côte pays homage to his chef, for stylistically and intellectually it's a perfect example of one important aspect of the cooking at Daniel: *la cuisine bourgeoise*, traditional preparations enriched by luxurious ingredients. The *poule-au-pot* is culinary wordplay, really, since *poule-au-pot* means "chicken in the pot"; this deeply flavorful rendition with foie gras and glistening gelée elevates potted chicken to its Platonic ideal. Oxtail, artichoke, and porcini terrine with black truffle is the epitome of rustic elegance; it reflects Boulud's propensity to elevate a humble ingredient (the oxtail) to unaccustomed height with the *richesse* of black truffle. And the striated terrine of braised rabbit in red wine with lentils and carrots drives home the point.

As the plates are on their way out, two by two, Drew Nieporent, whose Myriad Restaurant Group owns an impressive handful of restaurants, including Nobu, Montrachet, and Tribeca Grill in New York and Rubicon in San Francisco, comes looking for Boulud. Nieporent is a rotund, jolly front-of-the-house man who knows everyone in town; his favorite anecdote about himself is the time in the mid-1980s when a young David Bouley was working for him as chef at Montrachet, and Bouley made him so mad he threw him out on the sidewalk with all his pots and pans. Since Bouley is fond of telling the story as well, one surmises it must be true. Nieporent is acting as an emcee of sorts for the evening, during which, unbeknownst to Boulud, a roast of the chef is planned. Georgette Farkas, who has masterminded the roast, knows that Boulud would really prefer not to be in the dining room at all; she has told him only that he'll have to come out and say a few words several times, and that she'll send Nieporent to get him.

Having found Boulud, Nieporent is led back by the chef toward the dining room. *"C'est un peu le bordel, hein?"* Boulud tells him cheerfully. It's a little bit of a mess back here. Of course it is!

The first to speak is Daniel Johnnes, the wine director and sommelier at Montrachet, a partner in the Myriad Restaurant Group, and one of the most well-respected wine authorities in the country.

"When I was first asked to roast Daniel Boulud," Johnnes begins tonight, "the thought of a roasted chef was pretty funny to me. Then I realized I wasn't roasting just any old chef. I was to roast one of the world's greatest chefs."

Boulud stands beaming next to Johnnes.

"Here goes," says Johnnes. "My three-step recipe for Roast Chef. Step one: First, make sure to choose a tender one. One that is tough and nasty will always be just that: tough, nasty, and unpleasant. Step two: Marinate him with many years of friendship, well seasoned with ego-stroking compliments. The chef's ego is unusually large, especially if it belongs to one of the world's best chefs. It must be handled with care. Like a foie gras, if mishandled, its bile will leave a bitter taste. A pinch or two of sweet tender words will tenderize him. Which reminds me of a time I was working with Daniel as a waiter at Le Régence in 1984."

Boulud grins.

"Chef Daniel barked an order for me to pick up some food in the kitchen, and I, busy with something else, started to leave for the dining room. A split second later, a lobster shell blasted past my ear, missing me by a fraction of an inch. I returned the lobster with my best sidearm fastball and made a beeline for the dining room, sure not to return to the kitchen that day."

"It hit you, the lobster!" Boulud says, laughing. The crowd laughs along with him.

"Back to my marinade. Step three: the roast itself. Don't turn up the heat too high. The chef can quickly turn bitter and those many years of preparation and friendship can be lost in moments. Also, timing is important. How long to roast a chef? Too long and the unusually large ego can burst."

"It's too bad we don't have Bouley here!" says Boulud. The crowd roars.

After Johnnes finishes, it's Nieporent's turn. "Seventeen years ago and a hundred and fifty pounds ago," he begins an anecdote. At its conclusion, he raises his glass and puts his arm around a still-beaming Boulud. "The reason you are no longer one of the great New York chefs," he says, "is that you're one of the world's great chefs." The diners cheer enthusiastically, and Boulud quickly slips out.

"Okay, who is picking up the soup, *là*?" is the first thing out of the chef's mouth once he's on the other side of the swinging door. His smile drops into a frown the instant he crosses the threshold.

"Okay," says Bertin, "shrimp at six. Shrimp at six." That means that of Bertin's three chilled seafood soups, the shrimp nage goes at six o'clock, the position closest to the diner.

Michael Lawrence is on his way through with plates. "Consommé at six o'clock, guys," he says. It looks like a consommé because the nage is perfectly clear, but when the diners' spoons hit the little ocean floor of silken—almost custardy—tofu at the bottom, it brings up the dish to an alarming brilliance.

Thus Bertin's soups show another side of Daniel's cooking: that which brings together the rarefied flavors and textures of Japan and the uncompromising technique of France and pulls them up in a way that's mind-bogglingly new.

In the meantime, they're already twenty minutes behind schedule, and it's only the second course.

On the long table in the corridor, Bertin places three soups on a plate, Boulud places a bread stick strategically in the middle. A few seeds from the bread stick fall into the white soup. "Shit," says Boulud. He tries to fish them out with his finger.

Only eighty-five more to go.

Another gets screwed up. Toto comes and takes away the two ruined ones. Lawrence jumps in with others, ready to be garnished. "Here, Chef, take these."

Brett Traussi, wearing a suit, is at the other end of the long table, helping as well. The waiters stand four and five deep, waiting for plates.

"Allez-y, les enfants, allez-y!" shouts Toto.

Each waiter takes two and walks carefully down the middle. Cooks come through with ingredients from the prep kitchen, headed for the main kitchen.

Boulud goes halfway into the main kitchen. German, wearing a long, white jacket like Toto's, expedites on the chefs' side, calling out orders. "Help, please!" calls Boulud. "I need a couple of pumpkin soup." For someone who doesn't eat seafood, no doubt. He whistles, loud.

A minute and a half later, Joe brings them.

"Joe!" call Boulud and Traussi at the same time.

"One more," says Boulud.

Next is Alex Lee's raw fish course—a study in the essential, the harmonic. There's nothing extraneous here: thinly sliced hamachi topped with a tidy pile of golden osetra caviar, on a pool of leeks and caramelized lemon. A crown of luscious raw tuna filled with fresh edamame puree and punctuated with brightly flavored watermelon radish and pickled onions. A seviche of Thai snapper with his homegrown fennel seeds and a hat of cloverlike anise hyssop, tiny puddles of Peruvian seviche sauce, and two dots of cilantro oil. Minimalist and brilliant—utterly Alex Lee, which, after all, is utterly restaurant Daniel, and served side-by-side-by-side on an oblong white porcelain dish. The ahi limon peppers were grown by Tim Stark; Lee loves them because when you bite into them, your palate tricks you into thinking you're going to get a hot-pepper blast, but instead you get an amazing citrusy flavor. Boulud takes a pair of elegant, pointed black chopsticks and balances them artfully on the plate, using the circle of watermelon radish as a chopstick rest. Out they go.

"Next is table 8," says Lawrence, directing traffic.

Up in the skybox, a photographer and his assistant, hired by *Food Arts* magazine to document the evening, have set up a makeshift studio. Boulud has hired a video artist as well. As plates go out to the dining room, one of each course lands on Tolman's desk. Each, in its turn, is placed in a setup on Boulud's table in the inner office. After they're shot, the photographer and his assistant do what any sane people would do: They eat them.

"Whoever can take three, take three," says Lawrence, meanwhile, downstairs. "Okay? Because it's a very large party." The more agile servers take three plates at a time, rather than two.

Boulud holds a chart of the tables. "Let's go, Jean-Luc," he tells Le Dû. *"Ça fait dix minutes que j'attends encore.* I need five waiters here." Now he sticks his head into the main kitchen again. "I need runners here!" he shouts. "Now table 7. Now you take three. You cannot take three?" The video artist and assistant are taping in the corridor. The waiters go under their arms, London Bridge–style.

Coming down the skybox stairs, the photographer sees Brad Thompson walking past into the main kitchen. "How are you doing?" says the photographer to Thompson. "I photographed you at Café Boulud."

"Right," says Thompson. "How are you doing?"

Catherine, a French intern who has been helping the photographers in the skybox, comes down, too, and talks to Pascal, who's standing in the kitchen waiting for an order. "Pascal," she says, *"tu fumes?"* Do you smoke?

"De l'herbe uniquement," says Pascal. Only grass. *"Les cigarettes jamais."* His nose goes into the air, as if the mere thought of cigarette smoke might ruin his palate for cheese. *"Il faut demander à Charles,"* he adds, munificently.

Nine o'clock and it's still Alex Lee's course.

Georgette Farkas comes in from the banquet room. "How are you doing, Chef?" she asks Boulud.

"On perd du temps," he says. "Where's my wife, have you seen her?"

"I didn't talk to her," says Farkas.

"She doesn't want to eat too much. I hope she'll come and say hi," Boulud says a little wistfully. But the moment passes, and he's on to worrying about the guests. "Are they happy?" he asks Farkas. "It's not too hot in the room? Can we turn down the lighting a little bit more?"

Boulud looks at his watch: 9:15. "Okay," he announces, "we are a little bit behind now." He turns to Farkas again and asks when he has to come out.

Now Gallagher is up. He, Bertin, and another cook are plating: A large, perfectly seared sea scallop sits atop gratinéed asparagus and a drizzle of aged balsamic vinegar; two or three of his meticulously sugared slivered almonds are scattered around. Amazing to think of the preparation that has gone behind each element of each dish of each course—multiplied by ten! An eared cup holds his crispy langoustine with a bacon and chanterelle galette wrapped in Savoy cabbage; one of the beautifully roasted cipollini halves sits on top.

Ten waiters go out, taking Gallagher's course.

"Don't touch anything!" shouts Boulud. "*Attendez!* Where's the other one?" He goes into the banquet kitchen. "Okay," he says, coming out, "who wants to stand here? Now we need the waiters! Tell the guests please to start to eat and enjoy, eh? Tell them to start to eat; there's more coming behind."

"Daniel," says Traussi, "we're sending everything at once?"

"Yes, yes, yes," says Boulud.

"I need two more, Chef," says Anthony Francis, "for the first table. Of the little squares. Can I get two squares for the first table?"

Three cooks come through, having come from the prep kitchen, carrying trays over their heads. "*Chaud! Chaud! Chaud!*" they cry. They bring them into the banquet kitchen.

"Take six on a tray and two by hand every time," Boulud instructs the waiters.

"Brad, how long until the next course?" Toto asks Thompson. The next course is Thompson's.

"I'm coming up with the fish," says Thompson. "I'm going to present it, and then we're going to start."

"So about fifteen?" says Toto.

"Yeah, maybe." That would mean they're about twenty-five minutes behind.

"Can you make a nice plate for the photographer?" asks Catherine.

"They want to take a picture of the fish?" asks Thompson. "Where's the good olive oil?"

A *stagiaire* runs downstairs for it.

At 9:45, Thompson brings out the big fish. Spectacular it is, lying there on the sheet pan, covered with sliced roasted lemons, roasted tomatoes strewn about, and fennel. Aromatic herbs waft up. Deftly Boulud slides it onto a bed of herbs on a waiting serving platter. *"Comme à la maison,"* says Boulud, smiling. Just like at home.

"Happy birthday," says Thompson.

"C'est just like a ballet," Boulud answers.

Anthony Francis takes the fish out to the dining room to present it.

"The fish is seven minutes, eh?" says Boulud. "Seven minutes."

Thompson, in the banquet kitchen, puts herbs into a running blender, then turns up the speed. He stirs the contents, tastes, pours in salt, replaces the top. Whirs, stops, grinds pepper, stirs, tastes with a big silver spoon. You can hear the *whirrr* of the blender in the dining room. Thompson is flanked by Ayamu on one side and Katy, an Asian-American cook who also works with him on banquets, on the other. "Okay," he says, "and basil, too."

Nieporent squeezes through the corridor, past Johnny Iuzzini, and turns into the kitchen.

"How can you walk by and not say hello?" says Iuzzini. After all, Nieporent knows everybody.

Nieporent greets him. "It's gonna take a little time for the fish," he says.

Now Alex Lee comes from the main kitchen into the corridor to report a casualty. "Rob disappeared at three o'clock," he says, regarding a line cook who has been on the job only a few months. "He just walked out. It's a shame—I really liked him. He's technically sound." And he goes back into the kitchen.

Francis comes back, having presented the fish. His arms are cramped, stuck into the position they were in as they cradled the platter.

Thompson and his assistants start plating onto round china rimmed in squares of mustard yellow and white—a beautiful choice for the Mediterranean flavors of the plate. The roasted fish is garnished with tomato, fennel, redolent *jus,* and olive oil; a thin crouton balances on top. The baked bass, bathed in its sauce with chorizo, cockles, peppers, and parsley, sits on one corner. And completing the triangle is the little packet of steamed striped bass wrapped in lettuce with black truffle.

Now Nieporent pulls Boulud into the banquet room again. "Not too many speeches!" says Boulud, smiling, as he gets pulled in.

"Gotta do it!" says Nieporent.

In the banquet room, Georgette Farkas stands and tells the story about how Boulud threw her out of the kitchen when they first met. "It was my first year in the kitchen as a pastry apprentice," she remembers, "at the Plaza Athénée in 1985. I was about four years old. I think it was my first week there."

"Don't get too personal, Georgette!" warns Boulud, laughing.

"It was nice and safe in the pastry kitchen. They used to put the girls back there in those days. There was one day I was just learning to make the *palmier*. I didn't know that Daniel has *the nose*. I saw smoke coming out of the oven and realized I had them in there ten minutes too long. I said, Thank God the chef's out *there*. Well, he came in, having smelled the smoke, and he taught me the expression *'Quand c'est noir, c'est cuit,'* which means 'When it's black, it's cooked.' " General laughter. A couple of anecdotes later, she wraps up with, "Thank you, Daniel, for everything."

After more beaming, embraces, applause, Farkas turns the floor over to *New York Times* columnist Florence Fabricant, who regales the crowd with more Daniel stories and ends by talking about Boulud's role in Citymeals-on-Wheels, the charity that brings food to homebound elderly people.

Boulud thanks Fabricant and introduces Joel Smilow, "who never invested in a restaurant before," he says. "Thank you, Joel, for the risk you took."

Meanwhile, in the banquet kitchen, pandemonium.

"What are you waiting for?" Lawrence asks Pedro, the silver-haired head banquet waiter.

"What is it?" asks Pedro.

"It's all striped bass," says Lawrence.

"Okay," says Pedro to his team. "Let's go!"

Each waiter carries two plates.

Boulud, already in back, rubs his hands, then claps them, three times. "Start to clear!" he shouts. "Start to clear! Start to clear! Let's go!"

Meanwhile, Lee and Thompson have started plating Andrew Carmellini's course, Féculents à l'Italien: lasagne of organic fowl and white truffle, potato gnocchi with lentils and black truffle, heirloom tomato risotto with rosemary and Parmesan.

"Someone take one upstairs," says Lee, meaning up to the skybox to be photographed. "Come on! We need it! We have a few over here!" Now he turns to Boulud. *"Il manque neuf pièces."*

"How many more do you need?" asks Thompson.

"Nine," says Lee.

Sweat pours off Thompson's head.

"We're using the round ones for risotto, too?" asks Lee.

Bruno Jamais comes through. "Pasta next," he says.

"Le bordel" is Frédéric Côte's comment.

Traussi directs traffic from the waiters' side of the banquet pickup window, the pungent aroma of white truffles wafting up. Eleven cooks work the line in the tiny kitchen.

After the course is plated, a large dish of the pasta comes out—there's extra!—and lands back on the table. Michael Lawrence and Catherine, the office intern, stick spoons in it. It's 10:50 P.M., and Catherine didn't have time for family meal. Côte, J.P., Jamais, and Lee stick in spoons as well, tasting the rich lasagne. "Excellent," says Lee. In the banquet kitchen, Olivier heaps risotto onto a tiny plate.

Five minutes later, the veal has been presented, and Allannic and Côte put the leg onto the small pass of the banquet kitchen. *Sous-chefs* stand around admiring it for a minute before starting to slice and plate it.

The dinner is now forty-five minutes behind. Lee has returned to the pass in the main kitchen. In the cramped banquet service area, trays carrying two-thirds-full glasses of wine come back from the banquet room; the guests seem to be hitting their limit. Boulud finds Côte in the corridor. "Fred," he says, *"J'ai besoin de quelqu'un pour m'aider."* I need someone to help me.

"Il n'y a personne là-bas, hein?" There's no one downstairs?

They both go back into the banquet kitchen. After a moment, Boulud comes back out, wielding knives. Thompson, plating, seems ready to crack.

"Brad, where's the rest of the fucking team?" says Boulud.

And so it goes. The veal course is finished, the game course is served. By the time it is eaten, Johnny Iuzzini, on top of his game, has plated his entire autumn fruits dessert course. Rémy Fünfrock, Café Boulud's pastry chef, will follow, with *gourmandises au chocolat*.

"Can I put the dessert silverware down now?" asks a server. It's 11:55.

"Come on, guys!" shouts Lawrence. "We're not finished! Let's keep going!"

"If he doesn't come out soon . . ." Georgette tells Traussi.

"He's coming, he's coming," says Traussi.

Boulud, for his part, has made a decision: The guests seem overwhelmed, so he's not going to put them through two more courses. Both dessert courses will be served together as one course—a spectacle of desserts, rather than a parade of dessert. He goes downstairs to deliver the news to Iuzzini.

But Iuzzini has already pre-plated everything: the blackberry pyramid with pistachio nougat, the warm fig tart *feuilleté* with almond cream, the kaffir lime semifreddo with roasted plums and berries. Now he and his team must unplate everything, and replate it with Fünfrock's chocolate desserts. What a mess.

As Iuzzini and his team scramble, Boulud appears, having changed into a fresh jacket.

Inside the banquet room, Nieporent announces, "Ladies and gentlemen, at this time I'd like to introduce Michael Batterberry."

Batterberry, who with his wife, Ariane, is editor-in-chief of *Food Arts*, the glossy trade magazine for chefs, as well as a cofounder with her of *Food & Wine* magazine, gives his speech, which is more like an homage than a roast.

Then Boulud steps up. "I want to thank everyone," he says, "because I think in a very different way every one of you in my life challenged me. If you're a friend, a colleague, I always got challenged. I love to be challenged."

Now Boulud brings in all the chefs who have cooked tonight. As they file in, Jamais makes a barfing gesture. It's 12:15.

"We smell bad," says Allannic through his teeth as he smiles. *"J'ai chaud."*

"With this dinner," Boulud says as they come in, "I wanted to challenge everyone in the kitchen to do something they had never done before." He explains the scholarship fund and starts to introduce the chefs, one by one—Frédéric Côte, Bruno Bertin—telling a little story about each. When he gets to Alex Lee, the crowd roars, breaking into wild applause.

In the pickup area, Lawrence says, "Okay, we're clearing the dessert. Clear dessert! Clear dessert!"

"And he's often my bodyguard when I travel," Boulud is saying, having introduced Thompson.

When he gets to Iuzzini, Boulud says, "Johnny—he's been with me six years. He's been the executive *sous-chef* in pastry. Johnny has been the interim pastry chef, but he told me, 'I want to have the freedom to learn more.' But he's done a fantastic job. He's fantastic."

"I know it's late," says Boulud, after introducing Rémy Fünfrock, "and everybody wants to go home, but I'd like to introduce a few more." He goes on to present Jean-Luc Le Dû, Brett Traussi, Anthony Francis, and Michael Lawrence. "But most of all, everyone," he concludes, "I thank *you* very much for coming tonight."

Now Nieporent takes the microphone. "Twenty years of cooking in America!" he says, and then he points to the *sous-chefs*, who are still lined up in front. "The future of America!"

"Do you have the chocolate gifts?" Traussi asks Francis, and Francis points out the parting gift to be given out to each of the guests: gorgeous three-tiered gold boxes of petits fours made by Iuzzini—each tier is a drawer with nine treats—handmade chocolates better than anything you find at La Maison du Chocolat, gemlike fresh fruit jellies, tender *macarons*.

The *sous-chefs* and cooks clean up the kitchens, with much back-patting and congratulations all around. They've done it. And fabulously.

There's one chef, though, who isn't happy at all with the way the evening has gone: Johnny Iuzzini. He sits at Boulud's table up in the skybox, his head in his hands. The evening may have been a smashing success, but Iuzzini is devastated. As the youngest *sous-chef* on the brigade, this was his big chance to prove himself, and he blew it. All because of his overzealous rush to pre-plate everything. He knows that few of the guests would notice that a couple of the sauces were missing, a result of having had to unplate them, or that the kaffir lime semifreddo started to melt. Nor were they likely to care, after eight courses of twenty-seven dishes. But to him, it was an unmitigated disaster. The chefs would notice. And Boulud would notice. The worst part, he tells himself, is it's his fault for not planning better. He should have done desserts that could be held longer, desserts that could have been plated more easily.

What a shame, thinks Iuzzini. After taking so much care all the way through the early and middle parts of the evening, the end was just rushed through. What a total blur. And his big chance wasted.

For Boulud's part, he isn't quite ready to have the evening end. At 1:10, as the cooks clean the restaurant, congratulating one another on a job well done, and the last trays are removed from the banquet room, Boulud sits on the upper level of the lounge having a beer with a couple of friends: Daniel Johnnes, Mark Goldberg, the contractor responsible for the construction of the lounge in which they sit, and Bill Milne, the photographer. Five minutes later, the photographer says good night and Boulud is left chatting and joking with Johnnes and Goldberg. They discuss the recent renovation of the Belle-cour Room. Goldberg says he likes it but adds that the work's inferior.

"That's because you didn't do it!" says Boulud.

"Look at the sheen of the wood in this lounge," says Goldberg, stroking the rich, russet-colored wood lovingly. "It's all hand-rubbed."

The guests are gone, and most of the cooks and wait staff have finished their cleanup. Downstairs in the office, Farkas, Catherine, and Iuzzini sit at their desks, finishing up a few last things.

"Last one to leave," says Francis, "please turn off the lights."

"I have no idea where the lights are," says Farkas. "I've never been the last to leave."

Outside, a light drizzle has started to fall as Boulud walks out with his friends. Some might see a shimmering city. But all Boulud can see is the ongoing repairs in the middle of East Sixty-fifth Street, and water backed up in the gutter. He stops and looks at it.

"Mark," he says, "can you come tomorrow and put in a pipe from here"—he indicates another spot about twenty-five feet away—"to here?" Goldberg jokes about it, but Boulud is dead serious. His brigade of ten of the most talented young chefs in the country have just paid homage to him with the most outlandishly extravagant repast, planning for weeks and prepping and cooking for days, and Boulud is bothered over a blocked gutter.

"But they're in the middle of fixing the street," Johnnes points out.

"I know. I tried to slip them some money, but it didn't work," jokes Boulud.

"You've gotta put a table out here and give them a lunch," says Goldberg. "Don't insult them with money."

Eleven

FALL CLASSIC

I T'S TRUE WHAT THEY SAY about autumn in New York, and this is the height of the season. Since the summer was so wet, the trees leafed out lushly, and now the reds and golds and purples of Central Park are nothing short of spectacular.

By contrast, since the arrival of Alain Poitier two weeks ago, the pastry kitchen at Daniel is not the happiest place to be. The new executive pastry chef is thirty-two years old and single. He left his job in France, as *chef pâtissier* at Contanceau restaurant in La Rochelle, on the seventeenth of September and arrived in New York on the twenty-fifth, the day of the *"20 Ans en Amérique"* dinner. A few days later, he stepped into the pastry kitchen here and prepared to head up the team that refers to itself as Johnny's Angels. ("Nobody messes with my girls," says Iuzzini. "Nobody.") Fortunately, Poitier—whose command of English is less than fluent—has his *sous-chef* in tow, or else the pastry kitchen would be a lonely, lonely place for him.

As it is, the rest of the team—from Iuzzini on down to Jacqueline, Sam, Regina, Sonya, and the others—go about the business of making pastry with none of the élan that has infected the rest of New York during this best of all seasons.

• • •

Alex Lee and Brad Thompson are both out of the country—Lee is in Piedmont, eating and buying white truffles for the restaurant, and Thompson is guest-cheffing his bike tour through Burgundy.

At two o'clock, during a lull in lunch service, Michael Lawrence brings something that looks like a champagne cocktail into the kitchen and sets it in front of Daniel Boulud.

"A 'Normandie,' " announces Lawrence. Tara, the head bartender, has been busy concocting a new signature cocktail for fall. This one contains champagne, Calvados, and a drop of cranberry juice.

Boulud sips. Considers. He doesn't like the Calvados. "It's an eight," he says. "But we can get it to a ten."

Tara started working here in May, and she's been working out well. Her last job was at Windows on the World's bar, "The Greatest Bar on Earth." By three P.M. she's cleaning, polishing glasses, stocking—making sure she has everything she needs for this evening. At four o'clock she'll be joined by the evening bartender, Jacqueline. Tara's day is long: She comes in at ten A.M. to set up for lunch, and she'll stay till eleven P.M. Jacqueline will finish sometime between twelve-thirty and two in the morning.

The first thing Tara does when she comes in is to ask Michael Lawrence to unlock the iron bar that runs across the inside bottom of the bar, where most of the bottles are kept. Such precautions don't bother her; in every place she's worked during the past fourteen years, pilferage has been a problem. Rather than have to question people, she prefers that the goods be kept under lock and key; that way it's not an issue. The bottles on the upper shelves—those that are visible to anyone sitting at the bar—do not get locked up. Boulud wanted to have a cage built that would lock up the entire bar area, but the cost of twenty thousand dollars was excessive. Outright pilferage has not been a problem; still, they're always careful to lock up the Louis XIII cognac.

Tara, a thirty-six-year-old native of Joplin, Missouri, has been in New York for eleven years; she fell in love with the city the minute she arrived here. Like so many New Yorkers, Tara had planned on staying only for a year or two, but loved it so much that she never left. And like many Daniel employees, Tara lives in Queens, in Sunnyside. She comes to work either on the subway or the bus, though she prefers the bus—the Q32—since it can be a bit faster. And more important, she can always get a seat. That makes a difference when you're on your feet for thirteen hours. (Three weeks ago Tara had to go to the podiatrist, plagued by calluses and corns. She had already taken to wearing

EZ-Stride shoes. They're ugly, but she's behind the bar. Now, though, the podiatrist has ordered her to wear prescription shoes.)

So, what do people drink before embarking on the kind of marvelous repast they'll experience at Daniel? The most popular apéritif has been Lillet Blonde—that is, it was, until they ran out. Because of improper labeling, its importation came to a screeching halt a couple months ago; Tara can't get any more until they fix the problem. When someone orders it, she now suggests Dubonnet Blonde or Lillet Rouge.

The "in" drink of the moment, though, is the Cosmopolitan, the signature quaff of the HBO series *Sex and the City*. Tara makes hers with Triple Sec, vodka, and cranberry juice, along with a little lemon and lime. It comes out a nice, bright pink.

Of course, at a restaurant such as Daniel, the drinks have to rise above the ordinary—as does the bartender. Tara makes drinks the way they used to be made. No sour mixes. No Rose's lime juice. All the citrus juices are fresh: Oranges, grapefruits, lemons, and limes are squeezed three mornings a week, usually Monday, Wednesday, and Friday, so nothing is kept more than two days. The only prepared juices used at the bar are cranberry and pineapple. A gimlet, for instance, is gin with fresh lime and simple syrup. Tara always tells a guest that they're made with fresh lime, since there are actually some who prefer their drinks made with Rose's.

As far as Tara is concerned, what makes her a good bartender is that she enjoys talking to people. That and she can make a good drink. Her drinks are so good, in fact, that guests often say, "This is the best thing I've ever had." Last night a couple came in, regulars, and ordered old-fashioneds; Tara was in the back polishing glasses. "Would you like them perfect or sweet?" Jacqueline asked them. But when Tara came back to the bar, they still didn't have their drinks. "We want *you* to make them," they told her. That was instant gratification.

And that's what she likes about the job. Unlike cooks, who never get to see the guests' reaction to their work, Tara always gets to see her customers enjoying what she makes.

As far as talking is concerned, a good bartender needs to read people. Do they want to talk or be quiet? Many guests are from out of town, and "It's almost like being a concierge," as Tara puts it. A few nights ago a gentleman from San Francisco came in without a reservation and had dinner at the bar. He wanted an incredible meal, and he got it. As he ate, Tara gave him pointers for navigating the city: where to go in Times Square to get theater tickets, and where to eat. She recommended Union Square Cafe, Gotham Bar & Grill, and, of course, Café Boulud.

At four o'clock there's a managers' meeting, held this time in the dining room, sans Boulud. On the agenda: a new assistant captain named Brad. Everyone agrees he shouldn't be in the tip pool on his first day. Discussion turns to a new person, Nika, to try out on the reservations staff. "She's available to work nights," says Brett Traussi, "and she has a very nice telephone voice."

"We know how that will go," says Michael Lawrence. " 'I'm sorry we don't have a table, but maybe you can meet me for drinks.' "

Discussions ensue about new neckties for the wait staff, about the possibility of selling caviar from the restaurant, and about the Christmas card the restaurant will send this year.

And then plans for New Year's Eve—a big night in a restaurant such as this.

"We're going to publicize it in-house," says Georgette Farkas. "Our head maître d' is going to phone our thousand top clients."

Bruno Jamais is not amused. "It's not a thousand," he says.

"I'm only joking," says Farkas.

"How many would it be?" wonders Hilary Tolman.

"Thirty," says Jamais. "Forty. But that's not enough."

"So the idea is to call more," says Farkas.

"I can call schmucks, if you want," says Jamais. "You have nine hundred schmucks. There are really only thirty VIPs."

"Maybe the first call is a little awkward," says Farkas, "but the second one is a little less awkward. And by the year 2010, they'll all be waiting for that call."

"*We* have to make the calls," Lawrence notes.

Tolman asks, "Do you want us to go through that list and pick out more than Bruno's thirty?"

Farkas turns to Jamais. "How about if Hilary and Michael and I pick the next thirty? Thirty can be two hundred people. If ten of them book tables of ten, we're so happy."

"That's a hundred guests," says Lawrence.

Although the meeting is taking place on the side of the dining room farthest from the kitchen—a considerable distance away—compelling aromas have floated over. "There's no one from the kitchen here," continues

Lawrence. "We should say that the way the kitchen staff treats themselves and treats the dining room contributes to low morale and may lead to lawsuits, and we need to address that with the kitchen managers."

"Just some respect," says Jamais. "That's it."

By now it's 4:40, time for family meal. Waiters, runners, and busboys are bringing their plates into the dining room and digging in. A reservationist takes a plate into the reservations room.

"Can we touch on the eighty-six issue?" wonders Lawrence now. He's bothered by the fact that people can only get a reservation at ten-thirty or eleven, and when they come, they can't have the paupiette because the kitchen has run out of sea bass. "It's a Daniel Boulud signature dish," says Lawrence, "and then the guests are pissed, so we have to come to some solution."

Farkas points out that Boulud needs to keep a tight reign on what is ordered in order to avoid waste.

"Do we want pissed-off guests," asks Lawrence, "or do we want left-overs?"

"Maybe we have some eighty-six at six-thirty so we keep some for ten-thirty," suggests Jamais.

"How can we have some eighty-six at six-thirty?" says Farkas.

The problem doesn't get resolved; it's impossible without someone from the kitchen. They move on.

"The *Wine Spectator* Grand Award," says Traussi, opening the floor to Jean-Luc Le Dû, who has proposed expanding the wine cellar dramatically, in an effort to win the coveted award next year.

"We went through the cellar list a couple days ago," says Le Dû, "and we have just over eight hundred references on the list. If we get another eight hundred, we'll have sixteen hundred, and I think we're right in the ballpark."

"I think you'll need to get a third person," says Traussi, and then talk turns to David, the cellar steward. "Since he's come back in the cellar," says Traussi, "I'd like to propose him for employee of the month." Employees of the month—one from the front of the house and one from the back—have their photograph posted in a display case next to the one that displays Daniel's press clippings in the corridor leading to the locker rooms downstairs.

"I'm with him," says Toto.

"I have David and I have a *stagiaire*," says Le Dû, "a girl who is working well. So I don't think I need anything else. We're staffed."

"Okay," says Traussi.

"What is David's last name?" asks Lawrence.

"Neary," says Toto. He spells it.

Next topic is garbage. "The garbage carter," announces Traussi, "wants to go from twenty-five hundred dollars a month to fifteen thousand a month."

"It was an introductory rate," says Farkas.

"That's a hundred and eighty thousand a year," says Traussi. "All the garbage haulers, instead of being owned by the mob, now they're owned by Waste Management in New Jersey."

"Can you get somebody else?" asks Tolman.

"Maybe we can bring the mob back in to shake them down," says Lawrence, shaking his head. "Good Lord."

"At the next meeting," says Traussi, moving on, "I would like to do the holiday schedule. For the week of Thanksgiving and the week of Christmas. I think we should do this in front of Daniel, so everyone bring in a wish list. Should we elect to close on Tuesday the twenty-sixth for lunch?"

"Absolutely," says everyone. "Definitely." "Of course."

"Okay," says Traussi. "We close at lunch. Saturday we're open the full day, Sunday closed, Monday closed. Sunday is Christmas Eve."

"If you take Thanksgiving," says Le Dû, "you can't take Christmas."

Everyone agrees. Discussion turns to the other employee of the month.

"Who do you like for the front of the house?" asks Tolman.

"I don't like anybody right now," says Lawrence.

"Any of the reservationists?" suggests Farkas.

"It should be Pedro," says Anthony Francis, referring to the head banquet waiter. "He's been doing a good job for a year and a half."

"He's great," says Traussi.

"Pedro it is," says Lawrence.

"Next Wednesday we're picking up a party for eight hundred people on Fifty-seventh Street," announces Traussi, wrapping things up. "So it's going to be a little crazy."

"And be careful next week," adds Le Dû, mentioning that the Wine Experience, the huge Midtown event organized annually by *Wine Spectator* magazine, will bring thousands of wine professionals and wine and food journalists from all over the country into town. And the DiRoNA Awards, honoring Distinguished Restaurants of North America, will take place as well. So Thursday, Friday, and Saturday are likely to be heavy with industry VIPs.

"Tell the cooks to be nice" is all Toto has to say about it.

AS THE COOKS and *sous-chefs* do their prep downstairs, the topic turns not to the presidential election, coming up in a matter of days, but rather to the usual Wednesday topic: Grimes's review of the week in the *New York Times*.

"Oh, what a surprise," says Thompson, having returned from Burgundy. "Another small Italian restaurant in the Village or Brooklyn." Grimes seems to have something against ambitious uptown French restaurants.

Since Labor Day, Daniel has been busy nonstop.

Upstairs, Alex Lee waxes poetic about his trip with his brother to Piedmont, from which he's just returned. Most of what he talks about involves truffles—white, of course. (The black ones are from France and are harvested in the winter.) Cardoons, braised with Fontina cheese, garnished with white truffles. The richest tagliatelle imaginable, made with thirty egg yolks (well, twenty-seven: eighteen whole eggs and nine additional yolks to two kilos of flour), with butter and sage in a ragù with truffles. Lee has made this, too; he only does it when he gets eggs fresh from a farm. As he talks about what they ate, his eyes drift off. Culatello—the inner portion of a special prosciutto that rests only on one side to cure. Parmesan, celery hearts, and lardo (fatback pork) pressed between pieces of Carrera marble with rosemary and pepper. Piemontese beef carpaccio with tons of truffles. Two fried eggs with truffles on top. Sliced veal with a light cream sauce and truffles. Castomanio—a cheese that resembles a Parmesan—served with acacia honey.

Over the soup station, Joe, the lunchtime soup cook extern, has taped up a small printed sign:

> *Of all the items on a menu, soup is that which exacts the most delicate perfection and the strictest attention, for upon the first impression it gives to the diners, the success of the latter part of the meal largely depends.*
> —*Escoffier*

An interesting observation, and one that couldn't be truer. Yet curiously, along with the *garde-manger,* the soup station is where new cooks usually start when they first come to work at Daniel. This is because for both of these stations, most of the preparations are done well in advance, with very little *à la minute* cooking and much less pressure than on the hot line. Boulud, Lee, and the *sous-chefs* can offer guidance to the new cooks earlier in the day, so the risk of flops is minimal.

A new audio system has been installed in the kitchen, just under the video monitors, to improve morale, which has hit an all-time low. Bobby walked out during service last week, announcing at two o'clock, "I'm going to the bank." He never came back. Rob left, shortly before him. Another cook, a new guy, was here just two days before bolting. There are far fewer French cooks than there were at the beginning of the year, when they made up about half the brigade. Now it's just Allannic, Côte, David, Philippe, and a handful of others.

Allannic has been training for the New York Marathon for the past six months. The first two months, he lost fifteen pounds. The first step was quitting smoking, which he accomplished two years ago. He's now in fine form for the event, which will be on Sunday, November 5.

Leslie, the hot-apps cook, is out sick with bronchitis; it's the second time in seven years she's missed a day of work. Kosta, a line cook, covers her station.

There are four hundred reservations on the books for Saturday night—this despite the fact that New York City is in the grip of baseball fever, with the first Subway Series in forty-four years, the Yankees versus the Mets. Tonight is game four, to be played in Shea Stadium; the Yanks lead the series two games to one.

At 5:55, Neil Gallagher calls out the first order: "One crab, one terrine, followed by one skate, one squab, medium-rare."

Joe is still hanging around his station; he's been watching Chris, the nighttime soup cook, set up. "You got your cream in a squeeze bottle?" asks Joe.

"No," says Chris, "'cause it looks ugly when it comes out."

"I'm surprised we're not using a foam," says Joe.

"We've got too many foams."

"Order one artichoke, one crab salad," calls Gallagher, "followed by one short ribs, one venison, medium-rare. Two cauliflower soup, two ravioli, followed by one venison, two salmon, one shank."

In fact, there is foam on the artichoke soup—it's creamy and rich, very earthy tasting, made sublime by the addition of white truffles.

"William?" says Gallagher.

"Yes."

"Please tell the captain that there's no temperature on the salmon tonight." It's a salmon *mi-cuit*, "half-cooked." It's been warm-smoked for an hour and a half, then marinated in olive oil, rosemary, and cracked black peppers, and garnished with crushed Yukon Gold potatoes cooked off with thyme, butter, and lemon juice.

"Chris, did I ever tell you this story?" asks Joe. "Ever hear of Taillevent?"

Chris shakes his head. (Taillevent is the renowned Paris restaurant that has long held three stars in the *Michelin* guide.)

"Jed calls me right after I started this station and says I've got a *stagiaire* for you. I said great. So I'm showing him all this stupid stuff—like—the stupidest things! He's French. And I'm telling him this stuff like he's an idiot. So you ever hear of Taillevent?"

"No."

"It's a really important restaurant in France. And that's where he worked. And I'm telling *him* how to do stuff!"

"You should be getting out of here," says Gallagher.

"I'm closing the station down," says Joe.

Gallagher sends him downstairs to get some butter. Chris hands Gallagher a mushroom chip. "Chef," he says, "what do you think of this?"

Gallagher tastes it. "It gets stuck in your teeth," he says. "It rehydrates and gets stuck in your teeth. It's going in the soup, so that might be better, but . . ."

Joe comes back up with three pounds of butter—the French-style Plugra. Gallagher cuts it quickly into chunks and puts it in a pan.

"Fire 34, 54, 16, please," says William.

Gallagher pulls the tickets that have been written over with a Sharpie; he takes them to the meat station.

Lee eats a baked sweet potato, then he goes to watch Kosta making frogs' legs in the hot-apps station.

Chris mixes Gatorade powder with water in a big Snapple bottle to swig during service. He and Joe discuss the pumpkin soup—how the cream behaves differently if you add it in the first fifteen minutes of cooking, before you puree, versus adding it after you puree.

"Do you guys dream about work here?" Gallagher asks them.

"Oh, yeah," says Chris.

"And you?"

"Every night," says Joe.

"There are two books you should read," Chris tells Joe. "James Peterson's *Splendid Soups*. It's a really nice book. And Escoffier."

"You need Escoffier's big book to read the little one," Joe points out. Saturday will be his last day—he's going back to school—and it's clear he's going to miss working here terribly. "I'll come back if we can work *garde-manger* or something," he tells Chris.

"They have a really awesome *garde-manger* here," says Chris. "They do awesome terrines. Desserts are really good, too."

"I liked Thomas!" says Joe.

By eight o'clock the talk has turned to baseball. The Ecuadorian runners and busboys all like soccer, not baseball—the Ecuadorian team, of course, except Nelson, who likes Argentina. "He doesn't even like the team from his own country!" says Ernesto, scandalized.

Boulud, crazed on his way out to cook at the DiRoNA Awards at the Waldorf, runs up to the skybox and swivels the TV around and down so it can be seen by the cooks in the kitchen. He switches it to Channel 5.

Lee's head is still in Piedmont. In a pan over boiling water, he makes a rich sauce out of butter, egg yolks, and Fontina. He puts a hand blender into it and whirs it up until it's frothy, like a sabayon.

"Order sardines," calls Gallagher, but then he glances up to the 86 board. "Eighty-six the sardines," he says. "We don't have even one sardine left."

But actually they do have one, and Lee wants Tim, the *garde-manger* cook, to taste it. "Make one for yourself," Lee tells Tim.

"They're eighty-six," says Tim, confused.

"Just one," says Lee. "Here. A little garlic, and if you have a piece of arugula. You'll see how perfect it is."

Lee looks up to the skybox TV. "First pitch!" he yells. "Jeter hit a home run!" He pulls out the microphone. "First pitch, Jeter hit a home run! Boom boom, Cyrille!" Allannic is a diehard Mets fan, while just about everyone else roots for the Yankees. "We're gonna be in the shit, I know," adds Lee. He looks up to the TV again as he walks by. "Order a short ribs and a ravioli app!"

"You got a lot of *méridionales* working over there?" Gallagher asks the *garde-manger*. That's a *salade méridionale de légumes, mesclun, et ricotta salata au pistou:* artichoke, avocado, tomato, eggplant, and pepper salad with salted ricotta and a pesto dressing.

Chris is making cannelloni, piping in a mixture of mascarpone cheese, black and white truffle, black trumpet mushrooms, and foie gras. It's one of the richest, most luxurious dishes one can imagine. Tiny portions—perhaps two cannelloni—are offered to VIPs. It's a dish that's destined to become famous, a fall classic.

Everyone's moving very fast. One wonders if the pressure at Shea Stadium can be any greater than it will be here tonight.

By the time the last orders are out on the following night, the Yankees are once again the putative world champions of baseball (putative since the French cooks, fans though they might be, think it's a little silly for a series involving only North American teams to produce a "world" champion). For New Yorkers, though, it was a no-lose proposition.

The next week brings a spectacular, crisp autumn day, cool but not too cool, with an appealing snap in the air. Central Park is resplendent in red and gold. Classic fall.

"*Où est la Bible?*" Frédéric Côte asks Hilary Tolman, having pulled himself up to the skybox.

"*La Bible?*" asks Tolman.

"Le *New York Times.*" *Bien sûr.* It's Wednesday, once again, and in today's paper it's not just any restaurant that William Grimes has reviewed: It's Alain Ducasse at the Essex House.

Tolman hands the paper over to Côte, who reads avidly. Three stars for Ducasse. Three stars out of four for the only chef in the world who has ever presided simultaneously over two *Michelin* three-star establishments.

Although it wasn't entirely unexpected, Boulud himself can't help but be stunned by the implications. Ducasse was here just last night attending a book party to celebrate the publication of British chef Gordon Ramsay's new cookbook. Three stars for the chef who floored Daniel Boulud with his talent when he ate at his restaurant twenty years ago in Monte Carlo. Boulud was bowled over by the simplicity of Ducasse's cooking, dazzled by the incredible quality of the products, from the sea urchins to the *rouget* to the lamb to the ice cream. He had had a counter specially constructed for his ice cream, Boulud remembers, so the ice cream would never get too hard or too soft. He was impressed, too, with Ducasse's level of obsession. Thinking about it now reminds Boulud of one of the things he finds hardest about this life: not becoming a prisoner of his own passion, turning himself into a slave of what he loves to do.

Well, if Ducasse has three stars, at least that puts Daniel in excellent company. Now that he thinks about it, New York's three-star restaurants could certainly hold their own against New York's four-star restaurants. Perhaps he would take out an ad in the *Times:* The restaurants with three stars—Daniel, Alain Ducasse, Danube, and so on—would be printed down the left column, and those with four stars—Le Cirque 2000, Bouley Bakery, Jean Georges—down the right column. People would see how arbitrary it all was.

"*Il va repasser,*" predicts Côte as he finishes reading the review. Grimes will go back and review it again.

Tolman went to Alain Ducasse recently. Personally, she hated the room.

There were too many cushions on the banquette. Everything was perfectly cooked, she felt, yet there was not a single dish that *sent* her.

She made plenty of reservations for other VIPs from Daniel to go as well. Boulud went with Michael Lawrence. Bruno Jamais and Jean-Luc Le Dû have been several times. Georgette Farkas is going this week.

Le Dû comes upstairs. He met last Thursday with Boulud and Marcel Doron about whether to expand the wine program, with the idea of going after the *Wine Spectator* Grand Award. They've decided indeed to go full steam ahead. It will be a lot of work for Le Dû, but very exciting work, involving a lot of tasting, in order to expand the cellar from eight hundred selections to seventeen hundred (by his reckoning, the minimum required to get the award seems to be about fifteen hundred). Instead of five vintages of Château Pétrus, they should have fifty. Le Dû started tasting the day before the meeting. New shelving will be built to accommodate the bottles, and all the liquor that's now kept in the cellar will be moved out.

Downstairs in the prep kitchen, Brad Thompson shakes his head over the Ducasse review. "I just don't understand," says the big chef. "I want to open a small restaurant downtown now because that's all he likes."

Jed has left; he's gone to work at Union Square Cafe, although he had been saying he'd had enough of New York. He's been replaced by Mike McGhee, until recently the executive chef of Stone Mountain Resort in Burlington, Vermont. McGhee had applied for an executive *sous-chef* position, but when Boulud saw he had management experience, they offered him the position of food and beverage director.

Morale in the past week has sunk lower still. "I'm outta here by December" has become the common refrain among cooks at every level. With the restaurant boom, there aren't enough good cooks to go around, and it's causing a shortage even at restaurants like Daniel, where one would think the prestige alone might keep cooks there. But as one cook puts it, "If you want a good cook, you've got to pay fifteen or sixteen dollars an hour." Here the pay for line cooks is eight to twelve.

Has it affected the food? That all depends on whom you ask. The regulars seem happy as ever. Business is booming. But among themselves, some cooks and *sous-chefs* say quality has been slipping. It's no wonder: Turnover has been so high that half of the cooks are new, and many of the rest don't have a great deal of experience.

Still, Thompson believes in Boulud. Whereas Ducasse came to Manhattan with the idea of bringing a piece of France to New York, what Boulud has done and is still doing is utterly different. Boulud brings to the table his French traditions, but he creates a brilliant synthesis of French and American (accented by various global influences) that stunningly transcends either.

Friday morning, Thompson picks up the *New York Post* on his way downtown to shop for a new knife. He's floored by the giant headline he sees when he opens to the business page: BOULUD ON A ROLL, it screams. "Top chef opening 3rd eatery at City Club." Although Boulud hadn't announced his plans to any of the brigade, and he was nowhere near ready to announce them publicly, word had leaked within the Dinex Group, so Thompson did have an inkling this was happening. But how on earth did the *Post* get hold of it?

As it happened, Braden Keil, a *Post* reporter, unearthed the story by snooping around the construction site on West Forty-fourth Street in the new City Club Hotel space. Just across the street from the Royalton Hotel and next door to the newly revamped Iroquois Hotel, in which Steven Sobel, a former chef at Sign of the Dove, has opened a restaurant called Triomphe, Boulud's new restaurant, a French-Mediterranean place that will be more casual than either Daniel or Café Boulud, will open next spring right smack in the middle of a block that promises to be very hot.

Thompson ponders it all as he makes his way into a small shop in the industrial part of TriBeCa, Korin Japanese Imports. He rings the bell, next to which is a sign that says WHOLESALE ONLY. Inside he looks at the cases displaying knives, lusting after the two-thousand-dollar Masamotos, remembering his first Japanese knife, an inexpensive Mac, which is what they used when he worked at the Phoenician resort in Scottsdale. Finally he settles on a Suisin. He already owns a couple of Suisin's Inox carbon steel knives. Like their higher-carbon, higher-end cousins, they're sharp only on one side (left-handed chefs must order theirs specially), but the Inox is easier to sharpen than the Japanese high-carbon steel, and not as prone to rust. But now he's going for the big time—the Japanese high-carbon version. Although they are not practical for most home cooks, chefs who are good with knives can get a better edge with them. This he'll keep super-sharp, reserving it for precision work such as slicing fish. After he makes his selection, a six-inch model, he looks around a little more, thinking he'll buy Lupe, the butcher, a great cleaver for Christmas.

As he pays, his mind wanders back to Boulud's new restaurant. Boulud has not announced who the new chef will be—knowing him, he won't even decide until the very last minute. Could he be thinking of Thompson? In the meantime, Thompson knows that Boulud has big problems at home—at Daniel, that is—to contend with. The flight of cooks has become an exodus, and the grumbling in the kitchen has become a roar. Boulud has called a mandatory meeting for all kitchen staff, set for Monday morning at eleven o'clock. Will he be able to rally the troops?

Monday, November 6

CYRILLE ALLANNIC COULD use a little rest. Yesterday was the New York City Marathon, and he finished in a very respectable three hours, twelve minutes, sixteen seconds. A group of people from the restaurant came to cheer him on at Ninety-fifth Street: Michael Lawrence, Kevin, Philippe, Toto, Anthony Francis, and the interns Damien and Catherine, along with his wife, Rica, and her parents. Although he had hoped to finish in under three hours, he's still happy. But beat. Rica, for her part, made her debut as a journalist: She wrote a piece that ran last week in *Time Out New York* about restaurants and bars where people could get a curbside seat to watch the marathon.

This morning's meeting was supposed to last twenty minutes, but Boulud went on for two hours about what he expects from his cooks and what they can expect from him. They should take pride in their work, he told them, and he spoke, too, about the value of loyalty. What he can't stand is cooks who come and glean what they can from him as quickly as possible, tack Daniel proudly onto their résumé, and fly off posthaste to some other job. He addressed the *sous-chef* problem as well, dressing them down for not giving it their all. As far as Thompson and Iuzzini are concerned, this couldn't possibly have been directed at them; after all, they spend just about every waking hour in the restaurant.

Boulud is certainly inspiring. But will the pep talk be enough to pull the team together?

"I'm in the shit now," says Leslie, doing her prep in the downstairs kitchen, "but it's okay." It's still early afternoon, well in advance of the dinner service, but she knows exactly how long her preparations will take.

Fay walks in, wearing street clothes. She's having trouble making ends meet with the reduced pay she's getting at Peacock Alley, so she's come here to pick up some extra work. Boulud suggested she help Bruno Bertin, but Bertin shields himself, teasing her. "I'm going to put up flowers here," he says, "so nobody bothers me."

"Okay," says Fay, "then I'll go work for Alex. I miss Alex."

"Can you work for me in banquets?" asks Thompson.

"Yeah, maybe," says Fay.

"So, do you like the place?"

"Yes," she says, "it's great. The chef is great. The food is really nice quality."

"I read about what happened at the Waldorf," says Bertin. Fay wrinkles her nose; she doesn't know what he's talking about. Apparently there was a fire in the kitchen.

"Are you sure you work there?" asks Thompson.

"Look, Fay," says Bertin. "Waldorf is like *that*." He draws a Waldorf-style W, with crossed sticks. "But McDonald's is like *that*." He draws a McDonald's-style M, the same as the other but inverted.

"I make a mean hamburger," Fay points out.

Corey, the new cook responsible for meat garnishes, listens to them as he slices and chops, doing his prep. Little do they know that he actually worked at McDonald's.

Corey grew up in East New York, a rough-and-tumble Brooklyn neighborhood, surrounded by Caribbean culture—his father is from Guyana, and there were lots of Trinidadians and Jamaicans in his neighborhood. He got a job at McDonald's when he was sixteen and worked there for two years. Inspired by his grandmother, who cooked professionally at a hospital, Corey entered a cooking competition sponsored by C-CAP—Careers Through Culinary Arts Program, a ten-year-old national program that awards cooking-school scholarships to talented inner-city high-school students. He won a scholarship and enrolled at the CIA. While he was there, his fellow students spoke reverently of Daniel Boulud—to work at Daniel was considered the *ne plus ultra*. When Corey graduated, he got a job at JUdson Grill, chef Bill Telepan's well-respected Midtown restaurant. After eighteen successful months as *tournant*, Corey mentioned to Richard Grausman, C-CAP's founder, that he dreamed of working at Daniel, and Grausman put in a call to Boulud, while chef Bill Telepan picked up the phone and called Alex Lee. A month ago, the twenty-two-year-old was hired as *chef de partie*, the only black person on the brigade.

Corey happened to have found Boulud's talk inspiring, though it will put him in the weeds as well.

Upstairs, later in the afternoon, family meal comes out: hard taco shells, carnitas, lettuce, salsa. Plates are piled hugely high.

Roger, the cook in charge of fish garnishes, doesn't eat. To say he's in the shit is putting it mildly. A former truck driver who grew up in L.A., Roger says he started his career late—he's already thirty. Even on the best of days, he seems to be a little behind; he's always playing catch-up. "I don't seem to have the energy of these young guys," is the way he puts it, "though I'm sure I could drive a lot longer than most of them." Although he should be working six A.M. to six P.M. on most days, typically he comes in at four or four-thirty and leaves at six or six-thirty. "I never see the sun," he laments. Boulud, Lee, and Côte tell him he shouldn't be working so many hours, but if he doesn't, he can't get his *mise en place* done in time for service. (Normally he works lunch—he's here for Monday dinner because the day cooks and night cooks take turns covering Monday night.)

Roger is circumspect about Boulud's pep talk today. "The people who have pride in what they do will take it to heart," he says, "and their skills will improve a little bit. And the others will say, 'Oh, who cares.' You'll get a change for about a week, and then it will go back to the way it was."

No one at restaurant Daniel is discussing what the rest of the country is talking about: tomorrow's presidential election.

The next day is Election Day. In the days and weeks that follow, chads dangle and partisans vent and pundits predict and jurists opine, and the rest of America sits glued to CNN or the radio, listening for recount results and legal opinions and Supreme Court decisions that will determine who will assume the nation's highest office. But the cooks at Daniel have other fish to fry. Life goes on. People must eat.

Twelve

SELL TRUFFLES AND CAVIAR

B ARELY A MONTH after the New York City Marathon, and Cyrille Allannic is a wreck: He's put on five pounds; he has a bone spur in his foot and something like a hernia in his stomach. *Le bordel complet.*

And America still doesn't know who will be president.

Frédéric Côte, on the other hand, has announced he's leaving at the end of the month—which is also the end of the year, and in fact, the end of the official millennium—for it's now December 1. He's been offered a job as executive chef at Le Bec Fin, chef-owner George Perrier's legendary restaurant in Philadelphia. It will be the first time since the restaurant's opening in 1969 that Perrier has handed control of the kitchen over to another chef.

After lunch service is finished, Michael Lawrence, Brett Traussi, Alex Lee, Hilary Tolman, and Georgette Farkas head to the bar—not for a drink, but for a tasting session. Tara's been working on holiday cocktails. She's made one of each—about six in all—and she's lined up the beautiful, parti-colored drinks on the bar. Everyone crowds around.

"This one here is a Hemingway Daiquiri," Tara explains. "It has a splash of maraschino and a splash of fresh grapefruit juice."

"And what's that one?" asks Lawrence.

"That's a Twilight Martini."

"What's that again?" asks Lee.

"What can we do to make it more Christmasy?" wonders Lawrence. He then points to another. "Brett," he says, "look—this is our Christmas Margarita. How can we get the French thing in there?"

"Just put a little Cointreau in it," he says.

They all grab little straws and start sipping the various drinks, passing them around.

Farkas tastes the Apple Martini. "I'm all over the apple," she says.

"Go for it, Georgette," says Lee.

"You guys are drinking," she says. "I'm just sipping."

"I like it when you talk dirty," says Brett.

"Let's call it a Hemingway," says Lawrence.

Lee stares pensively.

"I don't like the color of the blue one," says Tolman.

"Some people like a blue drink," says Lawrence, facetiously.

"I had a Metropolitan at AZ that was great," says Traussi. "Someone should go steal the drink menu from AZ." Boulud dined at the Flatiron District restaurant recently with his family on a Sunday night, when Daniel was closed, naturally. Chef Patricia Yeo had taken the night off, but her staff alerted her that Boulud was in the restaurant and she appeared in her whites, paying homage tableside, by the time he was ready to order. AZ may have garnered three stars from the *New York Times,* theoretically putting it in Daniel's class, but everyone knew Boulud was a superstar.

"I can do it," says Tolman. "I don't live too far away."

"They have the 007," says Tara. "They probably put Cointreau in it or something."

"What's this one?" asks Traussi.

"A Gold Margarita." It's made with fresh prickly pear puree, Sauza Conmemorativo, Cointreau, fresh lime juice, and simple syrup, and rimmed with sugar.

"How do we get the French thing in there?" asks Lawrence.

"You serve half as much," says Traussi, "and charge two times the price."

"I could definitely drink one of those," says Farkas. "How about La Mexicaine?"

"It's good," says Lawrence, sipping. "Made with cactus pear."

"And this is called a Spiced Apple Martini."

"You should get one of those dried-apple rings," says Lawrence.

"We're gonna have spiced apple chips," says Lee, "but you have cinnamon in there. So maybe you could do a cinnamon stick."

"They don't do that in New Orleans, I bet," says Traussi.

"We don't have time for all that sweetness," says Lawrence. "We just pour more liquor in."

"A Hulla Boulud," says Farkas.

Lawrence approves. "It's Daniel's idea to use the damn cactus pear juice," he adds.

"He'll love it once you explain what it means," offers Tolman.

"Why can't we do a sake drink?" Traussi asks Lawrence.

"I can do a saketini," says Tara. "Everyone has a saketini, though."

Traussi agrees. "They're ubiquitous."

Tara goes over the ingredients of a red drink in a champagne flute: champagne, tequila, fresh lime juice, simple syrup, a dash of prickly pear juice, and maraschino liqueur. Dale DeGroff, the well-known bartender from the Rainbow Room, uses a lot of maraschino, Tara points out. He says it smoothes everything out.

Lawrence picks up the bottle and examines it. "Interesting," he says. "From Croatia. Just like our busboy Elvir."

Farkas points to the red drink. "Call that a Poinsettia," she says.

"No, call that eighty-six," says Lawrence. "Champagne and tequila just doesn't work."

At the end of the pre-dinner dining room staff meeting, Lawrence announces to the servers that a card describing the New Year's Eve dinners will be included in the check presenters—they're creating a little nightclub in the Bellecour Room; a gala four-course dinner and dancing will be offered in there and in the lounge for $290 (plus beverages, tax, and gratuities). There will also be a gala six-course tasting menu for $390 in the main dining room. Pre-theater dining will be à la carte, and gala seating will begin after pre-theater. Café Boulud will offer a five-course menu for $95 and a gala tasting menu for $225. "So let the festivities begin," he concludes.

"They can handle reservations through Georgette's office," adds Traussi. In fact, Farkas has sent out a flier about it today to a list of hotel concierges around town, in an effort to get the word out.

Traussi then has a word with the runners. "Pay very good attention to William in the kitchen," he says, "and keep your mouth shut. Everybody's trying to help, but there's too many chefs in the kitchen."

Alex Lee jumps in. "All you guys should know there's a time when it gets very, very busy, when apps and main courses are going out. It's hard fo

William to be in more than one place. I need you guys' help. You need to know the table. And not to talk, so when we put food in the pass, you should arrange your tables. Okay, the tasting tonight. We have crispy sardines from Portugal. With a little white toast, we cut them and add a little black truffle sauce. On top there's a classic celery and apple *rémoulade*. Excellent dish, we'd like you to sell that." Contrary to popular belief, the dishes that the chef wants sold are often among the best; he wants them pushed because he'd honestly like people to have the wonderful experience of enjoying them. It's really no more sinister than that. "Glazed porcini with roasted bay scallops and crispy potatoes with a truffled mushroom emulsion," continues Lee. "After that, we have a foie gras tonight, it's with the peppered pineapple. We just got six pounds of black truffles. There is a ten-dollar supplement on the scallops because they're very high right now, the truffles are very high. Duck is roasted on the spit tonight with a chutney of fall fruits, black trumpet mushrooms, and baby fennel, with a little bit of radicchio. It's the radicchio Italiano, not the round one. Pork belly with lentils. Lobster gratinée in a chanterelle crust with a really nice artichoke ragout and some parsley broth with the coral. Everybody gets foie gras and venison and short ribs on the tasting."

"Eighty-six sole?" asks Bernard Vrod.

"No," says Lee, "the sole just came in five minutes ago."

"Okay, guys, listen up, please!" says Lawrence.

"You guys, as busy as it was last night, we did really well with truffles and caviar," says Lee. For dishes involving these flashy ingredients, there *is* a financial incentive. "Last night we probably sold fifteen portions of caviar and two portions of white truffle, and that's going to boost the check average. It's the holidays, people want to have a good time, so we can sell the truffles and caviar."

"Pascal," says Lawrence. "Oh, Pascal."

"Yes, Michael."

"When we get very, very busy, it's not necessary to show the cart for the cheese tasting. Unless you think the guest will be upset not to see it. A lot of people won't be upset if we do a three-cheese tasting. So if we're in the shit and you don't have time to show the cart, we can do the tasting selection. But again, it's the captain's responsibility to gauge the guest."

One more order of business: Traussi has a business proposal for the busboys. He'll pay them ten dollars an hour to stuff envelopes for the Christmas card the restaurant is sending out, along with a bottle of wine, to eight hundred people.

"Okay," says Lawrence, "we've got people outside—it's five-thirty. Let's go."

In the kitchen, the line cooks are all wearing toques—the tall kind. Although cooks have complained in the past that they bumped the lights, for the moment no one seems bothered. And at some point, over these past twelve months, their getup has changed: Instead of wearing their aprons around their necks as they used to, they now fold them down and tie them only around their waist, the way the *sous-chefs* do. None of the *sous-chefs* wear the toques; as ever, it's a point of pride.

The pastry cooks still wear their aprons around their necks. The new executive pastry chef, Alain Poitier, wears a black turtleneck under his jacket.

Poitier doesn't seem to be happy here at all; Johnny Iuzzini thinks that the French chef is in over his head, and even though Iuzzini doesn't have the title, he's still running the show along with Poitier. Perhaps that's the way he likes it. Iuzzini talks often about his fierce loyalty to Boulud. He needs Boulud's approval and he wants his support. He wants to make him proud, like a father. Boulud, he says, pushes him to do better every single day. Iuzzini, in turn, indeed feels that he has to prove something every day, to himself, to Boulud. It still amazes him, after these six years, that Boulud sees everything. If Iuzzini so much as changes a spice in something, Boulud will detect the change right away.

Iuzzini's team has been behind him all the way, and it has been largely their support that has made his life here tolerable over the past couple months. It hasn't been easy to have an outsider come in as his boss when Boulud had considered him for the job. Iuzzini finds some consolation in the fact that a *sous-chef* is still a team leader; still, everything seems worse during the Christmas season.

It's not all bad in Iuzzini's life, though. Theresa moved in with him four months ago, and she helps keep him on an even keel. For instance, she doesn't let him go hang out in the clubs all night long, which he would be doing if he were alone. She bought him a tattoo recently: the logo of a party he used to go to when his life hit bottom. The tattoo, he says, will keep him in check. He's almost finished paying off his school loans, and he's paid off all but ten thousand dollars of the thirty thousand dollars in credit-card debt he'd accumulated during his out-of-control club days. Much of it is thanks to Boulud, who has always been behind him, pushing him.

Tonight Iuzzini will start the *bûche de Noël* production. For the past few days he's been making chocolate like mad: white chocolate trees decorated with red holly berries, milk chocolate drummer-boy lollipops. Chocolate even haunts his dreams. In one, he's making the confections and realizes halfway through that the chocolate's not tempered, and he wakes up in a cold sweat. Yesterday he almost fell into the chocolate machine because he's dopey from codeine, which he's been taking for an injury. He fractured a foot when his clog slipped as he was coming down the stairs. The doctor told him, "Try to stay off your feet." Ha.

A truffle the size of a softball sits on a plate on the pass. It's somewhat pitted, but as Alex Lee learned in Piedmont, the slugs, which eat the holes into them, go for the truffles that smell the most pungent. These pitted truffles don't fetch as high a price as the more cosmetically beautiful specimens, though—this one was only $1,800 per pound.

"Chef," says William, "can I have that?"

Lee hands it over. Fourteen orders are being plated, many of which will need a garnish of truffles.

"On the fly here, please," says William. "Table 95. Runners, pick up here, please. Let's go!"

They come running.

Upstairs in the skybox, the news is on, tuned to Election 2000 coverage. Brad Thompson glances up. "Oh," he says, deadpan, "was there an election?"

"Do you have anything else?" yells Lee to Kosta in the fish station.

"We have a lot of bay scallops," says Kosta.

"Push the bay scallops, okay?" yells Lee to the runners.

Bruno Jamais comes in, shaking his arms, looking hungry.

"You need a reservation," Thompson tells him. "We're all full."

Jamais pulls out an enormous roll of bills.

"What time would you like, sir?" says Thompson, smiling sweetly.

Wednesday, December 13

WINTER'S CHILL HAS set in early. Shortly after ten P.M. last night, the United States Supreme Court returned a decision that effectively ended the most curious and confusing presidential election in history.

But at Daniel, in the back of the house, no one's talking about it.

Johnny Iuzzini rolls out the pastry cart.

"Very nice," says Michael Lawrence as it goes by. "This is the best dessert cart in town."

Dominique, a handsome French waiter with very short, polished hair, starts to rearrange a couple of the pastries.

"Do that when you're at the table," says Lawrence.

"We don't have time."

"That's what assistant managers are for," says Iuzzini.

"We haven't had an assistant manager since me," says Lawrence, referring to his first job title here.

"What is J.P.?" asks Iuzzini.

"J.P. is maître d'," says Lawrence.

"What is Bruno?"

"Bruno is Bruno."

"What is Bernard?"

"Bernard is old."

"What is David?"

"David is a pain in the ass."

"Sounds like a management problem to me," says Iuzzini.

Lawrence holds the "out" door open. "Come on!" he says. "Let's roll the room, please!"

Up in the skybox, Hilary Tolman processes gift certificate requests—she's been doing about thirty of them a day this week. "If I die during the holiday season," she says, "it'll say 'Gift Certificate' on my headstone." On her computer screen, the phrase STRESS-FREE ZONE floats around, bouncing gently off the sides. The phone rings, and a fax comes in. "Let me guess," she says. "A gift certificate." Indeed it is.

Tolman looks forward to the managers' Christmas party next Monday—a lunch at the elegant Cello. In fact, she was surprised recently to learn that she was indeed a manger, so she'll be there with the other thirty-seven. Last week J.P. suggested to Tolman that they all chip in to buy Boulud a Christmas gift and surprise him with it at the party. They decided, since he travels so much, on a portable DVD player with deluxe speakers. J.P. spent hours on the Internet researching just which one they should buy. They also decided to give him three movies. Among the contenders: *Heavy Metal*, *Babette's Feast*, and some sort of self-help DVD about how to relax and take time for yourself.

It's one-thirty when Boulud comes upstairs; he's been down in a meeting with Marcel Doron about employee bonuses. As he puts on his whites, Toto bounds upstairs with a box for Boulud. He insists on opening any box for his chef just in case there's a bomb in it. (No matter that Boulud happens to be standing right next to him.) Toto opens it: Boom! It's a heavy crystal vase.

It's been a busy season, to say the least. Two days ago they did a party for Martha Stewart—six hundred people off-premises. Uncharacteristically, the team of ten cooks, plus Boulud, was ready to leave about a half hour ahead of schedule, and Boulud went into the banquet room, where the busboys were stuffing the Christmas cards into envelopes and slapping address labels on boxes containing bottles of wine. The wine being sent was a 1998 Graves that he and Le Dû selected on a buying and tasting trip to Bordeaux in March 1999, to be bottled and labeled their first private-label *cuvée*, "Daniel." The wine will be poured by the glass and offered by the bottle at the restaurant, and sold for $16.99 at the Sherry-Lehmann wine shop; including it with the Christmas card is the perfect (if extravagant) way to introduce it to eight hundred and four regular customers and press people. The chef surprised everyone by sitting down and stuffing envelopes along with the busboys. In ten days he'd be on vacation in Florida with Micky and Alix, and he can really use it.

Brett Traussi comes upstairs to hand Boulud some papers. Today is Traussi's birthday—he's thirty-five—and his buddy Brad Thompson brought him a huge bag of ribs from Virgil's, which together they devoured at Traussi's desk.

Tolman, for her part, has a boyfriend these days—someone who works in the restaurant. Although such relationships are not at all forbidden (Boulud actually gets a kick out of them), couples who become involved often try to keep it quiet. Tolman has been seeing this person for a month and a half and is very cagey about identifying him; all she'll reveal is he's back-of-the-house. The intensity of her blushing when she talks—or rather, *doesn't* talk—about it suggests that this is the first time she's been involved with someone on the staff. But her belly laugh at such a suggestion implies that there might have been a few more.

Monday, December 18

IT'S EARLY AFTERNOON, and all the managers—count 'em, thirty-eight—are reveling at their Christmas party at Cello, feasting on semismoked tuna and avocado salad with yuzu vinaigrette, hamachi carpaccio with ginger, olive oil, and marinated beets, seared Maine scallops and grilled foie gras with ketchup emulsion, bay scallops and foie gras risotto with white truffles, marinated Chilean sea bass with acacia honey and parsnip puree, potato-crusted halibut with a cappuccino of porcini mushrooms—all washed down with Clos Pegase Chardonnay "Mitsuko's Vineyard" 1998 and Volnay, Jean-Marc Boillot 1998. To say nothing of the procession of desserts that follows. The wine flows more than freely, and Brad Thompson, for one, is of the opinion that the party should have been after service, not before. Everyone's in a great mood now, he thinks, but when they come down off the alcohol, it'll be another story.

Thompson's stomach growls. He's still hungry. On the way back to Daniel he stops and gets a steak sandwich.

The line cooks, in the meantime, do their *mise en place* as usual. If there's any resentment about missing the exclusive management celebration, it takes a backseat to their elation at being there unsupervised.

Hideji, a new cook on the soup station, makes dumplings for pumpkin soup. He combines a thousand milliliters of ricotta that has been left to drain for two days with two whole eggs plus two extra yolks. Although he's only a line cook here, Hideji used to be *chef de cuisine* at Honmura An, the SoHo restaurant upon which Ruth Reichl bestowed three stars, shocking the food establishment. Boulud may have cooked for presidents, but Hideji has cooked for the Dalai Lama. No doubt no one on the brigade knows it, but at a dinner in New York several years ago presided over by a handful of star chefs, including Boulud, the Dalai Lama only actually ate the miso soup that Hideji had prepared. Hideji is here at Daniel as part of an ongoing effort to train himself in French cooking. He cooks with long, pointed chopsticks; his technique is impeccable. Across from him, in the hot-apps station, a sheet pan covers one side of the induction range, which got gouged in service Saturday night.

Patrice, now working the *saucier* station, cuts lengths of string with a knife, having looped it from a spoon up to the metal dowel that holds paper towels. He has recently started a romantic involvement, too. It's with someone who works in the skybox, but he doesn't want to say who. He lays bacon in lengthwise strips over a veal loin.

David pounds out a rhythm on the side of a *bain-marie*, dancing to his beat. Next to him, Roger pulls spinach out of water, squeezing it hard with gloved hands. He's recently given notice—he can't take the hours and the pressure anymore—but Boulud has asked him to stay through the holidays, and Roger didn't feel he could say no.

In the dining room, the waiters have just finished setting the tables. Now, their coats on the backs of chairs, they polish glasses.

At 3:25 the managers come back. Tolman comes into the kitchen, shows her menu to her paramour Patrice. She recounts how she and Le Dû sat at a table off to the side, ordering one of each dish, so they could taste everything.

Last Friday Boulud had been talking about doing a new menu for winter. "Just let me know when you need me to do it," Tolman told him.

On Saturday—her day off—he called her and asked, "Can you be here in fifteen minutes?" So today there's a new menu.

Lee comes in and tastes Patrice's sauces. "Look at this," he says. "This is too dark—it's almost black." Then Lee goes to the fish station. "How are you guys doing on lobster?" he asks. Okay, they say.

When Lee gets to the *garde-manger*, Bertrand, the cook who had hurt his back early in the year, wants to know how many orders of seviche he should do. Fifteen, Lee tells him.

Cyrille Allannic comes over and turns on the lights under the pass.

Frédéric Côte comes up. *"Alors?"* he says. So?

Lee says, "Cyrille, you do the ravioli. Leslie's not here." She and Lupe are both out sick with the same flu.

Boulud comes in, dressed from the Cello luncheon in an elegant black suit, blue shirt, and tie, with a short brown wool topcoat over it and a plaid muffler around his neck.

Patrice shaves black truffles, then chops them fine.

"Who talked to Leslie today?" asks Lee. *"Merde! Et Lupe, il vient demain?"*

At five-thirty Boulud and Lee go into the dining room for the staff meeting. Three hundred and thirty-five on the books tonight, including the usual assortment of VIPs and regulars. Plus Professor Silver, of apple tart fame. Fay, who's on the reservation sheet as "the former *sous-chef*, VIP per Alex," and the actor Gabriel Byrne.

"What kind of actor is he?" Boulud wants to know.

"A famous one," says Lawrence. "He's done a lot of movies and Broadway."

"He's young?" asks Boulud.

"No. Yes. Thirty-three." Lawrence is close: Byrne is fifty.

Jean-Luc Le Dû comes in, wrapped in his coat. "Hi!" he shouts.

"Hi, Jean-Luc," says Lawrence. It seems Le Dû is; he's looped from the lunch.

"Who's doing the pass?" a waiter wants to know. William is off tonight, and another runner will be expediting.

"And there's a big push between eight-thirty and nine-thirty, just like always," says Lawrence. "It's a little tight. We have to turn the tables. They're gonna come early, and they're gonna want to leave early, but we're still going to have to provide great service. But that's why you're captains."

Johnny Iuzzini comes in and explains the four *bûches de Noël*—chocolate, chestnut with marrons glacés, pistachio *Dacquoise,* and raspberry.

Back in the kitchen, Boulud shows Hideji how he wants the foie gras done. "No, bigger, bigger, like this," he says, making a rectangle with his hands. "Anyway, we're going to do about seven or eight portions. It's not cooked, so you have to finish it. We slice it and give it a flash of heat." He calls Roger over to see the presentation, in case Hideji needs help. "So the spice," continues Boulud, "a little bit on top."

"Two pieces of foie gras cut on a bias?" asks Roger.

"No," says Boulud, "one piece only." Now he sees the sheet pan on the induction, remembering there's a problem.

"We try not to use it, and if you have to, don't get it wet," says a cook.

"Should we put some tape on it?" Boulud wonders.

"Will it melt?"

"Get some electrical tape," suggests the chef.

Lee steps over. "Brett said we can use it," he says. "Just nothing heavy."

Boulud turns back to Hideji. "Did you get the baby mizuna?" he asks, fingering a different green. "No, this is no good. I don't want that."

"Arugula?" suggests Hideji.

"Yeah," says Boulud. "Arugula with mizuna. I want spicy, not bland."

Le Dû comes weaving through. Tolman ushers him up to her office. The cooks all look after him.

Bertrand calls Boulud over to the *garde-manger* to ask him what he wants done with the scallops. In a kitchen that's known for not being too hot, it's positively chilly in this corner.

"*Tu assaisones sel et poivre, un peu de wasabi machin,*" says Boulud. Season it with salt and pepper, and a little of that wasabi stuff. "You can do lime and olive oil. You make a little sea salt with water in case you need a little extra."

"Be careful of that oil," says Lee. "It's like thirty dollars a bottle."

"*Oui, oui,*" says Bertrand.

"Do you have any sea urchins?" Boulud asks. Bertrand does. "It would be nice to have one piece of sea urchin," says Boulud, working on the plate like a surgeon.

"*Ciboulettes?*" suggests Lee. Chives?

"So it's the oyster, the brininess, and then we have the lime with the scallops, and a little wasabi, just to give it a little bit of flavor," says Boulud. "The oyster is all about the brininess."

At 6:05, Lee calls out the first order. Le Dû sits up in the skybox across the table from Michael Lawrence, his head making oil spots on the window. Tolman talks to him, too. After a moment, Boulud goes up there, and Lawrence comes down.

A note up on the pass says:

For a customer in the building, dinner for four.

9 herb ravioli with sheep's milk ricotta, yellowfoot chanterelles, and Parm shavings

Spit-roasted free-range chicken with thyme, chanterelles, country bacon, cipollini onions, and potatoes

Light espresso and brownie cake with crispy phyllo dough and a caramel filling

Petit fours

To be delivered in her pots and pans. Client will use own silverware and china. Billing: $78 per person, tax and service charge not included.

After a minute, Boulud comes back down and takes the pass. "Ordering two *méridionale,* two crab, after that one sole, one paupiette." He slaps up the ticket. "Order one lobster, one tartare, after that one beef duo, one veal. Okay, make a *plateau* for 93 for four. Be sure to put on your toques! Foie gras terrine, lobster gratinée are doing well?" He looks around. "Where's Kosta? Where's Leslie? Leslie didn't come? Neither Kosta? Did Leslie say she was sick?"

Lee reassures him.

"*Est-ce qu'il y a des* extra bodies *en bas?*" he asks. Is there anyone downstairs who can help? "Order two mini-soup, two foie gras *poêlés,* after that two lamb, medium-rare."

"Tasting!" shouts Lee. "Two hot foie gras, then one lobster solo, one seviche, followed by one tuna, medium-rare, one halibut, followed by one pigeon, one venison, medium-rare."

"Hello!" bellows Boulud. "Lobster gratinée—let's fire!"

The short-staffed kitchen works nonstop at a furious pace. By 6:40 it feels like something or someone is about to explode.

Boulud grabs a plate. "Okay, where did you take those ravioli?" he asks a runner.

"That's for table 40 and 45, Chef."

"Do you have another lobster doing well?"

"Yes, Chef!" shouts the *poissonnier.*

"Hey, Daniel," calls Lee, "the ravioli!"

"Okay, what?"

"I have two extra lobsters, Chef," says a runner.

"No, it's for 45," says Lee. "What is that there? Fifteen and 34."

"I have a lobster for 47," says Boulud.

"Okay, Chef, 47 is done," says the runner expediting.

"Yeah, maybe we have one too many," says Boulud. "Bertrand, we have a problem."

"I need a crab right now!" yells Lee. "I need a *tartare caviar,* lobster salad! The ravioli, it's not ready."

There's a clanging of tongs in the pass. A loud sizzling from the meat station. Little talk, only what's necessary.

"Striped bass, striped bass," says Boulud, looking at a ticket. "Hello—it's a skate with striped bass." He wipes the plate. "And then I have a problem. It's all fucked up, this order." He pokes at the meat on a plate, sends it. "Who's taking the takeout in the building?"

"Me," says Allannic.

"Make sure the ravioli is tossed really well in the white cream. Hello, can you hear me? You have to make sure you have enough cream in there."

"What are you missing?" Lee asks him.

"Two artichokes, foie gras *chaud,*" says Boulud.

"They're coming," says Lee.

"Two artichokes!" yells a runner.

"Yeah, yeah, shut up, it's coming," says Boulud. "Hello, you have two more ravioli? Make sure they're cooked, those ravioli there."

Côte plates an order of foie gras, topping it with a jaunty beret of paper-thin dried pineapple.

"Hello, here's your tasting," says Lee, handing a plate to Boulud.

"Give me the other cannelloni, please." He turns to a runner. "Move it up! Move it up!" The runner scoots the plate closer to the chef, who shaves white truffles on it. "Okay, go! Sixty-four!"

"Sixty-four and 18 out?" asks Lee.

"Yes, Chef!" says the expediter.

"Fire 11?"

"Yes, Chef!"

"You have to listen to Daniel and me before the other guys," Lee tells him. This expediter is inexperienced, and it's really screwing things up.

"Ordering for the nutcase," calls Boulud. "One crab app, one tartare, no caviar, one lobster salad, no caviar, one seviche." He then has a fit about something going on in the pasta station. He goes over there, takes a plate, shaves black truffles on it. Some of it goes on the floor. "Oh, *merde*," he says.

At seven o'clock four orders come in rapid succession, including a tasting.

"I need cream!" calls Lee. "Heavy cream!"

"Yes, Chef!" says a runner. He runs into the coffee station to get it.

"Aarrgghh!" comes a cry from the line. One of the cooks burned himself.

David, the maître d', comes in, hands Boulud a ticket. "Chef, on 30 we have an add-on. A person who joined them."

"What do you want as an add-on?" asks Boulud, looking at the ticket. "A terrine of foie gras and a veal, medium-rare?" David says yes. "One more terrine of foie gras, Bertrand, ASAP. As fast as you can—it's an extra person!"

"Okay," says Lee, "can we set up the big table here?"

"Ordering!" cries Boulud.

"It's gonna be for table 30!" says Lee. "What is that there?" He points to a tray. "What is that there?!"

"You said table 23," says the expediter.

"Yeah, I'm sorry," says Boulud.

"Sixty-five," says the expediter.

"What are you saying is 23?" asks Boulud.

"No, 65," says the expediter.

"Sixty-five," says Boulud. "Coming up. Okay, let's go. And then one crab, one ravioli, please. Where is it? You have it? No, the other side there."

"No," says a runner, shaking his head. "I don't have it."

"Okay, get me another ravioli!" shouts Boulud. "Take the artichoke soup. Where is it? Okay, here for table 8. A ravioli and an artichoke for table 8."

"It's gone," says the expediter.

Boulud yells toward the *garde-manger*, "Where's that crab?!"

"Coming!"

Côte hand four plates to a runner. "Okay, go, go, go!"

"*Méridionale*, please, coming up," says Boulud. "Crab right here, please." The cook brings it.

"Where's the crab here? And the ravioli here?" Boulud turns to the runner. "Have you done 50 yet?"

"Yes, Chef!"

Lee yells from the back, "How are we doing on the big table 30?"

"I don't know," says Boulud. "I think there's a problem here." He looks at the expediter. "You're not calling the shots, you understand?"

"Yes, Chef."

"Give me a white truffle, please." Someone hands Boulud one, and a blizzard of white truffles rains down from the slicer onto an order of ravioli. "Call Michael for me," he says.

"Take these off," Lee tells a runner. "Come on!"

"Give me back that lobster, please," says Boulud, grabbing it. "Okay, go."

Lee, who has turned bright red, yells now, louder perhaps than he's yelled all year. "Can we take this out?! Come on, it's getting cold!"

"Where's Michael?" wonders Boulud.

"*Il est gentil et tout, mais il faut pas pousser,*" says Lee, referring to the expediter. He's nice and everything, but let's not kid ourselves. At this point, all the runners are going crazy trying to figure out the tickets.

Lawrence comes in, holding a truffle and a shaver in one hand. "Who's looking for me?" he asks.

"Put the white truffle here," Boulud tells him. "Michael, don't give me that guy again."

Lawrence looks forlorn.

"Just have him work till the end of the year. Next Monday we are closed."

Now there's the smell of something burning.

"*Mer-duh!*" says Boulud, shaving black truffles on lamb. "Wipe the plate on the side—you see that little thing?" he says.

Iuzzini and Thompson come through with two trays of *bûches de Noël*, yelling "*Boooche! Booooche!*"

It's 8:40, an hour and a half later, and things haven't improved any. And now Gabriel Byrne and Fay Bouchard have both arrived, and it's also time to start dealing with Professor Silver's apple tart. Boulud asks Iuzzini to bring up some *pâte feuilleté*—puff pastry.

He then turns his attention back to the pass. "Give me something for that actor," he continues, then turns to the runner. "What do you want to give him?" He looks at the tickets. On Byrne's it says:

3 méridionale
3 pasta bt
1 stripe
1 paupiette
1 sole
table 47

"What are you cooking all this ravioli for?" Boulud says to the hot-apps cook. "You sold them? *Ça va pas, non?* You have to count them. You cook them to order, no? You know how to count?"

He goes back to the pass. The bottom of another ticket says, "Very slow eater."

"Eighty-six pumpkin soup!" Boulud calls.

"Chef, we have it," says Hideji. He takes it out, and Boulud tastes it with a small spoon.

"Add a little chicken stock and seasoning," he says. "Hello! We have pumpkin soup! I'm sorry!"

He looks at the tickets once again. "Okay, for Fay!" he calls. "With Fay we're going to start with a *pâté de campagne* and a *terrine de foie gras.*" He goes to the *garde-manger* to do her plates.

Lee steps back to the pass. "Hello, is table 11 out?"

"Eleven and 20," says the expediter. "And 47."

"What about 91?"

"No, not yet, Chef."

Boulud comes back to the pass. "*Pour* Fay," he says to Lee, "what do we have as a second course?" They confer. "How many courses?" wonders Boulud. "Don't we have something else?"

"We don't have any bay scallops, right?" asks Lee.

Boulud interrupts the conversation to admonish the hot-apps cook again. "I'm sorry, Chef," he says, "I've never worked this station before."

Boulud and Lee go back to their huddle.

"Chef," says a runner, "the actor's gonna get something?"

"Yeah," says Lee. "Three mini-pasta, black truffle."

Iuzzini appears with the *pâte feuilleté* for the apple tart. Boulud, meanwhile, scrutinizes the plates going out for Fay as Lee wrestles with the pass. Boulud then goes to the video monitors, zooms in on table 12, Fay's table. "Three and 4," he says. "Pâté number 3. No, put the foie gras on number 3."

"Order two skate solo anytime," calls Lee.

"Okay, *pour* Fay," Boulud tells the *chef garde-manger* again, *"tu peux faire marcher une seviche pour elle et un tuna."* Fire a seviche for her and a tuna.

This is the thing that consumes Boulud most all evening: giving Fay—someone who quit her job as a line cook at Daniel—a great meal. In fact, he wants everyone to have a great meal. But it's of the utmost importance to him that his ex-employee have exactly the right meal for her. He's cooking for *her.* And that's Boulud.

Lee goes to the hot-apps station, points to a roiling pot of ravioli. "It can't be boiling and boiling like that," he says.

Bertrand puts two plates out. "Let's go, guys!"

Boulud goes to the pastry station to work with Iuzzini on the tart. Iuzzini cuts a freehand circle out of the *pâte feuilleté* with a pastry wheel, then rolls it gently around the rolling pin to pick it up, and lays it on a sheet pan covered with parchment.

"I'm going to put the apple warm on it," says Boulud, "so I want that to be very cold."

Iuzzini, of course, knows how to make an apple tart. But tonight Boulud wants to show him his grandmother's version—almost a cross between a tart and a turnover. Iuzzini puts the sheet pan on top of a stack of glasses crates, and Boulud spreads quince compote over it, smoothing it with the back of a spoon.

"I'll bake it downstairs," says Iuzzini.

"Johnny, hold it," says Boulud. "Put it in the freezer and I'll meet you down there."

As Iuzzini disappears downstairs, Boulud slices Gala apples with a paring knife from the pickup side of the pastry window. He does one, two, three, four of them, very fast, laying the slices on a plate. He brings the plate to the induction range to cook; he tastes a slice.

"Seviche *pour* Fay?" says Lee. "And *tartare caviar* VIP?" He calls out an order and then looks at the seviche. "Hello, this is for Fay! Did you put enough lime in there?"

Boulud sautées the apple in butter. He sprinkles sugar on top, makes them jump.

"Eighty-six sole!" cries David.

"Eighty-six sole!" echoes Lee.

• • •

Downstairs in the pastry kitchen, Iuzzini works on the apple tart. It's nice down there this time of night—peaceful. No one's around.

Boulud comes whizzing in with the apples. "Johnny, baby," he says, putting down the apples.

"Careful on the Silpat," says Iuzzini, "it's very expensive. When I inherit this company, I want to have some money left over."

Boulud trims the raw pastry with a pastry cutter and brushes the edge with egg wash. "You can give me the blowtorch," he says. He then brushes the outside with egg. "This is what I'm going to do in my second life," he says.

Iuzzini puts a pastry ring around it and puts it in the oven. "I would have put the Silpat directly on the stone," he says.

"Four hundred seventy-five, no?" says Boulud. "Ten, fifteen minutes. Nice and crispy. Let the sides juice up."

Thompson comes through. He and Iuzzini are going to a party after service, and they've asked Boulud to come with them. "Are you coming with us tonight?" Thompson asks him.

"Tonight?" says Boulud.

"Yes."

"Yessss!" cries Boulud.

But for Boulud, there will be no partying tonight, for the craziness upstairs continues on into the night.

And so goes the year, on into the holidays. Just before Boulud leaves for Florida, Alain Poitier, the French pastry chef, comes up to the skybox to tell him that things aren't working out; the feeling, as it turns out, is mutual. They'll go their separate ways.

On the cusp of the New Year, the United States of America has elected a president who has never visited France, and Daniel has a new co-executive pastry chef: Johnny Iuzzini. Another French pastry chef will be coming from France next year sometime to work alongside him, but this time they'll be equals; co-chefs, just as Boulud was first given his big chance as co-executive chef when he got his first job in New York, at the Westbury. He was so young at the time—just twenty-seven, a year older than Iuzzini—that the hotel didn't want to take a chance on handing him the whole thing.

And so the second year in the life of restaurant Daniel—the momentous year MM for the rest of the world—comes to a timely, if undramatic, close.

Thirteen

STELLAR

March 2001

T HE BEGINNING OF the actual new millennium has come and gone, and since George W. Bush took office in January, an economic downturn has the financial pundits whispering the word *recession*—a frightening prospect for restaurants in general, and even more devastating for luxury restaurants. New York City, in the past two years since Daniel has opened, has become obscenely expensive. Legions of dot-comers have come spilling out of folded Internet startups like so many obsolete floppy disks; not only can they no longer eat in expensive restaurants, many can't even pay their exorbitant rents. Indeed, compared with a year ago, when the Nasdaq composite index peaked and even mediocre restaurants brazenly priced entrées at thirty-plus dollars, New York's fine-dining business is looking somewhat lackluster.

On Monday, March 12, the economic picture turned from bad to worse: The Nasdaq fell 6.3 percent, falling below the 2,000 mark for the first time since Daniel opened. Not only is the index down a frightening 61.9 percent from where it was a year earlier, but it's now officially the first bear market since 1987.

In any case, for an expensive restaurant that depends on turning the tables at least two and a half times most evenings, the state of things has to be just a tad scary. At Daniel, business is a little slow, as it is for most restaurants these weeks in March.

On a positive note, the crazy turnover that the kitchen saw in the second half of 2000 has calmed down, aided no doubt by the slowdown in New York's restaurant business; there's no longer a labor shortage that makes it easy to jump ship. At the same time, morale has lifted somewhat as well.

At 9:20 on the following evening, a state of anxious excitement runs electric through the restaurant. Up in the skybox, Daniel Boulud, Alex Lee, Cyrille Allannic, Johnny Iuzzini, Brett Traussi, Bruno Jamais, Michael Lawrence, and Marcel Doron gather around the TV, which is tuned in to New York 1, the local cable news channel, affiliated with the *New York Times*. Soon they're joined by Erica Cantley, who's ducked out of her current post as head maître d' at Gotham Bar & Grill, where she's worked since leaving Esca several months ago; she wants to be back with her friends at Daniel at this nervous moment. (Unbeknownst to her, in six weeks she will be offered the position of head maître d' at Boulud's new restaurant, to be called DB. The new chef will not be an alumnus of Daniel, to Brad Thompson's chagrin, but one of the *sous-chefs* from Café Boulud, Jean-François Bruel.)

The cause for this gathering? There have been *visitations*—by William Grimes—and the restaurant has been alerted that it will be reviewed this week. A sneak preview of that review is about to air.

Every few minutes, the cooks below glance up at the skybox, eyeing Boulud and the others.

Could such a thing be possible? Can Daniel possibly be reviewed just a year and a half after its first review, when Le Bernardin hasn't been reviewed since 1995 and Le Cirque 2000, which few in the food world consider among the top echelon, hasn't been revisited since Ruth Reichl's 1997 four-star review?

Yet the improbable is happening. On Grimes's last visit, Boulud had all the video cameras possible trained on him, but somehow he couldn't get a fix on the critic's face; he always seemed to have his back toward the camera, no matter which one they switched to, almost as if Grimes knew where every camera was positioned. Boulud wasn't sure, but it seemed to him that Grimes was talking into his hand; in any case, the critic took no notes at the table. Did he have a tiny microphone hidden in his palm, with a wire going up his sleeve?

The last time Grimes reviewed Daniel, the crew had been confident they'd receive four stars. Champagne was ready, flutes lined up. It's impossible to convey the letdown that followed. Boulud will not make that mistake again. Although a photographer came to take Boulud's picture last Friday, another indication that the stars on upcoming review would likely number four, one could never be sure.

Finally, the newsreader on New York 1 announces the restaurant preview, William Grimes revisiting Daniel. And the result?

A mighty whoop comes from the skybox, followed by much gleeful yelling as a bottle of champagne is poured over Boulud's head; shouting and cheering from the kitchen comes immediately on its heels. It's a tremendous release, as if all the energy and industry and sweat and worrying and training and tweaking of the past two years has distilled itself in one moment of pure joy.

Four stars. So much work by so many people. Despite all the problems, Daniel's incredible accomplishment, the fulfillment of Boulud's dream of showcasing, of *perfecting*, the most ambitious food in the most ambitious restaurant New York has ever seen, has been realized—and applauded! Everything has come together. It's a beautiful and rare thing when the truly deserving are recognized.

The next morning, the headline on the front page of the *Times* dining section tells the whole story: IN NEW YORK, PROMISE FULFILLED. The four stars stretch themselves out symmetrically under the name Daniel.

If Hilary Tolman or Georgette Farkas had written the review, it wouldn't have glowed any more brightly. "It is now the Daniel that New York wanted and expected all along," writes Grimes, "a top-flight French restaurant, sumptuous and rather grand, but still very much the personal expression of its chef and owner, Daniel Boulud." He celebrates the "unmistakable spirit of generosity hovering over the dining room that makes Daniel unique. The name says it all." He raves about Boulud's style, which he calls "a seductive blend of qualities, robust and delicate at the same time, like a big-engine car that hits top speed with the merest toe-touch on the accelerator."

At another point Grimes applauds Daniel's inventiveness, writing, "Anyone worrying that French cuisine might be running out of gas should browse through a week's worth of menus at Daniel. The influences come from all over the Mediterranean, and as far afield as Japan and India, pulled in and made French with total assurance." If you read between the lines, this goes beyond annointing a new four-star restaurant; it's an allusion to the widely discussed crisis in French food in France. Critics have been complaining recently that in even the best restaurants, French cooking has been suffering from stasis. Grimes's proclamation puts Daniel at the very pinnacle not just of the New York restaurant scene, but of the world's: French food was dead, but Daniel has resurrected it. *(La cuisine française est morte—Vive la cuisine française!)* And though Grimes doesn't mention him by name, the compliment is due in no small part to the geographic expansiveness, the creative genius, the magic touch of Alex Lee.

In fact, other than Jean-Luc Le Dû, the sommelier, and Boulud himself, Grimes does not single out particular individuals in the review. Still, for those who have been killing themselves over the past two years to make Daniel great, it's the ultimate gratification. Iuzzini should be pleased that Grimes refers to a dessert menu that's "remarkable for its elegance and restraint." Grimes writes that he "felt sorry for the lighter-than-air warm almond cake, almost a horizontal soufflé, served with muscat-raisin ice cream. How could it hope to upstage the glamour parade just across the way, led by thin leaves of chocolate filled with gianduja and amaretto or the glistening, nearly black chocolate bombe, a smooth sphere that opens up to reveal an inner core of cassis, vanilla crème brûlée and cashew nougat?" Any pastry chef in his right mind would be thrilled by this. Not Iuzzini. First he was petrified that the review would come in and it would be only three stars because *the desserts stank.* Now he's stuck on the fact that the almond cake is Thomas Haas's creation, not his. Perhaps he hasn't read the review carefully enough, for it seems his bombe has upstaged his former boss's cake.

Grimes devotes a paragraph-plus to cheese, bringing a wide grin and a hint of color to Pascal's ghostly visage. "It is highly advisable," Grimes counsels, "to study the cheese trolley." He then goes on to swoon about a Selles-sur-Cher he had one visit, and recounts looking for the same cheese on a subsequent trip to the Loire Valley (he should have looked right on Bleecker Street).

For Bertrand, now a *saucier,* Grimes's declaration that the "reductions are so deep, they have no bottom" makes his herniated disk of last spring seem almost worthwhile. All the other *sauciers* of the past six months should take pride as well, for Grimes no doubt has tasted, and taken into account, their handiwork as well.

Two paragraphs celebrate the wine list, "a thrilling document."

The topper, though, comes in Grimes's penultimate paragraph. "The service has never needed any improvement at Daniel," he writes. "Confident and expert, it goes a long way to explain the neighborhood's love affair with

Daniel. Diners feel well cared for." *Soigné*. "There's none of the hovering that passes for attentive service at lesser restaurants. The tone is pitch-perfect, and as a result, patrons feel at ease." Michael Lawrence is beside himself, though he doesn't step out of character; his world-weary expression overrides his glee.

Nor has Boulud's endless tinkering with interior design elements been in vain. "The horrid sculpture has been removed from the dining room," notes Grimes. "Striped silk curtains across the archways have softened the architecture, and revised lighting now suffuses the dining room with a flattering, roseate glow."

Still, one can't help but ask oneself: What really happened during the year that has passed? "Four stars," muses one of the line cooks, "and we only lost twenty cooks in the process."

One could argue that the food at Daniel did not actually improve in the twenty months following Grimes's first (three-star) review. It was already extraordinary and frequently brilliant, even if there were sometimes rough spots or missteps that come with low morale and high turnover. Sure, the dining room has evolved into a more attractive and welcoming room, and the service has been polished to high gloss. But the food has not changed qualitatively. Daniel was twenty months ago, and is now, one of the very finest restaurants not only in New York, but indeed in the country. It may *be* the best restaurant in the country. To many food business observers (including this one), Daniel deserved four stars in June 1999 just as it deserves four stars in March 2001. So what changed enough to inspire William Grimes to upgrade Daniel?

To answer that, I must step out of the role I have embraced during the twelve months I spent behind the scenes at Daniel, the role of the proverbial fly on the wall. (Though if I had been an actual fly, I wouldn't have lasted fifteen seconds on those spotless walls!) While that role has limited what I could report in many cases, it has, at the same time, allowed me to record my observations of the goings-on at the restaurant with a flexible, and I hope penetrating, point of view.

But now I must emerge as a character in my own tale, for I need to get some answers.

I pick up the phone and call William Grimes. I have to know what he was thinking when he wrote that first review. And he surprises me by agreeing to an interview.

Naturally, Grimes is quite concerned about clueing in restaurateurs to his mysterious methods, so there are certain aspects of his job he won't discuss. I first ask him about his last two visits to the restaurant as recalled by Leslie

Lopez, the reservations manager and hostess. William Grimes came in, she has told me, under the name of Peter Collins, on March 7, with a party of four. "I certainly have used that name at one time or another," he confirms. On Wednesday, February 21, the staff says he had also come in, this time as Gary Tamboryn and again with a party of four. This name, however, he doesn't recognize at all—it couldn't have been him. "It's too creative," he tells me. "Gary Stevens, I've used. . . ." Imagine the meal that Gary Tamboryn, whoever he was, received when the kitchen thought he was William Grimes.

Grimes does confirm that he has made five or six visits over the last couple of months. At one, he tells me, one of the managers saw him coming out of the parking garage on his way into the restaurant. When he spotted Grimes, "he looked shocked, and his pace picked up."

He recounts, too, a story about his very first visit, in the spring of 1999. Grimes had gone to lunch at Daniel with a colleague from his paper, and as he tells it, they spent enough money that they aroused the management's interest. "By the end of the meal," he recalls, "a maître d' came over and started quizzing us, trying to figure out who we were." The maître d', he says, was fairly aggressive. "I don't know if he guessed who I was or he was hoping we'd become regulars, so he wanted our business cards. At the end he went away frustrated, and I felt he was overdoing it."

Grimes remembers the time when he was seated at table 66, that Siberia of locales next to the bus station. "That may have been my second visit," he recalls. "I was conscious that it wasn't a great table, but it didn't bother me. I was a little conscious that there was a waiter station there with napkins and silverware, so it wasn't a beautiful view. But for me, it's good when I get a table like that. I'd almost rather be at a table like that than front-row center. As long as I'm not physically uncomfortable."

In fact, Grimes doesn't care about table location and the prestige attached to a good table in general; he thinks the whole power table thing is a lot of hooey.

Grimes doesn't remember noticing that Daniel's staff figured out who he was halfway through the meal, but, he says, "I certainly know next time I came they knew who I was. The body language was different." Still, he says, there was not a huge difference in the way he was treated both times. "It's a restaurant with excellent service," he insists. "They didn't make the mistake that a lot of restaurants do, which is to overcompensate and put extra waiters on the table and make you feel swarmed. They played it reasonably cool, which is to their credit."

Does it ever occur to him, I ask, that when he's recognized, more care is taken with the food than it might otherwise be? "At a restaurant of that caliber," he says, "I don't think they're serving two kinds of food to two kinds of people."

I press the point. I've been behind the pass, and I see what happens. "Don't you think," I ask him, "that if Daniel knew you were there, he'd actually be cooking for you personally, and you might get something different than what a line cook could do?"

"A restaurant can't make itself better than what it is," Grimes answers. "What if I told you what the essay question was going to be tomorrow? You're only as smart as you are, and you only understand as much as you're going to understand about the novel you're writing about. You can't remake a stock."

We leave it at that. You can't remake a stock, and the sauces do depend on the stock. And no, the recipes won't be changed—the food they serve is the food they serve. But I think it's either naive or expedient to imagine that a cook with two months of experience can put together a shrimp, octopus, and squid salad with shaved fennel and a lime-mustard dressing like Alex Lee, or that a line cook with fourteen months under his belt can do as good a job with a risotto or a skate wing as can Daniel Boulud with his genius and a lifetime of cooking under his. And unless you're known to be someone very, very important, these two gentlemen will probably not cook your food. They'll keep an eye on what's going on—they'll taste sauces and make the quality-control rounds, but they will probably not touch your plate personally. If you do happen to find yourself among the lucky, lucky few who have the supreme good fortune to have one of them cook for you, the result will be something you will never forget.

When a restaurant receives four stars from the *New York Times*, you can be sure that what appeared on the reviewer's plate was the absolute best that the restaurant can do. And given that the reviewer will always be recognized (unless he or she is very new to the job), perhaps this is the fairest way of judging. For Grimes is partly right: No restaurant can do better than its best. And if he's comparing the best at every restaurant, at least the playing field is level. The food for the rest of us at these places may be down a notch from that ideal, but one hopes that brilliance will flash through now and then.

Grimes offers, to my delight, to shed some light on what the stars actually mean to him—his "impressionistic" sense of what they signify. "Let's say you've just gone to a movie and you've got reservations for dinner afterward," he supposes. "If you go to a one-star restaurant, I would say your conversation is mostly about the movie, punctuated by remarks about the food being pretty good. Two stars, the movie conversation gets interrupted each time new food comes. At this point, about one-third of the conversation is about the movie, two-thirds is about the food. Three stars, you're not talking about the movie anymore, you're talking about the food. And at a four-star restaurant, your eyes are sort of rolling into the top of your head, and you're thanking God for putting you in this place at this time. You're into the ooh and ahh territory."

We go back in time to the three-star review. I remind Grimes of his proclamation that "diners expect nonstop fireworks when [Boulud] gets within fifty feet of a stove, and he has encouraged those expectations, promising to outdo himself at the new Daniel."

"I took that to mean you didn't get those fireworks nonstop," I said, "and so you felt it didn't deserve four stars."

"Yes," answers Grimes. And then he pauses. "And there was maybe a slight annoyance on my part that there was a tremendous amount of hype surrounding the new Daniel, and a sort of built-in attitude that seemed to be saying, 'Well, of course we're going to get four stars; that's simply a settled question.' "

Had Grimes, then, in effect, *punished* Boulud for the efficacy of his PR machine? Was Grimes so bothered by Boulud's confidence in his own culinary powers that he needed to *teach him a lesson?*

Grimes reminds me that the first Daniel review was his first step into the spotlight. He believes that Ruth Reichl was asked by the *Times* to hold off, not to review Daniel before she left. "I had to take a deep breath to take that on," confesses Grimes. "That was sort of my first big test as the new kid on the block."

He had long meant to go back. And, in fact, when he revisited Daniel in early 2000, he had a meal that he thought indicated a real jump in quality. Other isolated visits followed. Finally it all started coming together for him. "I wouldn't have kept going back to proclaim the status quo," he says. "I felt that if this thing had really clicked into four-star territory, there was no point in letting it languish."

Still. Was there a change in the restaurant? Or was there a change in the heart of a critic?

The Tuesday night before the Wednesday review was published, champagne Krug flowed freely at restaurant Daniel. Boulud instructed Le Dû to open a double magnum of Château Mouton-Rothschild 1995 that had been a gift from a customer, used for display in the cellar ever since. "Now is the moment!" Boulud said, bringing out all the cheeses. Later he donned a Superman T-shirt and French gendarme cap and paraded around the banquet room, where friends and family were celebrating. Brett Traussi left early, at two-thirty A.M. The party went on until five in the morning.

In the harsh light of nine A.M., Wednesday, Daniel's staff dribbles in, bleary-eyed, past the extravagant lemon trees that stand in planters on either side of the entryway just past the coat check. A citrusy aroma pervades the air, looking beyond even spring, into summer. Boxes of tall, fringed, yellow tulips line the first two steps leading down from the entry into the front desk area; a box of thick lush grass sits below each on the bottom step.

The reservation lines are ringing off the hook, natch. On top of everything else, the books are opening today for a Saturday night. Leslie Lopez has put on an extra person to answer the phones, and she came in at nine A.M. instead of eleven, her usual start time. At around three o'clock she expects it to get even more crazy, and then again at around five, as people start thinking about leaving work.

On Boulud's desk in the skybox, the congratulations are piling up. Hilary Tolman has decided not even to try to do any paperwork today.

"Dear Chef Daniel:" says one e-mail message,

> *Congratulations on the 4 stars in the NY Times.*
>
> *I want to add that you are a star by yourself. I worked the Auction at the Essex House a year ago. That was me carrying boxes out of the hotel, after the auction, and having trouble balancing them. You came to the rescue like a knight in shining armor. I always thought you could not find a gentleman in NY anymore; you changed that impression.*
>
> *I was shocked that a famous and important person helped me to carry boxes!*
>
> *It showed what a real person you are and that is why I give you all the stars in the world.*
>
> *No reply necessary; I wanted to get this off my chest.*
>
> *Good Luck and Good Health, May God Bless you always.*
>
> *One of your fans.*
>
> *Cecilia*

Today, of all days, Raymond Blanc, the well-known two-star *Michelin* chef from Le Manoir aux Quat' Saisons in Oxford, England, is doing a stint as guest chef—a press lunch in the banquet room, dinner tonight, and a dinner tomorrow.

Wild-eyed, with a goofy grin and glasses on a long cord around his neck, Chef Blanc uses tongs to turn tied loins of venison as they brown in a pan on a burner at awkward thigh-height in the prep kitchen. The loins will be roasted, and served with braised endive and celery with a sauce *aigre-doux* (a sweet-and-sour *sauce gastrique*) with bitter chocolate. A shock of dark brown hair flops down over his eye. Brad Thompson looks on, worried, exhausted, fed up despite last night's exhilarating news. Blanc pours sea salt into his hand from a blue cylinder of La Baleine, sprinkles some lavishly onto the loins of venison from a great height, then tosses the extra salt in his hand onto the floor, where it falls through the hole-y rubber mat.

Mark the baker pulls apart some super-elastic dough for *pain au levain*, checking to see whether the gluten has developed. The farther he can stretch it, the more gluten there is.

Back in the chocolate lab, Johnny Iuzzini works with Peter Collins, a pastry cook Raymond Blanc brought with him. They attach chocolate handles to demitasses made entirely of dark chocolate—Iuzzini holds the ends of a curved handle to a warm pan, using the melted parts to solder it onto the side of a cup. These will be filled with a coffee parfait and kirsch sabayon.

Now Raymond Blanc stands in the Feast & Fêtes prep area, working on his first course: marinated eel, octopus, and Japanese spices. Aha, he tells Thompson: an idea. But it requires an ingredient they don't have in the house. Thompson clambers up the stairs to the main floor, and up the stairs to the skybox.

Boulud sits at his desk, attempting to work, but well-wishers on the phone keep interrupting him.

"Chef," says Thompson, "can you call Nobu? We need fresh seaweed for a little seaweed in the middle of the eel."

"No," says Boulud, "we have that."

"It's not fresh," says Thompson. "It's dried."

"We cannot get fresh," says Boulud. "He means preserved."

In the kitchen below, Alex Lee arrives, having returned late last night from another truffle hunt, this time for black truffles in France. On his way back, he paid a visit to Alain Ducasse's new location in Paris at the Plaza Athénée, and he recounts highlights of his spectacular meal to Neil Gallagher, Cyrille

Allannic, and Olivier Reginensi, a new *sous-chef*, whose last job was helping Alain Ducasse open his restaurant in New York. In fact, like Boulud, Lee, and the maître d' Bernard Vrod, Reginensi has also worked in this space before, when it was Le Cirque: In 1993 through 1994 he worked under Sylvain Portay, the chef who replaced Boulud when Boulud left Le Cirque. He started here two weeks ago.

Cyrille Allannic, by the way, no longer walks to work with his wife—a month ago Rica accepted a job as a publishing associate at Scribner. On her first day, faced with a manuscript Scribner didn't want to publish, she had to write a rejection letter. Who was she to reject somebody, she asked herself, on her very first day in publishing?

"Chef?" says Nelson, the thickset Ecuadorian runner, to Boulud as he walks by. Boulud stops and turns to him. *"Félicitations,"* says Nelson.

Boulud grabs his hand, shakes it warmly. "Thank you very much!" he says. "Oh, you weren't here last night. Thank you!" And then he starts thanking the few runners who didn't work last night.

Ducking into the coffee station as he's about to go the staff meeting, Nelson stops briefly at the Pensée du Jour, a daily saying concocted or collected by Lamine, who is in charge of the coffee station: *"Pourquoi vouloir décrocher la lune quand on a les étoiles?"* Why would you want to reach for the moon when you already have the stars?

Ten minutes to twelve, and Michael Lawrence rounds up the usual suspects for the pre-service staff meeting, now held in the main part of the dining room.

"Guys!" he yells. "What's happening with the menus while you're relaxing?" A few moments later, he claps his hands and says, "Let's go! Let's go! Okay, who was late this morning? I heard somebody was late this morning!" And then he mumbles under his breath, "But I was here till four-thirty, so I think I have an excuse. . . .

"Everybody," he continues, "we have to come to work on time. Because that's what it takes."

He looks at the reservation sheet, which naturally has swelled since nine o'clock this morning.

"Okay," he says. "We're up to seventy-something now. The general manager from the Plaza Athénée is coming. He's going to be on 40 with a six-top. Then we have the Danzigers. Three on 42 at one o'clock. Laurent, that's you and they're gonna get the *gougères*. They're making them now as a canapé.

Nelson, can you call Alex, please? We want to see if there's something he wants to offer them. But it's always something special.

"Mr. Litchfield, another regular. Seven guests. Fifty-three for seven at one o'clock, and then we have another seven on 33, which he has requested. Thirty-three. Okay, Dominique? He's coming with his family. So we have some very high-maintenance, needy guests today."

Next he talks about Karen Dannenberg, a food writer who's also coming, but confuses her with Karen Page, the wife and co-writer of Andrew Dornenburg. In fact, Linda Dannenberg is a cookbook author; he finally clears it up. "That's a VIP table as well," he concludes.

"Okay," he says, "I guess everybody saw the paper this morning. Thank you all for your hard work." The runners and busboys and captains and maître d's look around, nodding here and there. Lawrence barely cracks a smile.

"You know, we have four stars," he says, "but we're not perfect. Every day, every day, every day we learn. When we stop learning, that's the end of it."

ACKNOWLEDGMENTS

Although it is not the custom to acknowledge the subjects of a nonfiction work, I'd like to take this opportunity to thank Daniel Boulud and his entire staff for their openness, bravery, and kindness during my year-plus at Daniel.

A big thank-you to Jennifer Hershey, who first suggested I spend a year in a restaurant, as well as to Pam Krauss and Clarkson Potter for believing in me. Eternal gratitude to Janet Capron, the best reader and friend a writer could ever hope for, and to Erika Goldman, for wise counsel. Heartfelt thanks to Angela Miller for all the editorial and emotional support, as well as her good faith, patience, and friendship.

Finally, to my husband, Thierry, for everything, and to Wylie for being my bunny.